Economics of Information Security and Privacy III

Bruce Schneier

Editor

Economics of Information Security and Privacy III

 Springer

Editor
Bruce Schneier
Minneapolis
MN, USA
schneier@schneier.com

ISBN 978-1-4939-0036-7   ISBN 978-1-4614-1981-5 (eBook)
DOI 10.1007/978-1-4614-1981-5
Springer New York Heidelberg Dordrecht London

Printed on acid-free paper

Springer is part of Springer Science+Business Media (www.springer.com)

Preface

You have in your hands most of the papers—some are missing because of various publication requirements—from the Tenth Workshop on Economics and Information Securityor WEIS 2011.

The idea that economics has anything to do with computer security is only slightly older than this workshop. Ross Anderson and I seem to have stumbled upon the idea independently—he in his brilliant article from 2001, "Why Information Security Is Hard—An Economic Perspective" (http://www.cl.cam.ac.uk/~rja14/Papers/econ.pdf), and me in various essays and presentations from that same period. WEIS was inaugurated a year later at the University of California at Berkeley and has been held annually ever since in both the USA and Europe. It is the only workshop where security technologists get together with economists and policy makers and try to understand the economic problems related to computer security.

And economics has a lot to teach computer security. We generally think of computer security as a problem of technology, but it is a technological problem that has people as an essential element. Security designs need to take intelligent attackers into account, of course, but they have to take into account the interests and motivations of the users as well. This makes computer security unique, and opens up vast areas of failure that traditional computer engineering systems don't have to deal with. Often systems fail because of misplaced economic incentives, when the people who could protect a system are not the ones who suffer the costs of failure.

When you start looking, economic considerations are everywhere in computer security. Hospitals' medical records systems provide comprehensive billing-management features for the administrators who specify them, but are not so good at protecting patients' privacy. Automated teller machines suffered from fraud in countries like the UK and the Netherlands, where poor regulation left banks without sufficient incentive to secure their systems, and allowed them to pass the cost of fraud along to their customers. And one reason the Internet is insecure is that liability for attacks is so diffuse. In all of these examples, the economic considerations of security are more important than the technical considerations.

More generally, many of the most basic security questions are at least as much economic as technical. Do we spend enough on keeping hackers out of our computer systems? Or do we spend too much? For that matter, do we spend appropriate amounts on police and military services? And are we spending our security budgets on the right things? In the 10 years since the terrorist attacks of 9/11, questions like these have a heightened importance.

Economics can actually explain many of the puzzling realities of Internet security. Firewalls are common and e-mail encryption is rare—not because of the relative effectiveness of the technologies, but because of the economic pressures that drive companies to install them. Corporations rarely publicize information about intrusions; that is because of economic incentives against doing so. And an insecure operating system is the international standard; in part, that is because its economic effects are largely borne not by the company that builds the operating system, but by the customers who buy it.

Some of the most controversial cyberpolicy issues also sit squarely between information security and economics. For example, the issue of digital rights management: is copyright law too restrictive—or not restrictive enough—to maximize society's creative output? And if it needs to be more restrictive, will DRM technologies benefit the music industry or the technology vendors? Is Apple's strict control over iPhone and iPad applications good for security, or just another way for the company to lock its customers into its platforms? What are the costs and benefits of different Internet security proposals: systems that restrict anonymity, breach disclosure laws, or Internet "kill switches"? Any attempt to answer these questions becomes rapidly entangled with both information security and economic arguments.

WEIS 2011 was held at George Mason University, in Fairfax, Virginia (http://weis2011.econinfosec.org/). Over the course of two days, 95 attendees heard 20 talks, two invited speakers, and one panel. Topics covered included privacy, identity, security resilience, and the economics of computer crime.

This year marked a milestone for WEIS: ten conferences in 10 years. I've long said that the fundamental problems in computer security are no longer about technology; they're about applying technology. Workshops like WEIS help us understand why good security technologies fail and bad ones succeed, and that kind of insight is critical if we're going to improve security in the information age.

Minneapolis, MN, USA   Bruce Schneier

Contents

Contributors

Ryan Abman University of California, Santa Barbara, Santa Barbara, CA, USA

Ross Anderson University of Cambridge, Cambridge, UK

Adrian Baldwin HP Labs, Bristol, England, UK

Yolanta Beres HP Labs, Bristol, England, UK

Vincent Bindschaedler EPFL, Lausanne, Switzerland

Joseph Bonneau University of Cambridge, Cambridge, UK

Marco Casassa Mont HP Labs, Bristol, England, UK

Daegon Cho Carnegie Mellon University, Pittsburgh, PA, USA

Richard Clayton University of Cambridge, Cambridge, UK

Geoffrey B. Duggan University of Bath, Bath, England, UK

Benjamin Edwards University of New Mexico, Albuquerque, NM, USA

Dinei Florêncio Microsoft Research, Redmond, WA, USA

Stephanie Forrest University of New Mexico, Albuquerque, NM, USA

Julien Freudiger EPFL, Lausanne, Switzerland

Chris Hall Highwayman Associates Ltd., Leatherhead, UK

Cormac Herley Microsoft Research, Redmond, WA, USA

Steven Hofmeyr Lawrence Berkeley National Laboratory, Berkeley, CA, USA

Jean-Pierre Hubaux EPFL, Lausanne, Switzerland

Christos Ioannidis University of Bath, Bath, England, UK

Hilary Johnson University of Bath, Bath, England, UK

Richard A. Kemmerer University of California, Santa Barbara, Santa Barbara, CA, USA

Christopher Kruegel University of California, Santa Barbara, Santa Barbara, CA, USA

Chris Middup Open University, England, UK

Sabyasachi Mitra College of Management, Georgia Institute of Technology, Atlanta, GA, USA

Tyler Moore Harvard University, Cambridge, MA, USA

Evangelos Ouzounis European Network and Information Security Agency, Heraklion, Greece

Sören Preibusch University of Cambridge, Cambridge, UK

David Pym University of Aberdeen, Aberdeen, Scotland, UK

Sam Ransbotham Boston College, Chestnut Hill, MA, USA

Brent Rowe RTI International, San Francisco, CA, USA

Simon Shiu HP Labs, Bristol, England, UK

Douglas G. Steigerwald University of California, Santa Barbara, Santa Barbara, CA, USA

George Stelle University of New Mexico, Albuquerque, NM, USA

Brett Stone-Gross University of California, Santa Barbara, Santa Barbara, CA, USA

Panagiotis Trimintzios European Network and Information Security Agency, Heraklion, Greece

Giovanni Vigna University of California, Santa Barbara, Santa Barbara, CA, USA

Nevena Vratonjic EPFL, Lausanne, Switzerland

Julian Williams University of Aberdeen, Aberdeen, Scotland, UK

Dallas Wood RTI International, San Francisco, CA, USA

The Impact of Immediate Disclosure on Attack Diffusion and Volume

Sam Ransbotham and Sabyasachi Mitra

Abstract A significant debate in the security industry revolves around the vulnerability disclosure policy. We investigate the effects of immediate disclosure through an empirical study that analyzes security alerts for 960 clients of an US based security service provider. We find that immediate disclosure of vulnerabilities reduces delay in the attack diffusion process and slightly increases penetration of attacks in the population of target systems but slightly decreases the overall the volume of attacks.

1 Introduction

Most common types of attacks on computer systems exploit vulnerabilities present in the software running on these systems [5, 6]. These errors in software can be eliminated through corrective patches released by the software vendor, or their effects can often be contained through other protective measures initiated by security professionals. Thus, the impact of a software vulnerability depends on whether the software vendor and security professionals have the opportunity to eliminate the vulnerability (or otherwise protect systems) before the vulnerability is exploited by attackers. Consequently, the discovery and disclosure process for vulnerabilities plays a vital role in securing computer systems. The key question is how to design effective disclosure processes that advantage security professionals and disadvantage attackers.

S. Ransbotham (✉)
Carroll School of Management, Boston College, Chestnut Hill, MA 02467, USA
e-mail: sam.ransbotham@bc.edu

S. Mitra
College of Management, Georgia Institute of Technology, Atlanta, GA 30332, USA
e-mail: saby.mitra@mgt.gatech.edu

B. Schneier (ed.), *Economics of Information Security and Privacy III*,
DOI 10.1007/978-1-4614-1981-5_1,
© Springer Science+Business Media New York 2013

There are two primary methods for disclosing vulnerabilities discovered by security professionals. First, security professionals can disclose the vulnerability immediately after discovery such as through the BugTraq mailing list. We refer to this pathway as *immediate disclosure*. When disclosed through immediate disclosure, the vulnerability information is immediately disseminated to security professionals who can install countermeasures, to vendors who can develop patches, and to potential attackers who can also exploit the information to their advantage. Second, security professionals may report the vulnerability to CERT (Computer Emergency Response Team) or other similar agencies (e.g. the private vulnerability markets operated by iDefense and Tipping Point). We refer to this pathway as *non-public disclosure* [11]. These agencies immediately notify the software vendor and disclose the vulnerability to the public when a patch is available from the vendor, or after a specific period (typically 45–180 days after notifying the vendor). In non-public disclosure, security service providers and potential attackers receive notification at the time of public disclosure, while vendors are notified in advance so that they can develop patches. When a vulnerability is discovered by attackers, it is exploited first before it is discovered by security professionals (after an attack is detected) and finally reported to agencies like CERT.

A significant debate in the security industry revolves around the benefits and drawbacks of immediate disclosure. The dominant viewpoint, termed as *responsible disclosure,* encourages disclosure through CERT and other similar mechanisms that provide a reasonable time for the vendor to develop patches before the vulnerability is disclosed to the public. The basic motivation behind responsible disclosure, which is supported by many software vendors and security professionals, is that the alternative immediate disclosure creates an unsafe period when the vulnerability may be exploited before the patch is developed and deployed. Proponents of responsible disclosure therefore argue that responsible disclosure will lead to lower risk of attack, more protected systems, and a safer security environment. On the other hand, immediate disclosure is often motivated by the need to force unresponsive vendors to address a vulnerability and to create incentives for developing secure software [1, 2]. Proponents argue that immediate disclosure will lead to more responsive software vendors and more alert security service providers, and consequently a safer information security environment.

In this chapter, we shed light on this overall debate through an empirical study that compares vulnerabilities disclosed through the *immediate disclosure* and *non-public disclosure* mechanisms. Specifically, we evaluate the *impact* of immediate disclosure by analyzing over 2.4 billion information security alerts for 960 clients of an US based security service provider. We examine four measures of impact: (a) attack delay—does immediate disclosure speed the diffusion of attacks corresponding to the vulnerability through the population of target systems, (b) attack penetration—does immediate disclosure increase the number of systems affected by the vulnerability within the population of target systems, (c) attack risk—does immediate disclosure increase the risk that a computer system is attacked for the first time on any specific day after the vulnerability is reported, and (d) attack volume—does immediate disclosure increase the volume of attacks based on the vulnerability? Attack delay, attack penetration and risk of first attack are important because they affect the time that vendors have to release a patch and security professionals have to protect systems before they are attacked. Likewise, attack volume measures the overall amount of malicious attack activity [9].

There are two primary contributions of this research to the information security literature. First, while several analytical models have examined optimal vulnerability disclosure and patching policies [1–5], this research is one of a few that empirically evaluates the effect of disclosure policies through the examination of intrusion detection system data. Second, we empirically evaluate a research question that is of significant practical importance for policy formulation—whether immediate disclosure has a detrimental effect on information security. We believe that our findings are of practical interest to policy makers and vendors.

The rest of the chapter is organized as follows. In the next section, we summarize the hypotheses examined in this research. In the following section, we describe the data and empirical methods used to evaluate our hypotheses. We then describe the results of our empirical analysis, and the final section summarizes the implications of our analysis.

2 Hypotheses Development

2.1 Attack Delay and Risk of First Attack

The dominant view in the information security community is that immediate disclosure will lead to a less secure environment because public disclosure of the vulnerability can lead to systems being attacked before the vendor provides a patch or before security professionals can protect systems. In contrast, when a vulnerability is reported through CERT and other similar agencies, there is a lag between the discovery of the vulnerability and subsequent public disclosure. Consequently, responsible disclosure introduces a delay in the start of the diffusion process for attacks because attackers, on average, become aware of the vulnerability at a later date. Further, on any specific day after the vulnerability is discovered, the delay associated with responsible disclosure also reduces the risk of first attack corresponding to the vulnerability. The risk of first attack measures the probability that a target system is attacked on any specific day after the vulnerability is discovered, given that the target has not been attacked until that time. Both the attack delay and the risk of first attack are important metrics because they affect the time that the vendor has to correct the vulnerability and that security professionals have to otherwise protect systems. This discussion leads to the following two hypotheses.

H1: The diffusion of attacks through the population of target systems will have less delay for vulnerabilities reported through immediate disclosure.

H2: The risk of first attack for a target system on any specific day after the vulnerability is discovered will be higher for vulnerabilities reported through immediate disclosure.

2.2 Attack Penetration and Volume of Attacks

When a patch corresponding to a vulnerability is not available, specific coun-termeasures can provide partial protection against attacks through three types of countermeasures that limit the impact of a vulnerability [10]: (a) access control methods that limit access to the affected software, (b) feature control methods that disable functionality and features in the affected software and devices, and (c) traffic control methods that filter suspicious traffic based on the attack signature. Similar descriptions of countermeasures also appear in [11]. Countermeasures are easier to develop and deploy than patches, but they provide imperfect protection until the vulnerability is corrected through patches.

We argue that immediate disclosure induces a race between attackers who attack systems and security service providers who develop and install countermeasures to protect systems. This race, which is similar in concept to a patent race in the economics literature [7], raises urgency among security service providers and accelerates the development and deployment of countermeasures. Consequently, the time window for successful exploitation by attackers is small until countermeasures are installed, and the vulnerability has a short life span. The shorter life span leads to a lower penetration level of attacks among the population of target systems since many target systems have countermeasures installed and the population of vulnerable systems rapidly decreases. The short life span of the vulnerability and its lower penetration levels among target systems reduces the overall volume of attacks as attackers divert their attention to more profitable opportunities. This forms the basis of the following two hypotheses:

H3: The diffusion of attacks through the population of target systems will have reduced penetration for vulnerabilities reported through immediate disclosure.

H4: The volume of attacks will be lower for vulnerabilities reported through immediate disclosure.

3 Data and Methods

We utilize two main data sources for the study. First, we use a database of alerts generated from intrusion detection systems (IDS) installed in client firms of a security service provider. The dataset contains real alert data (as opposed to data from a research setting) from a large number of clients with varied infrastructure across many industries. The alert database contained over four hundred million alerts generated during 2006 and 2007 for over 900 clients of the security service provider. We created a panel dataset of the number of alerts generated every day during the 2-year period of our analysis, for each target firm and specific vulnerability. That is, each data point in our dataset is for a specific target firm—vulnerability combination, and it contains a count of the number of alerts generated for each day in the 2-year period (2006–2007).

We combine the above data set with information in the National Vulnerabilities Database [8] to obtain several characteristics of the vulnerabilities we study. The NVD obtains data from several other public vulnerability data sources such as CERT, BugTraq, XForce and Secunia. We match the records in our alert database with the data in the NVD through a CERT assigned unique ID for each vulnerability. We use the following variables from the NVD data as controls in our empirical analysis to ensure that the results we observe are due to immediate disclosure and not because of the characteristics of the vulnerability itself. The control variables are described below and shown in italics.

Once the attacker has access, vulnerabilities require varying degrees of complexity to exploit and are categorized by experts as *Low, Medium* or *High Complexity* and we include control variables for medium and high complexity, with low complexity as the base type. We also include an indicator variable (*Signature*) that is set to 1 if a signature was available at the time that the vulnerability was disclosed, 0 otherwise. The *Impact* of a vulnerability is categorized by experts into one or more categories, and we use an indicator variable for each impact category that is set to 1 if the potential for the specific impact is present, 0 otherwise. The NVD classifies vulnerabilities into several different *Types* based on the software defect that the vulnerability represents, and we used indicator variables to control for each vulnerability type. We also include an indicator variable (*Patch*) that is set to 1 if a patch was available on the focal day of analysis, 0 otherwise. We also include the *Age* of the vulnerability (log transformed) at the time of our analysis (measured by the number of days since the vulnerability was reported) to control for any age related effects. An additional variable (*Server*) indicates whether the software corresponding to vulnerability is desktop (0) or server (1) based.

Our focal variable (*Immediate Disclosure*) indicates if a disclosure was made through a public forum (e.g. BugTraq). An important caveat is that we classify a vulnerability as *immediate* if it is ever reported on a public forum, even if it may also have been reported through other reporting agencies. Thus, some vulnerabilities may be misclassified as immediate, making it more difficult to obtain significant results. Consequently, our results will be stronger if we could better identify immediately disclosed vulnerabilities. (Our research is ongoing to further clarify the *first* disclosure mechanism.)

Table 1 shows selected descriptive statistics for the vulnerabilities in our sample, divided into immediate and non-immediate disclosure vulnerabilities. The two types of vulnerabilities are similar in terms of the reported characteristics.

3.1 Modeling the Diffusion of Attacks

We model the diffusion of attacks through the population of target systems through a s-curve that has been extensively used to model the diffusion of innovations [12]. Let $N(t)$ be the cumulative number of target systems affected at time t where t is measured from the time the vulnerability is disclosed. Let P be the height of the

Table 1 Sample descriptive statistics

Variable	Value	Immediate disclosure		Non-immediate	
		Count	%	Count	%
Complexity	Low	270	61.04	347	51.87
	Medium	194	23.26	263	39.31
	High	68	15.70	59	8.82
Confidentiality impact	No	121	23.47	157	23.47
	Yes	411	76.53	512	76.53
Integrity impact	No	104	13.95	156	23.32
	Yes	428	76.68	513	76.68
Availability impact	No	106	19.77	97	14.50
	Yes	426	80.23	572	85.50
Vulnerability	Input	184	37.21	206	30.79
	Design	76	11.63	111	16.59
	Exception	44	6.40	72	10.76
Market disclosure	No	441	82.89	600	89.69
	Yes	91	17.11	69	10.31
Server application	No	513	96.43	651	97.31
	Yes	19	3.57	18	2.69
Contains signature	No	466	87.59	576	86.10
	Yes	66	12.41	93	13.90
Patch available	No	224	42.11	320	47.83
	Yes	308	57.89	349	52.17

s-curve, or the maximum number of target systems in the population affected by the vulnerability (referred to as penetration of the diffusion process). D is the time when $P/2$ systems are affected by the vulnerability (i.e. the s-curve reaches half of its ultimate penetration level) and captures the delay associated with the diffusion process. R is the slope of the s-curve and it is dependent on various factors such as the type of vulnerability and the complexity of developing exploits.

$$N(t) = \frac{P}{1 + e^{-(Rt-D)}} \tag{1}$$

We use non-linear least squares to estimate (1) with P, R and D as linear functions of our focal (*Immediate Disclosure*) and other control variables.

3.2 Analyzing the Risk of First Attack

We use the Cox proportional hazard model to examine the risk of first attack from a vulnerability. A hazard model explains the first exploitation attempt of a vulnerability for a specific target firm. We constructed a data set that contains for each target firm and vulnerability combination, the day of first attempt to exploit the vulnerability (960 firms and 1,201 vulnerabilities for a total of 1,152,406 observations). All vulnerabilities were aligned so that day 0 represented the date the vulnerability was reported to the reporting agencies or publicly disclosed. We incorporate our focal (*Immediate Disclosure*) and control variables as explanatory covariates in the hazard model.

3.3   Volume of Attacks

We use a two-stage Heckman model to analyze the number of alerts generated by a vulnerability for a specific firm. Recall that our data set has for each firm (960 firms) and each vulnerability (1,201 vulnerabilities), the number of alerts generated on each day of our research period. All vulnerabilities are aligned so that day 0 represents the day the vulnerability was first reported to the reporting agencies or disclosed publicly. Many vulnerabilities are never exploited in our alert data and ordinary least squares estimation will ignore the selection bias. The two-stage Heckman model allows us to incorporate selection bias in the volume of attacks. In the first stage, we use a selection model to investigate vulnerability attributes that affect overall likelihood of exploitation. In the second stage, we examine the number of alerts per day (with a natural log transformation). In this analysis, we control for all vulnerability covariates and we include monthly fixed effects based on attack date to control for changes in attack behavior over time. We also include 960 firm fixed effect indicators to control for potential differences in a firm's inherent risk of attack.

4   Results

Table 2 shows the results of the non-linear least squares estimation of (1). Based on the estimated parameters, we find that immediate disclosure reduces delay (D) of diffusion (accelerates the diffusion process) and slightly increases penetration (P) of attacks based on the vulnerability. To ease the interpretation of the estimated parameters, Fig. 1 plots the s-curve for immediate and non-immediate disclosure vulnerabilities. The figure shows that while immediate disclosure significantly reduces delay of the diffusion process by approximately 12 days, it has a small effect on the penetration level. Thus, we find support for H1 and our results slightly disagree with H3.

Table 3 shows the results of the Cox proportional hazard model to analyze the risk of first attack from a vulnerability for a specific target firm. Model 0 provides the results with only the control variables included, while Model 1 includes our focal variable (*Immediate*). The results in Table 3 show that immediate disclosure significantly increases the risk of first attack by an estimated 49.7%. Thus, our results support H2.

Table 2 Diffusion of vulnerability exploit attempts

Variable	Model 0			Model 1		
	P	R	D	P	R	D
Constant	72.921***	−0.045***	−23.822***	58.711***	−1.122***	76.100***
Confidentiality impact	−35.980***	−0.091***	71.715***	−32.475***	0.191***	135.880***
Integrity impact	−0.354	−0.015***	40.826***	11.739***	0.394***	91.899***
Availability impact	−10.909***	−0.147***	−40.211***	−11.125***	−0.776***	−156.507***
Input type	61.636***	−0.102***	89.354***	51.834***	0.504***	121.676***
Design type	−25.785***	−0.047***	−1.596***	−24.477***	−0.339***	9.165***
Exception type	22.260***	−0.608***	189.362***	−43.074***	−1.567***	27.602***
Medium complexity	207.046***	−0.060***	72.532***	174.273***	0.573***	136.684***
High complexity	45.598***	−0.002	10.702***	42.092***	0.573***	20.652***
Market disclosure	−78.618***	−0.740***	240.813***	−57.462***	−1.151***	278.744***
Server application	13.605***	−1.311***	466.265***	−3.054*	−0.104***	27.296***
Signature available	124.750***	0.300***	−47.806***	123.242***	1.415***	−141.577***
Patch available	−22.575***	0.104***	−98.445***	−19.941***	−0.597***	−140.865***
Immediate disclosure				3.686***	−0.094***	−5.765**
R^2	31.66			29.47		

132,768 daily observations of 333 vulnerabilities from 2006–2007. Robust (HC3) standard errors; significance: $^* p < 0.05$; $^{**} p < 0.01$; $^{***} p < 0.001$. Nonlinear regression on number of firms affected, $N(t) = \frac{P}{1+e^{-(Rt-D)}}$ where the cumulative penetration (P), the rate of diffusion (R) and delay (D) are linear functions of the variables shown in the table.

Fig. 1 The diffusion of immediate and non-immediate vulnerabilities

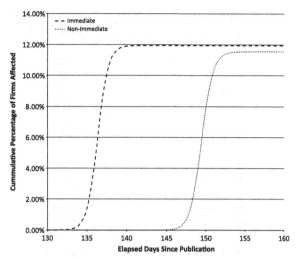

Table 3 Risk of exploitation of vulnerabilities

Variable	Model 0	Model 1
Confidentiality impact	−0.135***	−0.165***
Integrity impact	0.288***	0.298***
Availability impact	0.296***	0.339***
Input type	0.302***	0.289***
Design type	−0.388***	−0.359***
Exception type	−0.093**	−0.108***
Medium complexity	−0.215***	−0.188***
High complexity	0.227***	0.227***
Market disclosure	−1.508***	−1.594***
Server application	−0.620***	−0.658***
Signature available	1.034***	1.075***
Patch available	0.009	−0.001
Immediate disclosure		0.497***
Log likelihood	−111,736.2	−111,225.21
Wald χ^2	8,436.90***	8,504.00***

The results from our evaluation of H4 are reported in Table 4. The dependent variable is the number of attacks (log transformed) on a specific date for a specific client and for a specific vulnerability. Table 4 reports results from a two-stage Heckman selection model. The coefficient of the *Immediate* variable is negative and significant, indicating that immediate disclosure reduces the volume of attacks. However, based on the estimated parameter, immediate disclosure reduces volume of attacks by approximately 3.6%. Thus, we find only limited support for H4.

Although the effect size was small, our results indicate that immediate disclosure paradoxically increases the number of distinct firms attacked (increased penetration), but decreases the total number of attack attempts. This may indicate a unique search pattern shaped by the exploitation race. Attackers may attempt a broad search

Table 4 Volume of alerts per client firm per vulnerability

Variable	Model 0	Model 1
Constant	0.430***	0.465***
confidentiality Impact	0.037***	0.031***
integrity impact	−0.076***	−0.083***
Availability impact	−0.003	−0.005
Input type	0.145***	0.136***
Design type	−0.089***	−0.089***
Exception type	−0.132***	−0.128***
Age (ln)	−0.210***	−0.210***
Medium complexity	−0.042***	−0.050***
High complexity	−0.036***	−0.037***
Market disclosure	−0.101***	−0.098***
Server application	0.132***	0.130***
Signature available	0.170***	0.166***
Patch available	−0.024***	−0.019***
Attack month	Fixed effects	Fixed effects
Firm	Fixed effects	Fixed effects
Immediate disclosure		−0.034***
Inverse mills	−0.0812***	−0.095***
Constant	0.263***	0.329***
confidentiality impact	0.024***	0.015***
Integrity impact	0.503***	0.501***
Availability impact	−0.246***	−0.253***
Input type	0.146***	0.138***
Design type	−0.195***	−0.197***
Exception type	0.569***	0.572***
Medium complexity	0.111***	0.100***
High complexity	0.278***	0.280***
Market disclosure	−0.062***	−0.050***
Server application	−0.331***	−0.325***
Signature available	0.739***	0.738***
Patch available	−0.438***	−0.432**
Immediate disclosure		−0.067***
Publication month	Fixed effects	Fixed effects
Wald χ^2	2.16e+06***	2.16e+06***

to rapidly determine if countermeasures are in place. If countermeasures are found, then there is no utility for continued attempts within a firm and overall attack volume does not correspondingly increase with the increased penetration. This supports the conversion from broad untargeted reconnaissance activity to targeted attacks previously theorized [10].

Interestingly, we also find that public availability of an attack signature accelerates the diffusion process, increases penetration of attacks, increases risk of first attack, but slightly decreases the volume of attacks, indicating that the signature contains information that the attacker can utilize to build tools and exploit the vulnerability. Some of the other variables in the models also provide interesting insights. For example, vulnerabilities that require complex execution methods (e.g. social engineering) have delayed diffusion processes and lower attack volumes.

4.1 Summary and Implications

Contrary to the dominant view in the security industry and the practitioner literature, we find that immediate disclosure of vulnerabilities reduces delay in the attack diffusion process (as expected), but also slightly increases penetration of attacks in the population of target systems and slightly decreases the volume of attacks. Our results can be explained by viewing the attack process as a race between attackers who attack systems and security service providers who develop countermeasures, similar to a patent race that has been examined in the economics literature [7]. This race accelerates the attack diffusion process, but also increases awareness, forces security service providers to be more vigilant, accelerates the deployment of countermeasures, and reduces the window of opportunity for attackers before countermeasures are installed.

Our results have two important implications for policy makers, security organizations such as CERT, and software vendors. First, limited public disclosure of vulnerability information may combine the benefits of non-public and immediate disclosure to skew the race towards securing systems. For example, organizations such as CERT can immediately disclose the vulnerability to trusted security service providers (as well as the software vendor) so that they can develop countermeasures to protect systems for their clients until a patch is made available by the software vendor. This may provide an advantage to security service providers in the attack and countermeasures race without publicly disclosing the signature and other attack details. This limited disclosure to trusted security service providers is particularly important since our results indicate that public disclosure of signatures increases attack penetration and attack volume. Unfortunately, limiting disclosure is inherently difficult and, in the end, relies on obscurity to provide advantage to defenders.

Second, while immediate disclosure causes security service providers to be more vigilant and limits the volume of attacks based on the vulnerability, it is possible (and perhaps even likely) that the effect on those who are not protected through such services is in the opposite direction as attackers focus their attention on such targets in the absence of others. Also, a similar diversion-based argument applies to vulnerabilities not disclosed through immediate disclosure. In general, the attack and countermeasures race for immediate disclosure vulnerabilities may cause security service providers to adjust priorities and focus less on other (perhaps more critical) vulnerabilities.

It is important to note that our analysis focuses on exploitation attempts and we do not observe the costs associated with immediate or non-public disclosure. Immediate disclosure is likely to significantly increase costs to defenders because it requires urgent handling instead of routine processes. If all vulnerabilities were immediately disclosed, benefits from prioritization would likely diminish while defensive costs may increase. Overall, our analysis and results indicate that the effects of different disclosure methods are complex and nuanced, and represent a fruitful area of further research.

References

1. Arora A, Caulkins JP, Telang R (2006) Sell first, fix later: impact of patching on software quality. Manag Sci 52(3):465–471
2. Arora A, Telang R, Hao X (2008) Optimal policy for software vulnerability disclosure. Manag Sci 54(4):642–656
3. August T, Tunca TI (2006) Network software security and user incentives. Manag Sci 52(11):1703–1720
4. August T, Tunca TI (2008) Let the pirates patch? an economic analysis of software security patch restrictions. Inform Syst Res 19(1):48–70
5. Cavusoglu H, Cavusoglu H, Raghunathan S (2007) Efficiency of vulnerability disclosure mechanisms to disseminate vulnerability knowledge. IEEE Trans Software Eng 33(3):171–185
6. Cavusoglu H, Cavusoglu H, Zhang J (2008) Security patch management: share the burden or share the damage? Manag Sci 54(4):657–670
7. Denicolo V (2000) Two-stage patent races and patent policy. RAND J Econ 31(3):488–501
8. National Vulnerability Database (2008) http://nvd.nist.gov/. Accessed 23 Apr 2008
9. Park I, Sharman R, Rao HR, Upadhyaya S (2007) Short term and total life impact analysis of email worms in computer systems. Decis Support Syst 43:827–841
10. Ransbotham S, Mitra S (2009) Choice and chance: a conceptual model of paths to information security compromise. Inform Syst Res 20(1):121–139
11. Ransbotham S, Mitra S, Ramsey J (2011) Are Markets for Vulnerabilities Effective? MIS Quarterly 36(1):43–64
12. Rogers EM (2003) Diffusion of innovations, 5th edn. The Free Press, New York, NY

Where Do All the Attacks Go?

Dinei Florêncio and Cormac Herley

Abstract The fact that a majority of Internet users appear unharmed each year is difficult to reconcile with a weakest-link analysis. We seek to explain this enormous gap between potential and actual harm. The answer, we find, lies in the fact that an Internet attacker, who attacks en masse, faces a sum-of-effort rather than a weakest-link defense. Large-scale attacks must be profitable in expectation, not merely in particular scenarios. For example, knowing the dog's name may open an occasional bank account, but the cost of determining one million users' dogs' names is far greater than that information is worth. The strategy that appears simple in isolation leads to bankruptcy in expectation. Many attacks cannot be made profitable, even when many profitable targets exist. We give several examples of insecure practices which should be exploited by a weakest-link attacker but are extremely difficult to turn into profitable attacks.

1 Introduction: Why Isn't Everyone Hacked Every Day?

Internet security has a puzzling fact at its core. If security is only as strong as the weakest-link then all who choose weak passwords, re-use credentials across accounts, fail to heed security warnings or neglect patches and updates should be hacked, regularly and repeatedly. Clearly this fails to happen. Two billion people use the Internet; the majority can in no sense be described as secure, and yet they apparently derive more use from it than harm. How can this be? Where do all the attacks go?

We do not have to look far for evidence that things are bad. The range of attacks to which Internet users are subjected is enormous. Attack vectors seldom disappear, and new threats emerge all the time. Brute-forcing, Man-in-the-middle attacks and

D. Florêncio (✉) • C. Herley
Microsoft Research, Redmond, WA, USA
e-mail: dinei@microsoft.com; cormac@microsoft.com

B. Schneier (ed.), *Economics of Information Security and Privacy III*,
DOI 10.1007/978-1-4614-1981-5_2,
© Springer Science+Business Media New York 2013

session hijacking have been with us for some time, but have recently been joined by a host of new threats. Phishing emerged in the last decade. While it has not declined, exploits such as Cross-Site Request Forgery and keylogging Trojans have been added to the list. The previously unknown phenomenon of botnets has mushroomed into prominence in the last five years. In the last few years we have learned that DNS, on which the name structure of the Internet depends, Chip-and-PIN, which handles hundreds of millions of transactions per day, and SSL, which handles encrypted traffic online "are broken" [25, 29].

Against this backdrop, there are approximately two billion people using the Internet [30]. Larger services like Facebook, Yahoo! and Hotmail have hundreds of millions of users each. It is not speculation to say that the majority of Internet users ignore the majority of security advice they are offered. In spite of the large and growing set of attacks, numerous studies show that users choose weak passwords [12, 27], ignore certificate error warnings [10], cannot tell phishing sites from legitimate ones [9], are careless about the status of their anti-virus protection and re-use passwords across accounts liberally. A recent report by Webroot [1] found that 90% share password across accounts, 41% share passwords with others, 40% never use special characters in passwords, and 14% have never changed their banking password. Updating software, regarded as a vital security practice, is largely left to chance. As of Sept. 2010, fully 58% of Windows users were still running Windows XP [2], and 22% of Internet Explorer users still use IE6 more than 4 years after the launch of IE7, and a year and a half after IE8. Trustseer reported in 2009 that 80% of users were running un-patched versions of Flash [3]. Users are not alone in this negligence: Rescorla reports that even among system administrators fewer than 40% had installed a long-available patch against the Slapper worm [32].

Yet, if things are so bad, how come they're so good? It is not speculation to say that the majority of users are not harmed every day. Estimates place the number of users who have accounts hijacked each year at below 5% [14, 16]. So, 95% or more of users suffer no harm from account hijacking each year. Thus, most users fall well short of the effort required to "be secure" and yet they mostly escape harm. For example, the majority of the 90% from the Webroot survey who re-use passwords across accounts almost certainly escape harm. Equally, while Chip-and-PIN may be broken, it is involved in several hundred million transactions per day with apparently manageable levels of fraud. The great potential for harm of the Slapper worm was never fulfilled. Close to 50% of the DNS infrastructure remained un-patched at time of Kaminsky's disclosure, and yet, for all intents and purposes, nothing happened.

So, where do all the attacks go? In this paper we seek to explain this enormous gap between potential and actual harm. A weakest-link analysis seems unable to offer an explanation. The answer, we suggest, lies in a shortcoming of common threat models. The model where a single user Alice faces an attacker Charles fails to capture the anonymous and broadcast nature of web attacks. Indeed, it is numerically impossible: two billion users cannot possibly each have an attacker who identifies and exploits their weakest-link. Instead, we use a cloud threat model where a population of users is attacked by a population of attackers. Our main finding is that a crowd of users presents a sum-of-effort rather than a weakest-link defense. Many attacks, while they succeed in particular scenarios, are not profitable when averaged over a large population. This is true even when many profitable targets exist and explains why so many attack types end up causing so little actually observed harm. Thus, how common a security strategy is, matters at least as much as how weak it is. Even truly weak strategies go unpunished so long as the costs where the attack fails exceeds the gains from it succeeds. Why is this question important? If, as appears to be the case, a majority are insecure and yet unharmed it is important to understand why. These users are avoiding harm at far lower cost than is usually assumed to be necessary.

2   A Threat Model That Scales

System-centric threat models often describe the technical capabilities of an attacker. A defender Alice is pitted against an attacker Charles, who can attack in any manner consistent with the threat model. Generally Alice's security is regarded as being only as good as the weakest-link.

There are several things wrong with this threat model. It makes no reference of the value of the resource to Alice, or to Charles. It makes no reference to the cost of defence to Alice, or of the attack to Charles. It makes no reference to the fact that Charles is generally uncertain about the value of the asset and the extent of the defence (i.e., he doesn't know whether benefit exceeds cost until he attacks successfully). It makes no provision for the possibility that exogenous events save Alice, even when her own defence fails (e.g., her bank catches fraudulent transfers). It ignores the fact that Charles must compete against other attackers (we showed how this drives down returns in previous work [20]). It ignores scale: assuming that Internet users greatly outnumber attackers it is simply numerically impossible for every user to have an attacker who identifies and exploits her weakest-link. Some high-value users may face this threat model, but it is not possible that all do. Some or all of these shortcomings have been addressed by others; see the Related Work section for details. It is however one last failing that we are primarily interested in addressing. This model, where weakest-links are ruthlessly exploited, is unable to explain the reality we observe: 20% use a significant date or pet's name as password, yet 20% are not victimized. It is this inability to explain observations that we seek to address.

2.1   An Internet Threat Model

In our threat model a population of Internet users are attacked by a population of hackers. We call the Internet users Alice(i) for $i = 0, 1, \cdots, N' - 1$ and the attackers Charles(j) for $j = 0, 1, \cdots, M - 1$. Clearly $N' \gg M$: Internet users

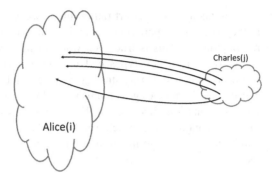

Fig. 1 Threat Model: a population of Internet users Alice(i) are attacked by a population of hackers Charles(j). Each user, Alice(i) receives attacks from numerous different attackers, each hacker Charles(j) attacks many different users. If Charles(j) successfully obtains access to Alice(i)'s account he then attempts to monetize the asset

outnumber attackers. Each Alice(i) is subjected to attack by many of the attackers. Each attacker goes after as many Internet users as he can reach. Cost is the main reason for this approach: it costs little more to attack millions than it does to attack thousands. The attackers' goal is purely financial. None of the Alice(i)'s are personally known to any of the Charles(j)'s. Thus, revenge, jealousy, curiosity and emotion play no role. The situation is depicted in Fig. 1. This threat model captures the large-scale broadcast attacks so familiar to Internet users: phishing, malware-bearing spam, for example. These attacks are similar to the parallel attacks that Schechter and Smith mention [36] and the scalable attacks that Herley studies [22] and the distributed attack network that Fulz and Grossklags study [15]. For more details on related work see Sect. 6.

Our threat model differs from others in several respects. First, we focus on end-users of the Internet. Thus we examine the consumer rather than the enterprize space. This is significant for a number of reasons. Consumers generally have less information and are less protected. They must decide for themselves a whole range of issues that affect their security from passwords to anti-virus to software updates. But they do so largely in ignorance. They do not have security professionals who monitor their network searching for problems and anomalies. They do not have well developed expectations as to where their weakest-links lie. Even after Alice(i) has an account hijacked or money stolen she has very little ability to carry out forensic examination and determine what happened. Second, rather than having an individual defender and individual attacker pitted against each other, we have a population of N' users facing M attackers. Attackers must strive, not merely to attack users, but also to compete with each other. While N' is large it is finite. Charles(j) faces the prospect that the most easily-attacked users will be victimized by several attackers. There is a chance that Charles(j) successfully attacks Alice(i) only to find that Charles($j - 1$), Charles($j - 2$) and Charles($j - 3$) have already been there. As all Internet users know: as far as spam, phishing, etc., are concerned there are no un-contacted populations. Third, the attacks we study happen in a competitive economic landscape. An attack is not merely a technical exploit but a business proposition. If it succeeds (and makes a profit) it is repeated over and over (and copied by others). If it fails (does not make a profit) it is abandoned and the energy is spent elsewhere. Fourth, attackers are playing a "numbers game": they seek victims in the population rather than targeting individuals. For example, if Charles(j) targets Paypal accounts, he isn't seeking particular accounts but rather any accounts that he happens to compromise. Charles(j) doesn't know the value, or security investment of any particular Internet user in advance. He discovers this only by attacking.

We freely admit that this threat model has some obvious short-comings. It excludes cases where the attacker and defender are known to each other, or where non-monetary motives are involved. It does not cover cases of attackers motivated by emotion, curiosity, revenge or the desire for fame or notoriety. It does not cover the case of Advanced Persistent Threats. It does not cover the case where the attacker is targeting Alice(i) alone or values her assets beyond their economic value. While restrictive, our model of an unknown, financially motivated attacker does cover a significant fraction of what most users are concerned with.

2.2 Expected Gain and Expected Loss

Our Internet user Alice(i) has assets that she must protect. For any particular asset there are many possible attacks, call them attack(0), attack(1), $\cdots$, attack($Q-1$). For example, keylogging, phishing, brute-forcing are all methods of attacking an Internet account. An attacker can choose whichever gives the best return for his effort.

We model Alice(i)'s expected loss as follows. The effort that Alice(i) devotes to defending against attack(k) is $e_i(k)$. $Pr\{e_i(k)\}$ is the probability that she succumbs to this attack (if attacked) at this level of effort. We assume that $Pr\{e_i(k)\}$ is a monotonically decreasing function of $e_i(k)$. This merely means that the greater effort Alice(i) spends on attack(k), the lower her probability of succumbing. L_i is the loss that Alice(i) endures when she succumbs to any attack, independent of the attack type. For example, it doesn't matter whether her password was stolen by keylogging or brute-force. In addition, to allow for external fraud checks, there is some chance that, even though she succumbs to attack, Alice(i) suffers no loss because she is saved because of exogenous events. For example, her bank password falls to Charles(j) but her bank detects the fraud and saves her from harm. Here, we use $Pr\{SP\}$ to denote the probability that her Service Provider saves Alice(i) from harm. Alice(i)'s loss then is the probability that exogenous events do not save her, times the probability that she succumbs to any of the attacks, times her loss, plus the sum of what she spends defending against all attacks:

$$(1 - Pr\{SP\}) \cdot \left(1 - \prod_{k=0}^{Q-1}(1 - Pr\{e_i(k)\})\right) L_i + \sum_{k=0}^{Q-1} e_i(k). \qquad (1)$$

The goal of Alice(i) is to minimize her expected loss under the range of attacks that she sees.

On the other side of the fence what is the expected gain for an attacker Charles(j)? We denote G_i as his gain (if successful) from Alice(i), and $C_j(N,k)$ as the cost to Charles(j) of reaching N users with attack(k). The expected gain of the attacker Charles(j) is the probability that exogenous events do not stop his fraud, times the sum of the probable gain over all attacked users, minus the total cost of the attack:

$$U_j(k) = (1 - Pr\{SP\}) \cdot \left(\sum_i Pr\{e_i(k)\}G_i\right) - C_j(N,k). \qquad (2)$$

The summation in (2) is over as many users, N, as Charles(j) attacks. We don't assume that all N' Internet users are attacked, however we assume that the number is large enough for statistical arguments to apply. This accords with our threat model: many Internet attacks have costs that grow far slower than linearly with the number of users attacked, so it makes sense to attack as many users as possible. The spam campaign documented by Kanich et al. [26], for example, attacked three hundred fifty million users. So assuming that Charles(j) attacks at least thousands is not overly restrictive. It also bears mentioning that many attacks might have a fixed cost that is almost independent of the number of users attacked. Charles(j) might be able to spam three hundred fifty million users for $100, but he can't reach 3.5 million for $1.

G_i is the gain that Charles(j) extracts from Alice(i). Now, Charles(j)'s gain, G_i, is not necessarily the same as Alice(i)'s loss, L_i. There are several reasons for this. We assume that the asset is rivalrous [28], which means that enjoyment of it by one party reduces enjoyment of it by another. Thus

$$G_i \leq L_i,$$

so that Charles(j) can at most gain whatever Alice(i) loses. It is possible that Charles(j) is not alone in successfully attacking Alice(i), so that he shares the loss that Alice(i) suffers with several others; i.e., $G_i \approx L_i/m$ for some number of attackers m. We explore this possibility in Sect. 4.3.

If the asset is non-rivalrous other possibilities exist. First, Charles(j) might benefit without harming Alice(i): e.g., if he uses Alice(i)'s machine simply to send spam and conceal his IP address he might derive significant value while Alice(i) would not suffer directly. Thus, $G_i \gg L_i$. An intriguing possibility, where $L_i < 0$, and Alice(i) makes a "pact with the devil" and benefits from the attack is explored by Bond and Danezis [6]. Finally, it is possible that $G_i \ll L_i$; this might be the case of vandalism. For example, if instead of attempting to monetize the asset Charles(j) set out to destroy it. We won't treat either of these cases further and instead concentrate on the rivalrous case.

3   The Internet Attacker Faces a Sum-of-Efforts Defense

Security is often described as a weakest-link game [8, 18], where security depends on the most easily breached part of a defence. This has colored much thinking in the space. It is hard however, to square this with the claim that 20% of users choose a pet's name or significant date as password, and the fact that password re-use across accounts is almost universal [12].

The weakest-link analysis makes perfect sense where a single attacker faces a single defender [8, 18]. Since the game is zero-sum (or negative sum) with only two players the threat that is most profitable for the attacker is the one that is most costly for the defender. However, for the Internet attack model that we are using, where a crowd of users face a crowd of attackers, this is no longer the case. The threat that is most profitable for the attacker need not be any individual user's weakest-link. Further, an individual user's weakest-link need not be exploited by the most profitable attack for any attacker. In fact, as we know show, the simple change in threat model changes the defense that an Internet attacker confronts from a weakest-link defense into a sum-of-efforts one. For example, the fact that users who choose their birthdate as password avoid harm is puzzling in a weakest-link analysis but makes prefect sense in our threat model.

Elements of weakest-link, sum-of-effort and best-shot games are all present in the formulation above, and their roles are crucial as we show now. An excellent analysis of these three games in a security setting is given by Varian [39]. An analysis of how these games differ in a protection and insurance environment is performed by Grossklags et al. [19] who also introduce the concept of a weakest-target game.

3.1   Attack Selection

Each attacker Charles(j) chooses the attack that maximizes his expected gain. That is, ranging over all attack(k), he selects $\max_k U_j(k)$. Not all attackers may have the same cost structure, so what is the best attack for one, may not be so for another. For example, for Charles(j) and Charles($j+1$) the best attack might be attack(k), while for Charles($j+2$) it might be attack(k'). This explains the co-existence of several attacks on the same asset class. For example, many different attacks on user credentials co-exist; this suggests that there is no single attack(k) which maximizes the expected gain for all attackers. However, it is likely that some attacks give the best return to a wide set of attackers, while some are best for almost none. It is also likely that this changes with time.

3.2 Sum-of-Efforts

Examining (2) we see that for greater than zero gain Charles(j) requires that his return exceeds his costs:

$$(1 - Pr\{\text{SP}\}) \cdot \left(\sum_i Pr\{e_i(k)\} G_i \right) > C_j(N, k).$$

Recall that $Pr\{e_i(k)\}$ is a decreasing function of user effort $e_i(k)$. The left-hand side is related to the sum-of-efforts of all attacked users, weighted by the gains. The greater the total effort of the user population the lower the return. Thus, the expected gain from any attack is a *sum-of-effort* game [39]. An attack can be unprofitable (i.e., $U_j(k) < 0$) if the sum-of-effort of users is great enough, even though individual users represent good targets. We examine this further in Sect. 4.1. The formulation of (2) is not precisely sum-of-effort. Increasing effort by those who are above the threshold to escape harm does nothing to reduce the return. Thus it is effectively a non-linear sum-of-efforts defense.

A sum-of-efforts defense is known to be far more effective than weakest-link. The well-known free-rider effect [38] ensures that many users escape harm, even at low levels of effort. This will play an important role in the remainder of the paper.

3.3 Best-Shot

Detection of fraud by the service provider is a *best-shot* game. That is, if any of a series defences catches the fraud, then Charles(j) fails. For example, a bank may have a series of checks in place to detect fraud. Accounts that have little history of outbound transfer, logins from geographies outside the user's pattern, transfers to a stranger's account may all alert suspicion. The success of credit card fraud detection illustrates that $Pr\{SP\}$ can be quite high based purely on customer usage patterns. If in the process of attempting to drain the account Charles(j) triggers any of them then his gain is zero. In fact Charles(j) faces a sum-of-effort defense, cascaded with a best-shot defense. That is, he must succeed first against a sum-of-effort defense (to successfully compromise enough users). Following this, he must succeed against a best-shot defense (to successfully evade the fraud detection measures of the service provider).

3.4   Contrast Between Internet Attacker and Individual Attacker

The difference between a sum-of-effort and weakest-link defenses is so great that it's worth reiterating how it comes about in our threat model. Our Internet attacker faces a crowd of users. He selects attack(k) that maximizes:

$$(1 - Pr\{SP\}) \cdot \left(\sum_{i=0}^{N-1} Pr\{e_i(k)\}G_i \right) - C_j(N,k).$$

By contrast the individual attacker is after a particular user, Alice(i_0), rather than a crowd. He thus selects attack(k) that maximizes:

$$(1 - Pr\{SP\}) \cdot Pr\{e_{i_0}(k)\}G_{i_0} - C_j(1,k).$$

This is clearly maximized by the attack for which $Pr\{e_{i_0}(k)\}/C_j(1,k)$ is highest. This is Alice(i_0)'s weakest-link: the highest probability of success/cost ratio. Facing such an attacker Alice(i_0) can indeed afford to neglect no defense. Even slight weaknesses can be exploited. Why then doesn't our attacker target each user in turn? The answer, of course, is his cost structure. Our Internet attacker gets to attack N users with attack(k) at a cost of $C_j(N,k)$. However he cannot afford to target users individually $C_j(1,k) \gg C_j(N,k)/N$. The circumstances that ensure our Internet attacker faces a sum-of-effort rather than weakest-link defense are intrinsic to his *modus operandi*. This is a key point of difference between our model and that produced by the weakest-target game [19]. As the name suggests, those who have invested least succumb in a weakest-target game. However, in our model even those who have invested little or no effort escape harm, so long as there aren't enough such users to make the overall attack profitable in expectation.

4   Why Do Attacks Fail?

We now turn to the question of why so many exploits and vulnerabilities fail to translate into harm experienced by users. One obvious reason why an attack may never inflict harm is that it has negative return, that is the expected gain is lower than the expected cost. While we often get the impression that cyber-criminals get money "for free" clearly they have costs, just as any legitimate business does. Looking at (2) we can determine several ways that expected gain can be negative. This requires:

$$(1 - Pr\{SP\}) \cdot \left(\sum_i Pr\{e_i(k)\}G_i \right) < C_j(N,k). \qquad (3)$$

We now go through several of the possibilities that can satisfy this condition.

4.1 Average Success Rate Is Too Low

The left-hand side of (3) is the expected return to Charles(j) of attack(k). The sum is an average of the gains to be had, G_i, weighted by the success likelihoods $Pr\{e_i(k)\}$. Each user makes some effort against attack(k); the greater the effort Alice(i) makes the smaller the probability that she succumbs to attack(k). Since $Pr\{e_i(k)\}$ is a monotonically decreasing function of $e_i(k)$, the greater the total effort of the user population the lower the expected return for Charles(j). Thus, if the average effort increases, average success decreases and expected gain decreases. If average success decreases enough (i.e., $1/N \cdot \sum_i Pr\{e_i(k)\} \to 0$), then attack($k$) is unprofitable. It is not necessary that every user increase effort merely that enough of them do.

This leads to a simple explanation of why some attacks fail to happen: the average success rate is low enough to make it uneconomic. Since $Pr\{e_i(k)\}$ is a monotonically decreasing function of $e_i(k)$ this means that average effort is too high. This might seem a far-fetched possibility given what we know of Internet user behavior. However, some attacks require only effort that we already know most users make. For example, if the attack is to password-guess using the top ten passwords from the RockYou dataset we know that these passwords account for about 2% of accounts. Thus 98% of users have made enough effort to resist this attack.

Consider an attack which is easy to defend against (i.e., for a small effort $e_i(k) > \varepsilon$ then $Pr\{e_i(k)\} \approx 0$). The vast majority of users invest the effort to evade the attack, but a very small number do not. This attack works very well against a tiny fraction of people. However, Charles(j) can determine whether it works only by trying it (i.e., investing the cost $C_j(N,k)$). If the attack works on too small a fraction of the population the attack is uneconomic.

Observe if the attack becomes uneconomic, that users who do not invest enough (i.e., $e_i(k) < \varepsilon$ and hence $Pr\{e_i(k)\} \approx 1$) nonetheless escape this attack. Since the average effort is enough to keep the average success low and make the attack unprofitable everyone escapes harm, both those who have invested adequately and those who have not. That sum-of-effort games allow for a free-rider effect is well known [38].

Thus, one major reason that some attacks fail to manifest themselves is that the attack succeeds only on a tiny fraction of the population. A very small set of people use their dog's name as password. A similarly small fraction also use the name of their cat, significant other, child, parent, favorite team, movie star or singer, or use a birthday or anniversary date. A small percent of people who make one of these choices have the name or date (i.e., the dog's name or birthday) discoverable in an automated way. Thus the success of any of these attacks is a small percent of a small percent. If Alice(i) follows one of these strategies it might seem that Charles(j) gets G_i for a small amount of effort. That is, if

$$(1 - Pr\{\text{SP}\}) \cdot Pr\{e_i(k)\}G_i > C_j(N,k)/N \qquad (4)$$

doesn't Charles(j) make a profit? This is not so. It is not the case that Charles(j) is attacking Alice(i) at a cost of $C_j(N,k)/N$, but rather that he is attacking a population of N users at a cost of $C_j(N,k)$. If the average gain across the attacked users is not positive then his attack fails. To pick and choose the best targets requires that Charles(j) knows in advance which users have invested least.

4.2 Average Value Is Too Low

For attack(k) to be unprofitable we saw that (3) had to hold. In addition to the possibility that the success rate is too low, there is the chance that the average value extracted G_i is too low. That is, Charles(j)'s expected return gives him the probability-weighted average of the gain expected from each user [i.e., the summation in the left-hand side of (3)]. If the average value of G_is is too low then the attack again fails to be profitable. Much the same dynamic is at work as in the previous section. The attacker gets the average return for the average cost: the fact that individual users represent profitable targets is of no use if they cannot be identified.

Which attacks fall into this class? A common class is those that are predicated on leveraging a low value asset into a high return. We explore these in Sect. 5.2.

4.3 Attackers Collide Too Often

An important aspect of our threat model is that attackers live in an environment where they compete with each other. While the pool of Internet users is large, it is finite, and attackers compete for a common asset pool. In Sect. 2.2 we introduced the possibility that attackers collide in pursuing the same asset. In a finite world collisions are inevitable. Indeed Enright et al. [11] mention the case of security research teams colliding in their study of the same botnet, raising the question of how either can be sure whether they are measuring the activity of the botmasters or of other researchers! More concretely, Sariou et al. [35] find that many malware-infected machines have multiple infections. For example, 71.8% of clients infected with eZula had at least one other infection. Are collisions infrequent enough to be discounted or do they meaningfully affect the analysis? If m attackers collide in successfully attacking Alice(i) then the expected gain must be divided m ways: $G_i = L_i/m$. We now examine how this can happen.

4.3.1 Outcome Is Deterministic

Consider the case where $Pr\{e_i(k)\}$ is binary, i.e., has value either zero or one depending on the user's effort:

$$Pr\{e_i(k)\} = \begin{cases} 1 & e_i(k) < \varepsilon \\ 0 & \text{otherwise} \end{cases} \tag{5}$$

Here, any effort greater than ε gives perfect immunity to the attack, while any effort below ε ensures that Alice(i) succumbs if she is attacked. To be concrete, suppose that the attack is brute-forcing passwords using a list of ten common passwords (e.g., the ten most common passwords from the RockYou [23] dataset). Any user who has chosen one of those ten passwords (e.g., "abcdefg") always succumbs to this attack, while all others escape unscathed. Now, if Charles(j) attempts this attack he ends up successfully hijacking the accounts of all users who chose these ten passwords. However, he is not alone. Every attacker who follows this strategy enjoys exactly the same success: they also enter each of these accounts. Thus, if m attackers follow this strategy we should have $G_i \approx L_i/m$.

A deterministic outcome is the limiting case of something that is more generally true. When attackers collide the expected return is reduced. Thus an estimate of the likelihood of collision is necessary in evaluating the attacker's expected gain. If there are m attackers and each enjoys an independent probability $Pr\{e_i(k)\}$ of compromising Alice(i) in any given attack then the expected number who succeed is $mPr\{e_i(k)\}$. Thus, for any attack where $Pr\{e_i(k)\} > 1/m$ the attacker Charles(j) must expect to share L_i with others. This is quite counter-intuitive, as it implies that victims who have a *high* probability of succumbing to attack(k) do not increase in value to Charles(j). As $Pr\{e_i(k)\}$ doubles, so does the number of attackers with whom the asset must be shared. The worst victims for Charles(j) are those who deterministically succumb. He ends up burgling a house with m other burglars, or looting a store whose shelves are already bare. This is self-limiting. Unless Alice(i) changes her behavior she ends up, not with one, but with hundreds of attackers in her account.

It is natural to wonder what happens if the first successful attacker shuts the other $m - 1$ out. For example, he might change the password, patch the machine or perform other actions to make sure that others do not get access to the asset in the same manner he did. This makes no difference to the expected return: whether the entire asset goes to the first successful attacker or it is shared among them the average return is unchanged.

4.4 Attack Is Too Expensive Relative to Alternatives

A further reason that attack(k) can fail to ever be observed is that

$$\text{For some } k': \quad U_j(k) < U_j(k')\forall j.$$

That is, there's an attack that's better, having either higher expected gain or lower cost.

Consider the example of a realtime MITM attack on a banking session. This threat can take the form of session hijacking, in which the attacker piggy-backs on the legitimate session, or credential replay, in which the attacker sends a time-varying credential within the time window. In either case the attacker must lie in wait until the user actually authenticates. In both cases the attacker only has a single login session to exploit the account. Clearly this attack, which has a time restriction, has greater cost than one that does not. Since the attacker must be ready to exploit the account whenever the opportunity arises there is a constraint on his time. Since all value must be extracted in one session there is no possibility of selling the account for exploitation by others. If the account has a limit on the maximum daily transfer, then this is the maximum that can be transferred out rather than the entire account balance. For all of these reasons, the cost is greater and the gain lower than an attack that involves gathering the password of an account. A password can be used at will, can be sold on, and can be used to login multiple times if necessary to drain the account. Thus if we consider two accounts, one protected by passwords, and one by a one-time password token, there is little reason to attack the latter unless the expected gain from the better protected account is higher. Financial institutions such as Paypal, which make such tokens available to their users fall into this category: while MITM attacks are possible there is little reason to mount them when a less expensive attack on comparably valuable assets exists.

Murdoch et al. [29] recently reported an elegant attack on the Chip and PIN protocol used by many European credit card issuers. The attack confuses a point of sale terminal into believing that it has received the correct PIN, even though this is unknown to the attacker. However, since US issued cards are accepted in Europe there is no need to mount this attack. Why assault the PIN when there is no shortage of equivalently valuable targets that do not have the protection can be attacked?

4.5 *Exogenous Fraud Detection Is Too High*

A final factor that decreases Charles(j)'s expected utility is the probability that exogenous events save Alice(i). That is, if $Pr\{SP\} \approx 1$ in (2) then it is exceedingly difficult for Charles(j) to make a profit, irrespective of how Alice(i) behaves. For example, suppose Alice(i)'s bank detects and halts most attempted fraudulent activity. In this case, the true protection is not the effort $e_i(k)$ that Alice(i) expends defending against attack(k), but the back-end protections that the bank has in place. It is difficult for Charles(j) to cover his costs if this is so.

5 Where Do All the Attacks Go?

We now examine some of the attacks which do not appear to succeed as often as a weakest-link analysis would suggest. Our goal is not to suggest that any of the practices described are advisable. We merely seek to close the gap between what analysis suggests should be happening, and what observation says is actually the case.

5.1 Choosing Your Dog's Name as Password

A dismissive description of a typically bad practice is "using your dog's name as password." Indeed Webroot found 20% of users had used a pet's name or significant date as password [1]. Similar strategies involve choosing one's favorite sport's team, actor or cartoon character as password. But this raises the obvious question: if the practice is really so bad, how do so many people get away with it? While this is certainly inadvisable we suggest that profiting from this is a lot harder than it looks. While, for some people this may be their weakest-link, enough people do not follow the practice to ensure that the sum-of-effort that an attacker trying to exploit it faces is enough to ensure that it is unprofitable.

Consider a user who has $100 in a bank account protected with her dog's name as password. This is an easy $100 for an attacker only if he knows exactly who follows this practice and never wastes his effort attacking those who don't. Otherwise, the gain is reduced by all the places where the attack fails. We saw in Sects. 4.1 and 4.2 that an attacker needs that the attack be profitable in expectation. So (3) must hold, not merely (4). Suppose that 1% of users choose their dog's name as banking password. Further suppose that 1% of users have their dog's name discoverable automatically (e.g., by running a crawling script at a social networking site), and 1% have their bank username discoverable automatically. This means that, in expectation, an attacker can get into one bank account for every million users he attacks. However, (as we saw in Sect. 4.3) if the attack is this simple (and the outcome deterministic), it will be attempted by many. Suppose that $m = 100$ attackers follow this strategy. Since the outcome is deterministic all of them succeed in the same accounts and fail in the same accounts, so the expected gain drops by another factor of 100. Thus, our attacker sees his average return drop by eight orders of magnitude from the easy money proposition that we began with. We can insulate ourselves from the error of survivor paradox by asking how an attack scales. For example, a dog's name as bank password seems like a sure thing for some attacker. Instead, we might ask how much it would cost to determine the dog's names of one million banking customers and how much that information would be worth.

5.2 Leveraging a Low-Value Account into a High One

It is sometimes claimed that attackers who gain access to a low value email account can use this to get to banking information, or reset banking passwords etc.. This may indeed be the case, and this approach probably succeeds some of the time. Again, however, a lot more people appear to use a low-value email as their bank contact than have their accounts emptied every year. In question is not whether this account escalation attack ever succeeds (i.e., does (4) hold for at least one user?) but is it profitable on average (i.e., does (3) hold?).

Suppose Charles(j) gains access to n webmail accounts. Some of these are used as the email account of record for banking sites. Some of those will have the bank username included (many banks exclude username in all email communications). Some of those banking sites will mail a password reset link to an email account (though often only after successfully answering secret questions). For each webmail account if all of these conditions are met Charles(j) gains access to a bank account, otherwise he simply gets to read a stranger's email. Thus, a percent of a percent of a percent of webmail accounts will have high value, while the rest are close to worthless. Profit for Charles(j) results only if the value of the percent of a percent of a percent of n webmail accounts that lead to banking information is greater than the cost of acquiring all n webmail accounts.

Just as in Sect. 4.1 the attacker needs (3) to hold not just (4). That individual users are profitable targets is not in doubt, however Charles(j) attacks his victims in bulk and needs the average gain to be positive. To pick and choose the best targets requires that Charles(j) is omniscient and knows in advance which users have greatest extractable value. It might seem that Charles(j) can boost his return by targeting those with high net-worth. However, high networth and extractable value are not necessarily correlated [22]. Targeting Bill Gates or Warren Buffet is not a sure path to increasing expected gain. In addition, as we saw in Sect. 3.4, targeting small segments violates Charles(j)'s cost model. He attacks a massive number of users for $C_j(N, k)$, but achieves very little reduction in cost by scaling down.

Again, just as in Sect. 4.1, sum-of-effort defense implies that there is a free-rider advantage. The average value that can be extracted from an email account is very low. Some email accounts allow access to far more valuable assets and thus represent profitable targets. However, determining which are profitable and which are not cannot be done without mounting (and incurring the cost of) the full attack. If the whole attack becomes unprofitable, then users who have high value escape along with those who have low. Those who have invested least escape, thanks to those who have invested more.

5.3 Domino Effect of Password Re-use

Another frequent claim is that attackers stealing the credentials of one account will exploit the well-known habit of users to re-use passwords across accounts. The thinking is that armed with, for example, a `facebook` password an attacker may be able to gain access to the Wells Fargo account of the user. "One weak spot is all it takes to open secured digital doors and online accounts causing untold damage and consequences" write Ives et al. of this possibility [24]. Again, however, we are left with the puzzle that this appears to happen a great deal less than it might. We know that the practice of re-using passwords across accounts is almost universal [1, 12]. If the practice is so common, and so bad why is there not greater evidence of harm?

The answer, we suggest, again, lies in the confusion between having an attack that occasionally works and one that can be made economic at scale. Some facebook passwords are doubtless used also for banking. However, determining the correct bank and the username is not straightforward. First, to be successful at scale, determination of the username must be automated: it is clearly impractical for Charles(j) to wade through a thousand compromised facebook accounts seeking hints as to the username. This is especially so since he doesn't know that the facebook and bank password are the same until he successfully logs in. Thus, the entire process must be automated. Hence, Charles(j) needs not merely that the passwords be the same, but that the bank username either be the same, or be easily determined in an automated way from the facebook account information. If 1% of users satisfy the first criterion and 1% the second then out of a thousand compromised facebook accounts Charles(j) has only a 1 in 10 chance of gaining access to a single bank account.

5.4 Fraud Detection

While it is unlikely that $Pr\{SP\} = 1$ in many domains it appears to be high. Persistent reports that credentials sell for fractions of a penny on the dollar [13] indicate that cashing out is hard. The fact that, at least in the US, consumers are protected from the financial consequences of fraudulent transfers and credit-card transactions suggests that banks have considerable ability to detect fraud (i.e., $Pr\{SP\} \approx 1$) even when all else fails.

In fact, since this term applies to all attacks, improving $Pr\{SP\}$ may be a better investment for a bank than any other. This protects all users, whether they are diligent or not. Indeed, highly successful fraud detection assuming that Alice(i) will become compromised may give better return on investment than new technologies that help Alice(i) avoid compromise.

5.5 Diversity Is More Important than Strength

In Sect. 4.1 we saw that even very poor security practices can go unpunished. If the fraction of users who succumb to a certain attack is too small then the entire attack is unprofitable. When this happens those who would succumb to the attack get a free ride. Those who choose their dog's name as password escape harm simply because not enough people do so to make the attack profitable. Equally, however many other poor security practices go unexploited because of the uneconomic nature of the attack when scaled up to the whole population. This leads to the interesting conclusion that a great many users can have poor security practices that go unexploited so long as a small enough minority follows the same practice. The use of the names of pets, friends, significant others and teams and birthdays as passwords are all bad practices, but each of them is probably rare enough (and hard enough to exploit in an automated way) to make attacking any of them unprofitable. The importance of diversity in computing ecosystems has been recognized since a paper on the subject by Geer et al. [17].

Let's look at the implications of the free-rider effect caused by the sum-of-effort nature of the expected return from an attack. If brute-forcing and password guessing is a problem, suppose that $N - 1$ of our Internet users finally decide to choose strong passwords for all of their accounts. One user, Alice(i_0), takes a pass and continues her practice of using "abcdefg" as password everywhere. Through no action on her part Alice(i_0)'s risk of harm from brute-forcing decreased dramatically. Brute-forcing is now an infeasible attack for most users and the expected return plummets. In fact, two things determine whether Alice(i_0) succumbs to attack(k). The first is Alice(i_0)'s own effort: the higher $e_{i_0}(k)$ the lower the probability $Pr\{e_{i_0}(k)\}$ that she succumbs *if attacked*. The second is whether she is attacked at all. That is, if attack(k) isn't profitable for any Charles(j) then the attack is never seen at all. One way this can happen is if all other users invest a lot more than Alice(i_0). She gets away with being sloppy, so long as enough users make the effort to make the attack unprofitable. Similarly, all users can be sloppy, so long as they are sloppy in different ways. Schechter et al. [33] similarly argue that it is popularity, rather than strength, of passwords that represents a vulnerability.

5.6 Effort Allocation Is Hard

Just as an attack can be unprofitable for Charles(j), effort can be unprofitable for Alice(i). From (1) the totality of Alice(i)'s effort is profitable only if:

$$(1 - Pr\{\text{SP}\}) \cdot \left(1 - \prod_k (1 - Pr\{e_i(k)\})\right) \cdot L_i > \sum_k e_i(k).$$

If this does not hold then Alice(i) is spending more on effort to avoid attacks than her expected loss. Further, her investment in effort against any particular attack(k) is profitable only if

$$(1 - Pr\{\text{SP}\}) \cdot Pr\{e_i(k)\} \cdot L_i > e_i(k).$$

When this occurs Alice(i) is rational to ignore the effort and run the risk of the harm. This is exactly the rational rejection of security effort against attack(k) described by Herley [21].

Since, Alice(i) does not know what her weakest-link is, effort allocation is extremely hard. If she defends against all attacks she is wasting a great deal of effort on attacks that are unprofitable for all attackers (and thus have very low probability of happening). However, her situation is improved by the fact that exogenous fraud detection reduces her risk of harm $(1 - Pr\{SP\})$. In fact, since effort from the service provider affects all attacks, while her effort must be allocated between them, it is likely that increasing $Pr\{SP\}$ has a greater influence than effort she can make against any of the attacks.

6 Related Work

The question of tradeoffs in security is not a new one. Numerous authors have pointed out that, even though security is often looked at as binary, it cannot escape the budgeting, tradeoffs and compromises that are inevitable in the real world. The scalable nature of many web attacks has been noted by many authors, and indeed this has often been invoked as a possible source of weakness for attackers. Anderson [5] shows that incentives greatly influence security outcomes and demonstrates some of the perverse outcomes when they are mis-aligned. Since 2000 the Workshop on the Economics of Information Security (WEIS) has focussed on incentives and economic tradeoffs in security.

There have been numerous studies documenting the enormous range of internet attacks. Sariou et al. [34] perform an interesting measurement study of internet attacks. Kanich et al. [26] document the result of observing a spamming botnet for a number of weeks. Their findings provide interesting insight into the scale and yield of large-scale Internet attacks. Prior to their work, we have had surprisingly little data on the cost and scale of spam campaigns. Stone et al. [37] also managed to take over a botnet for a period of weeks.

Varian suggests that many systems are structured so that overall security depends on the weakest-link [39]. Gordon and Loeb [18] describe a deferred investment approach to security. They suggest that, owing to the defender's uncertainty over which attacks are most cost effective, it makes sense to "wait and see" before committing to investment decisions. Boehme and Moore [8] develop this approach and examine an adaptive model of security investment, where a defender invests most in the attack with the least expected cost. Interestingly, in an iterative framework, where there are multiple rounds, they find that security under-investment can be rational until threats are realized. Unlike much of the weakest-link work, our analysis focusses on the attacker's difficulty in selecting profitable targets rather than the defender's difficulty in making investments. However, strategies that suggest that under-investment is not punished as severely as one might think spring also from our findings.

Schechter and Smith [36] examine the economics of an attacks on defensive systems deployed at large number of different locations. Their parallel attack model is similar in some respects to our threat model introduced in Sect. 2.1. However, their model does not include the cost of attack, instead the penalty is that an attacker risks apprehension and loss of winnings. Thus their framework is significantly different. They do not address the question of explaining missing attacks.

Grossklags et al. [19] examine security from a game theoretic framework. They examine weakest-link, best-shot and sum-of-effort games and examine Nash equilibria and social optima for different classes of attacks and defense. They also introduce a weakest-target game "where the attacker will always be able to compromise the entity (or entities) with the lowest protection level, but will leave other entities unharmed." A main point of contrast between our model and the weakest-target game is that in our model those with the lowest protection level get a free-ride. So long as there are not enough of the to make the overall attack profitable, then even the weakest targets escape.

Fultz and Grossklags [15] extend this work by now making the attacker a strategic economic actor, and extending to multiple attackers. As with Grossklags et al. [19] and Schechter and Smith [36] attacker cost is not included in the model, and the attacker is limited mostly by a probability of being caught. Our model, by contrast, assumes that for Internet attackers the risk of apprehension is negligible, while the costs are the main limitation on attacks.

In contrast to the work of Schechter and Smith [36] and Grossklags et al. [15, 19] this paper is mosty concerned with better explaining observations. That is, our starting point is the gap between what the weakest-link approach predicts and the reality we see. We devote all of Sect. 5 to explaining observations that fall naturally from our model.

In earlier work we offered a partial explanation for why many attacks fail to materialize [22]. If the attack opportunities are divided between targeted attackers (who expend per-user effort) and scalable attackers (who don't) a huge fraction of attacks fail to be profitable since targeting is expensive. This paper extends this work and shows that even scalable attacks can fail to be economic. A key finding is that attacking a crowd of users rather than individuals involves facing a sum-of-effort rather than weakest-link defense. The greater robustness and well-known free-rider effects that accompany sum-of-effort systems form most of the explanation for the missing attacks.

Barth et al. [7] examine the question of reactive security, and show that it can be effective in settings where the defender does not myopically over-react to the most recent attacks. While the theoretical framework is rather different, our findings do echo this result insofar as we also explain how under-investment in security can be a sensible approach.

Odlyzko [31] addresses the question of achieving security with insecure systems, and also confront the paradox that "there simply have not been any big cybersecurity disasters, in spite of all the dire warnings." His observation that attacks thrive in cyberspace because they are "less expensive, much more widespread, and faster" is similar to our segmentation of broadcast attacks. Schneier [4] argues that "one of the important things to consider in threat modeling is whether the attacker is looking for any victim, or is specifically targeting you." In previous work we showed that phishing is subject to the tragedy of the commons reducing the return for all parties [20]. This complements the present paper in demonstrating that attackers compete with each other for finite resources.

7 Conclusion

John Wanamaker famously declared that "Half the money I spend on advertising is wasted; the trouble is I don't know which half." This summarizes the Internet attacker's problem, except in the attacker's case it may be closer to 99.9999% waste. Charles(j) of course would prefer to direct all of his effort at those who have the highest likelihood of succumbing (i.e., $Pr\{e_i(k)\}$ is highest) or the greatest value (i.e., L_i is highest). However, target selection is costly and hard.

The threat model we propose goes some way to closing the gap between potential and actual harm. The constraint that attacks must be profitable in expectation removes a great many attacks that otherwise appear economic. It guarantees that the attacker sees a sum-of-effort rather than a weakest-link defense. It's not enough that something succeed now-and-then, or when the circumstances are right, or when all the ducks are in a row. When attacking users en masse, as Internet attackers do, attacks must be profitable at scale.

References

1. http://pr.webroot.com/threat-research/cons/protect-your-computer-from-hackers-101210.html
2. http://gs.statcounter.com/press/microsoft-internet-explorer- browser-falls-below-50-perc-of-worldwide-market-for-first-time
3. http://www.trusteer.com/files/Flash_Security_Hole_Advisory.pdf
4. http://www.schneier.com/blog/archives/2010/01/32_million_jewe.html
5. Anderson R (2001) Why information security is hard. In: Proceedings of ACSAC
6. Bond CM, Danezis G (2006) A pact with the devil
7. Barth A, Rubinstein BIP, Sundararajan M, Mitchell JC, Song D, Bartlett PL (2010) A learning-based approach to reactive security. Financial Crypto
8. Boehme R, Moore T (2009) The iterated weakest-link: a model of adaptive security investment. WEIS
9. Dhamija R, Tygar JD, Hearst M (2006) Why phishing works. CHI
10. Egelman S, Cranor LF, Hong J (2008) You've been warned: an empirical study of the effectiveness of web browser phishing warnings. CHI
11. Enright B, Voelker G, Savage S, Kanich C, Levhchenko K (2008) Storm: when researchers collide. login
12. Florêncio D and Herley C (2007) A large-scale study of web password habits. WWW 2007, Banff
13. Franklin J, Paxson V, Perrig A, Savage S (2007) An Inquiry into the Nature and Causes of the Wealth of Internet Miscreants. In: Proceedings of CCS
14. Federal Trade Commission (2007) Identity theft survey report. www.ftc.gov/os/2007/11/SynovateFinalReportIDTheft2006.pdf
15. Fultz N, Grossklags J (2009) Blue versus red: toward a model of distributed security attacks. Financial Crypto
16. Gartner (2007) Phishing survey. http://www.gartner.com/it/page.jsp?id=565125
17. Geer D, Bace R, Gutmann P, Metzger P, Pfleeger C, Quarterman J, Schneier B (2003) Cyber insecurity: the cost of monopoly. Computer and Communications Industry Association (CCIA), Sep, 24

18. Gordon LA, Loeb MP (2002) The economics of information security investment. ACM Trans Inform Syst Secur
19. Grossklags J, Christin N, Chuang J (2008) Secure or insure?: a game-theoretic analysis of information security games. WWW
20. Herley C, Florêncio D A profitless endeavor: phishing as tragedy of the commons. NSPW 2008, Lake Tahoe, CA
21. Herley C (2009) So long, and no thanks for the externalities: the rational rejection of security advice by users. In: NSPW 2009, Oxford
22. Herley C (2010) The plight of the targeted attacker in a world of scale. In: WEIS 2010, Boston
23. Imperva. Consumer password worst practices
24. Ives B, Walsh KR, Schneider H (2004) The domino effect of password re-use. In: CACM
25. Kaminsky D (2008) Its the end of the cache as we know it. Black Hat Briefings
26. Kanich C, Kreibich C, Levchenko K, Enright B, Voelker GM, Paxson V, Savage S (2008) Spamalytics: an empirical analysis of spam marketing conversion. In: Proceedings of the 15th ACM Conference on Computer and Communications Security, Alexandria, Virginia, USA, October, pp 3–14
27. Klein DV (1990) Foiling the cracker: a survey of, and improvements to, password security. Usenix Security Workshop
28. Mankiw NG (2007) Principles of economics, 4th edn
29. Murdoch SJ, Drimer S, Anderson R, Bond M (2010) Chip and pin is broken. In: IEEE Security&Privacy, Oakland
30. Odlyzko A (2003) Internet traffic growth: sources and implications. In: Proceedings of SPIE
31. Odlyzko A (2010) Providing security with insecure systems. WiSec
32. Rescorla E (2003) Security holes... who cares? Usenix Security Symp
33. Schechter S, Herley C, Mitzenmacher M (2010) Popularity is everything: a new approach to protecting passwords from statistical-guessing attacks. In: Proceedings of HotSec, 2010
34. Saroiu S, Gribble SD, Levy HM (2004) Measurement and analysis of spyware in a university environment. In: Proceedings of NSDI
35. Saroiu S, Gribble S, Levy H (2004) Measurement and analysis of spywave in a university environment. In: Proceedings of the 1st conference on symposium on networked systems design and implementation-volume 1, p 11. USENIX Association
36. Schechter S, Smith M (2003) How much security is enough to stop a thief? In: Financial cryptography. Springer, Berlin, pp 122–137
37. Stone-Gross B, Cova M, Cavallaro L, Gilbert B, Szydlowski M, Kemmerer R, Kruegel C, Vigna G (2009) Your botnet is my botnet: analysis of a botnet takeover. CCS
38. Varian HR (2001) Sytem reliability and free riding. WEIS
39. Varian HR (2004) System reliability and free riding. Economics of information security

Sex, Lies and Cyber-Crime Surveys

Dinei Florêncio and Cormac Herley

Abstract Much of the information we have on cyber-crime losses is derived from surveys. We examine some of the difficulties of forming an accurate estimate by survey. First, losses are extremely concentrated, so that representative sampling of the population does not give representative sampling of the losses. Second, losses are based on unverified self-reported numbers. Not only is it possible for a single outlier to distort the result, we find evidence that most surveys are dominated by a minority of responses in the upper tail (i.e., a majority of the estimate is coming from as few as one or two responses). Finally, the fact that losses are confined to a small segment of the population magnifies the difficulties of refusal rate and small sample sizes. Far from being broadly-based estimates of losses across the population, the cyber-crime estimates that we have appear to be largely the answers of a handful of people extrapolated to the whole population. A single individual who claims $50,000 losses, in an $N = 1,000$ person survey, is all it takes to generate a $10 billion loss over the population. One unverified claim of $7,500 in phishing losses translates into $1.5 billion.

1 Introduction

Inthe 1983 Federal Reserve Survey of Consumer Finances an incorrectly recorded answer from a single individual erroneously inflated the estimate of US household wealth by $1 trillion [4]. This single error added 10% to the total estimate of US household wealth. In the 2006 FTC survey of Identity Theft the answers of two respondents were discarded as being "not identity theft" and "inconsistent with the record." Inclusion of both answers would have increased the estimate by $37.3

D. Florêncio (✉) • C. Herley
Microsoft Research, Redmond, WA, USA
e-mail: dinei@microsoft.com; cormac@microsoft.com

B. Schneier (ed.), *Economics of Information Security and Privacy III*,
DOI 10.1007/978-1-4614-1981-5_3,
© Springer Science+Business Media New York 2013

billion [7]; i.e., made a 3× difference in the total estimate. In surveys of sexual behavior men consistently report having had more female sex partners than women report having had male sex partners (which is impossible). The difference ranges from a factor of 3 to 9. Morris [24] points out that a tiny portion of men who claim, e.g., 100 or 200 lifetime partners account for most of the difference. Removing the outliers all but eliminates the discrepancy.

How can this be? How can an estimate be so brittle that a single transcription error causes a $1 trillion difference? How can two answers (in a survey of 5,000) make a 3× difference in the final result? These cases have in common that the estimates are derived from surveys, that the underlying quantity (i.e., wealth, ID theft losses, or number of sexual partners) is very unevenly distributed across the population, and that a small number of outliers enormously influenced the overall estimate. They also have in common that in each case, inclusion of the outliers, caused an enormous error to the upside, not the downside. It does not appear generally understood that the estimates we have of cyber-crime losses also have these ingredients of catastrophic error, and the measures to safeguard against such bias have been universally ignored.

The common way to estimate unknown quantities in a large population is by survey. For qualities which are evenly distributed throughout the population (such as voting rights) the main task is to achieve a representative sample. For example, if the achieved sample over- or under-represents any age, ethnic or other demographic group the result may not be representative of the population as whole. Political pollsters go to great lengths to achieve a representative sample of likely voters.

With surveys of numeric quantities things are very different. First, some quantities, such as wealth, income, etc., are very unevenly distributed across the population. A representative sample of the population (i.e., all people have equal likelihood of being chosen) will give an unrepresentative picture of the wealth. For example, in the US, the top 1% and the bottom 90% of the population each controls about one third of the wealth [18]. A *representative* sample of 1,000 people would end up estimating the top third of the wealth from the answers of about ten people, and the bottom third from the answers of about 900 people. Thus, there are two orders of magnitude difference in the sample size for equivalent fractions of the wealth. We have far greater accuracy at the bottom than at the top. Second, for numeric quantities even a single outlier can greatly effect the survey estimate. The survey mean can be affected to an arbitrary extent by a single lie, transcription error or exaggeration. Self-reported numbers are known to have large sources of bias [19] and there is no guarantee that any survey respondent accurately reports the truth. If errors cancel then this error is unbiased (i.e., in expectation neither pulls the estimate up nor down). However, for non-negative quantities (e.g., prices, wealth, cyber-crime losses, number of sex partners etc.) errors have a lower bound, but no upper bound, so errors do not cancel and the bias is always upward. Finally, there are unique difficulties when surveying rare phenomena. Non-response error can be large, there is significant reduction in effective sample-size and it is difficult to overcome the fact that some fraction of the population routinely lies, exaggerates and misreports. If the phenomenon we wish to survey is rarer than the frequency of liars, our signal is effectively overwhelmed with noise, and no accurate estimate can be formed, at any survey size.

These three sources of error, that a representative sample of the population doesn't give a representative picture of the surveyed quality, that outliers can cause catastrophic errors, and for rare phenomenon we are measuring a signal weaker than the noise in which it is embedded pose a serious threat. In this paper we show that the estimates we have of cyber-crime come from surveys that suffer from all three of these sources of error. Cyber-crime losses follow very concentrated distributions where a representative sample of the population does not necessarily give an accurate estimate of the mean. They are self-reported numbers which have no robustness to any embellishment or exaggeration. They are surveys of rare phenomena where the signal is overwhelmed by the noise of misinformation. In short they produce estimates that cannot be relied upon. The difficulties presented have long been recognized in the areas of Robust Statistics [33] and Survey Science [18]. However safeguards against producing erroneous results seem largely ignored in cyber-crime surveys.

2   Sex and Lies

We begin with an example which illustrates one of the major sources of error. Surveys of sexual behavior consistently show a large gender discrepancy. Men report having had more female sex partners than women report having had male sex partners. The difference ranges from a factor of 3 to 9 (see Wiederman [34] and references therein). This discrepancy is repeated across many different surveys and countries (e.g., US, Britain, France, New Zealand and Norway). In a closed population with equal numbers of men and women, of course, this is impossible. The average lifetime number of heterosexual partners for men and women is the same.

Thus, the surveys of men and women give independent estimates of the same quantity, yet those estimates are mutually inconsistent. Clearly, there are sources of significant error in one, other or both of the estimates. Further, since men reliably report more partners than women, in surveys performed in different countries at different times and using different methodologies, those errors appear to pull consistently in one direction. This strongly suggests that each of the surveys has the same source of error. There are various possibilities. Selection bias which excludes women who have had many male partners might occur for this difference. Response bias, where women under- and men over-report their number of sexual partners, might also account for this error.

Morris [24] points out that the data has a heavytail distribution and most of the discrepancy is generated by a very small fraction of respondents who report large numbers of partners. Among the 90% of respondents who report having fewer than 20 partners the discrepancy between the reports of men and women all but disappears. This suggests a very simple explanation which accounts for most of the bias. The majority of women tell the truth, but perhaps under-report by a little. The majority of men also tell the truth, but perhaps over-report by a little. However, a small fraction of men tell whoppers: they exaggerate the number of partners they have had, not by a little, but by a lot. A man who claims to have had 100 lifetime sex partners (as about 1% in the dataset that Morris examines do) when the actual number is 50, adds enormous response error. It would take 16 men with the median number of partners understating by $2\times$ to cancel this single $2\times$ overstatement. Thus there is great asymmetry in the response error.

What has this to do with cyber-crime? Cyber-crime, like sexual behavior, defies large-scale direct observation and the estimates we have of it are derived almost exclusively from surveys. The sexual partner surveys are unique in that, while we don't know the correct answer, we have a cross-check (i.e., the result from the women) that shows that the estimate procedure is producing inaccurate answers. These surveys serve to illustrate two of the problems that are present also in cyber-crime surveys: the difficulty of achieving a representative sample of heavytail distributions, and the difficulty of telling representative outliers, which should be included, from unrepresentative ones (e.g., lies and exaggerations) which should not. A third difficulty, that of surveying very rare phenomenon amplifies both of these difficulties.

2.1   Sources of Error in Survey Research

When we wish to estimate any numerical quantity, x, over a large population we select some portion of the population. Call X the whole population and Y the contacted population (i.e., the set of people who are asked to respond). However, some of those who are contacted refuse, so we end up with a smaller responding population R. Clearly, $R \subset Y \subset X$. We call the averages over these populations $\bar{x}, \bar{y}$, and $\bar{r}$. When surveying a self-reported numerical quantity (such as salary, or hours of exercise per week) the observed answer is not necessarily the true answer. Thus, the true mean of those who respond is $\bar{r}$ but we observe $\overline{f[r]}$.

If the goal of the survey is to estimate $\bar{x}$, the mean of X, the survey error is $\bar{x} - \overline{f[r]}$. This error can be broken down into sampling error and non-sampling error [3]. The sampling error is $\bar{x} - \bar{y}$, or the difference between the mean of the whole population and that of the contacted population. The non-sampling error, $\bar{y} - \overline{f[r]}$, reflects the difference between the mean of the contacted population and that observed of the responding population. This in turn is generally split into non-response error and response error. Non-response error, $\bar{y} - \bar{r}$, is the difference between the mean of the contacted population and that of the responding population. Finally, response error, $\bar{r} - \overline{f[r]}$, is the difference between the true mean of the responding population and the observed mean (Fig. 1).The total survey error is then [3]:

$$\bar{x} - \overline{f[r]} = (\bar{x} - \bar{y}) + (\bar{y} - \bar{r}) + (\bar{r} - \overline{f[r]}).$$

Fig. 1 Venn Diagram. X is
the whole population, Y is the
contacted population, and R is
the achieved sample

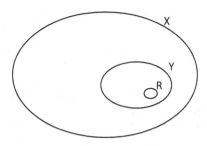

Non-response error, $(\bar{y} - \bar{r})$, is known to be particularly important where the refusal rate is high (i.e., the number of people in R is small relative to the number in Y). This has long been known in the crime survey literature. If the refusal rate is high there is a possibility that victims respond at a much higher or lower rate than the rest of the population which causes over- or under-estimation. For example if 10% of non-victims, and 50% of victims respond then R contains $5\times$ as many victims as Y. We examine this in Sect. 3.3.1.

Response error, $(\bar{r} - \overline{f[r]})$, is especially problematic when dealing with self-reported numbers. When there is no ability to verify the reported answers then there is no protection against lying or mis-statement, and the potential error can dwarf sampling error. We examine the role that this plays in Sect. 3.2. Sampling error is examined next.

3 Lies and Cyber-Crime

3.1 The Survey Mean Need Not Approximate the True Mean, Even When the Survey Is Representative

3.1.1 Heavytail Distributions

Many qualities are very unevenly distributed across the population. Some of them, such as height, weight, etc., are well-approximated by the familiar bell-curve, or normal, distribution. Of course, non-negative quantities such as height cannot precisely follow a normal distribution as the distribution has tails that extend infinitely in both directions: neither negative nor infinite heights are admissible. Heights nonetheless follow a normal pattern fairly closely. In particular, heights are more or less symmetrically distributed about the mean.

For some qualities the distribution is much more uneven. For height, even a factor of two difference is extreme. Wealth, income, fame etc., by contrast, are obvious examples where the quality is heavily concentrated among a small fraction of the population. A small number of people have a great deal (e.g., wealth or fame) and most have very little or none. These qualities are much better captured by heavytail distributions such as Pareto or Log-normal. Heavytail distributions have infinite tails that contain a large fraction of the probability mass. Because of the large mass in the tail the mean is generally much higher than the median. These are also know as distributions with positive skew.

The Pareto is a family of concentrated distributions, containing for example the well-known 80/20 distribution, which indicates that 80% of the phenomenon is concentrated among 20% of the samples. It is used, for example, to model the wealth distribution of households in the US [8,18]. In the Pareto distribution the probability of a randomly chosen individual having amount x is:

$$p(x) = Cx^{-\alpha}, \text{ for } \alpha > 2.$$

The fraction of the phenomenon accounted for by the top fraction P of the population is

$$W = P^{(\alpha-2)/(\alpha-1)}. \tag{1}$$

Observe that as $\alpha \to 2$, an arbitrarily small fraction P will control and arbitrarily large fraction W of the wealth. That is, $W \to 1$: more and more of the phenomenon will be held by a small fraction P of the population. For US wealth $\alpha \approx 2.32$. We now show that as the concentration increases even representative samples of the population will fail to give a representative picture of its statistics.

3.1.2 Representative Sampling Gives an Unrepresentative Estimate

Quantities that are unevenly distributed across the population are harder to survey than those that are evenly distributed. For a uniform distribution, every individual has an equally important contribution to make to the survey. Concentrated distributions are at the other extreme: a representative sample of the population gives a very unrepresentative picture of the quantity of interest. If we uniformly sample the population we end up with many samples from the part of the population that has little or no wealth, and very few samples from the part that has most of the wealth. Figure 2 shows the distribution of wealth among households in the US. The top 1% control approximately 33% of the wealth. In a sample of 1,000 where all households respond with equal likelihood we'll end up estimating one third of the wealth from the answers of ten households. If the average of those ten is not the true average of the upper 1% we end up with a misleading estimate.

The problem does not end there. The third that is held by the top 1% is just as unevenly distributed as the overall wealth [27]. Approximately a third of one third is held by the top 1% of 1%. That is 0.01% of the population holds 11% of the wealth. Table 1 summarizes the wealth concentration in the upper tail for the Pareto that closely models US wealth [18]. As can be seen, the concentration continues at different scales.

In fact, a representative sample of the population does not guarantee that the sample mean approximates well the true mean. That is, when things are very skewed we have $\bar{r} \not\approx \bar{x}$. This is so, since it is hard to achieve a representative sample with

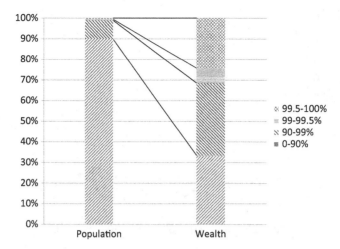

Fig. 2 Fraction of the wealth controlled by segments of the population [18]. The top 1% and bottom 90% each control about one third of the wealth. A survey that is representative of the population will be very unrepresentative of the wealth (having 90× fewer samples for the top third than the bottom)

Table 1 Concentration of Pareto distribution that approximates US wealth

Top fraction of population	Percent of wealth ($\alpha = 2.32$)
1%	32.7%
0.1%	18.7%
0.01%	10.7%
0.001%	6.1%

very few samples. And when a large portion of the wealth is concentrated among few hands the sample-size in that fraction of the wealth is tiny. Table 1 shows that for US wealth an $N = 1,000$ survey should expect ten and one respondents respectively for the top 33% and 19% of the wealth. Further, there is only a one in ten, and one in a hundred chance respectively of having a respondent from the top 11% and 6% of the wealth.

It is not possible to get a representative picture of that portion of the wealth with minuscule sample-sizes. While we can gather survey responses and average them, this can fail to give a representative picture of the wealth. If we repeat the trial we can get a very different answer. Figure 3 shows 100 trials of the sample mean of 1,000 representative samples of a Pareto ($\alpha = 2.32$, i.e., US wealth) distribution. As can be seen the sample mean varies considerably from the true mean (which is 4.125). This picture is simply for the Pareto that approximates US wealth distribution. If the concentration increases (i.e., $\alpha \to 2$) or the sample-size decreases the variations become more extreme. We will see that both of these conditions apply in the case of cyber-crime surveys (Sects. 3.1.3 and 3.3.1). The great variability is simply an artifact of the unreliability of the sample mean. As Newman writes [27]: "while

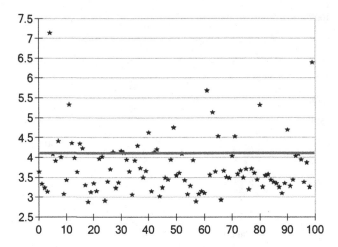

Fig. 3 Instances of sample mean for a Pareto ($\alpha = 2.32$, i.e., US wealth) distribution. There are 100 trials each with $N = 1,000$ samples. Even though there is no measurement error and the sampling is representative the sample mean shows considerable variance. This problem gets worse as concentration increases or sample-size decreases

we can quote a figure for the average of the samples we measure, that figure is not a reliable guide to the typical size of the samples in another instance of the same experiment."

The concentration is a problem for two main reasons. First, since so much of the phenomenon is in the tail it is difficult to adequately sample it unless a truly enormous survey is conducted. Second, the estimate is extremely brittle. An inordinate fraction of the estimate is coming from the answers of a handful of respondents. If those respondents are not representative, mis-remember, exaggerate, or entirely invent their answers the effect on the overall estimate is catastrophic. As, the 1983 Consumer Finances [4] and 2006 ID Theft [7] surveys show, an error or two can cause enormous increase. Expressed differently, since the majority of the estimate comes from a handful of people, great faith is being placed in their answers. The estimate is reliable to the degree that their answers are both representative and reliable.

The extreme difficulty of surveying heavytail phenomena has long been recognized. In the US the Survey of Consumer Finances a multi-layer sampling approach is used [18]. A first sample of 3,824 households were selected with equal probability, which gave a broad overview of wealth and finances in the overall population. A second sample of 438 households from two higher strata was conducted (the median net worth of households in these two strata were $50 million and $300 million). This allows formation of a far more accurate picture of the upper tail of the wealth distribution than is possible from a uniform sample. Considerable effort was taken to keep the refusal rate among those in the upper strata low (not surprisingly wealthy individuals have a far higher refusal rate than the population average).

3.1.3   Concentration in Cyber-Crime Surveys

Concentration in cyber-crime surveys is not merely a possibility. In fact those surveys that give enough information make clear that the distribution of losses is enormously concentrated, with a small fraction of respondents accounting for the bulk of the losses. For example, the Gartner 2007 phishing survey finds a median loss of $200, but a mean of $857. A factor 4.5× difference between mean and median is indicative of greater concentration than even the US wealth distribution. A Pareto distribution with this skew concentrates 59% of the wealth in the hands of the top 1%.

The FTC in 2006 report [7] great differences between mean and median, both of money and time lost, and the value the thief obtained. Even with the exclusion of the two outliers mentioned in the introduction the survey found a mean loss of $1,876 and median of $500, which is roughly comparable to the degree of concentration of US wealth. "The median value for the number of hours spent resolving problems by all victims was 4. However, 10% of all victims spent at least 55 h resolving their problems. The top 5% of victims spent at least 130 h."

The IC3 survey [14] finds a 9.7× ratio of mean/median: "Of those complaints reporting monetary loss that were referred to law enforcement, the mean dollar loss was $5,580 and the median was $575. The significant difference between the mean and median losses is reflected by a small number of cases in which hundreds of thousands of dollars were reported to have been lost by the complainant." This is simply an eye-popping level of concentration, indicating that almost all the losses were endured by a tiny number of complainants. In a Pareto distribution with this level of skew the top 1% controls 78% of the wealth.

The US Bureau of Justice Statistics produce bi-annual reports of Identity Theft [5]. The mean/median ratio varies across different theft categories, with 10× being typical. In some categories the ratio of the mean out-of-pocket loss to the median is as high as 14, indicating that almost the entire reported loss for the survey is derived from the answer of a single respondent.

Unfortunately, the majority of cyber-crime surveys give only the mean, $\bar{x}$, or total estimate $|X| \cdot \bar{x}$. While they refer to the concentration of the losses, failure to provide the median makes it impossible to do further analysis.

3.2   The Survey Mean Need Not Approximate the True Mean When There Is Measurement Error

The average response of the responding population **R** is:

$$\overline{f[r]} = \frac{1}{|R|} \sum_{i \in R} f[r_i]. \tag{2}$$

If $\overline{f[r]} \approx \overline{r}$ and $\overline{r} \approx \overline{x}$ then we can approximate the mean response of the responding population for that of x over the overall population.

As we saw above, for heavytail distributions, we can't assume that $\overline{r} \approx \overline{x}$. This, it turns out is only the beginning of our difficulties. Neither can we assume that $\overline{f[r]} \approx \overline{r}$. Unfortunately the sample mean is an extremely non-robust quantity: a single outlier is sufficient to distort the value.

There are various reasons that can produce measurement error (i.e., $f[r_i] \neq r_i$). Transcription error was the cause of a massive error in the 1983 consumer finance survey. It's possible that respondents mis-remember, or misunderstand the survey question. And, of course, not everyone tells the truth. The discrepancy in sexual partner reports emphasizes the lack of robustness when forming estimates of self-reported numbers. Morris' work shows that even when the majority of self-reports are accurate, the sample mean can be wildly inaccurate. A respondent who lies (i.e., $f[r_i] \neq r_i$) affects the average by $(f[r_i] - r_i)/|R|$. Since answers must be positive, the erroneous contribution to the mean is bounded below by $-r_i/|R|$, but is unbounded above. The larger $(f[r_i] - r_i)/|R|$ the larger the response error introduced. For example, if an individual has wealth r_i but it is incorrectly recorded as $f[r_i] = 10r_i$ no other individual understatement cancels this error. We needn't stop there, with self-reported numbers exaggerations by $100 \times 1,000\times$ or more are not merely feasible, but have been observed. Recall that the FTC 2006 survey excludes answers from two respondents who appear to be relating fictitious losses which (if included) would have added \$37.3 billion to the estimate. Since \$10k in a survey of $N = 1,000$ people translate into \$2 billion when applied to a population of two hundred million (see Sect. 4.1) the estimates are extremely fragile.

The extreme concentration of distributions of wealth (and cyber-crime losses) raises the stakes considerably. Since so much of the phenomenon is concentrated among a small fraction of respondents the accuracy of the estimate depends on the accuracy of their answers. Indeed, when concentration is high enough, most of the estimate is coming from a tiny fraction of the responding population. Just how much is coming from the highest reporting respondents is tabulated in Table 2. This shows the factor difference made to the entire estimate by the fraction P with the highest reports. That is, for example, how much higher the estimate is for inclusion of the top 1% as opposed to an estimate based solely on the other 99%. When $\alpha = 2.05$ for example (the concentration found in the IC3 survey [14]) the top 1% increased the estimate by $5.1 \times$. Here we tabulate $1/(1 - W)$, where W is as defined in (1). For increasing concentration a very small fraction of the population has an outsized influence. For example, when the survey size is small, and the phenomenon is rare a single respondent can be 5% of the response pool (and thus account for a $1.9, 3.4$ or $7.5\times$ increase).

Of course whether 1% of the survey is 100 people, ten, one or (in expectation) less than one depends on the sample-size. We'll see in Sect. 3.3.2 how 1% of the sample-size, on which 80% or so of the estimate is depending can be as little as one person.

Table 2 Factor difference that misrepresentation by a small fraction of respondents can make. For $\alpha = 2.32$, approximating the concentration of US wealth, invented numbers from the top 5% result in a 1.9× increase in the overall estimate

Percent	$\alpha = 2.32$	$\alpha = 2.13$	$\alpha = 2.05$
1%	1.5×	2.4×	5.1×
5%	1.9×	3.4×	7.5×
10%	2.4×	4.3×	9.6×

The essential problem we face, that, for non-negative quantities, the sample mean can be increased (but not decreased) by an arbitrary amount by the answer of a single respondent has long been known in Robust Statistics. In the best of circumstances (measurement error is rare, the phenomenon is evenly distributed and errors cancel) Tukey writes [33]: "If contamination is a real possibility (and when is it not?), neither the mean nor variance is likely to be a wisely chosen basis for making estimates from a large sample." However cyber-crime surveys are far from the best of circumstances. Sampling of heavytail distributions is far less robust than the normal distributions of which Tukey was writing.

Further evidence of the upward rather than downward bias of sample mean is found in a recent examination of the wisdom of the crowd effect by Lorenz et al. [20]. They find that the median gave a more accurate measure than the arithmetic mean of answers from a crowd. Of the six phenomena surveyed, the mean of the crowd answers always over-estimated, by an amount ranging from 59% to 1,365%.

3.2.1 Self-reported Numbers

If we had no measurement or reporting errors (i.e., we always have $f[r_i] = r_i$) things would be relatively simple. We would then merely have sampling error, $(\overline{x} - \overline{y})$, and non-response error, $(\overline{y} - \overline{r})$, to contend with. However, self-reported numbers are known to be generally inaccurate.

Self-reported numbers on calorie consumption and exercise are known to generally err on the optimistic side. In a weight loss survey [19]: "subjects under-reported their actual food intake by an average ($\pm$ SD) of 47 ± 16 percent and over-reported their physical activity by an average of 51 ± 75 percent."

The problem is twofold. First, that we have no ability to check the accuracy of any of the responses offered. Second, in concentrated phenomena most of the effect is reported by a handful of people. If the answers of those at the top are exaggerated or inaccurate we produce wildly inaccurate answers. There are numerous reasons why people may report inaccurately. In several cyber-crime surveys [7, 10] it appears the total estimate was based on how much respondents believe the thief obtained (rather than how much the victim lost). For example the median answer for the former was $500 but the latter was $0 in the FTC 2006 survey. Since respondents are being asked something of which they have no direct knowledge, over-estimation is highly likely. Vague and unclear categories may encourage respondents to "throw in" experiences that were not part of the survey intent. For example, an unsatisfactory online auction experience or dispute with a merchant might easily be conflated with "online fraud." The FTC survey which finds an individual respondent trying to report a claimed loss of $999,999 "theft of intellectual property" as ID theft is just such an example. Victims may be angry, and when offered an opportunity to complain be tempted to over-state rather than under-state their true losses. Finally, some percent of the population just lies and make things up.

3.3 Surveying Rare Phenomena

We've seen some of the difficulties of surveying unevenly distributed phenomena such as wealth. There is one further complication that makes accurate estimation of cyber-crime losses even harder: surveying rare phenomena is hard. Wealth and income may be unevenly distributed, but most of the population is involved and most responses can be used (although some answers are many times more useful than others in forming the overall estimate). If 1,000 people respond to a survey on wealth the answers of all of them will be useful in forming an estimate. For rare phenomena this isn't the case. For a phenomenon that affects 5% of people, 95% of the population will have nothing useful to say: their answers contribute nothing to the estimate. This complicates things in three respects. First, non-response bias can be high. When the phenomenon is rare there is a real risk that those who are affected respond at a much higher or lower rate than the overall population. Second, there is a raw reduction of sample-size. Third, some fraction of the population routinely lies and fabricates answers. This can cause our signal to be lost in the noise.

3.3.1 Achieving a Representative Sample

Suppose a small fraction of the population, X, are affected by phenomenon V. That is $|V|/|X|$ is small. Let's call the members of V victims, and all others non-victims. In doing a survey it is of paramount importance that the percent of victims in the responding population, R, be similar to that in X. It is not hard to imagine that people affected by phenomenon V may respond at a higher or lower rate than the rest of the population. Gamblers may be more likely than non-gamblers to respond to a survey on gambling, for example. People who have been victimized by a certain type of crime may be significantly more likely (or less) to respond to a survey on that crime.

The victimization rate is $V/(V+N)$. But if only a fraction V_r and N_r of victims and non-victims respectively respond we estimate the rate as

$$\frac{V \cdot V_r}{V \cdot V_r + N \cdot N_r}.$$

When the overall victimization rate is low (i.e. $V \ll N$ so that $V \cdot (V_r/N_r) + N \approx V + N \approx N$) we get [11]:

$$\frac{V \cdot V_r}{V \cdot V_r + N \cdot N_r} \approx \frac{V}{V + N} \cdot \frac{V_r}{N_r}.$$

Thus, our estimate of the victimization rate is the true rate, multiplied by V_r/N_r. Any difference in the victim and non-victim response rates enormously influences the estimate. So, if $V_r = 5N_r$ (victims are $5\times$ more likely to respond) then the estimated victimization rate is about $5\times$ the true rate. Exactly such a bias appears to occur in the Gartner [10] phishing survey which estimates the victimization rate a full factor of ten higher than the non-survey estimates of Florêncio and Herley [11], Clayton and Moore [23] and Trustseer [21].

3.3.2 Sample-Size Reduction

A further difficulty comes from the sheer reduction in effective sample size that surveying a rare phenomenon brings. If a phenomenon affects 5% of the population then in a representative sample of 1,000 people we expect only 50 answers that are of interest.

In Sect. 3.1 we saw the difficulty of surveying quantities that are unevenly distributed. It is almost impossible to avoid under-sampling the tail in a concentrated distribution. In addition we now find that rare phenomena are hard to survey, as most of the responses are wasted and cannot contribute to the estimate. However, cyber-crime losses suffer from both these problems: they are rare phenomena that are also extremely concentrated. That is, only a few percent of people suffer from ID theft. Even among those that do suffer from it the losses are extremely concentrated as we saw in Sect. 3.1.3. Thus cyber-crime losses are both confined to a small segment of the population, but also, have very uneven distribution within that segment. The rareness gives a reduction in the sample size. The concentration adds to the fragility of the sample.

To be concrete, consider a $N = 1,000$ survey of a phenomenon that affects 2% of the population. Our effective sample-size is now 20, not 1,000. A single individual counts for 5% of the response pool. Further suppose that the phenomenon is concentrated to the same degree as US wealth (i.e., Pareto with $\alpha = 2.32$). In this case 48% of the phenomenon is concentrated in the top 5%. Thus, we expect that fully one half of our estimate will be coming from a single individual.

Let's examine examples from actual surveys. The FTC 2006 survey [7] reached 4,917 respondents and found 3.7%, 1.4% and 0.8% rates of all ID theft, misuse of existing accounts, and misuse of new accounts respectively. However, these appear to correspond to sample sizes of 181, 68 and 39 respectively. Thus, for new account fraud the top 1% of respondents is less than one person. From Table 2, if these losses are as concentrated as US wealth, the top 5% (i.e., approximately two people) double the entire estimate.

As we move on from the FTC survey things only get worse. Gartner's 2006 survey [10] found a 3.2% phishing victimization rate. In a survey of 4,000 people this means approximately 128 claimed to be victims (recall we argue in Sect. 3.3.1 above that they over-estimate the true victimization rate by $10\times$). Thus the top 1% (which at the concentration level that Gartner finds accounts for 59% of losses) is about one person. Javelin in a survey of 4,000 [15] finds 4.25% have been ID theft victims and 1.7% of those have been phishing victims. This gives an effective sample size of three individuals!

3.3.3 Liars

Finally, in surveying rare phenomena it is hard to avoid the subject of liars [12]. There can be little doubt that some fraction of the population embellish, exaggerate and tell whoppers, even when there is no clear motive for doing so. We examined the difficulty that outliers present in Sect. 3.2. There, however, we tackled the general problem, where people report $f[r_i] = 10r_i$ or so (i.e., multiply their real wealth or number of sexual partners by 10). If there are a percent or two of liars in the population, they affect the estimate modestly unless any of them are outliers in the tail.

However, when surveying rare phenomena most of the population are unaffected, that is they have nothing to report. If the phenomenon affects 1% of the population and 1% of people are habitual liars then our survey can have up to 50% contributions from people who are offering pure invention by way of answers. If people who systematically exaggerate make up a fraction $p = 0.01$ of the population then the probability that a survey of $N = 1,000$ is exaggeration-free is $(1 - p)^N = 0.99^{1000} \approx 0.000043$ or 0.0043%.

4 Discussion

4.1 Total Estimate

We've seen that, when estimating $\bar{x}$, the survey error, $\bar{x} - \overline{f[r]}$, can be enormous. Often, however, it is the total, rather than the mean of X that we wish to estimate. That is we want $|X| \cdot \bar{x}$ rather than $\bar{x}$. This is the case, for example, in estimating total US household wealth [8], and losses in all cyber-crime surveys. Now, the response errors are amplified by backing into the overall population. The estimate becomes $|X| \cdot \overline{f[r]}$. Thus, from (2), each respondent adds $|X|/|R| \cdot f[r_i]$ to the estimate. For example, if the population size is $|X| = 200$ million and the survey size is

$|R| = 1,000$ then each dollar of losses claimed is multiplied by $|X|/|R| = 200,000$. In other words every dollar of claimed losses translates into \$200,000 in the estimate. A respondent who claims \$50,000 in ID theft losses adds \$10 billion to the overall loss estimate. Indeed five individuals, each of whom claim \$50,000 is all that is required to generate a \$50 billion loss estimate. Similarly, a single respondent who claims to have lost \$7,500 to phishing is all it takes to generate \$1.5 billion in estimated population-wide losses. Two such individuals is all it takes to give a loss estimate in the \$3 billion range.

4.2 Lack of Consistency

The variability of cyber-crime surveys is not merely theoretical. The FTC estimated Identity theft at \$47 billion in 2004 [6], \$15.6 billion in 2006 [7] and \$54 billion in 2008 [16]. Either there was a precipitous drop in 2006, or all of the estimates are extremely noisy.

The vagueness and lack of clarity about what has been measured allows for a large range of interpretation. In the last two years alone we find the following claims, which value cyber-crime at anywhere from \$560 million to \$1 trillion. "The spoils of cyber crime almost doubled in 2009. As a whole, losses totaled \$560m," Patrick Peterson, Cisco Fellow [28]. "Cyber crime costs corporate America \$10 billion every year!" [31]. "Damage caused by cyber-crime is estimated at \$100 billion annually," said Kilian Strauss, of the Organization for Security and Cooperation in Europe (OSCE) [26]. "Cyber-crime revenues are worth approximately \$1 trillion," Edward Amoroso, CSO, AT&T (written testimony to the US Senate Commerce, Science, and Transportation Committee, March 17, 2009).

4.3 Other Analyses of Cyber-Crime Surveys

Our assessment of the quality of cyber-crime surveys is harsh: they are so compromised and biased that no faith whatever can be placed in their findings. We are not alone in this judgement. Most research teams who have looked at the survey data on cyber-crime have reached similarly negative conclusions. Ryan and Jefferson [29], who perform a meta-study of 14 cyber-crime surveys, write "In the information security arena, there is no reliable data upon which to base decisions. Unfortunately, there is unreliable data that is masquerading as reliable data." Anderson et al. [1] find "there has long been a shortage of hard data about information security failures, as many of the available statistics are not only poor but are collected by parties such as security vendors or law enforcement agencies that have a vested interest in under- or over-reporting." Moitra produces a survey of various cyber-crime surveys [22]. He observes that "a lack of reliability and validity checks on the data that have been collected" and singles out exaggeration of losses, and self-selection bias as major sources of error not accounted for in the methodology. Brenner, in arguing that accurate measures and estimates for the incidence of computer-related crime are necessary writes: "We have never done this, even though the term 'cybercrime' and its various correlates [...] have been in use for decades." Herley and Florêncio [11] say that the cyber-crime survey estimates they examine "crumble upon inspection." Shostack and Stewart [30] write "today's security surveys have too many flaws to be useful as sources of evidence." The lack of faith in existing surveys is not limited to research teams. At the keynote at Workshop on Economics of Information Security (WEIS) 2010 Tracey Vispoli, VP and head of CyberSecurity Infrastructure at Chubb Insurance stated that [32] the insurance industry has "no expected loss data and no financial impact data."

4.4 Recommendations

What general conclusions can we draw from this? Survey science is hard. Mistakes can be made even when every care is taken (as the $1 trillion mistake in the Consumer Finance survey shows). The very term "survey" creates the impression of a broadly-based study which gives a representative snapshot of what is going on. When we deal with simple evenly distributed quantities, such voting intentions, this is the case. When we deal with concentrated phenomena, such as wealth, it is very far from the case. Extreme care (such as multi-layer sampling [18]) is required for concentrated phenomena. When we deal with phenomena that are both confined to a small segment, and concentrated within that segment all of the difficulties are amplified.

How may we recognize the danger signs in a survey? First, no weight can be given to surveys that fail to disclose methodology. The risks of catastrophic error are great even when things are done with care. Ensuring that the sample is representative, that concentration is not too great, that the upper tail has been adequately sampled and that outliers have been checked for gross error or fabrication: these are not matters on which benefit of the doubt can be extended. Second, evidence of the degree of concentration is important. The ratio of the mean to the median is a simple figure of merit for the concentration. For US wealth this number is about 4.12. At this level of concentration multi-layer sampling is essential. Ratios higher than this imply the need for infeasibly large sample-sizes. For example, the 2008 US Department of Justice ID theft survey [5] had a sample size of 56,480. ID theft is largely dominated by low-tech means (e.g. a credit card run twice, stolen wallet, etc.), and affects a rather large fraction of the population (i.e., up to 5%). The survey also indicates approximately 0.2% (i.e., 4% of the 5% ID theft victims) responded to a phishing e-mail or phone call. Thus, to achieve an estimate of phishing comparable in accuracy to the estimate of credit-card fraud would require a $25\times$ larger sample size (i.e., over one million people). If losses from cyber-crime are more concentrated than those from credit-card fraud then surveys of several million people would be required.

Estimates which fail to disclose the median as well as the mean, or which fail to give some measure of concentration, can be discarded. The reliability of the survey is inversely related to the concentration. Failure to declare concentration is as serious a failing as failure to state the sample size. In fact, as the concentration (i.e., the ratio of mean to median) increases the sample mean is not stable [27]: "while we can quote a figure for the average of the samples we measure, the figure is not a reliable guide to the typical size of the samples from another instance of the same experiment."

5 Related Work

Despite their ubiquity analyses of cyber-crime surveys have been relatively few. Andreas and Greenhill [2] examine the effect that bad estimates can have on policy and resource allocation. Ryan and Jefferson [29], perform a meta-study of 14 cyber-crime surveys and are largely unimpressed with the methodologies. Moitra produces a survey of various cyber-crime surveys [22]. He observes that "a lack of reliability and validity checks on the data that have been collected" and singles out exaggeration of losses, and self-selection bias as major sources of error not accounted for in the methodology. Herley and Florêncio [11] provide an extensive study of various phishing and ID theft surveys and conclude that all are considerable over-estimates.

The field of Robust Statistics has long studied the problem of estimating distributions from samples. Tukey was among the first to examine the difficulties of measurement (or response) error [33]. Morris [24] appears to have been the first to draw attention to the potential for extreme error when dealing with heavytail distributions and self-reported numbers. A series of papers by Kennilick and co-workers [17, 18] address the difficulties of estimating concentrated distributions from samples.

6 Conclusion

The importance of input validation has long been recognized in security. Code injection and buffer overflow attacks account for an enormous range of vulnerabilities. "You should never trust user input" says one standard text on writing secure code [13]. It is ironic then that our cyber-crime survey estimates rely almost exclusively on unverified user input. A practice that is regarded as unacceptable in writing code is ubiquitous in forming the estimates that drive policy (see, e.g., [25]). A single exaggerated answer adds spurious billions to an estimate, just as a buffer overflow can allow arbitrary code to execute. This isn't merely a possibility. The surveys that we have exhibit exactly this pattern of enormous, unverified outliers dominating the rest of the data. While we can sum user responses, and divide to get an average, the resulting calculation is not worthy of the term "estimate" unless we can have confidence that it reflects the underlying phenomenon. For the cyber-crime surveys that we have, statistical difficulties are routinely ignored and we can have no such confidence. Are we really producing cyber-crime estimates where 75% of the estimate comes from the unverified self-reported answers of one or two people? Unfortunately, it appears so. Can any faith whatever be placed in the surveys we have? No, it appears not.

References

1. Anderson R, Boehme R, Clayton R, Moore T (2007) Security economics and the internal market. Report for European network and information security agency, 2007
2. Andreas P, Greenhill K (2010) Sex, drugs, and body counts: the politics of numbers in global crime and conflict. Cornell University Press, New York
3. Assael H, Keon J (1982) Nonsampling vs. sampling errors in survey research
4. Avery R, Elliehausen G, Kennickell A (1988) Measuring wealth with survey data: an evaluation of the 1983 survey of consumer finances. Rev Income Wealth 34(4):339–369
5. Bureau of Justice Statistics. Victims of Identity Theft. http://bjs.ojp.usdoj.gov/content/pub/pdf/vit08.pdf
6. Federal Trade Commission (2003) Identity theft survey report. http://www.ftc.gov/os/2003/09/synovatereport.pdf
7. Federal Trade Commission (2007) Identity theft survey report. www.ftc.gov/os/2007/11/SynovateFinalReportIDTheft2006.pdf
8. Federal Reserve Board. Survey of Consumer Finances. http://www.federalreserve.gov/pubs/oss/oss2/scfindex.html
9. Florêncio D, Herley C (2010) Where do security policies come from? In: SOUPS 2010, Redmond
10. Gartner (2007) Phishing survey. http://www.gartner.com/it/page.jsp?id=565125
11. Herley C, Florêncio D (2008) A profitless endeavor: phishing as tragedy of the commons. In: NSPW 2008, Lake Tahoe, CA
12. Herley C, Florêncio D (2009) Nobody sells gold for the price of silver: dishonesty, uncertainty and the underground economy. In: WEIS 2009, London
13. Howard M, LeBlanc D, and Books I (2003) 24x7. Writing secure code, vol 2. Microsoft press, Washington
14. Internet Crime Complaint Center Annual Crime Report. http://www.ic3.gov/media/annualreports.aspx
15. Javelin (2003) Identity theft survey report. http://www.javelinstrategy.com/uploads/505.RF_Phishing.pdf
16. Javelin (2009) Identity theft survey report. http://www.javelinstrategy.com/uploads/505.RF_Phishing.pdf
17. Kennickell A (1998) Multiple imputation in the Survey of Consumer Finances. In: Proceedings of the section on business and economic statistics, 1998 annual meetings of the American statistical association, Dallas, Texas. Citeseer, 1998
18. Kennickell A (2009) Getting to the top: reaching wealthy respondents in the SCF. Washington, DC: Federal reserve board of governors, 2009
19. Lichtman S, Pisarska K, Berman E, Pestone M, Dowling H, Offenbacher E, Weisel H, Heshka S, Matthews D, Heymsfield S (1992) Discrepancy between self-reported and actual caloric intake and exercise in obese subjects. New Engl J Med 327(27):1893–1898

20. Lorenz J, Rauhut H, Schweitzer F, Helbing D (2011) How social influence can undermine the wisdom of crowd effect. Proc Natl Acad Sci 108(22):9020
21. Measuring the Effectiveness of In-the-Wild Phishing Attacks. (2009) http://www.trusteer.com/sites/default/files/Phishing-Statistics-Dec-2009-FIN.pdf
22. Moitra SD. Cyber security violations against businesses: a re-assessment of survey data. http://www.iimcal.ac.in/res/upd%5CWPS%20571.pdf
23. Moore T, Clayton R (2007) Examining the impact of website take-down on phishing. In: Proceedings of APWG eCrime summit, 2007
24. Morris M (1993) Telling tails explain the discrepancy in sexual partner reports. Nature
25. National Strategy for Trusted Identities in Cyberspace. Why we need it. http://www.nist.gov/nstic/NSTIC-Why-We-Need-It.pdf
26. New Scientist (2008) Cybercrime toll threatens new financial crisis. Nov. 20, 2008. http://www.newscientist.com/article/dn16092-cybercrime-toll-threatens-new-financial-crisis.html
27. Newman M (2005) Power laws, Pareto distributions and Zipf's law. Contemp Phys 46(5):323–351
28. Paterson P (2010) The Morphing IT Security Landscape. Nov. 18, 2010 https://vishnu.fhcrc.org/security-seminar/IT-Security-Landscape-Morphs.pdf
29. Ryan J, Jefferson TI (2003) The use, misuse, and abuse of statistics in information security research. In: Proceedings 23rd ASEM national conference, 2003
30. Shostack A, Stewart A (2008) The new school of information security research
31. Systems Solutions Group: Cyber Crime http://www.ssg-inc.net/cyber_crime/cyber_crime.html
32. TaoSecurity Blog: Brief Thoughts on WEIS (2010) http://taosecurity.blogspot.com/2010/07/brief-thoughts-on-weis-2010.html. July 14, 2010
33. Tukey J (1960) A survey of sampling from contaminated distributions. I. Olkin, 1960
34. Wiederman M (1997) The truth must be in here somewhere: examining the gender discrepancy in self-reported lifetime number of sex partners. J Sex Res 34(4):375–386

The Underground Economy of Fake Antivirus Software

**Brett Stone-Gross, Ryan Abman, Richard A. Kemmerer,
Christopher Kruegel, Douglas G. Steigerwald, and Giovanni Vigna**

Abstract Fake antivirus (AV) programs have been utilized to defraud millions of computer users into paying as much as one hundred dollars for a phony software license. As a result, fake AV software has evolved into one of the most lucrative criminal operations on the Internet. In this paper, we examine the operations of three large-scale fake AV businesses, lasting from three months to more than two years. More precisely, we present the results of our analysis on a trove of data obtained from several backend servers that the cybercriminals used to drive their scam operations. Our investigations reveal that these three fake AV businesses had earned a combined revenue of more than $130 million dollars. A particular focus of our analysis is on the financial and economic aspects of the scam, which involves legitimate credit card networks as well as more dubious payment processors. In particular, we present an economic model that demonstrates that fake AV companies are actively monitoring the refunds (chargebacks) that customers demand from their credit card providers. When the number of chargebacks increases in a short interval, the fake AV companies react to customer complaints by granting more refunds. This lowers the rate of chargebacks and ensures that a fake AV company can stay in business for a longer period of time. However, this behavior also leads to unusual patterns in chargebacks, which can potentially be leveraged by vigilant payment processors and credit card companies to identify and ban fraudulent firms.

B. Stone-Gross (✉) • R.A. Kemmerer • C. Kruegel • G. Vigna
Department of Computer Science, University of California, Santa Barbara, CA, USA
e-mail: bstone@cs.ucsb.edu; kemm@cs.ucsb.edu; chris@cs.ucsb.edu; vigna@cs.ucsb.edu

R. Abman • D.G. Steigerwald
Department of Economics, University of California, Santa Barbara, CA, USA
e-mail: ryan@econ.ucsb.edu; doug@econ.ucsb.edu

B. Schneier (ed.), *Economics of Information Security and Privacy III*,
DOI 10.1007/978-1-4614-1981-5_4,
© Springer Science+Business Media New York 2013

1 Introduction

Over the past few years, electronic crimes revolving around a class of malware known as *scareware* have become extremely lucrative ventures. The concept is simple; design a ploy through social engineering that exploits a computer user's fear of revealing sensitive information, losing important data, and/or causing irreversible hardware damage. The most common form of scareware is *fake antivirus* (AV) software, also known as "rogue security software." More specifically, a fake AV program impersonates an antivirus scanner and displays misleading or fraudulent alerts in an attempt to dupe a victim into purchasing a license for a commercial version that is capable of removing nonexistent security threats. Some fake AV programs may also lock down system functionality to prevent victims from accessing files or web sites or from creating new processes, such as Windows Explorer, Task Manager, and a Command Prompt under the false pretense that it is for the victim's own protection. In addition, we have observed fake AV software that contains hidden backdoor capabilities, enabling the program to be used for other malicious purposes, such as launching distributed denial-of-service (DDoS) attacks against adversaries.

Over the past year, we have been able to acquire backend servers for several multi-million dollar criminal operations selling fake AV products. These fake AV businesses are run out of Eastern Europe and utilize affiliate networks known as *partnerka* to distribute the rogue software [32]. These partnerka networks use various pseudonyms, and operate by recruiting affiliates to install their software on as many computers as possible. In exchange, the affiliates receive a commission for driving traffic to landing pages, malware installations (also known as *loads*), and fake AV sales. Moreover, some partnerka offer additional incentives to the most successful affiliates with prizes including expensive cars, computers, and cell phones [18].

Since we have access to the servers used by these criminal organizations, we are able to directly analyze the tools that are used to create the fake AV products, including programs that assist perpetrators in controlling the malware's behavior and brand names, as well as custom *packers* that obfuscate the malware to evade detection by legitimate antivirus products. Some fake AV groups even make use of third-party commercial services to track the detection rates by the most popular antivirus vendors (e.g., McAfee, Symantec, and Trend Micro) [19], and they tweak their obfuscation algorithms until a low detection rate is achieved. We also have access to the instruments that are used to direct traffic to fake AV web sites, the infrastructure that prolongs the longevity of the operations, and a very detailed view of the financial profits that fuel these illicit enterprises. Interestingly, the miscreants behind fake AV products even offer refunds to victims who are persistent, in order to reduce the amount of credit card chargebacks, which we will discuss in more detail later.

Although various aspects of fake AV software have been studied, there are many facets of these operations that are not well understood, including the modus operandi of the criminals, the amount of money involved, the victims who purchase the software, the affiliate networks that promote the campaigns, and the flow of money from the victims' credit cards, to the payment processors, to the bank accounts controlled by the criminals. In this paper, we attempt to fill this void by presenting the analysis of several criminal organizations that sell fake AV products. More specifically, we make the following contributions:

- We provide an in-depth analysis of fake AV operations and present detailed statistics based on the analysis of more than a dozen servers belonging to several criminal organizations. This is the most comprehensive, large-scale study of fake AV campaigns that highlights different aspects of their operations from the infection process, to the financial complexities of maintaining a fraudulent business.
- We examine how fake AV campaigns are managed and orchestrated, from the ringleaders' point of view. We discuss the software infrastructure that is utilized, the functionality it provides, and its role in the underground economy.
- We present an economic model that encapsulates financial patterns that are indicative of fake AV ventures. Our intent is to formalize the essential factors of these operations and to identify potential weaknesses that can be exploited to increase the criminals' functional and operational costs.

2   Technical Background

Before we present the financial logistics, we first discuss the methods that are utilized to infect machines with fake AV software and the infrastructure behind the process. In addition, we present details about three particular criminal operations running fake AV businesses. To protect ongoing law enforcement investigations, we refer to these three ventures as AV_1, AV_2, and AV_3. Note that we currently see ongoing activity (e.g., new malware samples, installations and online advertisements) from all three fake AV operations.

2.1   Infection Methods

There are three primary infection methods used by fake AV distributors to propagate their malware: social engineering, drive-by-download attacks, and botnets. In this section, we present how these strategies are used to infect as many computers as possible with fake AV malware.

One of the most popular infection methods uses social engineering techniques to convince a victim to voluntarily install the fake AV. To launch this attack, a malicious web page displays a window in the browser (e.g., via JavaScript or Adobe Flash) that pretends that the machine has been infected with malware. An example

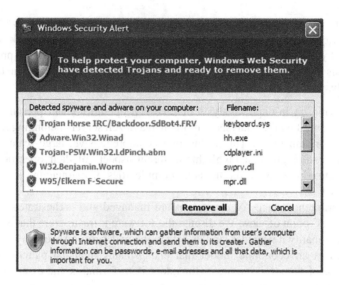

Fig. 1 Example alert from a fake antivirus advertisement displayed in a user's web browser

is shown in Fig. 1. To fix the security problem, the window also contains a link to a program that presumably helps to clean up the infection. Of course, this program is the fake AV software that attackers aim to install.

A second technique to install fake AV software is via drive-by download attacks. In a drive-by download attack, a web site is prepared with malicious scripts that exploit vulnerabilities in the web browser or one of its plugins. When the exploit is successful, the fake AV malware is installed automatically, without the user's knowledge or consent.

Both in the case of fake alerts and drive-by downloads, the initial goal of the attacker is to drive as many web visitors to their malicious web pages (sometimes called landing pages) as possible. In order to achieve this objective, attackers often make use of *blackhat search engine optimization* (SEO). Their intention is to poison search engine results by creating landing pages that contain popular search phrases. Many of these campaigns target current events such as the death of a celebrity, natural disasters, and holidays. Blackhat SEO relies on the fact that when search engine crawlers index a web site they identify themselves through the HTTP User-Agent field (e.g., googlebot). Thus, a site under an attacker's control can serve content that contains popular keywords that a search engine will use in the computation of the page rank. If the process is done correctly, the landing page is ranked high in the search engine's results for these popular keywords.

When a user clicks on a search engine result that leads to a blackhat SEO landing page, the server analyzes the user's web browser (via the User-Agent header), and the referring web site (through the HTTP Referer field). The tools that are used to manage these SEO campaigns are known in the underground economy as a *traffic direction system* (TDS). These TDSs can leverage the header information to distinguish between search engine bots and web browsers. In order to avoid detection, TDSs often take additional countermeasures such as resolving the visitor's IP address to a geographic location and recording the number of accesses. Once the TDS has verified the traffic, a user is redirected a number of times to a landing page. This landing page will then launch a social engineering or drive-by download attack, as described previously.

Note that most TDSs also define a *time-to-live* (TTL) value that specifies how long a particular redirection URL will remain active. Most TTL values are very short, which makes it more difficult for security researchers to track active campaigns.

An alternative approach to using blackhat SEO techniques for traffic generation is to exploit the distribution systems and ubiquity of online ad networks. An attacker may compromise a legitimate ad network, or sign up as an advertiser to display malicious advertisements disguised as free pornography, missing audio/video codecs, or virus scans that perform similar social engineering attacks to con visitors into installing their malware. Online ad networks are also frequently used in conjunction with drive-by-download attacks, known collectively as *malvertisements*, to covertly install the fake AV software (without user interaction or permission).

A third infection method is through *botnets*, a collection of compromised computers under the control of an attacker. Several large botnets, such as Koobface, Conficker, and Bredolab, have been known to distribute fake AV software to machines under their control, which is believed to be one of their top sources of revenue [17, 27, 38].

Once fake AV software has been installed on the victim's machine (either voluntarily through social engineering or involuntarily through a drive-by attack or botnet), intrusive nags will be shown continuously to the victim, warning of "malware infections" or "intrusion attempts" that pose a risk to the user's system. At this point, the fake AV software usually advertises itself as a free trial version with limited functionality (i.e., detection only). If a victim wants to remove the malware infections, they must upgrade to a commercial version by purchasing a license key. When a victim clicks the software's purchase button, they are taken to one of the fake AV company's web sites. After a victim enters their personal information and credit card, they are sent a license key (e.g., through email) that essentially deactivates the bogus malware alerts, providing the user with a sense that their purchase was valuable.

2.2 Infrastructure

Similar to any other legitimate online business, when a fake AV company's servers are down, they lose potential revenue streams. Therefore, there are a number of measures that these organizations take to ensure the availability of their infrastructure. The first strategy is to deploy an array of proxy servers that are publicly visible. The sole purpose of these proxies is to relay content to one or more backend servers

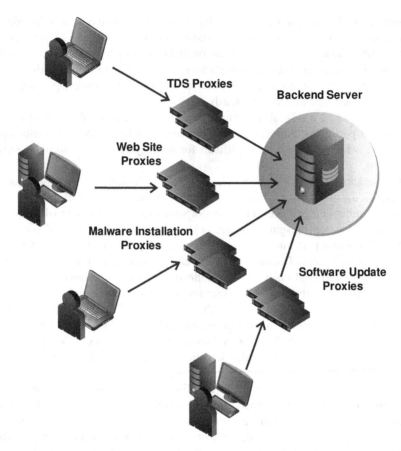

Fig. 2 Tiered infrastructure for many online criminal operations including fake antivirus businesses. We were able to obtain copies of three different fake AV organization's backend servers (in the *shaded circle* above) that control the entire operation

as shown in Fig. 2. More specifically, these machines communicate directly with users that are redirected to a landing page or infected hosts that purchase a license. The proxy servers are typically partitioned depending on the specific role that they fulfill (e.g., TDS servers are not reused for relaying sales information). The main purpose of the front-end servers is to thwart mitigation efforts. Hence, taking down one, or even several, of these machines often has little impact, since the domain name address records that point to these servers can be changed quickly and easily. These front-end servers are designed to be lightweight and expendable, and typically have an automated deployment program that accelerates the process of creating new proxy nodes.

The main drawback of proxies (from an attacker's point of view) is that when a defender obtains access to one of these front-end servers (or monitors their ingress and egress network traffic), she can learn the location of the backend infrastructure.

To address this problem and to further hide the location of the backend, the miscreants of fake AV operations may use multiple tiers of proxy servers. However, each extra tier will introduce additional network delay that could make a user who is purchasing a fake AV product more suspicious. In our experience, most fake AV operations use only one tier of proxy nodes. Thus, we were able to locate the backend infrastructure by tracking the network traffic from an infected host to a proxy node to the backend servers. By taking down the backend servers, the entire fake AV operation is disrupted (i.e., servers relaying sales, malware installations, and TDS become inoperable).

A second, important strategy is to register a large number of domain names. The domain names fulfill several purposes. First, it makes the fake AV web site look more legitimate (e.g., the domains are usually related to antivirus or security keywords). Second, the large number of domains makes takedown efforts more difficult, since the DNS records can be changed to point to any of their proxy servers. In addition, the reputation of a fake AV domain will decline as more people are defrauded, and many of the domains will become blacklisted. As a result, domain registrars may ultimately suspend some of the fake AV domains. Overall, the AV_1 crew purchased 276 domains, 17 front-end servers, and one back-end server. Similarly the AV_2 operation registered at least 188 domains, managed 16 front-end servers, and two back-end servers. We did not have complete visibility over the total number of domains used by AV_3, but from our observations, the infrastructure was similar to the others with a large number of free domains registered through the co.cc top-level domain (TLD), and approximately 20 front-end servers, and one back-end server.

3 Data Collection

In the following section, we describe the process that facilitated our efforts in obtaining access to these fake antivirus backend servers and the data we collected. The main tool that we utilized to analyze the fake AV malware was ANUBIS, a system that dynamically analyzes binary programs via runtime analysis [15]. ANUBIS runs a Windows executable and documents the program's behavior, including system modifications, processes creation, and network activity. ANUBIS is able to process on the order of tens of thousands of samples per day, providing us with a comprehensive view of the current malware landscape [1].

By searching through the network connections logged in the ANUBIS database, we were able to identify a number of unique network signatures commonly used by fake antivirus software. More specifically, when fake AV is installed, it often *phones home*, by connecting back to servers under the control of the fake AV criminal organization. For example, infected machines made an HTTP request similar to GET/install.php?aff_id=151&p=34&s=7&ip=192.168.1.3&cn=US, to notify the criminals of the installation and to credit the affiliate responsible for the infection. The parameters *p* and *s* provided details about the type and name of the malware.

After observing network signatures associated with these fake AVs, we contacted the hosting providers whose servers were being used for controlling these operations. We provided them with network traces, malware samples, and other evidence that revealed the location of the servers that were situated within their network. The hosting providers responded by taking these servers down, and they provided us with direct access to the information stored on them. Note that we had previously collaborated with a number of these vigilant ISPs in the U.S. and abroad through FIRE [34], our network reputation service that tracks where malicious content resides on the Internet.

In total, we were able to get a complete snapshot of 21 servers: 17 of which were proxy nodes, and 4 of which were backend servers. The information that we collected from these servers included data for AV_1 for approximately 3 months from January through April 2010, 16 months from January 2009 through May 2010 for AV_2, and from March 2008 through August 2010 for AV_3. From these data sources, we have a view of nearly the entire operation including web site source code, samples of the fake AV malware, and databases. The most interesting information is contained in the database records, which document everything from malware installations, fake AV sales, refunds, technical support conversations to the TDSs controlling the fake AV landing pages.

4 Following the Money Trail

Now that we have provided a summary of the fake AV infrastructure and our data sources, we will focus on the financial aspects that drive the sales of fake AV software. In particular, we analyze the flow of money from a victim to the criminals and their affiliates. In addition, we examine the ways in which the fake AV groups manage to stay under the radar when interacting with credit card payment processors.

4.1 Transaction Process

Before we present the detailed statistics of sales, revenue, chargebacks and refunds, we introduce an overview of the various entities involved in a fake antivirus business. The transaction process, as shown in Fig. 3, begins when a victim purchases the rogue AV software. This purchase is done through the fake AV company's web site (Step 1), where the victim enters her credit card information. The fake AV business (i.e., the merchant) then submits the credit card data to a third-party payment processor (Step 2). The payment processor forwards the information through one of the major credit card companies (Step 3), who requests authorization from the credit card issuer (Step 4). If the credit card issuer (i.e., a bank) approves the transaction, the victim's credit card is charged (Step 5), and the credit card company

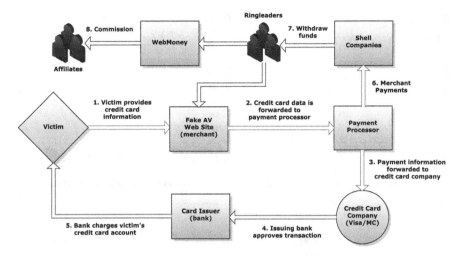

Fig. 3 High-level overview of the transaction process for fake antivirus businesses

notifies the payment processor of the successful sale. Periodically (e.g., biweekly or monthly), the payment processor deposits funds into bank accounts set up by the fake AV businesses (Step 6). The ringleaders of the fake AV operation then withdraw the funds (Step 7) and pay a commission to their affiliates (Step 8). We will provide more details about this process in the following sections.

4.2 Sales

There are a number of factors that contribute to whether a victim purchases a license, such as the aggressiveness of the fake AV software (e.g., frequency of alerts, type of threats, and whether system performance is affected). In addition, the price and subscription models offered by most fake antivirus products play an interesting role, with subscriptions that range from 6-month licenses to lifetime licenses. The AV_1 operation offered licenses for 6-months at $49.95, 1-year at $59.95, and 2-years at $69.95. These options were purchased almost uniformly with rates of 34.8%, 32.9%, and 32.3%, respectively. The AV_2 company's products also offered 6-month licenses at $49.95, 1-year at $69.95, and a lifetime license at $89.95. The 6-month option was the most popular (61.9%), followed by the lifetime license (24.6%) and the 1-year license (13.5%). The products sold by AV_3 were priced at $59.95 for a 1-year license and $79.95 for a lifetime license. All of AV_3's products were also bundled with a mandatory $19.95 fee for 24 x 7 customer support services, bringing the total price to $79.90 for the yearly license (purchased by 83.2% of victims) and $99.90 (purchased by 16.8% of the victims) for the lifetime license.

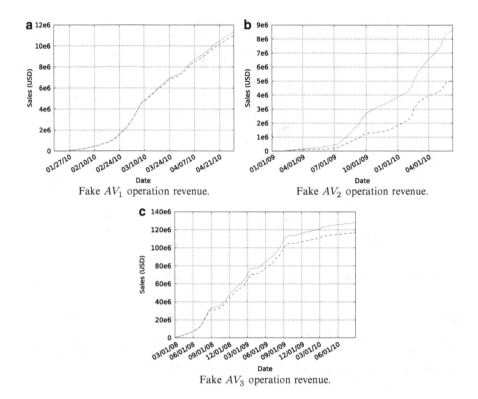

Fig. 4 Three criminal organizations' revenue from fake antivirus sales. The *solid line* displays the total revenue, while the *dotted line* displays the revenue after chargebacks and refunds

In total, AV_1 "trial" products were installed 8,403,008 times, which resulted in 189,342 sales, or upgrades to the "commercial" version (a conversion rate of 2.4%) in only 3 months. Likewise, AV_2's programs were installed 6,624,508 times, with 137,219 victims that purchased the fake antivirus over 16 months. That is a conversion rate of approximately 2.1%. The AV_3 business sold 1,969,953 licenses out of 91,305,640 installations from March 2008 through August 2010 (a conversion rate of approximately 2.2%).

The total victim loss from the three fake AV operations was $11,303,494, $5,046,508, and $116,941,854 from AV_1, AV_2, and AV_3, respectively. Figure 4 shows the cumulative daily revenue for each of these fake antivirus operations. If we extrapolate these profits over one year, the AV_1 crew was on track to earn more than $45 million dollars per year, while the AV_2 group earned approximately $3.8 million per year. The largest and most profitable operation was AV_3, which raked in an average of $48.4 million dollars per year.

As we will discuss in Sect. 4.4, some credit card transactions were reported to be fraudulent and were credited back to the victim. Interestingly, victim complaints force these illegitimate firms into a complex position with their payment processors, as we will discuss in the following sections.

4.3   Payment Processors

An interesting facet of fake AV sales is the process in which credit card transactions are handled. In particular, payment processors (also known as payment service providers) are an integral part of every sale. Without these processors, fake AV operations would not be able to accept credit card payments. This would make it not only harder for a victim to purchase the product (i.e., they would have to use an alternative form of payment, such as cash, check, or money order), but it would also likely raise red flags that the software may be fraudulent. Note that payment processors must maintain a degree of legitimacy, or they risk losing the ability to accept major credit cards. For instance, a payment processor known as ePassporte lost the rights to accept Visa credit cards, due to a large amount of fraudulent transactions, money laundering, and other questionable activities [20]. Note that the AV_2 crew at one point set up an ePassporte merchant account for processing credit card transactions.

Perhaps the most notorious payment service provider is Chronopay, which is headquartered in the Netherlands and operated by Russian businessmen. Chronopay has long been associated with processing transactions for various forms of online criminal organizations [24]. However, Chronopay also provides legitimate services to large organizations such as Electronic Arts, Kaspersky, and charities including the World Wildlife Federation, Greenpeace, and UNICEF. Because the volume of legitimate transactions from these businesses may far outweigh the fraudulent activities, major credit card companies may be hesitant to sever ties with Chronopay. Note that all three fake AV businesses that we analyzed used Chronopay's credit card payment services.

There were several other, smaller payment processors that the fake AV operations used for credit card transactions. Interestingly, we found communications between one of these small payment processors and the fake AV perpetrators that revealed that the payment service provider was well aware of the fake AV business and even offered advice to help the group sell more products. There are a number of tricks that some of these dishonest payment service providers perform in order to benefit from fraudulent transactions. First, payment processors may offer *high-risk merchant accounts*, where the processor may earn close to 15% for each transaction. These are typically for questionable businesses that have significant problems with customer complaints (e.g., online pharmacies or pornography). Second, we observed that some of these payment processors allow an illicit company to create multiple merchant accounts in which transactions are periodically rotated (approximately every 30–45 days) through each account, such that a single account is never flagged for fraudulent activities, since the transactions are distributed over all of the accounts.

4.4 Chargebacks and Refunds

Interestingly, all three fake antivirus groups that we studied offered a certain number of refunds to individuals who requested them. At first, it may seem counter-intuitive for a criminal operation that is selling fraudulent products to provide refunds to victims. However, it is important to keep in mind that these criminal organizations have to use legitimate (or semi-legitimate) credit card payment processors for every transaction. In addition, payment processors are required by statutory (federal regulations) and contractual obligations (PCI) to provide various levels of consumer protection against theft and fraudulent purchases. When a victim reports a fraudulent transaction to their credit card issuer, they are issued a credit, which is known as a *chargeback*. If a business receives too many chargeback complaints, the payment processor may sever ties with the company and prohibit further credit card transactions. Therefore, it is important to minimize the number of chargebacks, which has the effect of extending the lifetime of the fake AV operation.

Overall, AV_1 granted 5,669 refunds (3% of sales) at a cost of \$346,039 (in addition to 1,544 chargebacks worth \$94,963). In comparison, AV_2 issued 11,681 refunds (or 8.5% of sales) at a cost of \$759,666 (in addition to 3,024 chargebacks valued at \$183,107). AV_3 refunded 151,553 (7.1% of sales) for a total of \$10,951,191 (with 30,743 chargebacks valued at \$2,225,430). Note that the primary credit card processor for AV_3 temporarily froze AV_3's merchant account for approximately one month in March 2009, due to a high number of chargebacks. After this incident, AV_3 offered more refunds, and the number of chargebacks dropped accordingly.

Another important factor that has an impact on chargebacks and refunds is how frequently a fake AV business changes the name of their product. This is due to the fact that after a short interval (typically 3–7 days), victim complaints start appearing on consumer web forums that are in turn indexed by search engines. Thus, a victim may perform a Google search for the name of the fake AV and find that other users have similar grievances and complaints. Interestingly, we found that AV_2 had significant server problems and maintained the same product names for an extended period of time. As a result, they had the highest chargeback and refund rates.

As we will discuss in Sect. 6, the amount and timing of refunds follows an interesting pattern, which indicates that the criminals maximize their profits by refunding just enough sales to remain under a payment processors chargeback limit.

4.5 Affiliate Programs

The financial incentives for cybercrime play an important role both in the type and amount of fraud. In order to infect as many machines as possible and therefore maximize sales, fake AV businesses rely upon affiliate networks based primarily in Eastern Europe known as *partnerka*. The backend servers that we obtained contained payment records to these partners. The profits for some of the affiliates are immense, with members earning as much as 30–80% commission from sales leads. Remarkably, the top affiliate of AV_1 made more than $1.8 million dollars in approximately two months. Over the course of these two months, there were a total of 44 affiliates who were paid (out of 140 that enrolled), with four earning more than $500,000, 11 in excess of $100,000, and 15 more than $50,000. The average affiliate income was approximately $60,000 per month. In comparison, AV_2 had 98 active affiliates out of 167 total registered, and stored records for 9 months of payments to these affiliates. Overall, five of these affiliates made more than $300,000, 16 earned more than $100,000, and 22 earned more than $50,000. The AV_3 operation had a total of 1,107 affiliates with 541 who were active. The top AV_3 affiliate earned $3.86 million, and three others made more than $1 million. There were 15 AV_3 affiliates that earned over $100,000, and 23 that were paid more than $50,000.

By comparing the affiliate email addresses across the three different fake AV partnerka, we were able to determine that 70 affiliate members were involved in multiple groups. Interestingly, there was one affiliate who was associated with all three fake AV businesses.

The affiliate payments were made through WebMoney, a virtual electronic currency. There are several advantages that WebMoney provides for criminal activities. In particular, all transactions are anonymous and irreversible. That is, once a transfer has occurred it cannot be voided, regardless of whether it was fraudulent. Other benefits include a very low transaction fee (0.8%), and a large number of places, especially in Eastern Europe, that will exchange WebMoney for local currencies.

4.6 Shell Companies

One of the most important parts of the financial system from a fake AV company's perspective is the ability to *cash out* earned funds. Thus, a fake AV company must open one or more bank accounts to receive merchant remittances from their payment processors. These accounts are typically set up and registered to fictitious *shell companies*. We observed accounts registered primarily in Europe and Asia, including the Czech Republic, Finland, Cypress, and Israel. Once money is deposited into a shell account, the ringleaders can directly withdraw the funds. However, criminals who are more cautious may opt to use the services of *money mules*. A money mule is a person who is recruited (usually under the pretense of a work from home job) to accept a bank deposit, withdraw the funds, and wire the money (minus a service fee) back to the criminals. This greatly minimizes the risk that a criminal will be apprehended when receiving funds. Unfortunately, we were not able to determine the precise method used by these three fake AV groups to withdraw funds. Nevertheless, we believe the money was probably picked up directly by the ringleaders (or one of their close associates), based on the geographic locations of the bank accounts.

5 Victims

In this section, we analyze the victims that purchased fake AV software. In particular, we will study various characteristics of victims including: geographic location, operating systems, and institutions. In addition, we will examine the technical support and customer service provided by the three fake AV businesses.

The largest concentration of victims (by far) was in the U.S. (76.9%) followed by the U.K., Canada, and Australia. This is likely due to the fact that the fake antivirus products are primarily written for English speakers (only a few of them had been translated to other languages). The most popular, compromised operating systems were Windows XP (54.2%), Windows Vista (30.8%), and Windows 7 (14.8%). Internet Explorer 7 was the most commonly used browser (65.6%). The most frequently used email addresses of customers of fake AV products were Yahoo, Hotmail, AOL, Gmail, and Comcast. Other residential ISPs placed in the top 10 including AT&T, SBC Global, Verizon, and Bellsouth. This indicates that most victims probably purchased the fake AV software for their personal computers at home. However, there were a number of sales from victims at commercial, government, and military institutions.

All three of the fake AV companies offered various forms of customer service and technical support. Customer service for fraudulent products may seem contradictory, but its purpose is clear: to reduce the number of refunds and victim complaints. Overall, the fake AV groups offered two types of support systems. The first was an online system where victims could open tickets describing their problems, and technical support representatives would periodically reply to these tickets. The second type of support system was an interactive, live chat service, where a victim would talk in real-time with technical support personnel.

We were able to observe the communications in many of these support systems, and analyze how operators responded to questions, and how they handled irate customers. For the most part, victims were upset, realized that the fake AV software was a scam, and requested instructions for removing the malware from their system. The fake AV representatives typically responded with removal directions, but they warned users that their computer was still infected and made claims that competitors (i.e., legitimate antivirus vendors) were slandering their products.

We also performed automated data mining techniques to determine the relationship between complaints, sales, chargebacks, and refunds. To this end, we queried the fake AV groups' internal databases for patterns such as credit card numbers, unique identifiers (e.g., orders), email addresses, and various keywords (e.g., *fraud, scam, refund*, etc) that were relevant to disgruntled customer reactions. By correlating these database records, we examined whether a victim who purchased a fake AV product later filed a complaint through any of the support forums, and if a refund or chargeback was issued. Overall, only a small percentage (less than 10%) of victims actually sought refunds, and those who were issued refunds received their credit within 7 days on average. Note that the low rates of victim complaints that we discovered are similar to those reported by the computer security news investigation web site, KrebsOnSecurity [21].

6 Economic Model

In this section, we utilize the data that we have collected to identify behavior that is representative of a fake AV business. We then propose an economic model based on a key observation of refunds that may be used to detect other businesses that are engaged in illegal activities.

6.1 Refund Patterns

Fake antivirus software firms (hereafter, firms) act to maximize profits. To do so, the firms rely not only on the systematic transfer of funds to their accounts, but also on a return flow of refunds that mimics the behavior of legitimate providers. As this flow of refunds provides a clear pattern of behavior, we model the refund flow with consideration toward using it to detect and punish firms.

The flow of funds, and refunds, depends on two key players that act as intermediaries between the buyer of the fake software and the firm. As outlined in Fig. 3, the payment processor is a key player that serves to transmit credit information from the buyer to the credit card network. The second key player is the credit card network, which incorporates both the actual card company (e.g. Visa) and the bank that issues the card (and thereby hosts the buyer's account). The payment flow is from the buyer, through the payment processor and then the credit card network, to the firm.

The trigger for a refund is a request, made by a purchaser, for return of payment upon discovery that the software is fake (or not what they expected). The purchaser may then issue a request for a refund at any point after the sale. To construct a model of requests, we let s denote the number of sales in a given period and let rq denote the number of refund requests that result from s. We model requests in period t as a Poisson random variable:

$$rq_t = \lambda s_{t-1},$$

where λ captures the expected portion of buyers from period $t - 1$ who will issue a request for a refund in period t. Given the speed at which information is received and decisions are made, we are primarily concerned with periods corresponding to individual days.

When a refund request has been made, the firm can either ignore the request or grant a refund. If the firm ignores the request, then the buyer may contact the credit card network to obtain a refund. When the credit card network grants a refund to the buyer, the network must collect the funds from the firm by reversing the charge, hence refunds of this type are called chargebacks. This pattern is born out in the data as, for each of the firms under study, the average time to receive a chargeback is substantially longer than the average time to receive a refund (for AV_1, chargebacks average 23.7 days longer to process than refunds; the comparable numbers for the other firms are 21.4 days for AV_2 and 10.6 days for AV_3). For AV_1 and AV_2,

35–37% of all refunds occur within three days of sales. In contrast, only 1–6% of all chargebacks for AV_1 and AV_2 occur within three days of sales. For AV_3, only 12% of refunds occur within 3 days of sales but less than 1% of chargebacks occur within that same time.

If the firm ceases operations prior to a collection by the payment processor, then the processor must absorb the cost of the chargeback. Because a firm with a large number of sales in a period may decide to cease operations, leaving the processor at risk of absorbing a large number of chargebacks, the payment processor has an incentive to identify illegitimate firms and sever ties with them.

To model the interplay of requests, refunds (which are made directly by the firm to the buyer) and chargebacks, we must specify how payment processors monitor chargebacks to limit their risk. Let $\overline{cb}$ be a threshold, above which the credit card company denies all future transactions. In determining how many requests to refund, a firm that wishes to continue operations must balance the loss in current revenue from granting refunds against the loss of future revenue from being denied access to the credit card network. The number of refunds in a given period, rf, is thus an increasing function of the number of requests and a decreasing function of the number of chargebacks, cb,

$$rf = g(rq, cb).$$

Let the threshold $\overline{cb}$ apply to the sum of accumulated chargebacks over T periods. The decision rule of the credit card network is to sever ties with a firm if $\sum_{s=1}^{t} cb_s > \overline{cb}$, for any period $t \in 1, \ldots, T$. As a consequence, a firm will increase the rate of refunds as the sum of accumulated chargebacks approaches the threshold $\overline{cb}$. That is, refunds follow the pattern

$$rf_t = \alpha \cdot rq_t + \beta \cdot rq_t \cdot \left\{ \overline{cb} - \sum_{s=1}^{t} cb_s < D \right\}, \tag{1}$$

where $\{A\}$ takes the value 1 if the event A occurs and is 0 otherwise.

The desire to avoid crossing the threshold $\overline{cb}$ leads to a distinctive pattern of refunds and chargebacks. For a payment processor, (1) provides several patterns to distinguish these firms from legitimate software providers. For example, refunds from firms may increase at the periodic interval corresponding to T or may increase in reaction to an increase in chargebacks. Also, refunds should increase as the cumulated chargeback sum approaches $\overline{cb}$. For legitimate providers, no such dynamic pattern of refunds should emerge.

To understand the difference in the dynamic refund pattern between legitimate providers and fraudulent firms, note that in contrast to (1), refunds for legitimate providers follow the pattern

$$rf_t = \alpha \cdot rq_t \tag{2}$$

Because refunds are not a function of chargebacks in (2), refunds should depend only on requests for legitimate providers.

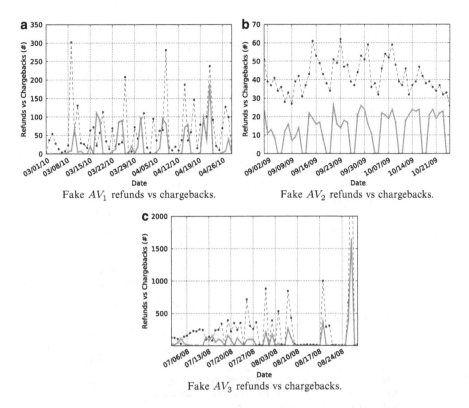

Fake AV_1 refunds vs chargebacks.

Fake AV_2 refunds vs chargebacks.

Fake AV_3 refunds vs chargebacks.

Fig. 5 Daily refunds and chargebacks from fake AV sales. The *dashed line* displays the number of refunds per day, while the *solid line* displays the number of chargebacks per day

To provide evidence that a firm's refunds respond to chargebacks, we display daily refunds and chargebacks for the firms in Fig. 5. For each of the firms, surges in daily chargebacks are closely followed by (or occur simultaneously with) surges in refunds. The only exceptions appear to be at the latter part of Fig. 5b.

While the figures reveal a dynamic pattern of refunds and chargebacks that is consistent with (1), isolating the impact of chargebacks on refunds requires that we control for the level of sales. We must do so because refunds are positively related to sales, so it is possible that sustained increases in sales could lead to increases in both chargebacks and refunds. To estimate the isolated impact of chargebacks, we construct the ordinary least squares estimates of the coefficients in

$$rf_t = \beta_0 + \beta_1 cb_t + \beta_2 cb_{t-1} + \beta_3 \overline{s_t} + u_t. \tag{3}$$

The coefficients β_1 and β_2 capture the increase in refunds on day t brought about by an increase in chargebacks on day t and day $t-1$, holding previous sales constant. The coefficient β_3 captures the increase in refunds due to an increase in average

Table 1 Coefficient estimates for (3)

AV_1 - Refunds	(I)	(II)	
Chargebacks	0.64	0.52	
	(0.24)*	(0.24)*	
Lagged Chargebacks	–	0.55	
		(0.21)*	
3-day Average Sales	0.008	0.009	
	(0.008)	(0.008)	

AV_2 - Refunds	(I)	(II)	(III)
Chargebacks	1.23	1.16	1.17
	(0.14)*	(0.15)*	(0.14)*
Lagged Chargebacks	–	0.26	0.25
		(0.12)*	(0.12)*
3-day Average Sales	0.043	0.041	0.041
	(0.004)*	(0.004)*	(0.004)*

AV_3 - Refunds	(I)	(II)	(III)
Chargebacks	0.72	0.71	0.72
	(0.24)*	(0.23)*	(0.23)*
Lagged Chargebacks	–	0.089	0.088
		(0.073)	(0.080)
3-day Average Sales	0.031	0.030	0.030
	(0.004)*	(0.004)*	(0.004)*

Note: Heteroskedasticity-robust standard errors are reported in parenthesis
Our results are not sensitive to the choice of a 3-day average sales window
*indicates significance at the 5% level

sales over the past three days ($\overline{s_t}$). As we do not observe the number of refund requests each day, we use $\overline{s_t}$ as a proxy. The quantity u_t is a random error that encompasses all other factors that influence refunds on that day.

Estimates of (3) are contained in Table 1. The column labeled (I) corresponds to (3) with $\beta_2 = 0$; that is, lagged chargebacks are not included (these lagged chargebacks are included in Column II). For each of the firms, chargebacks have a substantial impact on refunds after controlling for previous sales. For example, the estimate of 0.64 for firm AV_1 indicates that, after controlling for the average level of sales over the previous 3 days, an increase of 100 chargebacks leads to an increase of 64 refunds. In contrast, an increase in average sales of 100 leads to an increase of only 1 refund. The estimated standard errors describe the precision of our estimates: for this coefficient on chargebacks, the confidence interval of (0.16,1.12) indicates the range of plausible values for β_1. As the interval does not contain 0, the data is strongly supportive of a positive relationship between chargebacks and refunds.

In addition to controlling for sales, we also control for date of the month and day of the week to remove any monthly and daily trends. Column (III) in Table 1 corresponds to the coefficient estimates of (3) while controlling for monthly and weekly patterns. This was possible with AV_2 and AV_3 but not for AV_1 due to limited data.

Table 1 indicates significant correlation between chargebacks received and refunds granted while controlling for previous sales and monthly fluctuations among all three firms. Without knowing more firm-level details regarding their contracts with payment processors or restrictions from credit card networks further inference becomes difficult. However, we do interpret this as evidence that fraudulent firms seem to alter their refunds according to the chargebacks reported against them. Payment processors or credit card networks have more information and have a better understanding of the firm's chargeback constraints and may, therefore, be in a unique position to monitor these firms.

An important limitation to our analysis is that we lack comparable data for legitimate firms. Despite our findings above, we are unable to discern whether or not this pattern is distinctive to only illegitimate firms.

6.2   Detecting Fraudulent Firms

The previously described patterns in behavior could be observed by the payment processor since it knows the number of chargebacks against the firm at a particular time, the chargeback threshold faced by the firm, as well as the number of refunds the firm is offering (as these would have to pass through the payment processor). If the payment processor has an incentive to investigate its clients, the existence of this chargeback-responsive behavior could provide evidence that a particular antivirus company is fraudulent. The question is: Does the payment processor have an incentive to investigate its clients?

The payment processor (as noted in Sect. 4.3) receives a percentage of each transaction that occurs but faces a risk of losing business with a credit card company for too much fraudulent behavior. While losing a major credit card company like Visa would devastate a payment processor (as in the case of ePassporte), the credit card company may be hesitant to drop a payment processor if it does enough legitimate business (as in the case of Chronopay).

However, at any given time there is a risk that the fraudulent antivirus firm may be caught or may cease operations. In this case the firm will no longer be able to offer refunds and the payment processor will receive an increase in chargebacks from consumers who have no other way of receiving a refund. The payment processor would be forced to pay the entire amount of the chargeback (the chargeback fees as well as the entire refund amount) as it can no longer bill the firm. Depending on the volume of sales, the risk of future increases in chargebacks could be very costly. If this risk outweighs the revenue the payment processor receives from the firm's account, it may prefer to sever ties with the firm as to not be held liable for the potential chargebacks.

In the case when the firm is caught, credit card companies would have to pay the costs of the chargebacks if the payment processor is forced to shut down. The credit card companies may, therefore, be concerned if a small payment processor is serving an illegitimate firm that may be relatively large compared to the processor's overall volume. In these cases, credit card companies may have an incentive to investigate these firms if they are working with small payment processors. While the credit card company may not observe as much firm level information as the payment processor, it observes the chargebacks and refunds associated with a particular firm. Therefore, this could be a good technique for a credit card company to investigate fraudulent firms.

As mentioned above, we expect the rate of refunds offered by a fraudulent firm to vary in response to chargebacks incurred by the firm. As firms increase their sales, payment processors and credit card networks face increased risk of liability for future chargebacks if the firm ceases operations. This risk may warrant investigation of fraudulent firms using these observable patterns.

7 Ethical Considerations

The nature of the data that we collected raises a number of ethical concerns. In particular, we have a large amount of personal information for the victims who were defrauded by these three fake AV businesses. Thus, we took measures to protect the privacy and identity of the victims through the use of data encryption, automated program analysis, and by conducting our research according to established ethical principles in the field [2, 8, 12, 16]. We also obtained approval from the Institutional Review Board (IRB) at the University of California, Santa Barbara before performing our analysis. Finally, we provided all information that we obtained to U.S. law enforcement officials.

8 Related Work

In the past few years, there have been several studies that have analyzed various aspects of fraudulent businesses selling fake antivirus products. Researchers from Google described the techniques and dynamics used by cybercriminals to drive traffic to their sites via landing pages [30]. Other work analyzed the distribution and installation methods of rogue security software [10]. Various security vendors have reported on potential revenue from scareware operations based on the number of infections that they observed [4,37]. Cova et al. presented an analysis of the rogue antivirus structure and indirectly tried to measure the number of victims and profits based on poorly configured web servers used by several fake AV groups [6]. They estimated the conversion rate of infections to sales at 1.36%, which is slightly lower than the rates that we observed. We also found a similar geographic distribution of victims in the U.S., and number of domains registered by larger fake AV groups. In comparison, our data provides a much more complete view of large-scale fake AV operations, with information dating back more than two years. We also had visibility of refunds and chargebacks from fake AV sales, which has never been studied before.

Techniques to identify drive-by-download attacks have been proposed that analyze web sites for malicious content in a virtual or emulated environment to detect exploits [5, 14]. The prevalence of malicious web sites has been examined through crawler-based approaches that analyzed billions of web pages [28, 29]. Another study analyzed drive-by attacks via infiltration and provided insights into the compromised web servers used in the attacks as well as the security posture of potential victims [35].

A number of recent papers have analyzed the reasons that cause users to fall victim to phishing scams, which include lack of knowledge and attentiveness to browser and other security related cues [7, 9]. Several approaches have been proposed to detect phishing sites such as analyzing page content, layout, and other anomalies [22, 26, 31]. In addition, studies have analyzed the modus operandi of the criminal operations behind phishing [23], and the effectiveness of phishing defenses [25].

Previous work has investigated the Internet's underground economy, through advertised prices of web forums [39] and IRC chat rooms [11]. Holz et al. studied the drop zones used by botnets to store stolen information from victims [13]. Stone-Gross et al. hijacked the Torpig botnet and studied the data exfiltrated from infected computers, and estimated the value of the compromised financial information (e.g., credit card numbers and bank account credentials) [33]. The underground economy of large-scale spam operations was examined in [36]. The paper analyzed the complexity in orchestrating spam campaigns, and explored an underground forum used by spammers to exchange goods and services. Another type of scam, known as *One Click Fraud*, was studied by Christin et al. The fraud works through intimidation (similar to fake AV) by threatening unsuspecting web site visitors with potential embarrassment (e.g., the victim was browsing pornographic content) unless a payment is received for a nonexistent service. The authors presented an economic model to determine the number of users that must fall victim to the scam in order to remain economically viable, and estimated losses in the tens to hundreds of thousands of U.S. dollars [3].

9 Conclusions

In this paper, we have presented an in-depth study of how a particular type of scareware, namely fake anti-virus software, is deployed and managed. Our work is unique in that it is based on the information contained on a number of key servers that were part of the criminals' infrastructure. This unprecedented access allowed us to obtain ground truth about the type and sophistication of the techniques used to lure victims into paying for scareware, as well as the amount of transactions performed, including refunds and chargebacks.

We leveraged this data to build an economic model that shows how cybercriminals are very careful in performing refunds and chargebacks in order to maintain a balanced financial posture that does not immediately reveal their criminal nature. Nonetheless, the economic model also outlines how these operations have distinct characteristics that may differentiate these criminal endeavors from legitimate business operations.

Future work will extend the current model with detection capabilities that can be directly applied to payment data streams. The goal is to develop a tool based on the model that can identify scareware operations automatically.

Acknowledgments This work was supported by the Office of Naval Research (ONR) under Grant N000140911042 and by the National Science Foundation (NSF) under grants CNS-0845559 and CNS-0905537. We would also like to thank the anonymous reviewers for their valuable suggestions and insights.

References

1. Bayer U, Habibi I, Balzarotti D, Kirda E, Kruegel C (2009) A view on current malware behaviors. In: USENIX workshop on large-scale exploits and emergent threats (LEET), 2009
2. Burstein A (2008) Conducting cybersecurity research legally and ethically. In: USENIX workshop on large-scale exploits and emergent threats (LEET), 2008
3. Christin N, Yanagihara S, Kamataki K (2010) Dissecting one click frauds. In: ACM conference on computer and communications security (CCS), 2010
4. Correll S, Corrons L (2010) The business of rogueware: analysis of the new style of online fraud. http://www.pandasecurity.com/img/enc/The%20Business%20of%20Rogueware.pdf
5. Cova M, Kruegel C, Vigna G (2010) Detection and analysis of drive-by-download attacks and malicious javascript code. In: Proceedings of the international world wide web conference (WWW), 2010
6. Cova M, Leita C, Thonnard O, Keromytis A, Dacier M (2010) An analysis of rogue AV campaigns. In: Symposium on recent advances in intrusion detection (RAID), 2010
7. Dhamija R, Tygar J, Hearst M (2006) Why phishing works. In: Conference on human factors in computing systems (CHI), 2006
8. Dittrich D, Bailey M, Dietrich S (2009) Towards community standards for ethical behavior in computer security research. Technical report 2009–1, Stevens CS, April 2009
9. Egelman S, Cranor L, Hong J (2008) You've been warned: an empirical study of the effectiveness of web browser phishing warnings. In: Conference on human factors in computing systems (CHI), 2008
10. Fossi M, Turner D, Johnson E, Mack T, Adams T, Blackbird J, Low M, McKinney D, Dacier M, Keromytis A, Leita C, Cova M, Overton J, Thonnard O (2009) Symantec report on rogue security software. In: Whitepaper, 2009
11. Franklin J, Paxson V, Perrig A, Savage S (2007) An inquiry into the nature and causes of the wealth of internet miscreants. In: ACM conference on computer and communications security (CCS), 2007
12. Garfinkel S (2008) IRBs and security research: myths, facts and mission creep. In: Proceedings of the USENIX workshop on usability, psychology, and security, 2008

13. Holz T, Engelberth M, Freiling F (2008) Learning more about the underground economy: a case-study of keyloggers and dropzones. Reihe Informatik TR-2008–006, university of Mannheim, 2008
14. Ikinci A, Holz T, Freiling F (2008) Monkey-spider: detecting malicious websites with low-interaction honeyclients. In: Proceedings of Sicherheit, Schutz und Zuverlässigkeit, April 2008
15. International Secure Systems Lab (2010). Anubis: analyzing unknown binaries. http://anubis.iseclab.org
16. Kenneally E, Bailey M, Maughan D (2010) A framework for understanding and applying ethical principles in network and security research. In: Proceedings of the workshop on ethics in computer security research (WECSR), 2010
17. Kirk J (2010) Bredolab-infected PCs downloading fake antivirus software. http://www.pcworld.com/businesscenter/article/209031/bredolabinfected_pcs_downloading_fake_antivirus_software.html
18. Krebs B (2009) Massive profits fueling rogue antivirus market. In: Washington post, 2009
19. Krebs B (2009) Virus scanners for virus authors. http://krebsonsecurity.com/2009/12/virus-scanners-for-virus-authors/
20. Krebs B (2010) Following the money, ePassporte edition. http://krebsonsecurity.com/2010/09/following-the-money-epassporte-edition/
21. Krebs B (2010) Rogue antivirus victims seldom fight back. http://krebsonsecurity.com/2010/07/rogue-antivirus-victims-seldom-fight-back/
22. Ludl C, McAllister S, Kirda E, Kruegel C (2007) On the effectiveness of techniques to detect phishing sites. In: Proceedings of the conference on detection of intrusions and malware & vulnerability assessment (DIMVA), 2007
23. McGrath K, Gupta M (2008) Behind phishing: an examination of phisher modi operandi. In: USENIX workshop on large-scale exploits and emergent threats (LEET), 2008
24. Mick J (2010) Russian anti-spam chief caught spamming. http://www.dailytech.com/Russian+AntiSpam+Chief+Caught+Spamming/article18423.htm
25. Moore T, Clayton R (2007) An empirical analysis of the current state of phishing attack and defence. In: Workshop on the economics of information security (WEIS), 2007.
26. Pan Y, Ding X (2006) Anomaly based web phishing page detection. In: Annual computer security applications conference (ACSAC), 2006
27. Poulsen K (2009) Conficker doomsday worm sells out for $49.95. http://www.wired.com/threatlevel/2009/04/conficker-dooms/
28. Provos N, McNamee D, Mavrommatis P, Wang K, Modadugu N (2007) The ghost in the browser: analysis of web-based malware. In: USENIX workshop on hot topics in understanding botnets (HotBots), 2007
29. Provos N, Mavrommatis P, Rajab M, Monrose F (2008) All your iFRAMEs point to us. In: USENIX security symposium, 2008
30. Rajab M, Ballard L, Mavrommatis P, Provos N, Zhao X (2010) The nocebo effect on the web: an analysis of fake anti-virus distribution. In: USENIX workshop on large-scale exploits and emergent threats (LEET), 2010
31. Rosiello A, Kirda E, Kruegel C, Ferrandi F (2007) A layout-similarity-based approach for detecting phishing pages. In: Security and privacy in communication networks (SecureComm), 2007
32. Samosseiko D (2009) The Partnerka what is it, and why should you care? In: Annual virus bulletin conference, 2009
33. Stone-Gross B, Cova M, Cavallaro L, Gilbert R, Szydlowski M, Kemmerer R, Kruegel C, Vigna G (2009) Your botnet is my botnet: analysis of a botnet takeover. In: ACM conference on computer and communications security (CCS), 2009
34. Stone-Gross B, Moser A, Kruegel C, Kirda E, Almeroth K (2009) FIRE: FInding rogue nEtworks. In: Annual computer security applications conference (ACSAC), 2009
35. Stone-Gross B, Cova M, Kruegel C, Vigna G (2010) Peering through the iFrame. In: IEEE mini-conference on computer communications (INFOCOM), 2010

36. Stone-Gross B, Holz T, Stringhini G, Vigna G (2011) The underground economy of spam: a Botmasters perspective of coordinating large-scale spam campaigns. In: USENIX workshop on large-scale exploits and emergent threats (LEET), 2011
37. TrendMicro (2010) The business of cybercrime a complex business model. Technical report, 2010
38. Villeneuve N, Deibert R, Rohozinski R (2010) KOOBFACE: Inside a crimeware network. InfoWar monitor JR04–2010, The SecDev group, 2010
39. Zhuge J, Holz T, Song JGC, Han X, Zou W (2009) Studying malicious websites and the underground economy on the chinese web

The Inconvenient Truth About Web Certificates

Nevena Vratonjic, Julien Freudiger, Vincent Bindschaedler,
and Jean-Pierre Hubaux

Abstract HTTPS is the de facto standard for securing Internet communications. Although it is widely deployed, the security provided with HTTPS in practice is dubious. HTTPS may fail to provide security for multiple reasons, mostly due to certificate-based authentication failures. Given the importance of HTTPS, we investigate the current scale and practices of HTTPS and certificate-based deployment. We provide a large-scale empirical analysis that considers the top one million most popular websites. Our results show that very few websites implement certificate-based authentication properly. In most cases, domain mismatches between certificates and websites are observed. We study the economic, legal and social aspects of the problem. We identify causes and implications of the profit-oriented attitude of Certification Authorities (CAs) and show how the current economic model leads to the distribution of cheap certificates for cheap security. Finally, we suggest possible changes to improve certificate-based authentication.

1 Introduction

HyperText Transfer Protocol Secure (HTTPS) is a key factor of the growth of the Internet ecosystem. It is the de facto standard used to guarantee security of Internet communications such as e-banking, e-commerce and Web-based email. HTTPS notably provides authentication, integrity and confidentiality of communications, thus preventing unauthorized viewing of exchanged information. The security of HTTPS communications is increasingly relevant, given the popularity of Web services where users reveal private information.

N. Vratonjic (✉) • J. Freudiger • V. Bindschaedler • J.-P. Hubaux
School of Computer and Communication Sciences, EPFL, Lausanne, Switzerland
e-mail: nevena.vratonjic@epfl.ch; julien.freudiger@epfl.ch; vincent.bindschaedler@epfl.ch;
jean-pierre.hubaux@epfl.ch

B. Schneier (ed.), *Economics of Information Security and Privacy III*,
DOI 10.1007/978-1-4614-1981-5_5,
© Springer Science+Business Media New York 2013

Yet, in practice the provided security is dubious and HTTPS may not achieve the intended objectives for multiple reasons. In most of the cases, it is due to certificate-based authentication failures typically caused by one of the following four problems. First, certification authorities may fail to implement certificate-based authentication properly [20,38]. Second, websites may not deploy digital certificates in the correct way [11]. Third, users frequently do not attempt or are not able to verify the status of HTTPS connections [26, 27, 29, 36, 41]. Lastly, Web browsers may fail to meaningfully convey security threats to users [25, 39].

In order to implement HTTPS and certificate-based authentication, website administrators need a public/private key pair and a matching digital certificate [9]. The digital certificate authenticates the entity owning a specific website and the associated public key. $X.509$ certificates are standard on the Web and assume a hierarchical system of certificate authorities (CAs) issuing and signing certificates. Certificates notably contain information about the issuer (a CA), the certificate owner, the public key, the validity period, and the hostname (website). Website administrators can purchase trusted certificates from root CAs. The list of trusted CAs on top of the CA hierarchy (called root CAs) is usually pre-installed in Web browsers and varies from one Web browser to the next. If a website owns a certificate signed by a root CA, then a chain of trust is established and Web browsers can authenticate the website [9].

In cases of authentication failures, communication is vulnerable to man-in-the-middle attacks. Not only are sophisticated active attacks (e.g., session hijacking) possible, but also attacks such as *phishing* [32] and *typosquatting* [35] where a malicious party may impersonate a legitimate entity. These attack scenarios are more realistic because they do not require the attacker to modify users' communication on-the-fly, but rather to simply obtain a valid certificate for the relevant domains [6]. For example, an adversary may obtain a certificate for a domain name that is similar to the domain name of a legitimate entity (e.g., *paypaal.com* for the legitimate domain name *paypal.com*) and rely on typosquatting attacks (i.e., users accidentally mistyping the domain name in the URL) for users to initiate communication with the adversary. In these scenarios, consumers are frequently not aware that they are under attack as browser indicators of a secure connection are present and there are no security warnings. Thus, users may reveal sensitive information (e.g., a credit card number) to the adversary.

Compromise of HTTPS communications may have severe consequences for both users and Web service providers. Therefore, it is important to assess the scale of HTTPS' current deployment and evaluate the security it provides. In particular, it is crucial to investigate deployment practices of certificate-based authentication. We seek answers to the following research questions:

Q1: How much is HTTPS currently deployed?
Q2: What are the problems with current deployment of HTTPS and certificate-based authentication?
Q3: What are the reasons that led to these problems?

In this paper, we report the results of a large-scale empirical analysis of the use of HTTPS and certificate-based authentication, that considers the top one million websites.

Our results show that one-third of the websites can be browsed with HTTPS. Only 22.6% of websites with username and password fields implement user login via HTTPS. In other words, for 77.4% of websites users' credentials can be compromised because login pages are not securely implemented. We believe that for most websites the complexity and cost in operating HTTPS might deter administrators from implementing HTTPS.

More importantly, only 16.0% of the websites implementing HTTPS carry out certificate-based authentication properly, i.e., using trusted, unexpired certificates with valid signatures, deployed on proper domains. For most of the websites (82.4%), authentication failures are in most cases due to domain mismatch, i.e., the domain name that certificate is issued for does not match the domain name it is deployed for. Other authentication failures are caused by untrusted certificates, expired certificates and broken chains of trust. Untrusted certificates are certificates whose chain of trust does not originate at one of the root CAs trusted by Web browsers. This is the case with *self-signed certificates* which website administrators often produce, by signing certificates themselves, in order to avoid costs of purchasing certificates from CAs.

The results imply that website administrators either lack the know-how or the incentives to properly deploy certificates. To avoid domain mismatch warnings, websites need a different certificate for each subdomain or a wildcard certificate (that matches any subdomain). Obtaining such certificates from trusted CAs is expensive. Further, website administrators that deploy self-signed certificates might lack incentive to take the additional overhead of managing multiple certificates, because Web browsers do not trust self-signed certificates and will anyhow display security warnings to users.

Websites are not the only culprits as malpractices of CAs also contribute to weak certificate-based authentication. CAs sometimes do not follow rigorous procedures when issuing certificates and distribute *domain-validated only* certificates that do not provide trust in the identity of certificates' owners. These certificates are less costly, thus website administrators are tempted to choose such options.

Our results help to understand the modes of intervention to properly achieve the security promised by HTTPS. In particular, we need to rethink the economic incentives behind the certificate-based authentication system. Further solution approaches may utilize means of engineering (e.g., introducing a third-party that provides records of websites that deploy certificates properly, similarly to the *Google Certificate Catalog* project [15]), policy change (e.g., shifting the liability from users to the stakeholders), usability (e.g., preventing users to access websites that implement certificate-based authentication improperly) and reputation (e.g., maintaining public records on security (mal)practices of CAs or websites administrators).

The rest of the paper is organized as follows. In Sect. 2, we detail HTTPS underpinnings and provide related work on Web authentication including attacks and countermeasures. We explain the methodology used for data collection and processing in Sect. 3. The properties of the collected data are assessed in Sect. 4 and the main results of our study are presented in Sect. 5. We discuss possible causes of current status of affairs in Sect. 6 and conclude in Sect. 7.

2 Background and Related Work

Netscape Corporation introduced the Secure Socket Layer (SSL) protocol to secure Internet communications [2], later standardized by the Internet Engineering Task Force (IETF) as Transport Layer Security (TLS) [4]. HTTPS combines the Hypertext Transfer Protocol (HTTP) with SSL/TLS to securely transport HTTP over insecure networks.

A key part of HTTPS is authentication of Web servers. The authentication process is based on $X.509$ certificates and takes place when an HTTPS connection is initiated between a client and a server. We detail how $X.509$ certificates work and review the research literature identifying $X.509$ vulnerabilities and improvements.

Users can trigger HTTPS communications by using the *https://* prefix in URLs. Web browsers then initiate HTTPS connections by connecting on port 443 of Web servers [5]. If Web servers support HTTPS, they respond to the client by sending their digital certificate.

A digital certificate is an electronic document that binds a public key with an identity by relying on a digital signature. In a typical public key infrastructure (PKI), a trusted certificate authority (CA) generates the signature. A certificate allows third-parties to verify that a public key belongs to an individual, and thus to authenticate this individual. X.509 certificates include [9]:

- Version: X.509 version number.
- Serial Number: Uniquely identifies each certificate.
- Signature Algorithm: Algorithm used by issuer to generate digital signature and parameters associated with the algorithm.
- Issuer: Entity that issued the certificate (i.e., CA)
- Validity period: Date certificate is first valid from (Not Before) and expiration date (Not After).
- Subject: Identified entity.
- Subject Public Key: The public key.
- Extensions: Key Usage (e.g., encipherment, signature, certificate signing).
- Signature: Certificate's signature.

In practice, website operators obtain certificates from CAs by sending certification requests that contain the website name, contact email address, and company information. CAs should perform a two-step validation [21, 22]: (i) verify that the applicant owns, or has legal right to use, the domain name featured in the application; (ii) verify that the applicant is a legitimate and legally accountable entity. If both verifications succeed, CAs are entitled to sign certification requests, thus producing *Organization Validated (OV) certificates*.

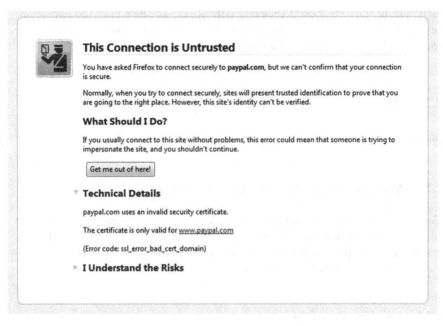

Fig. 1 Warning message for invalid certificates in Firefox

Web browsers verify certificates' authenticity by checking the validity of their digital signature and of their different fields. To check a digital signature, Web browsers need a second certificate that matches the identity of the Issuer. All Web browsers come with a built-in list of trusted root CAs. If browsers can verify the signature and trust the associated CA, then the certificate is trusted. Trust in a digital certificate is thus inherited from the entity that signed it and relies on the concept of *chain of trust* [9].

2.1 Certificate Verification Failure

Certificate verification can fail for the following reasons: (i) the certificate has expired, (ii) the domains certificate is valid for do not match the visited website, (iii) the signature is not valid, or (iv) the certificate issuer is untrusted. In the event of such failures, Web browsers usually warn users using pop-up windows. Users can either ignore such warnings and continue to the website, or decide not to proceed.

Firefox 4 redesigned its warnings and made them harder to skip, compared to Firefox 2. The goal is to encourage safe behavior from users [8]. In the example of Fig. 1, a user gets a warning because the certificate is valid for domain *www.paypal.com* and he tried to connect to *paypal.com*. If the user wants to continue to the site, he must click on "I Understand the Risks" and then the "Add Exception" button. The intention is to discourage unexperienced users from proceeding while enabling advanced users to take appropriate security decisions.

2.2 Attacks

Previous work introduced several attacks on HTTPS.

2.2.1 Attacking Certificate Authentication Failures

Certificate authentication failures may lead to man-in-the-middle attacks. An adversary can replace an original certificate with a rogue certificate. If users systematically bypass security warnings, they will not notice the subterfuge and their communications will be hijacked.

2.2.2 Attacking Root CAs

Sogohian and Stamm [37] introduce the *compelled certificate creation attack* in which government agencies may compel a certificate authority to issue false certificates that can be used by intelligence agencies to covertly intercept and hijack secure communications. They note that too much trust is put in CAs and challenge the current trust system calling for a clean-slate design approach that notably reduces the number of entities that could violate users' trust.

2.2.3 Attacking Weak Certificate Validation

CAs do not systematically perform a proper two-step validation before issuing a certificate. Such weak validation affects the quality of certificates. For example, some CAs only verify that the applicant owns the domain name (step 1 of validation) and do not validate the identity of the applicant [21]. A challenge is emailed to the administrator appearing on the Domain Name Registrar, and if CAs receive an appropriate response, they issue the requested certificate. However, when purchasing a domain name, the identity of the claimed owner of the domain is not properly verified. Consequently, Domain Name Registrars are untrustworthy and should not be used as a basis for user authentication. Acknowledging this, CAs often use the term "Organization Not Validated" in the certificate. Unfortunately, such certificates bypass browser security warnings. This practice introduces the notion of *domain validated only (DVO) certificate* that do not provide as much trust as *trusted OV certificate*.

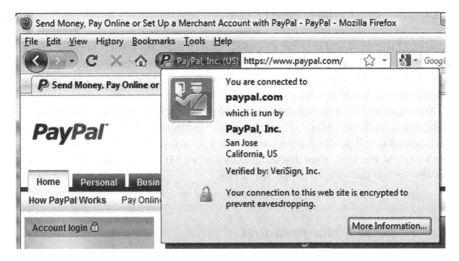

Fig. 2 User interface for EV SSL certificates in Firefox

Attackers can exploit the limitations of DVO certificates to their advantage. An adversary may register for the domain *bank-of-america.com* and obtain a corresponding DVO certificate.[1] By using an active redirection attack (e.g., DNS poisoning), or relying on typosquatting [35], users may connect to such fake websites. As Web browsers will not issue security warnings, the padlock will be displayed, and the URL will contain the bank's name, users may not realize they are on a phishing website. Most banking sites actually redirect their users from their main sites to e-banking URLs. Such URLs are sometimes long meaningless strings[2]. It is particularly hard for users to recognize a phishing URL from a legitimate one. These examples highlight the security risk associated with DVO certificates; they offer cheap untrustworthy authentication.

CAs have additionally introduced the concept of Extended Validation (EV) Certificates. To issue EV certificates, CAs use an audited and rigorous authentication method [12]. With EV certificate, Web browsers display an organization's name in green in the address bar as well as the name of the issuer (Fig. 2). Together with the displayed colors, this makes it difficult for adversaries to hijack communications. For example, Firefox colors in green the address bar for a website with EV certificate and in blue for regular certificates. Unfortunately, this distinction is often unknown to regular users [25].

---

[1] The legitimate domain is bankofamerica.com.

[2] E-banking URL of ubs.com:
https://ebanking1.ubs.com/en/OGJNCMHIFJJEIBAKJBDHLMBJFELALLHGKIJDACFGIEDK
HLBJCBPLHMOOKDAHFFKONKKKAMPMNAEDFPCIOENKBGNEGNBDKJNN6Aes21W
HTRFkGdlzvKKjjyZeB+GNeAGf-jzjgiO2LFw

2.2.4   Attacking Cryptographic Primitives

Ahmad [23] discovered that the OpenSSL library used by several popular Linux distributions was generating weak cryptographic keys. Although the flaw was quickly fixed, SSL certificates created on computers running the flawed code are open to attacks on weak keys.

Stevens et al. [38] demonstrated a practical attack to create a rogue CA certificate, based on a collision with a regular end-user website certificate provided by a commercial CA. The attack relies on a refined chosen-prefix collision construction for MD5 and has since then discouraged the use of MD5 to generate signatures of certificates and encouraged adoption of SHA.

2.3   Proposed Countermeasures

In order to limit the effect of such attacks, multiple countermeasures were proposed.

2.3.1   Surveillance of Self-Signed Certificates

Wendlandt et al. [40] improve the Trust-On-First-Use (TOFU) model used for websites that rely on self-signed SSL certificates. Web browsers securely contact *notary* servers, who in turn independently contact the webserver and obtain its certificate. A man-in-the-middle attack can be detected by the fact that the attacker-supplied SSL certificate differ from those supplied by notary servers.

2.3.2   Improve Web Browsers' Interface

Jackson and Barth [31] propose to protect users who visit HTTPS protected websites, but who are vulnerable to man-in-the-middle attacks because they do not type in the *https://* component of the URL. Their system enables a website to hint to browsers that future visits should always occur via a HTTPS connection.

Herzberg and Jbara [30] help users detect spoofed websites by prominently displaying the name of the CA that provided the sites' certificate in Web browsers.

2.3.3   SSL Observatory

Recently, the SSL Observatory project [20] led by Eckersley and Burns investigated security practices of CAs and properties of digital certificates. This project is the first large scale empirical analysis of SSL certificates gathering a large number of certificates. Current results identify bad practices of CAs, such as issuing EV certificates non-compliant with the standard (e.g., issued for unqualified host names or improper key lengths) and having a high number of subordinate CAs. Eckersley and Burns suggest that Web browsers only need between 10 and 20 root CAs to use SSL with most websites, rather than the current long lists of CAs.

In comparison with the SSL observatory, we consider a different approach. First, while the SSL Observatory project analyzes root certificates and certificates that have a valid chain of trust, we investigate all trusted and self-signed certificates served by the top one million websites. Second, we collect certificates by crawling different domains whereas the SSL observatory project crawls the entire IP address space. The key difference is that we can check how certificates are used in practice by websites. For example, we can measure the relation between domains, their popularity, their category and the quality of certificate deployment. We can measure the exposure of a user browsing the Web to different types of authentication failures. The data collected by the SSL observatory enables to check the type of certification construction and properties but not how they are used in practice. In other words, [20] gives an optimistic view of the current situation and our analysis complements their work.

3   Methodology

In this section, we describe the algorithms that are used for data collection and processing. We collect the data based on the HTTP and HTTPS connections established with Web servers of the most popular websites according to Alexa's ranking. In particular, we focus on understanding how certificates are deployed on these websites. To analyze the collected certificates we rely on OpenSSL [17] tools.

3.1   Algorithms for Data Collection

We conduct the survey on one million most popular websites (according to their Internet traffic), ranked by Alexa, a leading analytical firm that provides information on Internet traffic data [13]. This dataset imposes no limitations on websites' categories, countries, languages, or any other property. In order to determine if there is a significant difference in the results across different website categories, we additionally conduct the survey on 500 most popular websites from each of the Alexa's 16 categories: Adult, Arts, Business, Computers, Games, Health, Home, Kids and teens, News, Recreation, Reference, Regional, Science, Shopping, Society and sports.[3]

We crawl the websites from the list using a Python script whose pseudo-code is illustrated with Algorithms 1 and 2. For each *host* in the list, separately for

---

[3]To illustrate how Alexa sorts websites into categories, we provide the list of top five websites per category in Appendix.

Algorithm 1 HTTP data collection	**Algorithm 2** HTTPS data collection

for all *host* in *list* **do**
  retrieve(http://host)
  if success **then**
    store content and *URL*
    store cookies
    check for login
  else
    log connection failure
  end if
end for
	for all *host* in *list* **do**
	  retrieve(*https://host*)
	  if success **then**
	    store content and *URL*
	    store cookies
	    check for login
	    store certificate
	    store cipher suite
	    store HTTPS version
	  else
	    log connection failure
	  end if
	end for

HTTP and HTTPS, the script uses the retrieve function to initiate a connection and attempt to retrieve the content of the website. If redirections are encountered, they are followed unless the maximum of eight redirections per host has been reached. Given that some websites are accessible only at *www.host*, the retrieve function performs forced redirection to *www.host* if the script was not automatically redirected and the DNS lookup for *host* failed. If the connection is successfully established and all redirections have been followed, the script saves the content, cookies, and URL of the final page. At the same time, it checks the content of the webpage for login forms by looking for type="password" in the HTML source. Login forms use this property to instruct browsers to hide the characters typed into the text box. Whenever an HTTPS connection can be established to the host, the script additionally saves the websites' certificates and records the cipher suite and version of TLS used throughout the connection (lines colored in blue). Because of redirections, it is possible that the script encounters more than one certificate per host. In such a case, it only saves the certificate associated with the final URL, i.e., the one following the last redirection. The rationale behind this choice is that this is the certificate associated with the Web pages, users connecting to *https://host* can actually browse.

Having collected this data, we proceed to the verification and analysis of each certificate. This step is performed off-line with a second Python script. The latter relies on OpenSSL to verify the validity of certificates' signatures and extract values of some of the fields.

3.2 Verifying X.509 Certificates

The verification process includes several steps, the first of which is building a certificate's chain of trust. For each certificate, the chain of trust is built starting from the certificate that is to be verified. Building each new level of the chain requires retrieving the certificate of the Issuer (i.e., the parent certificate) of the previous certificate. Typically, each certificate contains *CA Issuers' URI* which can be used to download its parent certificate. If any of the certificates in the chain cannot be retrieved, the verification process cannot proceed and the chain is *broken*. When a certificate is its own Issuer (i.e., the Subject and Issuer fields match), it is considered to be a *root certificate* and the chain is complete.

After successfully building the chain of certificates, the signatures in the chain should be verified. If all of the digital signatures can be verified according to their cryptographic signature algorithm, the certificate has a **valid signature**. A certificate with valid signature is **trusted** if the issuer of the root certificate of the chain is trusted, otherwise it is **untrusted**. To establish trust, we rely on a well-known list of trusted root certificates provided in the *ca-certificate 20090814-3* package of the Archlinux distribution. This package contains most of the root certificates provided in Mozilla [14] software products. Among untrusted certificates, we distinguish between **self-signed** certificates (whose chain contains only itself) and **untrusted** certificates (whose chain contains at least two certificates, but whose root certificate issuer is not in the list of trusted certificates). Privately-signed certificates are a particular case of untrusted certificates, which are often used in large companies, where a self-signed certificate is produced and trusted as a root certificate to sign other certificates (e.g., for email and Web servers).

The actual verification performed by the script (for each certificate) uses OpenSSL *verify* tool [16]. The output of the tool is used to determine if the certificate signature is valid, and if so, whether the certificate is trusted, self-signed or untrusted (e.g. privately-signed). For each certificate that has a valid signature, we collect additional information. In particular, we extract the values of *Common Name* (CN) and *Country* from the Subject, and of the Not before and Not after fields. In addition, we extract *DNS name* entries from the *X509v3 Subject Alternative Name* extension, if it exists. Moreover, we obtain the root certificate of the chain and save the value of the Issuer field. Algorithm 3 illustrates the verification process.

Not before and Not after fields are used to compute the **validity period** of a certificate. If the current date is not within the validity period then the certificate is **expired**.

Domains for which a certificate is valid are specified in the subject *common name* field or the *DNS name* field of the *X509v3 Subject Alternative Name* extension. According to RFC 2818 [5], if the *X509v3 Subject Alternative Name* extension exists and contains at least one field of type *DNS name*, it must be used as identity for the server. Otherwise, if no such field exists, the subject *CN* fields are used. Therefore, to verify if a certificate is deployed for a proper domain (i.e., if there is a domain match), we match the DNS names or subject CN fields against *host* for which the certificate is saved (after following all redirections). As there might be several candidates (several *DNS name* fields, or several subject *CN* fields), we match each candidate according to the rules given by RFC 2459 [3]. Namely, we attempt to match each candidate (using case-insensitive matching) to *host*, taking into account possible wildcards.[4]

---

[4] A wildcard "*" stands for at most one level of subdomain, i.e. *.domain.tld* matches *subdomain.domain.tld* but not *subsubdomain.subdomain.domain.tld*.

Algorithm 3 Certificate verification

---

for all *cert* in downloaded certificates **do**
    current ← *cert*
    while *current* is not self-signed **do**
        if *parent* of *current* not available locally **then**
            try to retrieve parent
        end if
        if *parent* of *current* not available locally **then**
            return CHAIN BROKEN
        else
            current ← *parent*
        end if
    end while
    invoke openssl *verify* on *cert*
    if signature is valid **then**
        if *parent* of *current* is trusted **then**
            store "trusted"
        else if *cert* = *parent* of *current* **then**
            store "self-signed"
        else
            store "untrusted"
        end if
        invoke openssl *x*509 on *cert*
        store *subject country, subject CN*
        store *Not before, Not after*
        store *Alternative DNS name*
    else
        store "invalid signature"
    end if
end for
return SUCCESS

Based on the described comparison, there is a ***domain match*** if one of the following is true:

- *Host* and at least one of the candidate fields (case-insensitive) match exactly.
- The candidate field contains one or more wildcard (e.g. *.*domain*) and *host* matches the regular expression given by the candidate field.

If a match is found, the certificate is said to have a ***valid domain*** for *host*, otherwise there is a ***domain mismatch***.

We also classify certificates as DVO certificates and extended validation (EV) certificates. Checking whether a given certificate is an EV certificate is easy: it suffices to look for the EV Object Identifiers (OID) of the root CA. If the OID appears in one of the certificate's policy fields, then the certificate provides extended validation. OIDs can be obtained directly from authorized CAs' certificate policy statements (CPS) that can usually be downloaded from CAs' websites.

Determining whether a certificate is a DVO certificate is more complicated, because different CAs tend to indicate that a certificate is DVO in different ways.

Many of the DVO certificates contain $OU = Domain\ Control\ Validated$ string in their subject field. However, not all of the certificates that contain this string in the subject field are DVO. Indeed, for some of the certificates that contain this specific string in their subject field, we found that the subject organization had been validated as well. Moreover, some DVO certificates do not contain this string, but $O = Persona\ Not\ Validated$ string instead. However, as the number of root CA is (relatively) small and only a few of them signed a significant number of certificates, we examined a few certificates signed by each of the top CAs (in terms of the number of certificates signed) and looked for typical strings or indications that the certificate is DVO. Those strings (usually located in the subject field) are sometimes product names, such as *RapidSSL* or *QuickSSL*. In other cases, the presence of the string $OU = Domain\ Control\ Validated$ in the subject field and having an organization field identical to the CN field, is an indicator that the certificate is DVO. Based on these observations, we design an algorithm that determines if a certificate is DVO.

Summary of the certificate data set obtained in the survey is presented in Appendix (Fig. 17).

4 Data Collected

We store all the collected data in a SQLite [18] database. The database and some examples queries are available at http://icapeople.epfl.ch/vratonji/SSLSurvey/.

We create a list of unique hosts by merging the lists of top one million websites with 16 lists containing top 500 websites across categories. By including 787 hosts from the categories lists that were not in the top one million, we obtain a list of 1,000,787 unique hosts.

The script successfully established HTTP or HTTPS connections with 95.76% of unique hosts. Most connection failures were due to socket failures (connection timeout) or DNS failures (unable to resolve hostname). Other failures included redirections to invalid URLs or redirections to unknown protocols. *We consider the 958,420 working hosts for our survey*.

Based on the number of redirections (Fig. 3) that we observed with HTTP or HTTPS, *most websites perform one or no redirection at all*. We can also observe that *redirections occur more often for websites browsed via HTTP*. The results also justify our decision to allow the data collection script to follow up to eight redirections. For the few websites that had more than eight redirections, the browser entered an infinite loop without reaching a final page. Thus, for proper hosts, up to eight redirections were sufficient to successfully retrieve their content.

After following redirections, *in most cases, the landing page belongs to the same domain or www subdomain* (Fig. 4) with both protocols. The script obtained 1,032,139 Web pages with HTTP and 339,693 Web pages with HTTPS.

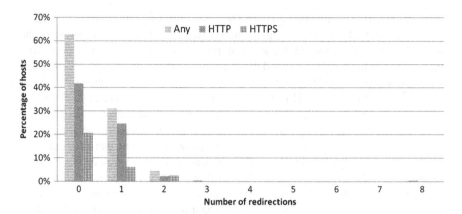

Fig. 3 Number of redirections with HTTP and HTTPS. Most of the websites perform one or no redirection at all. Redirections occur more frequently when websites are browsed via HTTP than via HTTPS

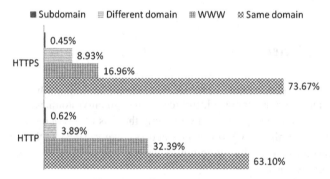

Fig. 4 Final domain after following redirections, compared to initial domain. Typically, the final page is in the initial domain or in the *www* subdomain with both HTTP and HTTPS

5 Analysis

To answer our research questions, we generate different statistics on the usage of HTTPS based on the collected data. We run a number of SQL queries to obtain the following results.

5.1 HTTPS Deployment on the Web

According to Fig. 5, *more than half (65.3%) of the one million websites can be browsed only via HTTP*, whereas *only one-third of websites can be browsed via HTTPS.* Among websites that implement HTTPS, 0.99% can be browsed exclusively via HTTPS (do not respond to HTTP or redirect users from HTTP to HTTPS) and the remaining 33.7% support both HTTPS and HTTP.

Fig. 5 HTTP vs. HTTPS. About 65% of the websites can be browsed only via HTTP and one-third can be browsed via HTTPS

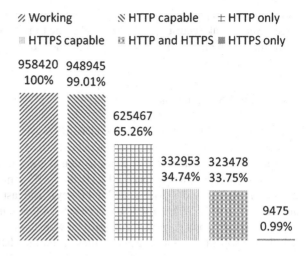

5.1.1   HTTPS Across Website Categories

Given that the data set for each category contains 500 websites, we cannot draw strong conclusions about HTTPS deployment across categories. However, we still observe some trends: *HTTPS is implemented most in categories Reference (33.75%), Health (33.41%) and Business (31.12%) and least in categories Arts (17.67%) and Sports (20.21%)*. Websites of universities belong to the *Reference* category and contribute to the high percentage of that category as most of them implement secure services, such as emails. In the *Health* category, websites may deal with sensitive medical data and we observe that a high percentage of them implements HTTPS. On the contrary, websites in categories *Sports* and *Arts* most likely do not need HTTPS, and we observe smaller deployment rate in those categories.

5.1.2   HTTP vs. HTTPS for Login Web Pages

We check whether websites that require users' login credentials (i.e., username and password) implement HTTPS. To do so, we searched for retrieved Web pages containing login and password fields. Surprisingly, *only 22.6% of Web pages with password fields were implemented via HTTPS!* In most cases, websites do not encrypt Web pages at all or use HTTPS encryption only partially, for parts of Web pages containing credentials. However, if the entire page is not transmitted over HTTPS, it can be compromised by man-in-the-middle attacks and lead to the compromise of credentials. Therefore, 77.4% of websites put users' security at risk by communicating users' credentials in clear text or by encrypting only parts of Web pages. Such weak security practices may be due to trade-offs between security and performance, the lack of know-how or the burden to implement HTTPS.

5.1.3 HTTPS Cipher Suites

The majority ($\sim$70%) of websites use DHE-RSA-AES256-SHA cipher suite. DHE denotes ephemeral Diffie-Hellman, where the Diffie-Hellman parameters are signed by a signature-capable certificate, itself signed by a CA. The signing algorithm used by the server is RSA, specified after the DHE component of the cipher suite name. The cipher used is AES with 256 bit keys. The last field notifies the message authentication code (MAC) used, in this case SHA that stands for a modified version of SHA-1. It is a good news that a majority of websites use this cipher suite, because it is in the top of the list of cipher suites recommended and preferred by major software companies (e.g., Mozilla). Most websites use 256 bits ($\sim$76%) or 128 bits ($\sim$22%). Surprisingly, there are some ($\sim$50) websites that still use 40 or 56 bit keys.

Nevertheless, our findings show that *good cipher suites are selected*. It means that the potentially weak part of establishing a secure HTTPS connection is server authentication.

5.2 Authentication Failures

Authentication failures are the major cause of improper implementation of HTTPS in practice. Besides malicious behavior, TLS-based authentication can fail for several reasons:

- **Broken chain of trust:** If a signature in the chain of trust cannot be verified, the chain of trust is broken.
- **Untrusted root certificate:** Trusted root certificates are self-signed certificates of CAs. Any other self-signed certificate is untrusted. In general, any certificate is untrusted if it is signed by an entity whose certificate is not among the trusted root certificate. Users must manually check whether they trust the Issuer of certificates untrusted by Web browsers.
- **Expired certificate:** Certificate validity period is defined using Not Before and Not After markups. Certificate validity varies from a few months to a few years, as agreed with CAs. Standards require that Web browsers check certificate validity periods and issue a warning to users in case of expiration. Certificate signatures can be verified even after a certificate expires because signature verification only guarantees the integrity of the certificate's content.
- **Domain mismatch:** Certificates apply to hosts identified in the Subject markup using the common name (CN) tag (e.g., *CN=www.epfl.ch*) or to the DNS name

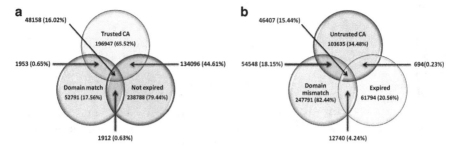

Fig. 6 Web browser authentication outcomes for websites that implement HTTPS and whose certificate signatures can be verified. Certificates of only 16.02% (48,158) of those websites allow for a correct authentication. When authentication fails, in 82.44% of the cases it is due to a domain mismatch. (**a**) Authentication success—no browser warnings (**b**) Authentication failure—browser warnings

specified in the Alternative Name Extension. If the host does not match exactly the name specified in the CN field or the DNS name of a certificate, Web browsers issue a domain mismatch warning. If another host is located at *login.epfl.ch*, then another certificate is required to identify this other host or the website can use a *wildcard certificate* (**.epfl.ch*) that is valid for any subdomain of the host.

Each problem occurs in our dataset and multiple combinations of problematic scenarios exist. Firstly, among 330,037 downloaded certificates, the signature of 300,582 could be properly verified. Our analysis is thus based on those certificates with valid signatures. Surprisingly, we observe (Fig. 6a) that *only 16.02% of all certificates with valid signatures allow for a correct authentication*, i.e., would not cause Web browsers to pop-up security warnings to users and HTTPS connection will be established transparently. It is only a minority (48,158) of all tested websites that enable proper Web authentication. The *domain mismatch failure is clearly the main cause of problems* (Fig. 6b). It accounts for 82.44% of failures, followed by untrusted, expiration date and broken chain failures. These results show that website operators fail to understand the domain to which acquired certificates apply to or do not wish to bear the cost of handling multiple certificates for one website.

5.3 Certificate Reuse Across Multiple Domains

While looking for an explanation for the high number of domain mismatch failures, we noticed that a high number of the same certificates (both trusted and self-signed) appear for a number of different domains. With the exception of a few wildcard certificates that can be valid for multiple domains, other certificates are usually valid for a single domain and when deployed on other domains will cause a domain mismatch failure. Figure 7 shows the distribution of unique certificates that appear

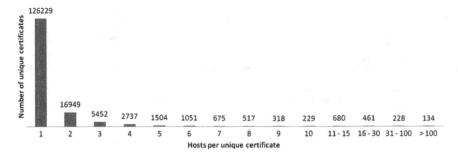

Fig. 7 Reusing certificates across multiple domains. A high number of certificates (both trusted and self-signed) that are issued for a single domain appear across a number of different domains. Deployment on those other (invalid) domains causes a domain mismatch authentication failure

Table 1 Certificate reuse due to internet hosting

Certificate validity domain	Number of hosts
*.bluehost.com	10,075
*.hostgator.com	9,148
*.hostmonster.com	4,954
*.wordpress.com	4,668
*.websitewelcome.com	2,912
*.justhost.com	2,908

across different hosts. *Among the 330,037 collected certificates, there are 157,166 (47.6%) unique certificates, 126,229 of which appear each on only one host.* The same certificate sometimes appears on more than 10,000 different domains! We find that there are 24 unique certificates that are reused across at least 500 domains each. In other words, 52,142 (26.5%) of the hosts that have a trusted certificate with valid signatures, have certificates that are reused across at least 500 domains. 20 of those certificates are certificates of Internet hosting providers (accounting for 46,648 hosts).

Typically, with virtual hosting (when many websites are hosted at same IP address) hosting providers serve the same certificate for all of the hosted websites. During the establishment of a TLS connection, the server does not know which website the client is requesting, because this information is part of the application layer protocol. Thus, the practice of hosting servers is to provide a default certificate, which is the behavior we observe. Table 1 shows a few examples with the number of hosts for which the certificate of a hosting provider is served and the domains for which the certificate is valid. In most of the cases, hosted websites do not belong to subdomains of hosting providers and rather have a completely different domain name, which causes domain mismatch warnings. Even though technically those websites are hosted at the provider's servers, the authenticity of those business should not be vouched for by the provider. Hosted websites should irrespectively obtain valid certificates for their domains from CAs and hosting providers should implement Server Name Indication (SNI), an extension of TLS which aims at solving this problem [7]. The main idea is that the client provides the domain name

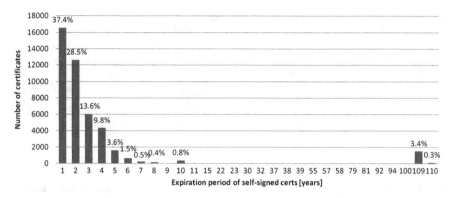

Fig. 8 Distribution of the expiration periods (in years) of self-signed certificates. In addition to being untrusted, most of the self-signed certificates are also expired (45.54%) and have a domain mismatch (97.48%). Even though self-signed certificates have almost no cost and are easy to generate, they are not maintained properly

of the requested website during the TLS negotiation phase, thereby allowing the server to serve an appropriate certificate. Nowadays, SNI is supported by most of Web browsers and Web servers. However, even if a client does not support SNI, servers should not serve default certificates that do not match domains of hosted websites, but rather refuse such connections.

A website often simply "borrows", i.e., uses a certificate of another website. If a certificate appears on a smaller number of domains, it might also be that the same administrator is in charge of these domains and then uses a single certificate for all of them. In either case, such certificate deployment is a bad practice.

5.4   Properties of Self-Signed Certificates

We investigate the differences in the deployment of trusted and self-signed certificates. *Among certificates with valid signatures, 65.6% are trusted (signed by trusted CAs) and the remaining 34.4% are self-signed* (Fig. 6a).

We observe that with self-signed certificates, in addition to being untrusted, at least one other authentication problem likely occurs (e.g., expired or domain mismatch). As self-signed certificates are free and easy to generate, it is to be expected that self-signed certificates are up-to-date and that they match domains they are used for. Our results show the opposite. We observe that *almost half of the self-signed certificates are already expired*. Some certificates expired a long time ago (e.g., 100 years).[5] Distribution of the time validity periods of the non-expired self-signed certificates is presented in Fig. 8: most of the self-signed certificates are valid for one or two years. We also notice a number of certificates that have a validity of 100 years.

---

[5]Expiration periods are computed with respect to February 2010.

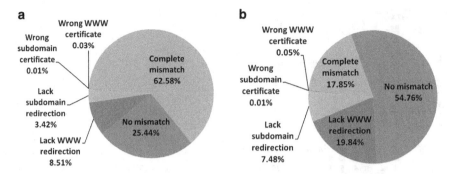

Fig. 9 A majority of trusted certificates are deployed for non-matching domains. Partially, domain mismatch happens because of certificate reuse across different domains (e.g., due to Internet hosting). After excluding reused certificates, the major problem that causes domain mismatch is deployment of certificates issued for *subdomain.host* on *host* domains. Simply by automatically redirecting to *subdomain.host*, about 27% of the websites would avoid security warnings being displayed to users when visiting their websites. (**a**) Domain matching for trusted certificates with valid signatures (**b**) Domain matching for unique, trusted certificates with valid signatures

Interestingly, *97.48% of the self-signed certificates have an invalid domain*. This shows that website administrators either do not know how to properly manage certificates or simply do not care what kind of warnings are displayed to users, as there will be one for a self-signed certificate anyway (due to the lack of trust in certificates' issuer). It is unclear whether users would trust self-signed certificates more if other fields (e.g., validity and domain) are correct, or whether it does not make a difference.

5.5 Properties of Trusted Certificates

In the following, we consider only trusted certificates with valid signatures. We observe that *among trusted certificates with valid signatures, only 7% are expired, but 74.5% have a domain mismatch*.

5.5.1 Domain Matching for Trusted Certificates

By comparing domains certificates are deployed for (i.e., *host*) with domains certificates are valid for (i.e., common names (CN) and DNS names in the subject alternative name extension fields of X.509 certificates), we observe the following cases (Fig. 9):

No mismatch: *Host* matches one of the domains certificate is valid for.

Lack subdomain redirection: The certificate is valid for *subdomain.host* and deployed on *host*. Automatic redirection from *host* to *subdomain.host* would resolve the domain mismatch problem in this case.

Lack www redirection: The certificate is valid for *www.host* and deployed on *host*. Automatic redirection from *host* to *www.host* would resolve the domain mismatch problem in this case. This case is a specific instance of the previous case and we look into it separately.

Wrong subdomain certificate: The certificate is valid for *host* and deployed on *subdomain.host*. To resolve the domain mismatch problem in this case website administrator has to obtain a certificate valid for *subdomain.host*.

Wrong www certificate: The certificate is valid for *host* and deployed on *www.host*. To resolve the domain mismatch problem in this case website administrator has to obtain a certificate valid for *www.host*. Again, this is a specific instance of the previous case.

Complete mismatch: (i) The *host* does not match the domains certificate is valid for, (ii) the *host* is not a subdomain of the domains certificate is valid for, or (iii) the domains certificate is valid for are not subdomains of *host*.

From the results in Fig. 9a we observe that *trusted certificates are mostly (62.58%) deployed for domains that are completely different from the domains certificates are valid for*. For 11.93% of the websites with trusted certificates, the domain mismatch problem could be easily solved with automatic redirection: to *subdomain.host* or *www.host*.

Because we have seen that certificates are often reused (mostly due to hosting providers) we narrow our analysis to unique certificates only and, as expected, results are better. *Domain mismatches happen for 45.24% of the unique trusted certificates with valid signatures* (Fig. 9b). The number of complete mismatches is thus drastically reduced from 62.58% to 17.85%. A possible interpretation for the remaining complete mismatches is that online businesses and major companies require at least one certificate and understand that the certificate has to be up-to-date and timely renewed, for the purposes of its online transactions or simply for a good reputation. However, as most certificates are valid for a single domain (with the exception of rarely used wildcard certificates), websites need to obtain multiple certificates for multiple domains. This cost is most likely too high, and website administrators rather deploy the same trusted valid certificate across different domains. A very common case is that websites obtain certificates for *subdomain.host* and use it for *host* domain as well. In these situations, browsers also issue security warnings due to domain mismatch. This problem can be solved if websites automatically redirect to *subdomain.host* when visiting *host*. *With automatic redirection to subdomain.host, about 27.32% of websites with trusted certificates would avoid domain mismatch warnings* (Fig. 9b). In particular, redirecting to *www.host* would resolve domain mismatch problem for about 20% of the websites. In a small percentage of cases (0.06%), websites have certificates that are valid for *host* and it is used on *subdomain.host*.

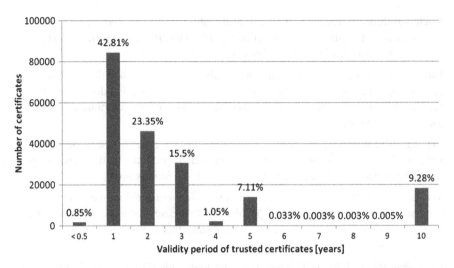

Fig. 10 Distribution of validity periods (in years) of trusted valid certificates. Almost half of the certificates are issued for one year, indicating that it might be too costly for businesses to pay for certificates valid for several years or that they do not favor long term investment. It might also be due to unwillingness of CAs to trust websites for too long, as it limits the risk of bad publicity in case a malicious websites is actually issued a certificate

5.5.2   Validity Period of Trusted Certificates

Figure 10 shows the validity time distribution of trusted certificates. We notice that almost *half of the trusted certificates have a validity of 1 year*. Typically, CAs offer certificates for periods of 1, 2 and 3 years. Similarly as for obtaining certificates for multiple domains, it seems that it is too costly to obtain certificates for more than one year. We found a surprising number (almost 10%) of certificates that have a validity of 10 years or more. However, it appears that all of those certificates are DVO and the price of such 10-year DVO certificates is approximately the price of a properly validated 1-year OV certificate. CAs have incentives to issue short term certificates in order to minimize the risk of being associated and vouching for an organization that might turn out to be compromised.

5.6   (Mal)practices of CAs

We looked into how many certificates were issued by each CA (Fig. 11) and the common (mal)practices of CAs when issuing certificates. Notably, we focus on investigating whether CAs issue: (i) DVO certificates (ii) certificates based on MD5 hash-functions and (iii) certificates with keys of inappropriate length with respect to their time validity.

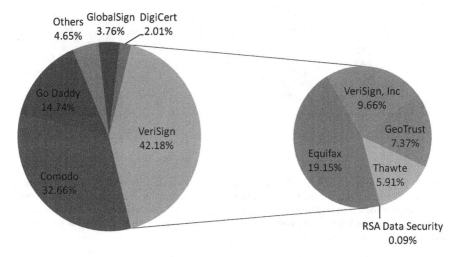

Fig. 11 CA root certificates. VeriSign has the largest share of the market, followed by Comodo. The certificates issued by GeoTrust, Thawte and Equifax are counted as VeriSign certificates as these CAs were acquired by VeriSign

VeriSign, together with its acquired CAs (Equifax, Thawte and GeoTrust), has the largest part of the market, issuing (42.2%) of the certificates, followed by Comodo with 32.7% of the certificates (Fig. 11).

5.6.1 DVO, OV and EV Certificates

We investigate the usage of DVO, OV and EV certificates. Bad news is that 54.2% of trusted certificates with valid signatures are only domain-validated (Fig. 12a). In other words, *half of the certificates issued by CAs are issued without properly verifying the identity of certificates' owners*. As previously discussed, these certificates do not guarantee trust and do not provide the security that users expect. In addition, there are no explicit security warnings to notify users about the difference in provided security.

Results from Fig. 12b show that among the small number (48, 158) of valid certificates, *users should not trust about 61% of them as the legitimacy of the organizations behind these certificates was not properly verified by CAs*.

Only about 3% (5, 762) of trusted certificates with valid signatures are EV (Fig. 12a). But *only 2,894 EV certificates are actually not expired and valid for the requested domain* (Fig. 12b). OV certificates are traditional SSL certificates that are issued by CAs after the proper two-step validation, but not following special EV recommendations. OV certificates can as well authenticate the organization owning the certificate.

Essentially, *18,785 websites have valid certificates that can prove the identity of the organization owning a certificate (either with EV or OV certificates)*.

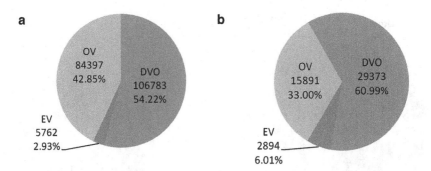

Fig. 12 Types of certificates: EV, OV and DVO. A small number of websites have certificates (EV or OV) that provide the trust in the identity of the organization owning a certificate. About 61% of the certificates trusted by Web browsers do not guarantee the legitimacy of the owner, i.e., are DVO. (**a**) Trusted certificates with valid signatures (**b**) Certificates that allow for successful authentication by web browsers

5.6.2 Certificates Using MD5

To sign a certificate, CAs first produce the hash of the certificate (typically with MD5 or SHA-1 hashing functions) and then encrypt the hash with their private keys. MD5 is not a collision resistant hashing function as it has been shown that it is possible to create two files that share the same MD5 checksum and consequently, to fake SSL certificates [38]. After the discovery of this attack, VeriSign announced [10] that it immediately discontinued the use of flawed MD5 cryptographic function for digital signatures, while offering a free transition for customers to move to certificates using the SHA-1 algorithm. Unfortunately, we found that certificates with MD5 are still in use. In our study, we found 2071 **trusted, not expired certificates that use MD5 and are all issued by Equifax** (belonging to VeriSign). Some certificates are valid until year 2014. Perhaps, some of these websites are not willing to go through the hassle of obtaining new certificates and decide to keep potentially vulnerable certificates. Nevertheless, CAs should not allow for such websites that expose customers to serious security threats.

5.6.3 Certificate Public Key Length wrt. Expiration Date

CAs may issue certificates with keys of inappropriate length with respect to their time validity. We extract the expiration date (**Not After** field) and key length from certificates and we represent them in Fig. 13. The size of a bubble in the graph corresponds to the number of data points that have the same value and the center of the bubble to the (Expiration year, Key length) point. We also plot the recommended (optimistic) key length that is considered to be secure in a given point in time [34]. Data points (centers of bubbles) that are above the recommended curve are acceptable and represent well chosen keys. Data points that are below the curve are

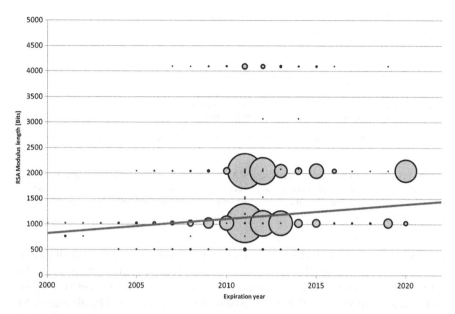

Fig. 13 Appropriateness of the key length wrt. expiration time. Data point (Expiration Year, Key Length) is represented with the center of a bubble and the size of the bubble represent a number of data points with the same value. Data points above the recommended key length curve (linear) are well chosen, the ones below are not considered to be secure at the time they are used. About half of the trusted certificates have inappropriate key length with respect to their time validity

badly chosen and are considered to be vulnerable at the point in time they are used. In aggregate, *about a half (97,436) of the trusted certificates have inappropriate key length with respect to their time validity*. Ideally, these certificates should not be used and CAs should rigorously follow the recommendations about the key length.

5.7 Correlation of the Authentication Failure Rate with Other Parameters

To better understand the underlying reasons for the observed certificate deployment, we correlate the authentication failure rate with other parameters such as issuing CAs, subjects' countries, website categories and rank.

5.7.1 Authentication Failure Rate wrt. CAs

Since CAs are only responsible for issuing certificates, not for managing how they are deployed, it might not be fair to correlate authentication success rate to certificates' issuing CAs. Given that the authentication success rate mostly depends

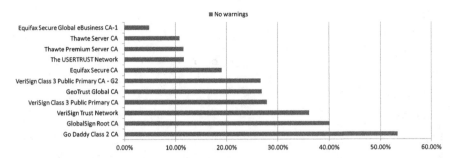

Fig. 14 Authentication success rate across CAs. Certificates issued by GlobalSign, GoDaddy and VeriSign achieve higher authentication success rate. Either they help their clients manage certificates properly or their customers are more security conscious and resourceful and take better care of their certificates

on whether a certificate is deployed on a matching domain, it is a responsibility of the organizations who purchased the certificates to properly maintain them and make sure that they allow proper authentication. Nevertheless, it is interesting to compare authentication success rate that is achieved with certificates issued by different CAs (Fig. 14). We limit our results to those CAs for which we collected at least 4,000 trusted valid certificates.

We observe that certificates issued by GoDaddy, GlobalSign and VeriSign obtain a higher authentication success compared to others. Interestingly, certificates that are signed by root certificates belonging to smaller and perhaps less famous CAs (Equifax, Thawte and UserTrust)[6] have a smaller success rate.

There are different hypotheses to explain this. GlobalSign, GoDaddy and VeriSign are well-established and trusted CAs with major clients. Their certificates typically have a larger price than competitors. Hence, only resourceful companies may afford to purchase such certificates and these organizations may care more about properly deploying certificates in order to provide good security. On the contrary, less security-conscious website administrators may opt for inexpensive and easier to obtain certificates, that are typically issued by other CAs. Given their lack of incentives, it follows that they might not bother deploying certificates properly. Another possibility is that GlobalSign, GoDaddy and VeriSign only issue certificates after a proper two-step validation process or that they make sure that their customers know how to properly deploy certificates.

---

[6]Even though some CAs (e.g., Equifax and Thawte) were acquired by VeriSign, we refer to them as separate CAs as they offer different products and services and have different policies.

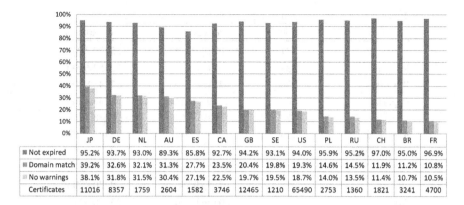

	JP	DE	NL	AU	ES	CA	GB	SE	US	PL	RU	CH	BR	FR
▨ Not expired	95.2%	93.7%	93.0%	89.3%	85.8%	92.7%	94.2%	93.1%	94.0%	95.9%	95.2%	97.0%	95.0%	96.9%
▧ Domain match	39.2%	32.6%	32.1%	31.3%	27.7%	23.5%	20.4%	19.8%	19.3%	14.6%	14.5%	11.9%	11.2%	10.8%
▨ No warnings	38.1%	31.8%	31.5%	30.4%	27.1%	22.5%	19.7%	19.5%	18.7%	14.0%	13.5%	11.4%	10.7%	10.5%
Certificates	11016	8357	1759	2604	1582	3746	12465	1210	65490	2753	1360	1821	3241	4700

Fig. 15 Certificate validity across countries. Organizations from Japan, Germany, and Netherlands have the best, whereas France, Brazil, and Switzerland have the poorest practices in deploying certificates. The major reason for authentication failure is due to domain mismatch, as most of the certificates are not expired

5.7.2 Authentication Failure Rate wrt. Countries

We investigate whether organizations from different countries differ in the way they deploy certificates. In Fig. 15, we show properties of trusted certificates with valid signatures for organizations across several countries. We consider countries for which we observed more than $1,000$ certificates. We compute the statistics based on the total number of trusted valid certificates we have collected for each country (the last row in Fig. 15). The results confirm that the major reason for authentication failure is due to domain mismatch, as most of the certificates are not expired. Therefore, the total percentage of certificates that do not cause any certificate warnings is dictated by the certificates being properly deployed for the domain they are issued for. We observe that organizations from Japan are most successful in the proper certificate deployment, having successful authentication with 38.1% of certificates. Second best are organizations from Germany with 31.8% of their certificates leading to successful authentication, followed by Netherland with 31.5%. The US is in the middle, having a percentage 18.7% that is closer to the average number observed across the top one million websites (16.02%). Poorest deployment practices are in France, Brazil and Switzerland. The major factor for a low authentication success rate among Swiss websites is due to the fact that many of them are hosted by an Internet hosting provider that serves its certificate for each hosted website.

5.7.3 Authentication Failure Rate wrt. Website Categories

If we look at the authentication success across different categories of websites, firstly we observe that websites from Computer category have a remarkably high

Table 2 Certificate deployment across website categories

Category	Total	Trusted	No warnings
Computers	121	109 (90.08%)	85 (70.25%)
Reference	133	116 (87.22%)	70 (52.63%)
Business	130	122 (93.85%)	57 (43.85%)
Regional	99	93 (93.94%)	43 (43.43%)
Shopping	129	126 (97.67%)	50 (38.76%)
Recreation	129	105 (81.39%)	45 (34.88%)
Kids and teens	87	71 (81.60%)	29 (33.33%)
Games	113	87 (76.99%)	35 (30.97%)
Society	126	97 (76.98%)	39 (30.95%)
Arts	75	50 (66.67%)	23 (30.67%)
Science	131	101 (77.09%)	40 (30.53%)
Health	146	115 (78.77%)	41 (28.08%)
Adult	100	61 (61.0%)	26 (26.0%)
Home	103	73 (70.87%)	26 (25.24%)
News	85	64 (75.29%)	18 (21.18%)
Sports	93	71 (76.34%)	13 (13.9%)

percentage 70.25%. Typically sites of technological companies belong to this category and it seems that they have a good know-how and understand the relevance of properly deploying certificates (Table 2). Reference, Regional and expectedly Business category are also significantly better than the average with more than 40%. It is understandable as Reference sites include University sites, Business websites have e-commerce services and Regional include tech companies such as Google, Yahoo, and Apple. Sports, News, Home, and Adults category have the lowest number.

5.7.4 Authentication Failure Rate wrt. Websites Ranks

We looked at how the authentication success changes with respect to websites' rank. We divide the ranked one million websites into bins of 50,000 websites each, and compute the number of certificates found among those 50,000 websites that allow for a proper authentication and the number of unique certificates (the corresponding two plots in Fig. 16a). The number of certificates with a certain property is expressed in percentages with respect to the total number of certificates found in the corresponding bin. We observe that the authentication success is significantly better for the first 50,000 websites and then it decreases for lower ranks. This is expected as popular websites generate more revenue from users' traffic and thus may afford better security practices (or perhaps because better security practices attract more users to these websites). We provide in Appendix a few examples of well ranked websites that suffer from authentication failures.

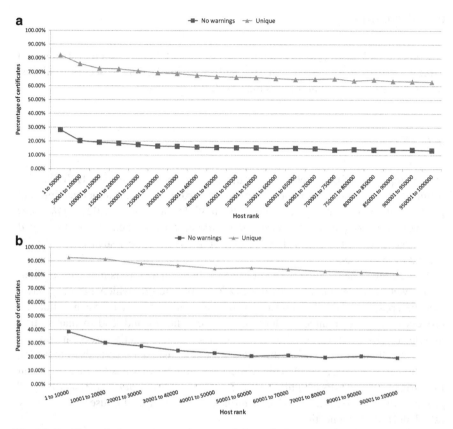

Fig. 16 Certificate deployment properties vs. website rank. It appears that the proper certificate deployment, in terms of authentication success and using unique certificates, is correlated to the rank. Higher ranked websites have better practices in implementing certificates properly. (**a**) Top one million websites (**b**) Top 100,000 websites

Given that certificate reuse across domains contributes to domain mismatch and leads to authentication failure, we also found the number of unique certificates. One may notice a strong correlation between the shapes of the two curves, authentication success and unique certificates, which might confirm that indeed certificate reuse across domains is a significant contributor to authentication failure. Since we observe higher dynamics for the highest ranks, we zoom into the highest 100,000 ranked websites (Fig. 16b). We draw the same conclusions as for one million websites and observe correlations between all the rank, the authentication success rate and the usage of unique certificates.

6 Discussion

We outline and interpret most interesting results of Sect. 5 where we obtained several weaknesses of certificate-based authentication leading to security failures. Economic, legal and social reasons may explain these issues.

6.1 Failures

Out of top one million websites, about 35% can be browsed via HTTPS. Unfortunately, most of them poorly implement certificate-based authentication and generate authentication problems. *Only about* 48, 158 *websites (16.02% of the ones with verifiable certificate signatures) have valid certificates*, i.e., certificates issued by trusted CAs, not expired, deployed on domains they are issued for, and with verifiable signatures.

Successful authentication does not necessarily mean that users may trust authenticated websites. CAs increasingly issue DVO certificates, for which they only verify that the applying entity has registered for the requested domain. Such validation process may not guarantee the legitimacy of certificates and lead to man-in-the-middle attacks (putting users' security at risk). Consequently, users should not systematically trust all websites that their browsers trust. Our results show that 61% of valid certificates are DVO. This reduces the number of websites that users can fully trust to 18,785. Essentially, *only 5.7% of the websites that implement HTTPS properly implement certificate-based authentication* and enable users to securely establish HTTPS connections.

6.1.1 Economics

Our investigations showed many domain mismatches were due to improper handling of certificates by websites. Several reasons can explain this, mostly boiling down to *misaligned incentives*. Websites typically offer several services on different subdomains and should obtain a certificate for each of them. This is complex, as it requires technical understanding, and expensive, as it requires obtaining several certificates. Hence, website operators often prefer to reuse a single-domain certificate across a number of (sub)domains, leading to domain mismatches. For example, if people lacking technical know-how (e.g., business managers) were responsible for obtaining certificates, they may focus on cost reduction, whereas people with technical know-how (e.g., engineers) may not invest sufficient time to carefully design certificate-based authentication systems. Certificate management is a cost and does not directly generate revenue compared to other services. Hence, *most website operators have an incentive to obtain cheap certificates.*

CAs are also culprits for authentication failures. CAs' business model depends on the price and the number of certificates sold. From an economic point of view, *CAs have an incentive to distribute as many certificates as possible* in order to increase profit. CAs segment their market and apply differentiate pricing. Consequently, they created different forms of certificates: Domain-validated only certificates, EV certificates and regular certificates.

In our results, we observed that *most website operators choose cheap certificates leading to cheap Web authentication*. Domain-validated only certificates are popular amongst small websites because they are easy and fast to obtain. They require minimum effort from CAs. Several CAs even offer free trials where websites can be certified for free for short periods of time. EV certificates differ from regular certificates and DVO certificates in that they require rigorous verifications. They are a preferred option for large websites dealing with important user information. Information asymmetry plays a large role in pushing cheap certificates. As website operators cannot tell the difference between good and bad security (i.e., market for lemons), they might as well take the cheaper option, thus pushing race to the bottom price.

A positive result is the low number of expired certificates we observed. This is probably because CAs strongly encourage renewal to increase revenue. This shows that *CAs could provide incentives to push proper adoption of certificates*. Yet, most trusted certificates were not deployed properly showing that CAs do not make that investment.

6.1.2   Liability

Liability should be assigned to the party that can best manage risk. Unfortunately, *most CAs transfer their liability onto their customers*. This reduces their risk and involvement in providing security. For example, Verisign License agreement version 5 [1] states that Verisign "SHALL NOT BE LIABLE FOR (I) ANY LOSS OF PROFIT, BUSINESS, CONTRACTS, REVENUE OR ANTICIPATED SAVINGS, OR (II) ANY INDIRECT OR CONSEQUENTIAL LOSS". It caps to $5,000 for total liability for damages sustained. This exhibits a serious flaw of the system: although CAs distribute an essential element of Web security, they do not take responsibility for it.

In this three-body problem, CAs pass their liability onto websites that in turn transfer it to users through their website policies. This tendency to push liability to others is another example of misaligned incentives reinforced by information asymmetry. CAs are not encouraged to protect users and rather focus on risk-reducing strategies. This problem appears in other situations, such as security economics of banking [24]. It may be difficult to expect full liability from CAs but a reasonable involvement could dramatically improve the current situation.

Lack of liability is known by economists to generate a moral-hazard effect [24]: As CAs know that customers cannot complain, they tend to be careless in the distribution of certificates, leading to erroneously distributed certificates such as [19].

6.1.3 Reputation

Man-in-the-middle attacks caused by the use of weak certificates can harm websites' and CAs' reputation. Hence, CAs should have an incentive to provide good security. Our results show that *well-established CAs tend to properly issue certificates and rely on a number of less prominent subsidiaries to issue certificates far less rigorously.* This helps preserve their reputation, while not missing good business opportunities. In addition, our results show that CAs tend to provide short-lived certificates, e.g., for one year. This limits the risk of bad publicity in case a malicious website is actually authenticated.

For websites, we observe that mostly large corporations get EV certificates in order to limit risk for their customers. Even if they could afford the cost of a MitM attacks, they wish to protect their own reputation and provide good security. *Most less exposed websites select DVO certificates.* In other words, they are fine with cheaper certificates. This may be because website administrators underestimate the value of the data they handle and wish only to reduce security costs. In addition, peer influence from other websites adopting similar weak security practices, may encourage websites administrators to choose DVO certificates.

6.1.4 Usability

For most users, security is secondary as they seek offered services. The variety of options of certificate-based authentication (e.g., domain validated, EV certificates, self-signed certificates and notion of certificates) actually makes it difficult for users to understand the system. Users may misinterpret security warnings as annoyances that prevent them from using Web services. Bad certificate management leads to more security warnings. *The more interruptions users experience, the more they learn to ignore security warnings.* This is counter-productive. Regardless of how compelling, or difficult to ignore SSL warnings are, users may think they are of little consequence because they also see them at legitimate websites [27]. A recent study about SSL warnings' effectiveness shows that users' attitudes and beliefs about SSL warnings are likely to undermine certificates' effectiveness [39] and it suggests to avoid warnings altogether and make security decisions on behalf of users.

Finally, *Web browsers have little incentive to limit access to websites* whose certificates are issued by untrusted CAs and thus stop users from accessing websites they could access from other browsers. Firefox currently tries to discourage users from communicating to websites with self-signed certificates by showing users complex warnings. Such approach spurred agitated debates on the usability of Firefox for Web authentication. In addition, we have seen that unfortunately there are situations (with domain-validated certificates) where users cannot entirely rely on browsers to help them decide whom to trust.

6.2   Countermeasures

We observe that proper incentives to secure the certificate-based authentication systems are missing. The current deployment of digital certificates, mostly based on self-regulation, is moving towards a business model that does not put the emphasis on security and needs a change. We suggest multiple regulation options to modify incentives and improve the situation.

- **New Third-Parties:** An independent third-party could change the current equilibrium of the system. This third-party could be managed by users with an open website (e.g., wiki), by an association of CAs or by Web browsers directly. Basically, such third-party could interfere with the current free-market approach to introduce information related to performances of CAs, and steer the system in a better direction.

  This independent third-party could provide transparency by providing information similar to our results about security performances of CAs (Fig. 14). This may stimulate competition among CAs to provide better security. CAs would actually have to worry about how certificates are used by websites. Similarly, it could agree with a small set of trusted root CAs, more transparent, hierarchical and localized. Finally, it could also monitor how well websites use certificates and rate websites based on the security they provide.

  Users could also run themselves a third-party to form groups of users sharing information with each other. This could reduce the problem of asymmetric information.

- **New Policies:** Changing legal aspects is a difficult and slow process, but may be very effective. It is important that CAs take responsibility for certificate-based authentication. They should be liable for the security of the system as responsibility should follow those that earn revenue. In order to tackle the asymmetric information problem, previous work suggests the use of certification schemes in order to guarantee the quality of provided certificates [33]. Such certificates could be operated by governments (e.g., Orange book) or commercial companies (e.g., Common criteria). However, regulation is costly. One-model-fits-all approach is hard to put in place, especially for smaller companies [28].

  Another option is to force websites to be responsible for properly implementing certificate-based authentication. However, websites are customers of the system and it is difficult to blame them for not understanding how to invest money in security.

  Finally, Web browsers could pressure CAs in order to improve the quality of CAs' practices. For example, Web browsers could have the policy to trust only the top performing root CAs in terms of provided security.

  In general, even though websites generate most authentication failures, we believe that policies should focus on certification authorities and Web browsers.

7 Conclusion

We crawled the top one million popular websites and investigated how they deploy certificate-based authentication. Our results show that nearly one-third of websites can be browsed with HTTPS, but only 18,785 (5.7%) of them properly implement certificate-based authentication. In other words, only 5.7% of the websites that implement HTTPS, do so without causing security warnings in Web browsers and with providing trust in the identities of certificates' owners.

We discuss multiple reasons that may have led to the failure of the current model for Web security. We argue that the current free market approach, where utility-optimizing entities try to maximize profits at minimum cost, is the root of the problem. We can compare the current situation to a *market for lemons*: information asymmetry occurs because CAs know more about certificates than websites and users. Hence, most website administrators acquire cheap DVO certificates and poorly implement them on their servers. Only a fraction of elite website administrators achieves high security by obtaining EV certificates and installing them properly. We also observe strategic behavior from CAs that rely on subsidiaries to sell less trustworthy certificates and maximize profits. This situation is not satisfactory as it affects the global security of the Internet ecosystem. We believe that the right incentives are not in place and suggest multiple policy changes to solve this issue. Notably, we suggest to make CAs liable for the proper use of certificates, web browsers to trust only top performing CAs, and the creation of an open-source community checking on root CAs.

Appendix

To illustrate how Alexa sorts websites into categories, we provide the list of top 5 websites per category in Table 3.

A few examples of well ranked websites that suffer from authentication failures are given in Table 4.

Summary of the certificate data set obtained in the survey is presented in Fig. 17.

Table 3 Top five websites by categories

Category	Rank (within category)				
	1	2	3	4	5
Adult	LiveJasmin.com livejasmin.com	Youporn youporn.com	XNXX Galleries xnxx.com	Adult Friend Finder adultfriendfinder.com	Streamate.com streamate.com
Arts	Facebook facebook.com	YouTube—Broadcast yourself youtube.com	The Internet Movie Database imdb.com	BBC Online bbc.co.uk	CNN Interactive cnn.com
Business	PayPal paypal.com	Yahoo Finance finance.yahoo.com	ESPN espn.go.com	Alibaba.com alibaba.com	EzineArticles.com ezinearticles.com
Computers	Google google.com	Facebook facebook.com	YouTube—Broadcast yourself youtube.com	Yahoo! yahoo.com	Gmail mail.google.com
Games	IGN ign.com	GameSpot gamespot.com	Pogo.com pogo.com	MiniClip.com miniclip.com	Yahoo! Games games.yahoo.com
Health	National Institutes of Health (NIH) nih.gov	WebMD webmd.com	PubMed ncbi.nlm.nih.gov/ pubmed/	Mercola mercola.com	Focus on Digestion medicinenet.com
Home	Yahoo Finance finance.yahoo.com	eHow ehow.com	Yelp yelp.com	Open DNS opendns.com	Google Product Search google.com/products
Kids and teens	W3 Schools w3schools.com	Thesaurus.com thesaurus.reference. com	GameSpot gamespot.com	Weebly weebly.com	Universal Currency Converter xe.com/ucc/

News	Yahoo News news.yahoo.com	BBC Online bbc.co.uk	CNN Interactive cnn.com	The New York Times nytimes.com	BBC News bbc.co.uk/news/
Recreation	Metacafe metacafe.com	TripAdvisor tripadvisor.com	Booking.com booking.com	Expedia.com expedia.com	XE.com xe.com
Reference	Yahoo! Answers answers.yahoo.com	Google Maps maps.google.com	StumbleUpon stumbleupon.com	Stack Overflow stackoverflow.com	WikiAnswers—Q&A wiki wiki.answers.com
Regional	Google google.com	Yahoo! yahoo.com	Google India google.co.in	Amazon.com amazon.com	Google UK google.co.uk
Science	Google Translate translate.google.com	NCBI ncbi.nlm.nih.gov	CNET News.com news.cnet.com	Urban Dictionary urbandictionary.com	Time and Date timeanddate.com
Shopping	Amazon.com amazon.com	eBay ebay.com	Netflix netflix.com	Amazon.co.uk amazon.co.uk	Wal-Mart Online walmart.com
Society	Digg digg.com	deviantART deviantart.com	OMG omg.yahoo.com	hi5 hi5.com	Yahoo! Shine shine.yahoo.com
Sports	AOL aol.com	ESPN espn.go.com	Yahoo Sports sports.yahoo.com	NBA nba.com	Yahoo! Sports: NBA sports.yahoo.com/nba/

Table 4 Top websites' implementation failures

Rank	Host	Cause of failure
31	fc2.com	Domain mismatch (CN=fc2server.com)
269	techcrunch.com	Domain mismatch (CN=*.wordpress.com, wordpress.com)
322	nfl.com	Domain mismatch (CN=a248.e.akamai.net, *.akamaihd.net)
336	stackoverflow.com	Domain mismatch (CN=stackauth.com, *.stackauth.com)
377	39.net	Self-signed & Domain mismatch (CN=cms.39.net)
394	www.informer.com	Expiration

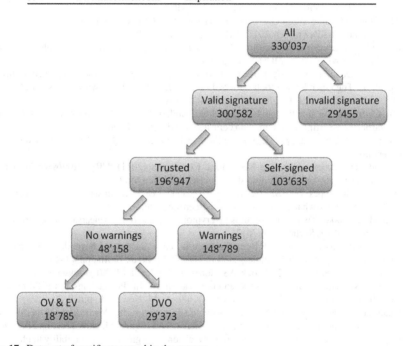

Fig. 17 Data set of certificates used in the survey

References

1. VeriSign Inc.   URL http://www.verisign.com/ssl/buy-ssl-certificates/secure-site-services/index.html
2. The SSL Protocol, Version 3.0 (1996)   URL http://tools.ietf.org/html/draft-ietf-tls-ssl-version3-00
3. Internet X.509 Public Key Infrastructure Certificate and CRL Profile (1999) URL http://www.ietf.org/rfc/rfc2459.txt
4. The TLS Protocol, Version 1.0 (1999) URL http://tools.ietf.org/html/rfc2246
5. HTTP Over TLS (2000) URL http://tools.ietf.org/html/rfc2818

6. Cardholders targetted by Phishing attack using visa-secure.com (2004) URL http://news.netcraft.com/archives/2004/10/08/cardholders_targetted_by_phishing_attack_using_visasecurecom.html
7. Transport Layer Security (TLS) Extensions (2006) URL http://tools.ietf.org/html/rfc4366
8. Has Firefox 3 certificate handling become too scary? (2008) URL http://www.betanews.com/article/Has-Firefox-3-certificate-handling-become-too-scary/1219180509
9. Internet X.509 Public Key Infrastructure Certificate and Certificate Revocation List (CRL) Profile (2008) URL http://tools.ietf.org/html/rfc5280
10. Tim Callan's SSL Blog, MD5 attack resolved (2008) URL https://blogs.verisign.com/ssl-blog/2008/12/on_md5_vulnerabilities_and_mit.php
11. EV and SSL Certificate Trends For The Top 100 Retailers (2010) URL http://www.lexiconn.com/blog/2010/09/ev-ssl-top-100-retailers/
12. Guidelines For The Issuance And Management Of Extended Validation Certificates (2010) URL http://www.cabforum.org/Guidelines_v1_3.pdf
13. Alexa the Web Information Company (2011) URL http://www.alexa.com/
14. Home of the Mozilla Project (2011) URL http://www.mozilla.org/
15. Improving SSL certificate security (2011) URL http://googleonlinesecurity.blogspot.com/2011/04/improving-ssl-certificate-security.html
16. OpenSSL: Documents, verify(1) (2011) URL http://www.openssl.org/docs/apps/verify.html
17. OpenSSL: The Open Source toolkit for SSL/TLS (2011) URL http://www.openssl.org/
18. SQLite Home Page (2011) URL http://www.sqlite.org/
19. SSL Certificate for Mozilla.com Issued Without Validation (2011) URL http://www.sslshopper.com/article-ssl-certificate-for-mozilla.com-issued-without-validation.html
20. The EFF SSL Observatory — Electronic Frontier Foundation (2011) URL http://www.eff.org/observatory
21. Trusted Certificates vs. Browser Recognized Certificates (2011) URL http://www.instantssl.com/ssl-certificate-support/guides/ssl-certificate-validation.html
22. What are the types of SSL Certificates? (2011) URL http://www.globalsign.com/ssl-information-center/what-are-the-types-of-ssl-certificate.html
23. Ahmad D (2008) Two years of broken crypto: debian's dress rehearsal for a global pki compromise. IEEE Secur Priv 6:70–73
24. Anderson R, Moore T (2007) Information security economics—and beyond. In: Cryptology conference on advances in cryptology, CRYPTO '07. Springer, Berlin, pp 49–49
25. Biddle R, van Oorschot PC, Patrick AS, Sobey J, Whalen T (2009) Browser interfaces and extended validation SSL certificates: an empirical study. In: Proceedings of the 2009 ACM workshop on cloud computing security, CCSW '09. ACM, New York, pp 19–30
26. Dhamija R, Tygar JD, Hearst M (2006) Why phishing works. In: Proceedings of the SIGCHI conference on human factors in computing systems, CHI '06. ACM, New York, pp 581–590
27. Downs JS, Holbrook MB, Cranor LF (2006) Decision strategies and susceptibility to phishing. In: Proceedings of the second symposium on usable privacy and security, SOUPS '06. ACM, New York, NY, pp 79–90
28. Ghose A, Rajan U (2006) The economic impact of regulatory information disclosure on information security investments, competition, and social welfare. In: Workshop on the economics of information security, WEIS'06, Robinson College, University of Cambridge, England
29. Good N, Dhamija R, GrosTERMklags J, Thaw D, Aronowitz S, Mulligan D, Konstan J (2005) Stopping spyware at the gate: a user study of privacy, notice and spyware. In: Proceedings of the symposium on usable privacy and security, SOUPS '05. ACM, New York, pp 43–52
30. Herzberg A, Jbara A (2008) Security and identification indicators for browsers against spoofing and phishing attacks. ACM Trans Internet Technol 8(4):16:1–16:36
31. Jackson C, Barth A (2008) ForceHTTPS: protecting high-security web sites from network attacks. In: Proceedings of the 17th international conference on world wide web, WWW '08. ACM, New York, pp 525–534

32. Jakobsson M, Myers S (2006) Phishing and countermeasures: understanding the increasing problem of electronic identity theft. Wiley, Hoboken
33. Landwehr CE (2004) Improving information flow in the information security market. Econ Inform Secur 12:155–163
34. Lenstra AK (2004) Key length. Contribution to The Handbook of Information Security, Lucent Technologies and Technische Universiteit Eindhoven, Mendham, NJ
35. Moore T, Edelman B (2010) Measuring the perpetrators and funders of typosquatting. In: Lecture notes in computer science. Springer, Berlin
36. Schechter SE, Dhamija R, Ozment A, Fischer I (2007) The emperor's new security indicators. In: Proceedings of the 2007 IEEE symposium on security and privacy, SP '07. IEEE Computer Society, Washington, DC, pp 51–65
37. Soghoian C, Stamm S (2011) Certified lies: detecting and defeating government interception attacks against SSL. In: Proceedings of the 15th international conference on financial cryptography and data security, FC'11. Springer, Berlin, pp 250–259
38. Stevens M, Sotirov A, Appelbaum J, Lenstra A, Molnar D, Osvik DA, Weger B (2009) Short chosen-prefix collisions for MD5 and the creation of a rogue CA certificate. In: Proceedings of the 29th annual international cryptology conference on advances in cryptology, CRYPTO '09. Springer, Berlin, pp. 55–69
39. Sunshine J, Egelman S, Almuhimedi H, Atri N, Cranor LF (2009) Crying wolf: an empirical study of SSL warning effectiveness. In: Proceedings of the 18th conference on USENIX security symposium, SSYM'09. USENIX Association, Berkeley, CA, pp 399–416
40. Wendlandt D, Andersen DG, Perrig A (2008) Perspectives: improving SSH-style host authentication with multi-path probing. In: USENIX 2008 annual technical conference on annual technical conference, ATC'08. USENIX Association, Berkeley, CA, USA, pp 321–334
41. Whalen T, Inkpen KM (2005) Gathering evidence: use of visual security cues in web browsers. In: Proceedings of Graphics Interface 2005, GI '05. Canadian Human-Computer Communications Society, School of Computer Science, University of Waterloo, Waterloo, Ontario, Canada, pp 137–144

Resilience of the Internet Interconnection Ecosystem

Chris Hall, Ross Anderson, Richard Clayton, Evangelos Ouzounis, and Panagiotis Trimintzios

Abstract In 2010 the European Network and Information Security Agency (ENISA) launched a study to investigate the resilience of the Internet's interconnection system and come up with policy recommendations. A large number of stakeholders were contacted, and their expertise has been reflected in the study. The formal outcome of the study was the publication by ENISA in early 2011 of a detailed technical report, *"Inter-X: Resilience of the Internet Interconnection Ecosystem"*. This paper presents a much abridged version of the ENISA report. In it, we present a summary of the problems that the Internet faces in keeping its interconnection system resilient, along with the recommendations proposed to policy makers.

1 Introduction

The Internet has been pretty reliable thus far, having recovered rapidly from most of the incidents that have occurred in its history. The effects of natural disasters such as Hurricane Katrina [21], terrorist attacks such as "9/11" [60], and assorted technical failures have all been limited in time and space [67, 68]. It is impossible to say whether we have just been lucky, and that sooner or later some event will

C. Hall (✉)
Highwayman Associates, Woodvill Cottage, Woodvill Road, Leatherhead, KT22 7BP, UK
e-mail: chris.hall@highwayman.com

R. Anderson • R. Clayton
Computer Laboratory, University of Cambridge, Cambridge, CB3 0FD, UK
e-mail: ross.anderson@cl.cam.ac.uk; richard.clayton@cl.cam.ac.uk

E. Ouzounis • P. Trimintzios
European Network and Information Security Agency, PO Box 1308,
Heraklion, 71001, Greece
e-mail: evangelos.ouzounis@enisa.europa.eu; panagiotis.trimintzios@enisa.europa.eu

B. Schneier (ed.), *Economics of Information Security and Privacy III*,
DOI 10.1007/978-1-4614-1981-5_6,
© Springer Science+Business Media New York 2013

catch us out. However it does appear likely that the Internet could suffer a systemic failure, leading perhaps to localised collapse and system-wide congestion, in certain circumstances:

- A regional failure of the physical infrastructure on which the Internet depends (such as the bulk power transmission system) or the human infrastructure needed to maintain it (for example, if pandemic flu causes millions of people to stay at home out of fear of infection).
- Cascading technical failures, of which some of the more likely near-term scenarios relate to the imminent changeover from IPv4 to IPv6. Common-mode failures involving updates to popular makes of router (or PC) may also fall under this heading.
- A coordinated attack in which a capable opponent disrupts the routing fabric, perhaps by broadcasting many thousands of bogus routes from a large ISP, or from a large number of compromised routers.

There is evidence that some implementations of the Border Gateway Protocol (BGP), the Internet's inter-domain routing protocol, are surprisingly fragile. There is evidence that some concentrations of infrastructure lack resilience and that significant disruption could be caused by localised failure. There is evidence that the health of the interconnection system as a whole is not a high priority for the networks that make up that system—by and large each network strives to provide a service which is reliable most of the time, at minimum achievable cost. The economics do not favour high dependability of the system as a whole as there is no incentive for anyone to provide the extra capacity that would be needed to deal with large-scale failures.

To date, we have been far from equilibrium: the rapid growth in Internet capacity has masked a multitude of sins and errors. However, as the Internet matures, as more and more of the world's optical fibre is lit, and as companies jostle for advantage, the dynamics may change.

There may well not be any immediate cause for concern about the resilience of the Internet interconnection ecosystem, but there is certainly cause for concern about the lack of good information about how it works and how well it might work if something went very badly wrong.

In 2010 the European Network and Information Security Agency (ENISA) launched a study to investigate the resilience of the Internet's interconnection system and come up with policy recommendations. A large number of stakeholders were contacted, and their expertise reflected in the study. The formal outcome was the publication by ENISA in early 2011 of a detailed 230 page technical report, "*Inter-X: Resilience of the Internet Interconnection Ecosystem*" [24] which goes into great detail on the security and economics of Internet routing, covering everything from the mechanics of route leaks to the financial conditions of the largest players (the Tier 1 transit providers).

In this paper we only present a brief canter through the landscape in Sects. 2–14 before discussing the main recommendations in Sect. 15. The interested reader is referred to the full report for all the details.

2 Scale and Complexity

The Internet is very big and very complicated! The interconnection system we call the Internet comprises (in March 2011) some 37 000 "Autonomous Systems" or ASs (ISPs or similar entities) and 350 000 blocks of addresses (addressable groups of machines), spread around the world [37].

This enormous scale means that it is hard to conceive of an external event which would affect more than a relatively small fraction of the system—as far as the Internet is concerned, a large earthquake or major hurricane is, essentially, a little local difficulty. However, the failure of even a small fraction of the Internet may still have a significant impact on a great many people. When considering its resilience it is necessary to consider not only the global issues, but also a large number of separate, but interconnected, local issues.

The complexity of the system is not just a matter of its sheer scale and the number of interconnections between ASs, but is compounded by a number of factors:

- Modelling interconnections is hard because we only ever have a partial view. The Internet has a number of layers, each with its own properties and each interacting with the other layers. For example, the connections between ASs use many different physical networks, often provided by third parties, which are themselves large and complicated. Resilience depends on the diversity of interconnections, which in turn depends on physical diversity—which can be an illusion, and is often unknown.

    While it is possible to discover part of the "AS-level topology" of the Internet (which ASs are interconnected) [59], it would be more valuable from a resilience perspective to know the "router-level topology" (the number, location, capacity, traffic levels etc. of the actual connections between ASs). If we want to estimate how traffic might move around when connections fail, we also need to know about the "routing layer" (what routes the routers have learned from each other) so we can estimate what routes would be lost when given connections failed, and what routes would be used instead. That also touches on "routing policy" (the way each AS decides which routes it will prefer) and the "traffic layer"— where end-user traffic is going to and from. This last is perhaps the most important layer, but very little is known about it on a global scale.

- The interconnection system depends on other complex and interdependent systems. The routers, the links between them, the sites they are housed in, and all the other infrastructure that the interconnection system depends on, themselves depend on other systems—notably the electricity supply—and those systems depend in their turn on the Internet.

- The interconnection ecosystem is self-organising and highly decentralised. Decisions to interconnect are made independently by the ASs, driven by their need to reach, and be reachable from, the entire Internet. The same holds at lower levels: the administrators of an AS configure their routers to implement their routing policy, then the routers select and use routes. But different routers in the same AS may select different routes for a given destination, so even the administrators may not know, a priori, what path traffic will take [27].

- The interconnection ecosystem is dynamic. Its shape changes all the time as new connections are made, or existing connections fail or are removed. At the corporate level, transit providers come and go, organisations merge, and so on. At the industry level, the recent rise of the content delivery networks (CDNs) has changed the pattern of interconnections [26, 30].
- The patterns of use are also constantly evolving. The rise of the CDNs also changed the distribution of traffic; and while peer-to-peer (P2P) traffic became a large proportion of total volumes in the early-to-mid 2000s, now video traffic of various kinds is coming to dominate in terms of both volume and growth [16, 44].
- The Internet is continuing to grow. In fact, just about everything about it continues to grow: the number of ASs, the number of routes, the number of interconnections, the volume of traffic, etc. [37, 38, 58, 64].

The scale and complexity of the system are hard to grasp. Resilience is itself a slippery concept, so the "resilience of the interconnection system" is non-trivial to define—let alone measure!

3   The Nature of Resilience

There is a vast literature on reliability where engineers study the failure rates of components, the prevalence of bugs in software, and the effects of wear, maintenance etc.; the aim being to design machines or systems with a known rate of failure in predictable operating conditions [70]. Robustness relates to designing systems to withstand overloads, environmental stresses and other insults, for example by specifying equipment to be significantly stronger than is needed for normal operation. In traditional engineering, resilience was the ability of a material to absorb energy under stress and release it later. In modern systems thinking, it means the opposite of "brittleness" and refers to the ability of a system or organisation to adapt and recover from a serious failure, or more generally to its ability to survive in the face of threats, including the prevention or mitigation of unsafe, hazardous or detrimental conditions that threaten its existence [34]. In the longer term, it can also mean evolvability: the ability of a system to adapt gradually as its environment changes—an idea borrowed from systems biology [41, 76].

For this study we follow Xie et al. [80] and define the resilience of a system as *the ability to provide and maintain an acceptable level of service in the face of various faults and challenges to normal operation*—i.e. the ability to adapt itself to recover from a serious failure and more generally to survive in the face of threats. A given event may have some impact on a system and hence some immediate impact on the service it offers. The system will then recover, service levels improve and at some time full service is restored.

Resilience therefore refers both to failure recovery at the micro level, as when the Internet recovers from the failure of a router so quickly that users perceive a connection failure of perhaps a few seconds (if they notice anything at all); through coping with a mid-size incident, as when ISPs provided extra routes in the hours immediately after the 9/11 terrorist attacks by running fibres across co-location centres; to disaster recovery at the strategic level, where we might plan for the next San Francisco earthquake or for a malware compromise of thousands of routers. In each case the desired outcome is that the system should continue to provide service in the event of some part of it failing, with service degrading gracefully if the failure is large.

There are thus two edge cases of resilience:

1. The ability of the system to cope with small local events, such as machine failures, and reconfigure itself, over a time scale of seconds to minutes, in an essentially automated manner. This enables the Internet to cope with day-to-day events with little or no effect on service—it is reliable. This is what most network engineers think of as resilience.
2. The ability of the system to cope with and recover from a major event, such as a large natural disaster or a capable attack, on a time scale of hours to days or even longer. This type of resilience includes, first, the ability to continue to offer some service in the immediate aftermath, and second, the ability to repair and rebuild thereafter. The key words here are "adapt" and "recover". This "disaster recovery" is what civil authorities tend to think of when they use the term "resilience".

We are interested in the resilience of the ecosystem in the face of events which have medium to high impact and which have a correspondingly medium to low probability. We thus emphasise the second of these cases.

Robustness is an important aspect of resilience. A robust system will have the ability to resist assaults and insults, so that whatever some event is throwing at it, it will be unaffected, and a resilient response is not required. While resilience is to do with coping with the impact of events, robustness is to do with reducing this impact in the first place. The two overlap, and from the users' perspective the distinction may be a fine one; what the user wants is for the system to be predictably dependable.

Resilience is context-specific. Robustness can be sensibly defined only in respect of specified attacks or failures, and in the same way resilience also makes sense only in the context of recovery from specified events, or in the face of a set of possible challenges of known probability. We call bad events of known probability "risk", but there is a separate problem of "uncertainty" where we do not know enough about possible future bad events to assign them a probability at all. In the face of uncertainty, it is difficult to assess a combination of intermediate levels of service and recovery/restoration times, especially when what is acceptable may vary depending on the nature and scale of the event.

Moreover, no good metrics are available to actually assess the performance of the Internet or its interconnects. This makes it harder still to specify acceptable levels of service. For the Internet the problem is compounded by scale and complexity (see above) and by lack of information (see below), which makes it hard to construct a model which might be used to attach numbers to resilience. It is even hard to assess what impact a given single event might have—an earthquake in San Francisco of a given severity may have a predictable impact on the physical infrastructure, but that needs to be translated into its effect on each network, and hence the effect on the interconnection ecosystem.

Given these difficulties (and there are many more), service providers commonly fall back on measures which improve resilience in general terms, hoping that this will improve their response to future challenges. This qualitative approach runs into difficulty when the cost of an improvement must be justified on much more restricted criteria. For the Internet as a whole, the cost justification of investment in resilience is an even harder case to make.

4 The Lack of Information

Each of the ASs that make up the Internet has a Network Operation Centre (NOC), charged with monitoring the health of the AS's network and acting when problems occur. There is no NOC for the Internet.

In fact it is even worse than that. ASs understand their own networks but know little about anyone else's. At every level of the interconnection system, there is little global information available, and what that is available is incomplete and of unknown accuracy.

In particular:

- There is no map of physical connections—their location, capacity, etc.
- There is no map of traffic and traffic volume.
- There is no map of the interconnections between ASs—what routes they offer each other.

The Internet interconnection system is, essentially, opaque. This opacity hampers the research and development communities in their attempts to understand how the Internet works, making it hard to develop and test improvements; it makes the study and modelling of complex emergent properties such as resilience even harder still.

The lack of information has a number of causes:

- **Complexity and scale**. To maintain accurate maps of the networks of fibre around the world might be a tractable problem. But many different logical connections run over these physical fibres, each of which will carry network traffic for numerous providers, which in turn support yet more providers' networks and circuits—rapidly multiplying up the combinations and permutations of overlapping use of the underlying fibre. Furthermore, much of this is dynamic— providers reroute existing networks and circuits as they extend or adapt their networks. Meticulous record keeping is required, but even within a single AS it is not always achieved. It would be even more complex to extend this mapping so as to measure the traffic volumes, given the sheer number of connections between networks.

- **The information hiding properties of the routing system** [6, 11, 15]. When mapping connections by probing the system from the outside, each probe will reveal something about the path between the two (inside and outside) points in the Internet at that specific time. But the probe reveals little about what paths may exist at other times, or what path might be taken if any part of the usual path fails, or what the performance of those other paths might be.
- **Security concerns**. Mapping the physical layer is thought to invite people with bad intentions to improve their target selection; so those maps that do exist are seldom shared [7].
- **The cost of storing and processing the data**. If there was complete information, there would be a very great deal of it, and more would be generated every minute. Storing it and processing it into a usable form would be a major engineering task.
- **Commercial sensitivity**. Information about whether, how and where networks connect to each other is deemed commercially sensitive by some. Information about traffic volumes is quite generally seen as commercially sensitive. Because of this, some advocate powerful incentives to disclose it, possibly in anonymised and aggregated form.
- **Critical information is not collected in the first place, or not kept up to date**. Information gathering and maintenance costs money, so there must be some real use for it before a network will bother to gather it or strive to keep it up to date. The Internet Routing Registries (IRRs) are potentially excellent resources, but are not necessarily up to date, complete or accurate, because the information seldom has operational significance (and may in any case be deemed commercially sensitive) [69].
- **Lack of good metrics**. While there are well-known metrics for the performance of connections between two points in a network, there are none for a network as a whole or, indeed, for a network of networks.

The poor state of information reflects not only the difficulty of finding or collecting data, but also the lack of good ways to process and use it even if one had it.

4.1 Incidents as a Source of Information

Small incidents occur every day, and larger ones every now and then. Given the lack of information about the interconnection system, the results of these natural experiments tell us much of what we presently know about its resilience. For example, we know the following:

- It is straightforward to divert traffic away from its proper destination by announcing invalid routes [8, 9, 14, 18, 62, 75], and in one well-known incident in February 2008 YouTube became inaccessible for a few hours [10, 53, 54, 66]. More publicity, and political concern, was raised by a 2010 incident during which China Telecom advertised a number of invalid routes, effectively hijacking 15% of Internet addresses for 18 min [4, 5, 19, 50, 52].

- Latent bugs in BGP implementations can disrupt the system. Most recently, in August 2010, an experiment which sent an unusual (but entirely legal) form of route announcement triggered a bug in some routers, causing their *neighbours* to terminate BGP sessions, and for many routes to be lost [67, 68]. The effects of this incident lasted less than two hours.
- In some parts of the world a small number of cable systems are critical. Undersea cables near Alexandria in Egypt were cut in December 2008 [29]. Interestingly, three cable systems were affected at the same time, and two of those systems had been affected similarly in January/February of that year [61, 72]. This seriously affected traffic for about two weeks [83–85].
- The Internet is critically dependent on electrical power and the August 2003 blackout in the Northeastern US and Canada had a widespread effect on connectivity, although the largest provider networks stayed up [20]. A large power outage in Brazil in November 2009 caused significant disruption, though it lasted only four and a half hours. Previous blackouts in Brazil had been attributed to "hackers", suggesting that these incidents are examples of the risk of inter-dependent networks. However, this particular conspiracy theory has been refuted [71].
- The ecosystem can work well in a crisis. The analysis of the effect of the destruction at the World Trade Centre in New York on 11th September 2001 shows that the system worked well at the time, and in the days thereafter, even though large cables under the buildings were cut and other facilities were destroyed or damaged. Generally, Internet services performed better than the telephone system (fixed and mobile) [3].

These sorts of incident are well known. However, hard information about the exact causes and effects is hard to come by—much is anecdotal and incomplete, while some is speculative or simply apocryphal. Valuable information is being lost. The report *The Internet under Crisis Conditions: Learning from September 11* [60], is a model of clarity; but even there the authors warn:

> "... while the committee is confident in its assessment that the events of September 11 had little effect on the Internet as a whole ..., the precision with which analysts can measure the impact of such events is limited by a lack of relevant data."

5   Resilience and Efficiency

There are fundamental tensions between resilience and efficiency. Resilience requires spare capacity and duplication of resources, and systems which are loosely coupled (composed of largely independent sub-systems) are more resilient than tightly coupled systems whose components depend more on each other [51]. But improving efficiency generally means eliminating excess capacity and redundant resources.

A more diverse system is generally more resilient, but it will also be more expensive and complex. Diversity of connections is most efficiently achieved using infrastructure whose cost is shared by many operators, but collective-action problems can undermine the resilience gain. It is efficient to avoid duplication of effort in the development of software and equipment, and efficient to exploit economies of scale in its manufacture, but this reduces the diversity of the equipment that is used. It is efficient for the entire Internet to depend on one protocol for its routing, but this creates a single point of failure. Setting up and maintaining multiple, diverse, separate connections to other networks costs time and effort and creates extra complexity to be managed.

The Internet is a loosely coupled collection of independently managed networks. However, at its core there are a few very large networks, each of which strives to be as efficient as possible both internally and in its connections to other networks. So it is an open question whether the actual structure of the Internet is as resilient as its architecture would suggest. In the past it has been remarkably resilient, and it has continued to perform as it has evolved from a tiny network connecting a handful of research facilities into the global infrastructure that connects billions today. However, as elsewhere, past performance is no guarantee of future results.

6   Resilience and Equipment

A particular concern for the Internet interconnection system is the possibility of an internal technical problem having a systemic effect. The imminent changeover to IPv6 will provide a high-stress environment in which such a problem could be more likely to manifest itself, and the most likely proximate cause of such a problem is bugs in BGP implementations, which could be serious given the small number of router vendors. There have been a number of incidents in which large numbers of routers across the entire Internet have been affected by the same problem, when something unexpected triggers a bug in the software—and occasionally even in the specification of BGP [67].

No software is free from bugs, and universal dependence on BGP and universal connectedness makes bugs more serious. ISPs may test equipment before buying and deploying it, but those tests concentrate on issues directly affecting the ISP, such as the performance of the equipment and its ability to support the required services. Manufacturers test their equipment too. But both ISPs and manufacturers are mostly concerned that the equipment works well under normal circumstances. Individual ISPs cannot afford to do exhaustive testing of low-probability scenarios for the benefit of the Internet at large, while for their part the manufacturers balance the effort and time spent testing against their customers' demands for new and useful features, new and faster routers and less expensive software. Of lesser concern, unfortunately, is how secure routers and routing protocols might be against deliberate attempts to disrupt or suborn them.

A number of respondents to the consultation exercise which informed the writing of our report felt that money spent on more strategic testing of equipment and protocols would be money well spent.

7 Service Level Agreements and "Best Efforts"

In any market in which the buyer has difficulty in establishing the relative value of different sellers' offerings, it is common for sellers to offer guarantees to support their claims to quality. Service Level Agreements (SLAs) perform that function in the interconnection ecosystem. From a resilience perspective, it would be nice to see ISPs offering SLAs that covered not just their own networks but the interconnection system too, and customers preferring to buy service with such SLAs. Unfortunately, SLAs for Internet access in general are hard, and for transit service are of doubtful value. In particular, the SLAs that are offered do not extend beyond the borders of that network, so whatever they do guarantee does not cover the interconnection system—the part between the borders of all networks.

Providers do not attempt to guarantee anything beyond their borders because they cannot. An end-to-end guarantee would require a back-to-back system of contracts between networks so that liability for a failure to perform would be borne by the failing network. That system of contracts does not exist, not least because the Internet is not designed to guarantee performance. It is fundamental to the current Internet architecture that packets are delivered on a "best efforts" basis— the network will do its best but it does not guarantee anything. The Internet leaves the hard work of maintaining a connection to the end-points of the connection—the "end-to-end" principle. The Transmission Control Protocol (TCP), which carries most Internet traffic (apart from delay-sensitive traffic such as voice), will reduce demand if it detects congestion—it is specifically designed to adapt to the available capacity, not to guarantee some level of performance.

The other difficulty with SLAs is what can (or should) be measured. For a single connection between A and B it is clear what can be measured, but it is not clear what level of performance could be guaranteed. But now consider a connection from A in one network to F in another network, which traverses four other networks (B, C, D, E) and the connections between them, as shown in Fig. 1.

All these networks are independent, and have their own SLAs, each extending only as far as their borders. If we follow the money, A is paying directly for a

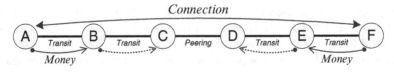

Fig. 1 How the flow of money fails to match the flow of traffic

connection to B and indirectly for packets sent from B to C. Similarly, F is paying directly for a connection to E and indirectly for the connection from E to D. C and D (who could well be global "tier one" providers) have their own arrangements. But if E has low standards, or is having a bad day, to whom does A complain? B has a contract with A, and offers an SLA, but that does not extend beyond B. B also has a contract with C, with a different SLA, but even if B complained to C about its customer's problem we have come to the end of the money trail: C may not be able to hold D to account, as it peers with D, and it has no relationship with E.

Even if it were possible to establish an end-to-end SLA for this connection, and pin liability on the failing network, there are hundreds of thousands of paths between network A and the rest of the Internet. So whatever value SLAs may have, they do not offer a contractual framework through which customers can influence the resilience of the interconnection system, even if they wished to do this. Few customers understand the issue, or care to do anything about it. Generally the Internet is remarkably reliable, so a customer's principal interest in choosing a supplier is price—possibly moderated by the supplier's reputation.

8 Reachability, Traffic and Performance

While end-users care about traffic and performance, the basic mechanism of the interconnection system—the BGP protocol [65]—only understands reachability. Its function is to provide a way for every network to reach every other network, and for traffic to flow across the Internet from one network to another. All ASs (the ISPs and other networks that comprise the Internet) speak BGP to each other, and reachability information spreads across the "BGP mesh" of connections between them. BGP is the heart of the interconnection system, so its many deficiencies are a problem.

The problems within the protocol itself include:

- There is no mechanism to verify that the routing information distributed by BGP is valid. In principle traffic to any destination can be diverted—so traffic can be disrupted, modified, examined, or all three. The security issues are covered further below.
- There is no mechanism in BGP to convey capacity information—so BGP cannot help reconfigure the interconnection system to avoid congestion [82]. When a route fails, BGP will find another route to achieve reachability, but that route may have insufficient capacity for the traffic it now receives.
- The mechanisms in BGP which may be used to direct traffic away from congestion in other networks—"inter-domain traffic engineering"—are strictly limited [13, 63, 81].
- When things change, BGP can be slow to settle down ("converge") to a new, stable, state [32, 33].
- The ability of BGP to cope, or cope well, under extreme conditions is not assured [78].

End-users expect to be able to reach every part of the Internet, so reachability is essential. But they also expect to be able to move data to and from whatever destination they choose, so they expect their connection with that destination to perform well. As BGP knows nothing about traffic, capacity or performance, network operators must use other means to meet end-users' expectations. When something in the Internet changes, BGP will change the routes used to ensure continuing reachability, but it is up to the network operators to tinker with the automated choices to ensure that performance is adequate, and take other steps if it is not.

Service quality in a "best efforts" network is all to do with avoiding congestion, for which it is necessary to ensure that there is always sufficient capacity. The most effective way to do that is to maintain enough spare capacity to absorb the usual short-term variations in traffic and provide some safety margin. Additional spare capacity may be maintained to allow time (weeks or months, perhaps) for new capacity to be installed to cater for long-term growth of traffic. Maintaining spare capacity in this way is known as "over-provisioning"; it is key to day-to-day service quality and to the resilience of the interconnection system.

Each operator constantly monitors its network for signs of congestion and will make adjustments to relieve any short term issues. In general the pattern of traffic in a network of any size is stable from day to day and month to month [1]. An operator will also monitor their network for long term trends in traffic. The management of capacity is generally done on the basis of history, experience and rules of thumb, supported by systems for gathering and processing the available data. The levels of spare capacity in any network will depend on many things, including how the operator chooses to balance the cost of spare capacity against the risk of congestion.

A key point here is that capacity is managed on the basis of actual traffic and the usual day-to-day events, with some margin for contingencies and growth. Capacity is not managed on the basis of what might happen if some unusual event causes a lot of traffic to shift from one network to another. If an event has a major impact, then the amount of spare capacity within and between networks will determine the likelihood of systemic congestion. So each individual network's degree of over-provisioning makes some contribution to the resilience of the whole—though it is hard to say to what extent.

If an event disables some part of the Internet, BGP will work to ensure that reachability is maintained, but the new paths may have less capacity than the usual ones, which may result in congestion. For many applications, notably web-browsing, the effect is to slow things down, but not stop them working. More difficulties arise with any sort of data that is affected by reduced throughput or increased delay, such as VoIP (voice over Internet Protocol) and streaming video. Congestion may stop these applications working satisfactorily, or at all [43, 77].

The important distinction between reachability and traffic is illustrated by considering what appears to be a simple metric for the state of the Internet: the percentage of known destinations which are reachable from most of the Internet, at any given moment. This metric may be used to gauge the impact of a BGP failure, or of the failure of some critical fibre, or any other widely felt event. But while the significance of, say, 10% of known destinations becoming unreachable is obviously extremely high for the 10% cut off, it may not be terribly significant for the rest of the Internet. We'd prefer to know the amount, and possibly the value, of traffic that is affected. If the 10% cut off is largely self-contained in traffic terms, or insignificant in economic terms, the failure has less impact. If the 10% cut off accounts for a large proportion of the remaining 90%'s traffic, the impact could be significant. So when talking about the resilience of the system, what is an "acceptable level" of the "best efforts" service? Are we aiming at having email work 95% of the time to 95% of destinations, or streaming video work 99.99% of the time to 99.99% of destinations? The answer will have an enormous effect on the spare capacity needed! Each extra order of magnitude improvement (say from 99.9% to 99.99%) could cost an order of magnitude more money; yet the benefits of service quality are unevenly distributed. For example, a pensioner who uses the Internet to chat to grandchildren once a week may be happy with 99%, while a company providing a cloud-based business service may need 99.99%.

8.1 Traffic Prioritisation

In a crisis it is common to restrict access to some resources, to shed demand and free up capacity. For telephony a traditional approach is to give emergency services priority. But restricting phone service to "obvious" emergency workers such as doctors is unsatisfactory. Modern medical practice depends on team working and can be crippled if nurses are cut off; and many patients who depend on home monitoring may have to be hospitalised if communications fail.

If capacity is lost in a disaster and parts of the system are congested, then all users of the congested parts may suffer a reduction in service, and some sorts of traffic (notably VoIP) may stop working entirely. If some types, sources or destinations of traffic are deemed to be important, and so should be given priority in a crisis, then serious thought needs to be given to how to identify priority traffic, how the prioritisation is to be implemented and how turning that prioritisation on and off fits into other disaster planning.

It is not entirely straightforward to identify different types of traffic. So an alternative approach may be to prioritise by source or destination. It may be tempting to consider services such as Facebook or YouTube as essentially trivial, and YouTube uses a lot of bandwidth. However, in a crisis keeping in contact using Facebook may be a priority for many; and shutting down YouTube—thus preventing the free reporting of events—would require solid justification. On the other hand, rate limiting ordinary users, irrespective of traffic type, may appear fair, but could affect essential VoIP use, and cutting off peer-to-peer traffic could be seen as censorship.

Hence, should a crisis occur, it would be inappropriate to expect ISPs to be the organisations to decide to discriminate between different sorts of traffic, or between customers of the same type (although premium customers at premium rates might expect to get better performance). It is not even clear that ISPs are, in general, capable of prioritising traffic on any given basis. So, if some traffic should be prioritised in a crisis, who will make the call, and will anyone be ready to act when they do?

8.2 Traffic Engineering

Traffic engineering is the jargon term for adjusting a network so that traffic flows are improved. In a crisis that would mean shifting traffic away from congested paths. This is less controversial than traffic prioritisation, but no less difficult.

When some event creates congestion in some part(s) of the interconnection system it would be convenient if networks could redirect some traffic away from the congested parts. When a network is damaged its operators will work to relieve congestion within their network by doing internal traffic engineering, adding temporary capacity, repairing things, and so on. One of the strengths of the Internet is that each operator will be working independently to recover their own network as quickly and efficiently as possible.

Where a network's users are affected by congestion in other networks, the simplest strategy is to wait until those networks recover. This may leave spare capacity in other networks unused, so is not the optimum strategy for the system as a whole. But, there are two problems with trying to coordinate action:

1. There is no way of telling where the spare capacity is.
2. BGP only provides very limited means to influence traffic in other operators' networks.

In effect, if networks attempt to redirect traffic they are blundering around in the dark, attempting to make adjustments to a delicate instrument with a hammer. Their attempts to redirect traffic may create congestion elsewhere, which may cause more networks to try to move traffic around. It is possible to imagine a situation in which many networks are chasing each other, creating waves of congestion and routing changes as they do, like the waves of congestion that pass along roads which are near their carrying capacity.

With luck, if a network cannot handle the traffic it is sent and pushes it away to other networks, it will eventually be diverted towards routes with spare capacity, and after a while all the traffic will have been appropriately redistributed. It is impossible to say how much time would be required for this process; it would depend on the severity of the capacity loss, but it could be days or even weeks.

Strategic local action will not necessarily lead to a socially optimal equilibrium, though, as the incentives may be perverse. Since any SLA will stop at the edge of its network, a transit provider may wish to engineer traffic away from its network in order to meet its SLAs for traffic within its network. The result may still be congestion, somewhere else, but the SLA is still met.

8.3   Routing in a Crisis

Experience shows that in a crisis the interconnection system can quite quickly create new paths between networks to provide interim connections and extra capacity, and we've already discussed how the loss of facilities in New York City on 9/11 was quickly dealt with.

The interconnection ecosystem has often responded in this way, with many people improvising, and working with the people they know personally. This is related to traffic engineering, to the extent that it addresses the lack of capacity by adding extra connections to which traffic can be moved. The response of the system might be improved and speeded up if there were more preparation for this form, and perhaps other forms, of co-operation in a crisis.

In the end, if there is insufficient capacity in a crisis, then no amount of traffic engineering or manual reconfiguration will fit a quart of traffic into a pint of capacity. In extreme cases some form of prioritisation will be needed.

9   Is Transit a Viable Business?

The provision of transit—contracts to carry IP traffic to every possible destination[1]—is a key part of the interconnection system, but it may not be a sustainable business in the near future.

Nobody doubts that the cost of transit has fallen fast, or that it is a commodity business, except where there is little or no competition [56,73]. In the USA, over the last ten to fifteen years, transit prices have fallen at rate of around 40% per annum— a rate which results in a 99% drop over a ten year period. In other parts of the world prices started higher, but as infrastructure has developed, and transit networks have extended to into new markets, those prices have fallen as well—for example, prices in London are now scarcely distinguishable from those in New York.

Where there is effective competition, the price of transit falls, and consumers benefit. In a competitive market, price tends towards the marginal cost of production. The total cost of production has also fallen sharply, as innovation reduces the cost of the underlying technologies and with increasing economies of scale. Yet every year industry insiders feel that surely nobody can make money at today's prices, and that there must soon be a levelling off. So far there has been no levelling off, though the rate at which prices fall may be diminishing.

---

[1]Contrast transit with peering, where an ISP will arrange with another to carry traffic to and from each other's customers. Since peering with every network in the world is impractical, ISPs will purchase transit contracts to carry the traffic that cannot be handled by peering relationships. Note that transit traffic is invariably paid for, whereas peering (which is usually only with other ISPs of a similar size, or between "content" and "eyeball" ASs) is generally free.

The reason is simple: the marginal cost of production for transit service is generally zero. At any given moment there will be a number of transit providers with spare capacity: first, network capacity comes in lumps, so each time capacity is added the increment will generally exceed the immediate need; second, networks are generally over-provisioned, so there is always some spare capacity—though eating into that may increase the risk of congestion, perhaps reducing service quality at busy times or when things go wrong.

The logic of this market is that the price for transit will tend towards zero. So it is unclear how pure transit providers could recoup their capital investment. The logic of the market would appear to favour consolidation until the handful of firms left standing acquire "market power".

At a practical level, the provision of transit may be undertaken not to make profits but just to offset some of the cost of being an Internet network. For some networks the decision to offer transit at the market price may be increasingly a strategic rather than a commercial decision. Another significant factor is the recent and continuing increase in video traffic and the related rise in the amount of traffic delivered by the content delivery networks (see below). This means that the continued reduction in the unit price of transit is not being matched by an increase in traffic over transit links, so the transit providers' revenues are decreasing.

The acknowledged market leader, Level 3, lost $2.9 billion in 2005–2008, a further $0.6 billion in 2009, and another $0.6 billion in 2010 [47–49]. It is not possible to say what contribution their transit business made to this; industry insiders note that Level 3 did not go through bankruptcy as some other players did, and would make a small profit were it not for the cost of servicing its debt. However, the industry as a whole is losing large amounts of money.

10   The Rise of the Content Delivery Networks

Over the past four years or so, more and more traffic has been delivered by content delivery networks (CDNs). Their rise has been rapid and has changed the interconnection landscape, concentrating a large proportion of Internet traffic into a small number of networks [44]. This shift has been driven by both cost and quality considerations. With the growth of video content, of ever richer web-sites, and of cloud applications, it makes sense to place copies of popular data closer to the end users who fetch it. This has a number of benefits:

- Local connections perform better than remote connections—giving a quicker response and faster transfers.
- Costs are reduced because data-files are not being repeatedly transported over large distances—saving on transit costs. However, the key motivation for CDN customers is not to reduce the cost of delivery, but to ensure quality and consistency of delivery—which is particularly important for the delivery of video streams;

- The data-files are replicated, stored in and delivered from a number of locations—improving resilience.

This has moved traffic away from transit providers to peering connections between the CDNs and the end-user's ISP. In some cases content is distributed to servers within the ISP's own network, bypassing the interconnection system altogether.

One CDN claims to deliver some 20% of all Internet traffic [2]. Since the traffic being delivered is the sort which is expected to grow most quickly in the coming years, this implies that an increasing proportion of traffic is being delivered locally, and a reducing proportion of traffic is being carried (over long distances) by the transit providers.

Another effect of this is to add traffic at the Internet Exchange Points (IXPs),[2] which are the obvious way for the CDNs to connect to local ISPs. This adds value to the IXP—particularly welcome for the smaller IXPs, which have been threatened by the ever falling cost of transit (eating into the cost advantage of connecting to the IXP) and the falling cost of connecting to remote (larger) IXPs (where there is more opportunity to pick up peering traffic).

There is a positive effect on resilience, and a negative one. The positive side is that systems serving users in one region are independent of those in other regions, so a lot of traffic becomes less dependent on long distance transit services. On the negative side, CDNs are now carrying so much traffic that if a large one were to fail, transit providers could not meet the added demand, and some services would be degraded. CDNs also concentrate ever more infrastructure in places where there is already a lot of it. If parts of some local infrastructure fail for any reason, will there be sufficient other capacity to fall back on?

Finally, it is possible to count a couple of dozen CDNs quite quickly, but it appears that perhaps two or three are dominant. Some of the large transit providers have entered the business, either with their own infrastructure or in partnership with an existing CDN. There are obvious economies of scale in the CDN business, and there is now a significant investment barrier to entry. The state of this market in a few years' time is impossible to predict, but network effects tend to favour a few, very large, players. These players are very likely to end up handling over half of the Internet's traffic by volume.

11 The "Insecurity" of the BGP Protocol

A fundamental problem with BGP is that there is no mechanism to verify that the routing information it distributes is valid [12, 39]. The effect of this is felt on a regular basis when a network manages to announce large numbers of routes for

---

[2]An IXP is a location to which many ISPs (and CDNs) connect. For the cost of a single link, they can exchange traffic (usually peering traffic, but sometimes transit) with all the other ISPs and CDNs who are IXP members.

addresses that belong to others; this can divert traffic into what is effectively a black hole. Such incidents are quite quickly dealt with by network operators, and disruption can be limited to a few hours, at most.

The great fear is that this insecurity might be exploited as a means to deliberately disrupt the Internet, or parts of it. There is also a frequently expressed concern that route hijacking might be used to listen in on traffic, though this can be hard to do in practice.

Configuring BGP routers to filter out invalid routes, or only accept valid ones, is encouraged as best practice [42]. However, where it is practical (at the edges of the Internet) it does not make much difference until most networks do it. Where it would make most immediate difference (in the larger transit providers) it is not really practical because the information on which to base route filters is incomplete and the tools available to manage and implement filters at that scale are inadequate.

More secure forms of BGP, in which routing information can be cryptographically verified, depend on there being a mechanism to verify the "ownership" of blocks of IP addresses, or to verify that the AS which claims to be the origin of a block of IP addresses is entitled to make that claim. The notion of title to blocks of IP addresses turns out not to be as straightforward as might be expected. However, some progress is now being made, and the Resource Public Key Infrastructure (RPKI) initiative [45] should allow ASs to ignore announcements where the origin is invalid—that is, where some AS is attempting to use IP addresses it is not entitled to use [55]. This is an important step forward, and might tackle over 90% of "fat finger" problems.

But the cost of RPKI is significant. Every AS must take steps to document their title to their IP addresses, and that title must be registered and attested to by the Internet Registries. Then, every AS must extend their infrastructure to check the route announcements they receive against the register. What is more, the problem that RPKI tackles is, so far, largely a nuisance not a disaster. When some network manages to announce some routes it should not, this is noticed and fixed quite quickly, if it matters. Sometimes a network announces IP addresses nobody else is using—generally they are up to no good, but this does not actually disrupt the interconnection system. So the incentive to do something about the problem is currently weak, although the number of incidents is expected to rise when IPv4 addresses are finally exhausted in late 2011.

Further, a route may pass the checks supported by RPKI, and still be invalid. A network can announce routes for a block of IP addresses, complete with a valid origin, but do so only to disrupt or interfere with the traffic (apparently) on its way to its destination. The S-BGP extensions to BGP (first published in 1997 [40]) try to solve the problem more completely, and there have been revised proposals since [12]; however they make technical assumptions about routing (traffic greed and valley-free customer preferences) that don't hold in today's Internet. Details of a new initiative, BGPSEC, were announced in March 2011. The aim is that this should lead to IETF standards by 2013 and deployed code in routers thereafter [46].

During the standardisation process in 2011–2013 a key issue will be security economics. ASs see the cost of BGP security as high, and the benefit essentially zero until it is very widely deployed.

Ideally, implementation and deployment strategies will give local, incremental benefit, coupled with incentives for early adopters. One possible mechanism is for governments to use their purchasing power to bootstrap adoption; another is for routers to prefer signed routes [31].

Technical issues that must the studied during the standardisation phase include whether more secure BGP might, in fact, be bad for resilience. Adding cryptography to a system can make it brittle. The reason is that when recovering from an event, new and possibly temporary routes may be distributed in order to replace lost routes, and if the unusual routes are rejected, because they do not have the necessary credentials, then recovery will be harder.

Finally, BGPSEC will not be a silver bullet, there are many threats [39], but it should tackle about half of the things that can go wrong after RPKI has dealt with origin validation.

To sum up, most of the time BGP works wonderfully well, but there is plenty of scope to make it more secure and more robust. However, individual networks will get little direct benefit in the beginning from an improved BGP, despite the significant cost. We will probably need some new incentive to persuade networks to invest in more secure BGP, or a proposal for securing BGP that gives local benefits from incremental deployment.

12   Exercises ("War Games")

The practical approach to assessing the resilience of the interconnection system is to run large scale exercises in which plausible scenarios are tested. Such exercises have a number of advantages and benefits:

- They start with real world issues. These exercises are not cheap, so there is an incentive to be realistic: planners consider what really are the sorts of event that the system is expected to face.
- They can identify some dependencies on physical infrastructure. By requiring the participants to consider the effects of some infrastructure failure, an exercise may reveal previously unknown dependencies.
- They can identify cross-system dependencies. For example, how well network operations centres can communicate if the phone network fails, or how well field repairs proceed if the mobile phone network is unavailable?
- They exercise disaster recovery systems and procedures. This is generally a good learning experience for everybody involved, particularly as otherwise crisis management is generally ad hoc.

Such scenario testing has been done at a national level [23] and found to be valuable, and recently an exercise at a multi-national scale has also been proved to be valuable.

On 4th November 2010 the European Member States organised the first pan-European cyber exercise, called CYBER EUROPE 2010, which was facilitated by ENISA. The final ENISA report [25] explains the importance of such exercises and calls for future activities based on the lessons learned.

13   The "Tragedy of the Commons"

The resilience of the Internet interconnection system benefits everyone, but an individual network will not in general gain a net benefit if it increases its costs in order to contribute to the resilience of the whole.

This manifests itself in a number of ways:

- In Sect. 11 above, we discussed the various proposals for more secure forms of BGP from S-BGP in 1997 to BGPSEC in 2011, none of which has so far been deployed. There is little demand for something which is going to cost money to implement and whose direct benefit is limited.
- There exists best practice for filtering BGP route announcements [42], which, if universally applied, would reduce instances of invalid routes being propagated by BGP and disrupting the system. But these recommendations are difficult to implement and mostly benefit other networks, so are not often implemented.
- There is an IETF BCP[3] for filtering packets, to reduce "address spoofing", which would mitigate denial of service attacks [28]. These recommendations also mostly benefit others, so are not often implemented.
- A smaller global routing table would reduce the load on all BGP routers in the Internet, and leave more capacity to deal with unusual events. Nevertheless, the routing table is about 75% bigger than it needs to be [37], because some networks announce extra routes to reduce their own costs. Other networks could resist this by ignoring the extra routes, but that would cost time and effort to configure their routers, and would most likely be seen by their customers as a service failure (not as a noble act of public service).
- The system is still ill-prepared for IPv6 [35], despite the now imminent (c Q3 2011 [36]) exhaustion of IPv4 address space.

It is in the clear interest of each network to ensure that in normal circumstances "best efforts" means a high level of service, by adjusting interconnections and routing policy—each network has customers to serve and a reputation to maintain. Normal circumstances include the usual day-to-day failures and small incidents.

---

[3]An Internet Engineering Task Force (IETF) Best Common Practice (BCP) is as official as it gets on the Internet.

The central issue is that the security and resilience of the interconnection system is an externality as far as the networks that comprise it are concerned. It is not clear is that there is any incentive for network operators to put significant effort into considering the resilience of the interconnection system under extraordinary circumstances.

14 Regulation

Regulation is viewed with apprehension by the Internet community. Studies such as the one created by ENISA [24] are seen as stalking horses for regulatory interference, which is generally thought likely to be harmful. Despite having its origins in a project funded by DARPA, a US government agency, the Internet has developed since then in an environment that is largely free from regulation. There have been many local attempts at regulatory intervention, most of which are seen as harmful:

- The governments of many less developed countries attempt to censor the Internet, with varying degrees of success. The "Great Firewall of China" is much discussed, but many other states practice online censorship to a greater or lesser extent. It is not just that censorship itself is contrary to the mores of the Internet community—whose culture is greatly influenced by California, the home of many developers, vendors and service companies. Attempts at censorship can cause collateral damage, as when Pakistan advertised routes for YouTube in an attempt to censor it within their borders, and instead made it unavailable on much of the Internet for several hours.
- Where poor regulation leads to a lack of competition, access to the Internet is limited and relatively expensive. In many less developed countries, a local telecomms monopoly restricts wireline broadband access to urban elites, forcing the majority to rely on mobile access. However the problem is more subtle than "regulation bad, no regulation good". In a number of US cities, the diversity of broadband access is falling; cities that used to have three independent infrastructures (say from a phone company, a cable company and an electricity company) may find themselves over time with two, or even just one. In better-regulated developed countries (such as much of Europe) local loop unbundling yields price competition at least, thus mitigating access costs, even if physical diversity is harder. Finally, there are few countries which impose a universal service provision on service providers; its lack can lead to a "digital divide" between populated areas with broadband provision, and rural areas without.
- There has been continued controversy over surveillance for law-enforcement and intelligence purposes. In the "Crypto Wars" of the 1990s, the Clinton administration tried to control cryptography, which the industry saw as threatening not just privacy but the growth of e-commerce and other online services. The Communications Assistance for Law Enforcement Act (CALEA) was passed in

1994 to mandate the co-operation of telecommunications carriers in wiretapping phone calls. The EU has a controversial Data Retention Directive that is up for revision in 2011 and there is interest in both the UK and USA in how wiretapping should be updated for an age not only of VoIP but diverse messaging platforms. This creates conflicts of interest with customers, raises issues of human rights, and leads to arguments about payment and subsidy.

- Governments which worry about Critical National Infrastructure may treat Internet regulation as a matter of National Security, introducing degrees of secrecy and shadowy organisations, which does nothing to dispel concerns about motivation—not helped by a tendency to talk about the problem in apocalyptic terms [74].[4]

Whatever the motivation, government policies are often formulated with insufficient scientific and technical input. They often manage to appear clueless, and in some cases will make things worse. The present study is an attempt to help alleviate this problem.

We have identified a number of areas where the market does not appear to provide incentives to maintain the resilience of the interconnection system at a socially optimal level. However, any attempt to tackle any of the issues by regulation is hampered by a number of factors:

- The lack of good information about the state and behaviour of the system. It is hard to determine how material a given issue may be. It is hard to determine what effect a given initiative is likely to have—good or bad.
- The scale and complexity of the system. Scale may make local initiatives ineffective, while complexity means that it is hard to predict how the system will respond or adapt to a given initiative.
- The dynamic nature of the system. Content delivery networks have been around for many years, but their emergence as a major component of the Internet is relatively recent; this is a testament to the system's ability to adapt quickly (in this case, to the popularity of streamed video).

Up until now, the lack of incentives to provide resilience (and in particular to provide excess capacity) has been relatively unimportant: the Internet has been growing so rapidly that it has been very far from equilibrium, with a huge endowment of surplus capacity during the dotcom boom and significant capacity enhancements due to optical communications technology improvements since then. This cannot go on forever.

One caveat: we must point out that the privatisation, liberalisation and restructuring of utilities worldwide has led to institutional fragmentation in a number of critical infrastructure industries which could in theory suffer degradation of reliability and resilience for the same general microeconomic reasons we discuss

---

[4]For a popular perception of the problems that government is grappling with see *Fight Cyber War Before Planes Fall Out of Sky* [79].

in the context of the Internet. Yet studies of the electricity, water and telecomms industries in a number of countries have failed to find a deficit thus far [22]. In practice, utilities have managed to cope by a combination of anticipatory risk management and public-private partnerships. However it is sometimes necessary for government to act as a "lender of last resort". If a router fails, we can fall back on another router, but if a market fails—as with the California electricity market—there is no fallback other than the state.

In conclusion, it may be some time before regulatory action is called for to protect the resilience of the Internet, but it may well be time to start thinking about what might be involved. Regulating a new technology is hard; an initiative designed to improve today's system may be irrelevant to tomorrow's, or, worse, stifle competition and innovation. For example, the railways steadily improved their efficiency from their inception in the 1840s until regulation started in the late nineteenth century, after which their efficiency declined steadily until competition from road freight arrived in the 1940s [57].

The prudent course of action for regulators today is to start working to understand the Internet interconnection ecosystem [17].

The most important package of work is to increase transparency, by supporting consistent, thorough, investigation of major outages and the publication of the findings, and by supporting long term measurement of network performance. The second package is to fund key research in topics such as distributed intrusion detection and the design of security mechanisms with practical paths to deployment, and the third is to promote best practice, to encourage diverse service provision and to promote the testing of equipment. The fourth package includes the preparation and relationship-building through a series of Private Public Partnerships (PPPs) for resilience. Modest and constructive engagement of this kind will enable regulators to build relationships with industry stakeholders and leave everyone in a much better position to avoid, or delay, difficult and uninformed regulation.

Regulatory intervention must after all be evidence-based; and while there is evidence of a number of issues, the workings of this huge, complex and dynamic system are so poorly understood that there is not enough evidence yet on which to base major regulatory intervention with sufficient confidence.

15 Recommendations

The recommendations come in four groups. The first group is aimed at understanding failures better, so that all may learn the lessons.

Recommendation 1: Incident Investigation

An independent body should thoroughly investigate all major incidents and report publicly on the causes, effects and lessons to be learned. The appropriate framework should be the result of a consultation with the industry and the appropriate regulatory authorities coming into a constructive dialogue. Incident investigation might be undertaken by an industry association, by a national regulator or by a body at the European level, such as ENISA. The last option would require funding to support the work, and, perhaps, powers to obtain information from operators—under suitable safeguards to protect commercially sensitive information.

Recommendation 2: Network Performance Measurement

Europe should promote and support consistent, long-term and comprehensive network performance measurement. At present some realtime monitoring is done by companies such as Arbor Networks and Renesys, and some more is done by academic projects—which tend to languish once their funding runs out. This patchwork is insufficient. There should be sustainable funding to support the long-term collection, processing, storage and publication of performance data. This also has a network management/law enforcement angle in that real-time monitoring of the system could help detect unusual route announcements and other undesirable activity.

The second group of recommendations aims at securing funding for research in topics related to resilience—with an emphasis not just on the design of security mechanisms, but on developing an understanding of how solutions can be deployed in the real world.

Recommendation 3: Research Network Performance and Resilience

Europe should sponsor research into better ways to measure and understand the performance and resilience of huge, multi-layered networks. This is the research aspect of the second recommendation; once that provides access to good data, the data should help clever people to come up with better metrics.

Recommendation 4: Develop and Deploy Secure Interdomain Routing

Europe should support the development of effective, practical mechanisms which have enough incentives for deployment. This may mean mechanisms that give local benefit to the firms that deploy them, even where deployment is incremental; it may require technical mechanisms to be supplemented by policy tools such as the use of public-sector purchasing power, subsidies, liability shifts, or other kinds of regulation.

Recommendation 5: Research into AS Incentives

Europe should support research into economic and legal mechanisms to increase the resilience of the Internet. Perhaps a system of contracts can be constructed to secure the interconnection system, starting with the connections between the major transit providers and spreading from the core to the edges. Alternatively, researchers might consider whether liability rules might have a similar effect. If the failure of a specific type of router caused loss of Internet service leading to damage and loss of life, the Product Liability Directive 85/374/EC would already let victims sue the vendor; but there is no such provision relating to the failure of a service from a transit provider.

The third group of recommendations aims to promote best practice.

Recommendation 6: Sponsor Best Practice

Europe should sponsor and promote best practice in network management. Where best practice exists its adoption may be hampered by practical and economic issues. The public sector may be able to help, but it is not enough to declare for motherhood and apple pie! It can contribute various incentives, such as through its considerable purchasing power. For that to be effective, purchasers need a way to tell good service. The first three of our recommendations can help, but there are some direct measures of quality too.

Recommendation 7: Independently Test Equipment and Protocols

Europe should sponsor the independent testing of routing equipment and protocols. The risk of systemic failure would be reduced by independent testing of equipment and protocols, looking particularly for how well these perform in unusual circumstances, and whether they can be disrupted, suborned, overloaded or corrupted.

Recommendation 8: Regular Disaster Recovery Exercises

The consultation noted that these are effective in improving resilience at local and national levels. European Member States should consider involvement in regular Europe-wide exercises, which ENISA has already expressed a willingness to facilitate. These might provide an umbrella for a number of useful activities, such as investigating what extra preparation might be required to provide more routes in a crisis.

The final group of recommendations aims at engaging policymakers, customers and the public.

Recommendation 9: Contingency Plans for Transit Market Failure

It is possible that the current twenty-odd largest transit providers might consolidate down to a handful,[5] in which case they might start to exercise market power and need to be regulated like any other concentrated industry. If this were to happen just as the industry uses up the last of its endowment of dark fibre from the dotcom boom, then prices might rise sharply. European policymakers should start the conversation about what to do then. Action might involve not just a number of European actors but also national regulators from other parts of the world (such as the US Federal Communications Commission). Recommendations 1, 2, 3, and 5 will prepare the ground technically so that regulators will not be working entirely in the dark, but we also need political preparation.

Recommendation 10: Traffic Prioritisation

If, in a crisis, some Internet traffic is to be given priority, and other Internet traffic is to suffer discrimination, then the basis for this choice requires public debate—and mechanisms to achieve it need to be developed. Given the number of interests seeking to censor the Internet for various reasons, any decisions on prioritisation will have to be taken openly and transparently, or public confidence will be lost.

Recommendation 11: Greater Transparency

Finally, transparency is not just about openness in taking decisions on regulation or on emergency procedures. It would greatly help resilience if end-users and corporate customers could be educated to understand the issues and send the right market signals. Further investigation is needed on mechanisms that can be developed to give the means to make an informed choice. This might involve combining the outputs from recommendations 2, 3, 5, 6, and 7 into a "quality certification mark" scheme.

---

[5]Just as the final version of the ENISA report was submitted, Level 3 (the transit provider with the largest market share) announced that it was acquiring Global Crossing (the second largest market share) for $3 billion ($1.1 of which is debt assumption), giving the merged company just over half of the market [86].

16 Conclusions

The Internet has been remarkably resilient up till now, and has shrugged off quite major incidents such as Hurricane Katrina and 9/11. However our civilisation has come to depend on the Internet, and it is now just as much a critical utility as water or electricity.

We have studied what sort of failures or attacks might cause significant service outages, and we have concluded that while the Internet is in pretty good shape, and does not need regulation in the way that electricity markets are regulated, there are still some things that the policy makers and industry might usefully do to improve its robustness and resilience. These include understanding failures better, funding research in resilience, promoting good practices and engaging with both public and private sectors in a constructive dialogue.

These activities will enable the decision makers in Europe and beyond to understand the Internet better, so that whether regulation is avoided, or is required in five or ten years' time, they will be in a position to propose informed and effective policies.

Acknowledgements We would particularly like to thank all the industry, academic and public sector stakeholders that took part in the survey we conducted as part of the study.

References

1. Agarwal S, Chuah C, Bhattacharyya S, Diot C (2004) The impact of BGP dynamics on intra-domain traffic. SIGMETRICS/Performance'04, ACM, pp 319–330
2. Akamai Inc. (2010) Facts & Figures. http://www.akamai.com/html/about/facts_figures.html#6
3. Alleman J, Liebenau J (2004) Network resilience and its regulatory inhibitors. Bohlin E et al. (eds) Global economy and digital society, Elsevier, Amsterdam, pp 379–394
4. Alperovitch D (2010) US-based internet traffic redirected to China. McAfee blog. http://blogs.mcafee.com/mcafee-labs/u-s-based-internet-traffic-redirected-to-china
5. Alperovitch D (2010) April route hijack: sifting through the confusion. McAfee blog. http://blogs.mcafee.com/mcafee-labs/april-route-hijack-sifting-through-the-confusion-2
6. Augustin B, Krishnamurthy B, Willinger W (2009) IXPs: mapped? IMC'09, pp 336–349
7. Blumenfeld L (2003) Dissertation could be security threat. Washington Post. http://www.washingtonpost.com/ac2/wp-dyn/A23689-2003Jul7
8. Blunk LJ (2005) New BGP analysis tools and a look at the AS9121 incident. http://iepg.org/march2005/bgptools+as9121.pdf
9. Bono VJ (1997) 7007 Explanation and apology. NANOG mailing list. http://www.merit.edu/mail.archives/nanog/1997-04/msg00444.html
10. Brown MA (2008) Pakistan hijacks YouTube. Renesys blog. http://www.renesys.com/blog/2008/02/pakistan_hijacks_youtube_1.shtml
11. Bush R, Maennel O, Roughan M, Uhlig S (2009) Internet optometry: assessing the broken glasses in internet reachability. IMC'09, pp 242–253
12. Butler K, Farley TR, McDaniel P, Rexford J (2010) A survey of BGP security issues and solutions. Proc IEEE 98(1):100–122
13. Caesar M, Rexford J (2005) BGP routing policies in ISP networks. IEEE Network 19(6):5–11

14. Chadd A (2006) Murphy's Law strikes again: AS7007. Murphy's law mailing list. http://lists. ucc.gu.uwa.edu.au/pipermail/lore/2006-August/000040.html
15. Chang H, Willinger W (2006) Difficulties measuring the internet's AS-level ecosystem. Information sciences and systems, pp 1479–1483
16. Cisco Systems (2010) Cisco visual networking index: forecast and methodology, 2009–2014. White paper. http://www.cisco.com/en/US/solutions/collateral/ns341/ns525/ns537/ns705/ ns827/white_paper_c11-481360.pdf
17. Claffy KC (2008) Ten things lawyers should know about the internet. http://www.caida.org/ publications/papers/2008/lawyers_top_ten/
18. CNet News Staff (1997) Router glitch cuts net access. CNet News. http://news.cnet.com/2100-1033-279235.html
19. Cowie J (2010) How to build a cybernuke. Renesys blog. http://www.renesys.com/blog/2010/ 04/how-to-build-a-cybernuke.shtml
20. Cowie JH, Ogielski AT, Premore BJ, Smith EA, Underwood T (2003) Impact of the 2003 blackouts on internet communications. Renesys. http://www.renesys.com/tech/reports/ Renesys_BlackoutReport.pdf
21. Cowie J, Popescu A, Underwood T (2005) Impact of hurricane Katrina on internet infrastructure. Renesys. http://www.renesys.com/tech/presentations/pdf/Renesys-Katrina-Report-9sep2005.pdf
22. De Bruijne M (2007) Systems that should have failed: critical infrastructure protection in an institutionally fragmented environment. J Contingencies Crisis Manag 15(1):1–29
23. ENISA (2009) Good practice guide on national exercises. ENISA technical report. http://www. enisa.europa.eu/act/res/policies/good-practices-1/exercises/national-exercise-good-practice-guide
24. ENISA (2011) Inter-X: resilience of the internet interconnection ecosystem. ENISA technical report. Available at http://www.enisa.europa.eu/act/res/other-areas/inter-x.
25. ENISA (2011) Cyber Europe 2010—evaluation report. ENISA technical report. Available at http://www.enisa.europa.eu/act/res/cyber-europe-2010/cyber-europe-2010-report
26. Faratin P, Clark DD, Bauer S, Lehr W, Gilmore PW, Berger A (2008) The growing complexity of internet interconnection. Comm Strat 72:51–71
27. Feamster N, Winick J, Rexford J (2004) A model of BGP routing for network engineering. SIGMETRICS/Performance'04, ACM, pp 331–342
28. Ferguson P, Senie D (2000) Network ingress filtering: defeating denial of service attacks which employ IP source address spoofing. RFC 2827, RFC Editor
29. Fried M, Klemming L (2008) Severed cables in mediterranean disrupt communication. Bloomberg http://www.bloomberg.com/apps/news?pid=newsarchive&sid=aBa0lTN.dcoQ
30. Gill P, Arlitt M, Li Z, Mahanti A (2008) The flattening internet topology: natural evolution. Unsightly barnacles or contrived collapse? Ninth passive and active measurement conference (PAM)
31. Gill P, Schapira M, Goldberg S (2011) Let the market drive deployment: a strategy for transitioning to BGP security. Boston University Computer Science, Technical report BUCS-TR-2011-003. http://www.cs.bu.edu/~goldbe/papers/sbgpTrans.html
32. Griffin TG, Premore BJ (2001) An experimental analysis of BGP convergence time. ICNP'01, pp 53–61
33. Griffin TG, Shepherd FB, Wilfong G (2002) The stable paths problem and interdomain routing. IEEE ACM T Network 10(2):232–243
34. Hollnagel E, Woods DD, Leveson N (2006) Resilience engineering: concepts and precepts. Ashgate Publishing, Surrey, UK
35. Huston G (2009) The ISP column: is the transition to IPv6 a "market failure"? http://www. potaroo.net/ispcol/2009-09/v6trans.pdf
36. Huston GIPv4 Address Report.http://www.potaroo.net/tools/ipv4/
37. Huston G et al. CIDR Report. http://www.cidr-report.org
38. ISC. The ISC domain survey. http://www.isc.org/solutions/survey

39. Kent S (2011) Threat model for BGP path security. Working draft. http://tools.ietf.org/html/draft-kent-bgpsec-threats-01
40. Kent S, Lynn C, Seo K (2000) Secure border gateway protocol (S-BGP). IEEE J Sel Area Comm 18(4):582–592
41. Kitano H (2002) Systems biology: a brief overview. Science 295:1662–1664
42. Kuhn R, Sriram K, Montgomery D (2007) Border gateway protocol security—recommendations of the National Institute of Standards and Technology. NIST. http://csrc.nist.gov/publications/nistpubs/800-54/SP800-54.pdf
43. Kushman N, Kandula S, Katabi D (2007) Can you hear me now?! It must be BGP. SIGCOMM Comput Commun Rev 37:75–84
44. Labovitz C, Iekel-Johnson S, McPherson D, Oberheide J, Jahanian F (2010) Internet inter-domain traffic. SIGCOMM'10, ACM, pp 75–86
45. Lepinski M, Kent S (2011) An infrastructure to support secure internet routing. Working draft. http://tools.ietf.org/html/draft-ietf-sidr-arch-12
46. Lepinski M, Turner S (2011) An overview of BGPSEC. Working draft. http://tools.ietf.org/html/draft-lepinski-bgpsec-overview-00
47. Level 3 Communications, Inc. 2006 FORM 10-K For the fiscal year ended. http://lvlt.client.shareholder.com/secfiling.cfm?filingID=1104659-07-88481
48. Level 3 Communications, Inc. (2008) FORM 10-K For the fiscal year ended. http://lvlt.client.shareholder.com/secfiling.cfm?filingID=1047469-09-2002
49. Level 3 Communications, Inc. (2010) FORM 10-K For the fiscal year ended. http://lvlt.client.shareholder.com/secfiling.cfm?filingID=1047469-11-1410
50. Leyden J (2010) China routing snafu briefly mangles interweb—cockup, not conspiracy. The register. http://www.theregister.co.uk/2010/04/09/china_bgp_interweb_snafu/
51. Longstaff P Security, resilience, and communication in unpredictable environments such as terrorism, Natural disasters and complex technology. (2005) http://pirp.harvard.edu/pubs_pdf/longsta/longsta-p05-3.pdf
52. Magnuson S (2010) Cyber experts have proof that China has hijacked US-based internet traffic: UPDATED. National defense blog. http://www.nationaldefensemagazine.org/blog/Lists/Posts/Post.aspx?ID=249
53. McCullagh D (2008) How Pakistan knocked YouTube offline (and how to make sure it never happens again). CNet. http://news.cnet.com/8301-10784_3-9878655-7.html
54. McPherson D (2008) Internet routing insecurity: Pakistan nukes YouTube? Arbor networks blog http://asert.arbornetworks.com/2008/02/internet-routing-insecuritypakistan-nukes-youtube/
55. Mohapatra P, Scudder J, Bush R, Austein R (Eds.) (2011) BGP prefix origin validation. Working draft. http://tools.ietf.org/html/draft-ietf-sidr-pfx-validate-01
56. Norton B (2010) Internet transit prices—historical and projected. http://drpeering.net/white-papers/Internet-Transit-Pricing-Historical-And-Projected.php
57. Odlyzko A (2010) Collective hallucinations and inefficient markets: the British railway mania of the 1840s. http://www.dtc.umn.edu/~odlyzko/doc/hallucinations.pdf
58. Odlyzko A. Minnesota Internet Traffic Studies (MINTS). http://www.dtc.umn.edu/mints/
59. Oliveira R, Pei D, Willinger W, Zhang B, Zhang L (2010) The (in)completeness of the observed internet AS-level structure. IEEE ACM T Network 18:109–112
60. Partridge C et al. (2002) The internet under crisis conditions: learning from September 11. The National Academies Press, Washington
61. Popescu A (2008) Deja Vu all over again: cables cut in the mediterranean. Renesys blog. http://www.renesys.com/blog/2008/12/deja-vu-all-over-again-cables.shtml
62. Popescu AC, Premore BJ, Underwood T (2005) The anatomy of a leak: AS9121. NANOG 34 http://www.renesys.com/tech/presentations/pdf/renesys-nanog34.pdf
63. Quoitin B, Pelsser C, Swinnen L, Bonaventure O, Uhlig S (2003) Interdomain traffic engineering with BGP. IEEE Comm Mag 41(5):122–128
64. Radovcic S (2010) European Internet Exchange Association 2010 Report on European IXPs. https://www.euro-ix.net/resources/reports/euro-ix_report_2010.pdf

65. Rekhter Y, Li T, Hares S (2006) A border gateway protocol 4 (BGP-4). RFC4271, RFC Editor
66. RIPE NCC (2008) YouTube hijacking: A RIPE NCC RIS case study. http://www.ripe.net/news/study-youtube-hijacking.html
67. Romijn E (2010) RIPE NCC and Duke University BGP Experiment. http://labs.ripe.net/Members/erik/ripe-ncc-and-duke-university-bgp-experiment
68. Romijn E (2010) Re: did your BGP crash today? NANOG mailing list. http://www.merit.edu/mail.archives/nanog/msg11505.html
69. Siganos G, Faloutsos M (2004) Analysing BGP policies: methodology and tool. INFO-COM'04, IEEE, pp 1640–1651
70. Smith DJ (2005) Reliability, maintainability and risk. 7th edn. Elsevier, Amsterdam
71. Soares M (2009) Brazilian blackout traced to sooty insulators, not hackers. Wired. http://www.wired.com/threatlevel/2009/11/brazil_blackout/
72. Telegeography 2008 Four international cable breaks in a week. http://www.telegeography.com/cu/article.php?article_id=21567
73. Telegeography (2010) IP transit prices continue their downward trend. http://www.telegeography.com/cu/article.php?article_id=35206
74. UK Cabinet Office (2010) Cyber security. Fact Sheet 18. http://download.cabinetoffice.gov.uk/sdsr/factsheet18-cyber-security.pdf
75. Underwood T (2005) Internet-wide catastrophe—last year. Renesys blog. http://www.renesys.com/blog/2005/12/internetwide_nearcatastrophela.shtml
76. Wagner A (2008) Robustness and evolvability: a paradox resolved. Proc Biol Sci 275:91–100
77. Wang F, Mao, Z.M., Wang J, Gao L, Bush R (2006) A measurement study on the impact of routing events on end-to-end internet path performance. SIGCOMM'06, ACM, pp 375–386
78. Wang L, Zhao X, Pei D, Bush R, Massey D, Mankin A, Wu SF, Zhang L (2002) Observation and analysis of BGP behavior under stress. IMW'02, ACM, pp 183–195
79. Wilson G (2010) Fight cyber war before planes fall out of sky. The Sun. http://www.thesun.co.uk/sol/homepage/news/3186185/Security-chiefs-warn-Britain-must-protect-itself-against-cyber-warfare-amid-government-cuts.html
80. Xie L, Smith P, Banfield M, Leopold H, Sterbenz J, Hutchinson D (2005) Towards resilient networks using programmable networking technologies. IFIP IWAN
81. Yang YR, Xie H, Wang H, Silberschatz A, Kroshnamurthy A, Liu Y, Li LE (2005) On route selection for interdomain traffic engineering. IEEE Network 19(6):20–27
82. Yannuzzi M, Masip-Bruin X, Bonaventure O (2005) Open issues in interdomain routing: a survey. IEEE Network 19(6):49–56
83. Zmijewski E (2008) Mediterranean cable break—Part II. Renesys blog. http://www.renesys.com/blog/2008/01/mediterranean-cable-break-part-1.shtml
84. Zmijewski E (2008) Mediterranean cable break—Part III. Renesys blog. http://www.renesys.com/blog/2008/02/mediterranean-cable-break-part.shtml
85. Zmijewski E (2008) Mediterranean cable break—Part IV. Renesys blog. http://www.renesys.com/blog/2008/02/mediterranean-cable-break-part-3.shtml
86. Zmijewski E (2011) A closer look at the "Level 3 + Global Crossing" union. CircleID. http://www.circleid.com/posts/20110414_a_closer_look_at_the_level_3_and_global_crossing_union/

Modeling Internet-Scale Policies for Cleaning up Malware

Steven Hofmeyr, Tyler Moore, Stephanie Forrest, Benjamin Edwards, and George Stelle

Abstract An emerging consensus among policy makers is that interventions undertaken by Internet Service Providers are the best way to counter the rising incidence of malware. However, assessing the suitability of countermeasures at this scale is hard. In this paper, we use an agent-based model, called ASIM, to investigate the impact of policy interventions at the Autonomous System level of the Internet. For instance, we find that coordinated intervention by the 0.2%-biggest ASes is more effective than uncoordinated efforts adopted by 30% of all ASes. Furthermore, countermeasures that block malicious transit traffic appear more effective than ones that block outgoing traffic. The model allows us to quantify and compare positive externalities created by different countermeasures. Our results give an initial indication of the types and levels of intervention that are most cost-effective at large scale.

1 Introduction

Many Internet-connected computers are infected with malicious software, or *malware*. Malware can harm the infected computer user directly, for example, by installing a keystroke logger to collect confidential information surreptitiously. It can also place the machine into a botnet consisting of thousands or even millions

S. Hofmeyr (✉)
Lawrence Berkeley National Laboratory, Berkeley, CA 94720, USA
e-mail: shofmeyr@lbl.gov

T. Moore
Harvard University, Cambridge, MA 02138, USA
e-mail: tmoore@seas.harvard.edu

S. Forrest • B. Edwards • and G. Stelle
University of New Mexico, Albuquerque, NM 87131, USA
e-mail: forrest@cs.unm.edu; bedwards@cs.unm.edu; stelleg@cs.unm.edu

B. Schneier (ed.), *Economics of Information Security and Privacy III*,
DOI 10.1007/978-1-4614-1981-5_7,
© Springer Science+Business Media New York 2013

of computers that carry out attacks of the operator's choosing, such as sending email spam or launching denial-of-service attacks. Infected machines can also become vectors for further malware spread, as in the case of Conficker, which initiates attacks from infected machines to recruit new computers to the botnet [31].

In economic terms, malware imposes negative externalities by harming innocent third parties [3]. Negative externalities are a form of market failure, which suggests that there will be an oversupply of the resource (in this case, malware) in equilibrium. Policy makers are interested in correcting this market failure to reduce the social cost of malware. Although many stakeholders could potentially help control the spread of malware, the emerging consensus is that Internet Service Providers (ISPs) are best positioned to intervene [2, 15, 27].

It is less clear, however, what kind of intervention is most appropriate. The possibilities range from simply notifying infected customers to actively quarantining them until the malware has been demonstrably removed. It is difficult to gauge the impact of policies and ISP-level interventions until they have been tried, and it is expensive (both financially and in terms of political capital) to adopt industry-wide policies. Consequently, it is important to get it right the first time.

One way to address this issue is through modeling. In this paper we model potential intervention strategies for controlling malware and compare their likely impact. We use an agent-based model called ASIM [20], which represents the Internet at the autonomous system (AS) level, the level at which policy interventions are being actively considered. ASIM incorporates traffic, which is key to understanding the spread of malware, geography, which is key to investigating country-level effects, and economics, which is is key to understanding the cost and benefits of interventions.

Through a series of experiments we study several questions, reporting some findings that are unsurprising and others that are counterintuitive. For example, our experiments show, as we would expect, that a few of the largest ISPs acting in concert are more effective than a randomly chosen subset of all ASes intervening unilaterally. However, the numbers involved are more surprising: Intervention by the top 0.2% of ASes is more effective than intervention by 30% of ASes chosen at random. Our results also suggest that when only the largest ASes intervene, it is better to simply filter out malicious traffic (especially transit traffic) than to attempt to remediate end-user infections. We also explore briefly the impact of interventions on the growth of the network, and demonstrate that policies that are beneficial in the short term could be harmful in the long-term. For example, the collateral damage caused by blacklisting malicious traffic sources promotes those ASes that profit from receiving more malicious traffic.

The remainder of the paper is structured as follows. We review in greater detail the policy interventions currently under consideration worldwide in Sect. 2. In Sect. 3, we explain how ASIM works and how the cybersecurity interventions are implemented. In Sect. 4 we describe how we empirically validated ASIM, and Sect. 5 reports experimental results. We discuss related work in Sect. 6 and the findings and limitations in Sect. 7. Finally, we conclude in Sect. 8.

2 Policy Interventions

There are several reasons why ISPs are a promising point of intervention. First, ISPs are the gatekeeper to the Internet for many computers and thus in a unique position to inspect traffic to and from their customers. Infections are often detected remotely by scanning for outgoing connections to known command-and-control servers used by botnet operators [24]. In this scenario, only the ISP can link an IP address to customer details, a crucial step if customers are to be notified and assisted.

A second reason is that ample opportunity exists for reducing the prevalence of malware by enlisting the help of ISPs. Using several years' worth of data on computers sending spam (a natural proxy for botnet activity), van Eeten et al. [15] found that most compromised computers were customers of legitimate ISPs, and that infection rates vary dramatically across ISPs and countries. Their evidence suggests that differences in security countermeasures, not merely target selection by attackers, can affect infection rates at ISPs.

However, incentives for ISPs to implement security countermeasures are weak. As mentioned above, much of the harm caused by malware is externalized, but the cost of intervention would fall largely on the ISP. Although the infected host is often unharmed by malware, the ISP is definitely not directly harmed. However, the cost of notification and cleanup can be substantial. According to an OECD study, one medium-sized ISP reported that it spent 1–2% of its total revenue handling security-related support calls [14]. Thus, there is a strong disincentive for ISPs to notify infected customers and also pay for any resulting support calls.

Despite weak incentives, ISPs in many countries have begun exploring a variety of remedial interventions, either with government cooperation or to preempt the imposition of more burdensome regulatory requirements. Interventions by ISPs usually do not include the detection of malware, only remediation once malware is detected. For notifications of misbehaving or compromised customers, ISPs rely on third parties, such as the operators of email blacklists, botnet trackers, other ISPs and security companies,

Once a threat is identified, most ISPs choose to do nothing, waiting until the abuse team has time to act or for additional warnings about the customer to accrue. However, some ISPs have begun to notify customers. In the US, Comcast automatically notifies customers of infections with a browser pop-up that links to instructions for removing the malware [10]. The customers are responsible for completing the clean-up process, and it is inevitable that not all malware will be removed successfully even after notification. As a further step, Comcast has partnered with Symantec to offer remediation by a skilled technician for $100. A similar approach is being rolled out by Australian ISPs [6].

A more aggressive step is to place infected computers into "quarantine." Once in quarantine, users are required to download and install anti-virus software and malware removal tools. They leave the quarantine only after the security software is installed and the computer passes a network-based scan for malware. Quarantine is considerably more expensive than the notification-only approaches, and the the ISPs that use them do so only for a minority of affected customers. Recently, the Dutch ISPs announced a signed agreement to notify and quarantine affected customers [16].

Both ISPs and policy makers have realized that tackling widespread infection can be made more effective if ISPs coordinate their interventions. In both the Dutch and Australian case, many ISPs have joined together in common action, prodded by their governments. This collective action is designed in part to allay the fear that customers might switch providers rather than fix the underlying problem.

Some countries are weighing more active intervention. If the cost of customer support is really the greatest impediment to ISP action, then the German government's decision to establish and subsidize a nationwide call center could really help [21]. Under this plan, ISPs will identify infected customers and pass along the information to the call center. Clayton describes a proposal under consideration by Luxembourg to subsidize the cost of voluntary cleanup whenever a customer has been notified of infection [9]. Instead of such "carrot"-based incentives, "sticks" could also be tried. Anderson et al. recommended that the European Commission introduce fixed penalties for ISPs that do not expeditiously comply with notifications of compromised machines present on their networks [2].

Finally, policy makers could coordinate their defenses by aggregating notifications of infection. A survey of Dutch ISPs revealed that they notify or quarantine only about 10% of infected customers [13] even though they claim to notify all customers known to be infected. This occurs because their individual lists of infections are incomplete. Data incompleteness is a widespread problem in information security [26], as firms often jealously guard their incident information as trade secrets. To combat this trend, the Australian Internet Security Initiative now aggregates data on compromised machines into a single feed and passes it along to Australian ISPs [6].

3 Model Description

ASIM [20] is an agent-based model of Internet growth at the Autonomous System (AS) level. ASes roughly correspond to ISPs. While there are differences between ASes and ISPs (e.g., a single ISP can use several AS numbers), more extensive and reliable data is available describing ASes than ISPs. This eases empirical validation and explains why most of the literature has studied Internet topology at the AS level. We summarize the important features of ASIM here, highlighting differences between the original implementation and the version used in this paper.

ASIM is based on highly simplified implementations of four key features of ASes: network structure, traffic flow, geography, and economics. These features are sufficient to enable ASIM to generate networks with topologies, dynamics, and spatial distributions similar to those of the Internet. There are conceptual similarities between ASIM and some earlier Internet models such as HOT [7, 8], although many of the details are different. For example, ASIM adds explicit economic considerations and accounts directly for population density.

ASIM attempts to reproduce large-scale features of the AS level of the Internet by modeling localized and well-understood network interactions. Instead of simply reproducing a macroscopic pattern using statistical fitting or phenomenological models, ASIM specifies a set of primitive components (the agents) and interaction rules that mimic the architecture of the real system. The model is run as a simulation, and macroscopic behaviors (e.g., degree distribution) are observed and compared to real-world data. The objective is to provide a parsimonious explanation of how a system works by hypothesizing a small set of simple but relevant mechanisms.

In ASIM each AS is an economic agent, which manages traffic over a geographically extended network (referred to as a *sub-network* to distinguish it from the network of ASes) and profits from the traffic that flows through its network. We assume a network user population distributed over a two-dimensional grid of locations. Traffic is generated between source and destination with a probability that is a function of the population profile. The model is initialized with one agent that spans one grid location. At each time step a new agent is added to a single location. As time progresses, each agent may extend its sub-network to other locations, so that the sub-networks reach a larger fraction of the population. This creates more traffic, which generates profit, which is then reinvested into further network expansion. In addition, agents link to each other, potentially routing traffic between sub-networks other than their own. A necessary, but not sufficient, condition for two agents to be connected is that they overlap in at least one location. Through positive feedback, the network grows until it covers the entire population.

For this paper, we have reimplemented ASIM in order to make it run efficiently in parallel.[1] In the process, we have simplified the model, without reducing the accuracy with which the model simulates AS-like networks. The major changes are described below.

3.1 Simplifying the Original ASIM

In the original model described in Holme et al. [20], a variable number of agents could be added every time step, sufficient to maintain the correct average degree. In the new model, we simply add one agent per iteration, regardless. This follows realistic observed growth curves where the number of new agents grows at an almost perfectly linear rate. In our analysis of the real world data, we find that about 5.5 new ASes are added per day, so in our simulation, one time step is the equivalent of approximately 4.4 hours. Each new agent is added to a single, already occupied location,[2] chosen at random (weighted according to population).

---

[1] Code available at http://ftg.lbl.gov/projects/asim.

[2] Except for the very first agent, of course.

Instead of a packet-switched model, we use the gravity model [19]. For the gravity model, the traffic flow T between a pair of agents A and B is

$$T(A,B) = \frac{pop(A)pop(B)}{d(A,B)^2},$$

where, $pop(A)$ is the population served by A, $pop(X)$ is the population served by B, and $d(A,B)$ is the shortest path distance on the AS graph from A to B. Once we have determined the flow between A and B, we propagate it across the graph on the shortest path and every agent along that path gets its count of traffic increased accordingly. If there are multiple shortest paths, we randomly choose one. This traffic flow computation is performed for every pair of agents.

The traffic model is run every 16 time steps, corresponding to every three days of simulation time. Computing paths and carrying out traffic flow is expensive and most paths do not change significantly in the short term. We find experimentally that running the traffic model every 16 time steps provides a good balance between computational overhead and maintaining accuracy. Note that there is no notion of capacity, as there was in the original model.

There are two major differences in the modeling of geography. First, we disregard geographic distance, i.e. the cost of expanding to a new location is constant, regardless of where an agent expands to. By contrast, in the original model, the greater the distance from an agent's existing locations to a new location, the higher the cost of expansion. Second, in the new ASIM, an agent expands to a randomly chosen location, weighted by populace, regardless of how many other agents exist at that location. This differs from the original model, where the location chosen was the one with the highest shared[3] population within reach.

The mechanism for earning revenue in the new implementation is very similar to the original model. In the original model, an agent earns money for every packet it transits. In the new ASIM, we do not have a packet-switched model, and so an agent simply earns money every iteration proportional to the volume of traffic that it transits in either direction.

It does not cost an agent to link, unlike in the original model. There are two circumstances in which new links are added. First, when a new agent is placed at a location, it is linked to an agent that is chosen uniformly at random from those already at that location. This ensures the graph remains connected. Second, as in the original model, a number of links is added on every iteration, sufficient to maintain the desired average degree. In this case, when a link is added, the source is chosen uniformly at random from all agents, and the destination is chosen by first choosing an occupied location (weighted according to population), and then selecting uniformly at random one of the agents at that location. If the source does not exist at that location, it expands to that location. This ensures that agents can only link if they share a location, as in the original model.

---

[3]The population of the location, divided by the number of agents with presence at that location.

3.2 Adding Cybersecurity to ASIM

We use ASIM to compare the effectiveness of different policy interventions that counter the proliferation of malware infections. For simplicity, we assume that every AS can implement interventions, i.e. we do not focus on ISPs alone. We define insecurity by assigning a *wickedness rate* to each AS: the fraction of machines that are infected with malware. Depending on its size, each AS has a corresponding *wickedness level*: the absolute number of infected machines. Sometimes we will simply refer to wickedness as an abbreviation of wickedness level. We define the wickedness rate w_i for each AS i according to the exponential distribution:

$$w_i = \min(-\overline{w}\ln(1 - r_i)), 0.5),$$

where r_i is a value selected uniformly at random from the interval $[0,1]$, and $\overline{w}$ is the average wickedness. In Sect. 4 we explain why this distribution is a reasonable match to observed empirical measurements of wickedness.

In ASIM, the *wicked traffic* that flows from a source AS A to a destination AS B is directly proportional to the wickedness level at A. We define the *wicked traffic rate* at B as the fraction of all traffic destined for end users at B that is wicked. Hence we do not count transit traffic when measuring wickedness, although wicked traffic is passed through the network. We are only interested in the impact of wicked traffic on end users, and so are only concerned with the volume of traffic that reaches the destination.

We model five types of interventions that can be undertaken by each AS:

1. **Do nothing:** This is the baseline where the AS makes no active intervention.
2. **Reduce egress wickedness:** This captures a range of AS interventions that remediate customer infections. The percentage reduction of wicked egress traffic depends on the aggressiveness of the intervention—automated notifications are less successful than quarantine, etc.
3. **Reduce ingress wickedness:** An AS can deploy filters that drop some portion of incoming wicked traffic. The proportion dropped depends on the effectiveness of wicked traffic detection, the capacity of filtering on the routers, and other factors. Ingress filtering can be applied to both end-user traffic and transit traffic.
4. **Reduce egress and ingress wickedness:** An AS can deploy methods 2 and 3 simultaneously.
5. **Blacklist wicked traffic sources:** An AS can drop all traffic originating from known wicked sources, typically dropping all traffic that comes from another AS that is known to have high infection rates. Hence there is collateral damage because legitimate as well as wicked traffic is dropped. We model this by having an AS drop all traffic (both wicked and legitimate) from other ASes with sufficiently high wickedness rates. We also model the notion of an AS being *too big to block*, i.e. an AS will only blacklist smaller ASes because blacklisting large ASes is expected to result in an excessive loss of legitimate traffic.

Another intervention under consideration by policy makers is increased *data sharing*, where an AS learns about infections from an amalgamation of sources. We do not treat data sharing as a separate intervention in the model; rather, we can observe the effect of increased data sharing by increasing the effectiveness of ingress and egress interventions.

Separately, we model which ASes choose to intervene as follows:

1. **Unilateral:** Some ASes choose to intervene unilaterally, and there is no coordination between ASes or regulatory pressure on a particular subset of ASes to intervene. We implement this by randomly selecting a subset of ASes to adopt intervention strategies.
2. **Large ASes act in concert:** A selection of large ASes together adopt one of the AS-level interventions. There are several variations on this:

   (a) *Global coordination:* All the largest ASes adopt one of the AS-level interventions.
   (b) *Country-specific coordination:* All of the largest ASes in one country adopt one of the AS-level interventions. We implement this in the model by randomly selecting a fraction of the largest ASes to apply interventions.
   (c) *Small AS inclusion:* Smaller ASes also adopt the interventions.

4 Validating the Model

The original ASIM [20] was validated on real world data and shown to be a close match on a number of metrics. That work dates from 2006, so we have collected more recent data to perform more extensive validation of the new ASIM. First, we gathered data on the real topology of the AS graph using the standard method of inferring links from BGP dumps, which we collected from the RouteViews[4] and RIPE[5] databases. These data were used to validate ASIM on 12 different graph-based metrics; the results are too extensive to include in this paper.[6]

Second, we gathered data on the distributions of locations among ASes in the real world by matching geoip information from MaxMind[7] with the IP prefixes of ASes collected from the BGP dumps. We used this data to confirm that the characteristics of the geographical distribution of agents in ASIM correspond closely with the real Internet. We also used MaxMind to gather population data for cities matched to locations inferred from the geoip data. We could thus confirm that the characteristics of the population distribution in ASIM closely follow that in the real world.

---

[4] www.routeviews.org.

[5] www.ripe.net.

[6] Data and tools available at http://ftg.lbl.gov/projects/asim.

[7] www.maxmind.com.

Obtaining data to validate the cybersecurity extensions to ASIM is a more challenging task. Reliable data are difficult to find for the most important quantity: the distribution of wickedness rates over the ASes. Perhaps the best data comes from a study by Van Eeten et al. [13] of botnet activity at Dutch ISPs. The authors aggregate data on IP addresses observed to be sending email spam, participating in the Conficker botnet, or appearing in the logs of intrusion detection systems for suspected attack behavior. They found that between 2% and 7% of the customers of the nine largest Dutch ISPs were infected and exhibiting botnet activity.

Van Eeten et al. also collected similar data on global Internet activity, finding that Dutch ISPs experience slightly lower than average rates, with the worst-performing countries experiencing a rate several times higher than that of of the Dutch ISPs. However, the authors do not report rates for other countries, because some countries make more extensive use of DHCP than the Netherlands, which could lead to overestimates. To incorporate the potential for higher rates, for our experiments we selected an average wickedness rate $\overline{w} = 0.1$, slightly higher than the highest Dutch ISP value.

Although we can derive the average wickedness rate from the Dutch data, we are also interested in how wickedness is distributed across ISPs. To that end, we collected per ISP data from two sources of malicious activities. First, we collected data from maliciousnetworks.org, where academic researchers have constructed a system that tallies the level of malicious activity at each AS [33]. They aggregate reports of botnet, phishing and malware servers observed at each AS. Second, we analyzed a single-day snapshot from the SANS Internet Storm Center, which publishes a list of over one million IP addresses exhibiting attack behavior.[8] We then determined the AS associated with each IP address in the SANS list and tallied the total number of IP addresses observed at each AS to arrive at measures of wickedness levels for the ASes. Note that in both of these cases, we can determine only wickedness levels, not rates, because the number of customers served by each AS is not publicized.

Figure 1 plots the complementary cumulative distribution function (CCDF) of wickedness levels obtained from maliciousnetworks.org, the Internet Storm Center, and ASIM. We can see that our use of an exponential distribution for the wickedness levels in ASIM results in a simulated CCDF that falls between the two empirical data sets. From this, we conclude that the method used in ASIM for generating wickedness rates for ASes is reasonable.

Even less data are available to evaluate the effectiveness of the different policy interventions described in Sect. 2. To our knowledge, the only data on interventions comes from the same Dutch study mentioned above [13]. The authors surveyed ISPs about how often they notified or quarantined customers infected with malware, and then compared this to their own measurements of wickedness levels. They found that ISPs notified between 1% and 50% of infected customers, and that around 20–25% of this number were also placed into quarantine. As a baseline, in ASIM

---

[8]http://isc.sans.edu/feeds/daily_sources.

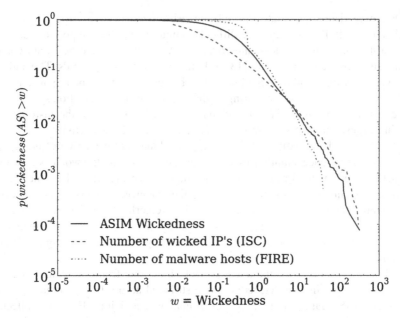

Fig. 1 The distribution of wickedness levels generated by ASIM and in two real world data sets (Normalized)

we assume that standard intervention reduces wicked traffic by 20%, although in Sect. 5, we also explore the impact of varying the remediation efficacy. We place the different intervention techniques on a continuum: notification is less effective than quarantine, and both can be substantially improved by sharing notifications.

5 Experimental Results

We carried out a number of experiments to explore the impact of the various cybersecurity interventions modeled in ASIM. First, in Sect. 5.1, we investigate the simulation at a single point in time, and second, in Sect. 5.2 we study the simulation as the network evolves. In both cases, we measure the impact of an intervention as the percentage by which it reduces the wicked traffic rate (as defined in Sect. 3.2) compared to when no intervention is adopted. When interventions occur, they filter out 20% of wicked traffic, except for blacklisting, where all traffic from a blacklisted AS is dropped, both legitimate and wicked. For all experiments, we used the default parameter settings for ASIM V0.3.[9]

---

[9]`av_degree = 4.2, extent_cost = 1.5, base_income = 5, pop_distr_exp = -1, wickedness = 0.1`.

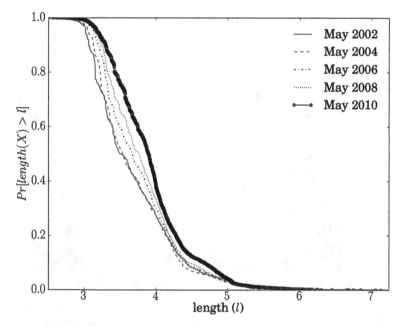

Fig. 2 The change over time of the complementary cumulative distribution (CCDF) for the average path length between every pair of ASes in the real Internet

5.1 Impact at a Single Instant

For our study of the effect of interventions at a single point in time, we used ASIM to grow a network of 10,000 ASes, and used that network as the basis for all experiments. For each intervention, we started with the same 10,000 AS network, set the parameters appropriately, and ran ASIM for a single time step. The traffic component of ASIM always updates at the end of a run, so this yields a single update of the traffic patterns, changed according to the intervention, and always starting from the same state.

We used 10,000 ASes, rather than the current approximately 34,000 in the real Internet,[10] to reduce the running time of the simulation. This should have no substantive impact on the experimental results because the key characteristics of the AS-level graph do not change significantly as the network grows, either in our simulations or in reality. For example, Fig. 2 shows that the distribution of average path lengths has remained roughly unchanged over the last decade, even as the number of ASes has grown more than threefold.

---

[10] As of May 2010.

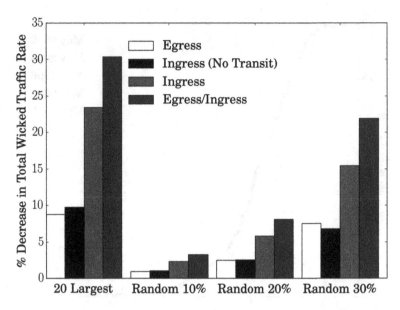

Fig. 3 The impact of interventions on wicked traffic rate. "20 largest" is the effect when the 20 largest ASes intervene; "random $x\%$" is the effect when x percent of all ASes intervene

We first examine how applying interventions to different ASes can affect wicked traffic levels. Figure 3 shows how wicked traffic decreases when only the 20 largest ASes (as measured by degree) adopt interventions, as compared to a random selection of between 10–30% of all ASes. This illustrates the case where interventions are coordinated at the largest ISPs to a hands-off approach where ISPs decide for themselves whether or not to adopt countermeasures. The graph clearly demonstrates that targeting the largest ASes is a superior strategy, given that targeting just the 20 largest ASes (0.2% of the total) reduces traffic by more than applying interventions to even 3,000 randomly selected ASes.

It is not particularly surprising that targeting the largest ASes is the most effective strategy, given the structure of the AS graph. In our simulations, the largest ASes route up to six orders of magnitude more traffic than the smallest. Nonetheless, the results reinforce the argument that remediation policies can be more successful by focusing on a small group of the largest ASes, unless a majority of all ASes can be persuaded to unilaterally respond.

What is more striking is the comparison between ingress and egress filtering. Filtering ingress traffic destined for end users only (i.e. not filtering transit traffic) is about as effective as filtering egress traffic (around 10% when the largest ASes intervene). Ingress filtering of both end-user and transit traffic at the largest ASes, by contrast, reduces wicked traffic by a factor of 2.7 over egress alone. This is a more surprising finding, as it suggests that filtering incoming wicked traffic is more effective than stopping outgoing traffic. When ASes act unilaterally, the difference is not as large (a factor of 1.8) because the smaller ASes transit less traffic.

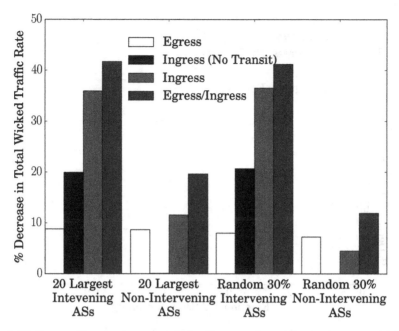

Fig. 4 The impact of interventions on wicked traffic rate on those ASes that intervene, and those that do not. "20 largest" is the effect when the 20 largest ASes intervene; "random *x*%" is the effect when *x* percent of all ASes intervene

Most policy interventions under discussion have focused on ISPs' remediating customer infections, which is akin to egress filtering. While this does reduce wicked traffic levels, our results suggest that resources might be put to better use by filtering incoming and transit traffic for wickedness.

Figure 4 compares the decrease in wicked traffic at ASes that implement the interventions to the reduction at ASes that do not adopt any interventions. The benefits for non-intervening ASes represent a way to measure the positive externalities of security interventions in the network. As expected, filtering egress traffic creates substantial positive externalities, with non-intervening ASes experiencing similar reductions in wicked traffic rates as intervening ASes. This effect holds for both the largest ASes and a random selection of ASes. By contrast, filtering ingress traffic has positive externalities only if wicked transit traffic is blocked. In this case, the greatest benefits accrue to the intervening ASes. This indicates that when filtering ingress traffic, the incentives for adopting countermeasures are more aligned, and there should be less fear of free-riding.

Furthermore, the positive externalities of ingress filtering (including transit traffic) can vary greatly depending on which ASes intervene. The benefits to non-intervening ASes are more than twice as large when the largest ASes intervene rather than when ASes unilaterally intervene at random. This is because large ASes attract more transit traffic, and so their filtering has a greater impact.

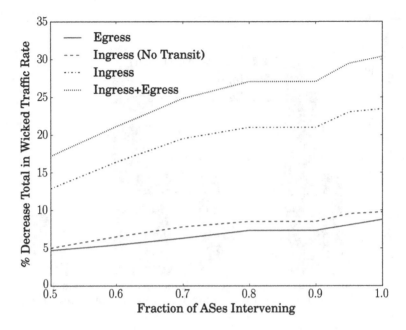

Fig. 5 The effect of the intervention of a fraction of the largest ASes

Even if having the largest ASes implement an intervention is the preferred strategy for reducing wicked traffic on the Internet, it may not be possible to enlist the support of all ASes. For example, even if all large US-based ISPs adopted ingress and egress filtering, operators in other countries might choose not to participate. To investigate the impact of incomplete adoption, Fig. 5 explores how varying the proportion of large ASes that participate in the intervention affects the reduction of malicious traffic.

Although wicked traffic falls as more ASes participate, the effect is non-linear. For example, the differences between 80% and 100% of ASes intervening are not great (from 27% to 30% wicked traffic reduction, an 11% change), whereas the differences between 60% and 80% are much greater (from 21% to 27%, a 29% change). This suggests that country-level interventions are much more likely to be effective if they include the majority of large ASes. For example, if the all the largest ISPs based in the US were to intervene, that would constitute at least 75% of all large ASes.

In all the experiments reported previously, the ingress and egress filtering effectiveness was set at 20%. However, some interventions are likely to be more effective than others. Notification-based schemes will filter less egress wicked traffic than active quarantine, and increased data sharing could raise the success rate of both ingress and egress filtering. It is very difficult to get reliable information on the efficacy of these different approaches. Instead, in Fig. 6 we explore how different combinations of values for the success rates of ingress and egress filtering affect

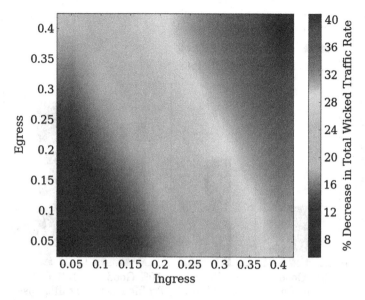

Fig. 6 The change in wicked traffic rate when varying the success rate of ingress and egress filtering. The scale indicates on the right the reduction in wicked traffic, from 0 to 40%

the wicked traffic rates. Ingress filtering is consistently more effective at reducing overall wickedness. For instance, ingress filtering 35% of wicked traffic and no egress traffic reduces the wicked traffic rate by the same amount as 20% ingress and 40% egress filtering.

We also study the more aggressive intervention of completely blocking all traffic originating from blacklisted ASes with unacceptably high wicked traffic rates. Blacklisting results in a trade-off between reducing wicked traffic and collateral damage caused by blocking innocent traffic. We consider only the case where interventions are carried out by the 20 largest ASes (those of degree≥170), because, as seen previously, interventions are most successful when the largest ASes act in concert.

There are two choices to make when applying blacklisting: first, the selection of the level of wickedness above which ASes are blacklisted, and second, the selection of whether to not blacklist larger ASes. We explore three levels of AS size: blacklisting all ASes above the wickedness level, or those of degree <170, or those of degree <10. For each choice of AS size, we select levels of wickedness that result in losses of legitimate (good) traffic of 2%, 5%, 10% and 15%.

Figure 7 shows that the best strategy when applying blacklisting depends very much on the level of legitimate traffic loss we are willing to tolerate. For very low losses (2%) the strategies have similar results. For more moderate losses (5%), we should blacklist all but the 20 largest ASes. Beyond that, it is more effective to blacklist all ASes. However, we see diminishing returns as the level

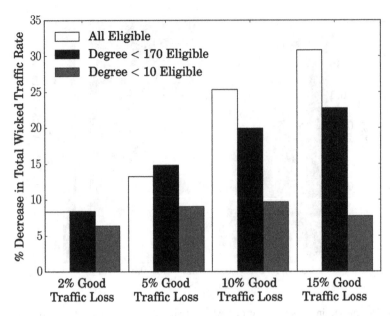

Fig. 7 The trade-off between reducing wicked traffic and losing legitimate traffic when blacklisting

of acceptable loss increases. For example, when blacklisting all ASes, a 50% increase in acceptable loss, from 10% to 15%, only reduces the wicked traffic by an additional 23%.

In fact, increasing the level of acceptable loss does not always reduce wicked traffic. As can be seen in Fig. 8, the largest reduction of wicked traffic happens around a wickedness level of 0.08. Furthermore, there is a range over which the wicked traffic reduction changes little; thus, the best choice of wickedness level would probably be around 0.12 for this example; anything lower increases the loss of legitimate traffic with no beneficial wicked traffic reduction.

5.2 Impact on Network Growth

The effect of malicious activity on the growth of the AS network is a complex issue, one that we do not have the space to investigate in depth in this paper. As an illustration of some of the potential for modeling chronic attacks in ASIM, we briefly consider how the cost of intervention influences network growth. Blacklisting is the simplest intervention to incorporate into the economics of ASIM, because ASes earn money according to how much traffic they route. Blacklisting reduces the amount of traffic (both legitimate and wicked) seen by ASes and hence should change the evolution of the network.

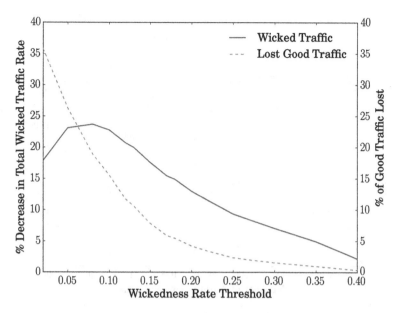

Fig. 8 The reduction in wicked traffic and the loss of legitimate (good) traffic when blacklisting all ASes of degree <170

We carried out experiments where the 20 largest ASes intervene to blacklist all traffic originating from ASes of degree less than 170. We set the wickedness level for blacklisting to be 0.18, which results in moderate legitimate traffic loss. At this level, according to Fig. 7, the best strategy is to blacklist all sufficiently wicked ASes of degree less than 170.

Figure 9 shows how wicked traffic and lost legitimate traffic change as the network evolves from 5,000 to 13,000 ASes. The wicked traffic increases slightly (by about 9%) and the lost legitimate traffic decreases significantly (by about 66%). To understand why this happens, consider two classes of ASes: those that lose incoming traffic due to blacklisting (class A) and those that do not (class B). In ASIM, every AS depends on traffic for revenue, and so ASes in class A will earn less and hence grow more slowly than ASes in class B. The ASes in class A will have reduced levels of wicked traffic and increased levels of lost legitimate traffic compared to those in class B. Thus, as ASes in class B grow more than those in class A, the overall level of wicked traffic will increase, and the overall level of legitimate traffic lost will decrease. This is exactly what we see in Fig. 9.

Although blacklisting tends to promote ASes that receive more wicked traffic, the rate at which wicked traffic increases is much slower than the rate at which lost legitimate traffic decreases. Hence, blacklisting could still be considered a viable strategy for reducing overall wickedness, at least in the short term. Persuading individual ASes to voluntarily adopt blacklisting, however, would be hard. Mandatory participation would likely be necessary.

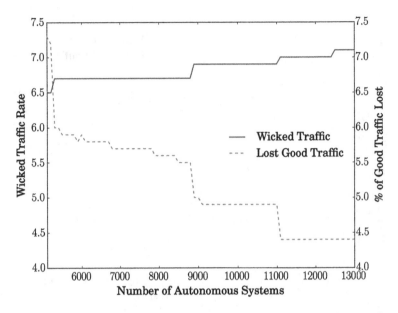

Fig. 9 The change in wicked traffic and loss of legitimate traffic over time as the network grows from 5,000 to 13,000 ASes. The wicked traffic rate is the percentage of all traffic that is wicked

6   Related Work

Few studies have modeled the costs and benefits of intervention to prevent the spread of malware across a network. LeLarge [22, 23] used an agent-based model to investigate the economics of interventions that counter the spread of malware. However, LeLarge's model is much more abstract than ASIM: agents exist on a random network, over which there is a probabilistic spread of infections. Agents can choose either to secure themselves (at a cost) or to remain unsecured and risk loss. There is no notion of geography or traffic. Varian [34] proposed a game-theoretic model to understand how security impacts the decisions of other rational actors, but without considering network topology or how infections may spread. Subsequently, a number of authors [5, 29] have proposed models of computer-infection spread that combine game theory with network topology. These models focus on optimal strategies to combat a binary state of infection.

By contrast, a number of models have been developed to explore the spread of malware, such as computer worms [17]. Compartmental models of disease spread (whether biological or electronic) are attractive methods for investigating the progress of epidemics [4]. For example, Ajelli et al. describe the spread of a botnet using such a model [1]. Other work incorporates additional factors into differential equation models, such as locations based on time zone [12] and peer-to-peer protocols [32]. These approaches focus on the spread of a single type of malware, such as a particular worm or botnet. By contrast, our approach is to model all malware in a generic way, incorporating both the economics of interventions, and the way interventions affect the spread of malicious traffic on the Internet topology at the AS level.

A major difference between agent-based models, such as ASIM, and differential equation models, such as those described above, is that the latter assume that populations are "well-mixed"; consequently they do not capture the effect of skewed network topologies. Various extensions, such as percolation methods and generating functions [28], have been proposed as a method for overcoming this limitation, spawning a great deal of interest in epidemics on network topologies [18]. Other extensions include using packet-level data generated by computer network traffic simulators [35]. In addition to investigating the spread of malware across network topologies, mitigation strategies such as quarantining malicious hosts [11, 25, 30] have been investigated. However, to the best of our knowledge, there are no studies that use these models to investigate intervention policies at the ISP or Internet-level.

7   Discussion

ASIM simplifies many aspects of routing on the real Internet. For example, traffic in ASIM always follows the shortest path, whereas real traffic is also influenced by agreements between ASes, following various conventions such as the "valley free" rule. In ASIM ASes earn money from all traffic they route, whereas in reality ASes earn money from their customers and pay their own upstream providers. But we found in preliminary investigations that these added complexities do not improve the accuracy of the model, at least in terms of measures such as average path length, degree distribution, etc. More detailed modeling is a topic for future research and may lead to have implications for the study of policy interventions.

Other model enhancements would allow us to study more carefully the impact of interventions on the economics of network growth. We have presented a simple initial approach, using blacklisting, but in future we intend to explore other aspects, such as the cost of carrying out various interventions. Blacklisting is simple in that packets from a particular source are dropped, whereas filtering only wicked traffic would likely be much more expensive, requiring a sophisticated intrusion detection system (IDS). Because of the performance requirements, it may be infeasible to filter traffic using an IDS at the level of the powerful routers used in the largest ASes. In this case, blacklisting and improving end-user security may be the only reasonable options.

In our experiments with network growth, we kept the level of wickedness, or compromised hosts, constant. This is clearly unrealistic as the number of compromised hosts changes over time as some are cleaned up and others infected. Furthermore, we expect that the amount of wicked traffic reaching end-users will also influence infection rates. It is difficult to find good data on how these rates change over time, and so it will be difficult to validate a model that captures these aspects. One topic for future research is to model dynamic wickedness levels, perhaps following an epidemiological model where there is some rate of recovery from infection, and some rate of reinfection, which is to some degree dependent on wicked traffic flow.

8   Conclusions

The results of our experiments using ASIM indicate that when filtering wicked traffic, the best targets for intervention are a small group of the largest ASes. Specifically, we find that intervention by the top 0.2% of ASes (in terms of size) is more effective than intervention by a randomly chosen subset of 30% of all ASes. However, we show that this efficacy rapidly drops off if less than three quarters of that top 0.2% intervene. This is an issue of importance if not all the largest ASes fall within the same regulatory domain, such as a nation-state.

Our experiments also illustrate the relative effectiveness of filtering ingress and egress traffic. We show that filtering ingress traffic (including transit) is more than twice as effective as filtering egress traffic alone. Unsurprisingly, the effect of filtering is felt most strongly by those actively filtering the data, although positive externalities can be seen if outgoing or transit traffic is filtered. In our model, filtering egress traffic is also a proxy for end-user remediation, which suggests that the current focus on cleaning up ISP customers is not the most effective strategy.

In the case of blacklisting, we show that the choice of which ASes should be exempt from blacklisting depends on how much legitimate traffic loss we are willing to tolerate. If moderate levels of legitimate traffic loss are acceptable, then large ASes should be exempt; however, if higher levels of traffic loss are acceptable all ASes should be eligible for blacklisting. The threshold for which ASes are blacklisted does not relate linearly to the reduction in the wicked traffic rate. This is likely due to attrition of good traffic, raising the fraction of wicked traffic seen.

Our investigations of the impact of interventions on the evolution of the network are brief and are limited to modeling the effect of blacklisting traffic on growth. We show that blacklisting traffic results in a gradual increase in wicked traffic, and a more rapid reduction in the loss of legitimate traffic. Although this is beneficial in the short term, in the long-term those ASes that profit most from wicked traffic will prosper at the expense of more secure ASes, and so global effectiveness will decline.

We believe that the results reported in this paper are a good proof-of-concept demonstration of how agent-based modeling can be useful to policy makers when considering different interventions. We hope in future that our approach will provide additional interesting results and tools to help policy makers determine the best way to respond to the growing malware threat.

Acknowledgements The authors gratefully acknowledge the support of DOE grant DE-AC02-05CH11231. Stephanie Forrest acknowledges partial support of DARPA (P-1070-113237), NSF (EF1038682,SHF0905236), and AFOSR (Fa9550-07-1-0532).

References

1. Ajelli M, Lo Cigno R, Montresor A (2010) Modeling botnets and epidemic malware. In: 2010 IEEE international conference on communications (ICC), pp 1–5
2. Anderson R, Böhme R, Clayton R, Moore T (2008) Security economics and European policy. In: Johnson ME (ed) Managing information risk and the economics of security, Springer, Berlin, pp 55–80
3. Anderson R, Moore T (2006) The economics of information security. Science 314(5799):610–613
4. Anderson RM, May RM (1992) Infectious diseases of humans dynamics and control. Oxford University Press, Oxford
5. Aspnes J, Rustagi N, Saia J (2007) Worm versus alert: who wins in a battle for control of a large-scale network? In: Proceedings of the 11th international conference on principles of distributed systems, OPODIS'07, Springer, Berlin, pp 443–456
6. Association II (2010) Internet service providers voluntary code of practice for industry self-regulation in the area of cyber security. http://iia.net.au/images/resources/pdf/iiacybersecuritycode_implementation_dec2010.pdf
7. Chang H, Jamin S, Willinger W (2003) Internet connectivity at the AS-level: an optimization-driven modeling approach. In: MoMeTools '03: Proceedings of the ACM SIGCOMM workshop on models, methods and tools for reproducible network research, ACM, New York, NY, USA, pp 33–46. DOI 10.1145/944773.944780
8. Chang H, Jamin S, Willinger W (2006) To peer or not to peer: modeling the evolution of the Internet's AS-level topology. In: Proc. IEEE INFOCOM
9. Clayton R (2010) Might governments clean up malware? In: Workshop on the economics of information security. http://weis2010.econinfosec.org/papers/session4/weis2010_clayton.pdf
10. Comcast: Comcast.net security—constant guard. http://security.comcast.net/constantguard/
11. Coull SE, Szymanski BK (2005) A reputation-based system for the quarantine of random scanning worms
12. Dagon D, Zou C, Lee W (2006) Modeling botnet propagation using time zones. In: In Proceedings of the 13th network and distributed system security symposium NDSS
13. van Eeten M, Asghari H, Bauer JM, Tabatabaie S (2011) Internet service providers and botnet mitigation: a fact-finding study on the Dutch market. Technical report, Netherlands Ministry of Economic Affairs, Agriculture and Innovation, The Hague. http://rijksoverheid.nl/ministeries/eleni/documenten-en-publicaties/rapporten/2011/01/13/internet-service-providers-and-botnet-mitigation.html
14. van Eeten M, Bauer JM (2008) Economics of malware: security decisions, incentives and externalities. Technical report, OECD STI Working paper 2008/1. http://www.oecd.org/dataoecd/53/17/40722462.pdf
15. van Eeten M, Bauer JM, Asghari H, Tabatabaie S (2010) The role of internet service providers in botnet mitigation: an empirical analysis based on spam data. Technical report, OECD STI Working Paper 2010/5. http://www.oecd.org/officialdocuments/publicdisplaydocumentpdf/?cote=dsti/doc(2010)5&docLanguage=En
16. Evron G (2009) Dutch isps sign anti-botnet treaty. Dark Reading. http://www.darkreading.com/blog/archives/2009/09/dutch_isps_sign.html
17. Fei S, Zhaowen L, Yan M (2009) A survey of internet worm propagation models. In: Broadband network multimedia technology, 2nd IEEE International Conference on IC-BNMT '09, pp 453–457

18. Ganesh A, Massouli L, Towsley D (2005) The effect of network topology on the spread of epidemics. In: IEEE INFOCOM, pp 1455–1466
19. Haynes KE, Fotheringham A (1984) Gravity and spatial interaction models. Sage Publications, Beverley Hills, CA
20. Holme P, Karlin J, Forrest S (2008) An integrated model of traffic, geography and economy in the internet. ACM SIGCOMM Computer Commun Rev 38(3):7–15
21. Karge S (2010) The german anti-botnet initiative. In: OECD workshop on the role of internet intermediaries in advancing public policy objectives. http://www.oecd.org/dataoecd/42/50/45509383.pdf
22. Lelarge M (2009) Economics of malware: epidemic risks model, network externalities and incentives. In: Proceedings of the 47th annual allerton conference on communication, control, and computing, pp 1353–1360
23. Lelarge M, Bolot J (2009) Economic incentives to increase security in the internet: the case for insurance. In: INFOCOM 2009, IEEE, pp 1494–1502
24. Mody N, O'Reirdan M, Masiello S, Zebek J (2009) Messaging Anti-abuse working group common best practices for mitigating large scale bot infections in residential networks. http://www.maawg.org/system/files/news/MAAWG_Bot_Mitigation_BP_2009-07.pdf
25. Moore D, Shannon C, Voelker G, Savage S (2003) Internet quarantine: requirements for containing self-propagating code. In: INFOCOM 2003. Twenty-second annual joint conference of the IEEE computer and communications. IEEE societies, vol 3, pp 1901–1910
26. Moore T, Clayton R (2008) The consequence of non-cooperation in the fight against phishing. In: Anti-phishing working group eCrime researchers summit (APWG eCrime), pp 1–14. URL http://people.seas.harvard.edu/~tmoore/ecrime08.pdf
27. Moore T, Clayton R, Anderson R (2009) The economics of online crime. J Economic Perspect 23(3):3–20
28. Newman MEJ (2002) Spread of epidemic disease on networks. Phys Rev E 66(1)
29. Omic J, Orda A, Van Mieghem P (2009) Protecting against network infections: a game theoretic perspective. In: INFOCOM, IEEE, pp 1485–1493
30. Palmieri F, Fiore U (2008) Containing large-scale worm spreading in the internet by cooperative distribution of traffic filtering policies. Comput Secur 27(1–2):48–62
31. Porras P, Saidi H, Yegneswaran V (2009) An analysis of conficker's logic and rendezvous points. Technical report, SRI International. http://mtc.sri.com/Conficker/
32. Schafer J, Malinka K, Hanacek P (2008) Malware spreading models in peer-to-peer networks. In: Security technology, 42nd annual IEEE international Carnahan conference on ICCST 2008, pp 339–345
33. Stone-Gross B, Moser A, Kruegel C, Kirda E, Almeroth K (2009) FIRE: FInding Rogue nEtworks. In: Proceedings of the annual computer security applications conference (ACSAC). Honolulu, HI
34. Varian HR (2004) System reliability and free riding. In: Economics of information security, Kluwer Academic Publishers, Dordrecht, pp 1–15
35. Wei S, Mirkovic J, Swany M (2005) Distributed worm simulation with a realistic internet model. In: Principles of advanced and distributed simulation, Workshop on PADS 2005, pp 71–79

Fixed Costs, Investment Rigidities, and Risk Aversion in Information Security: A Utility-theoretic Approach

Christos Ioannidis, David Pym,* and Julian Williams

Abstract This paper addresses the question of determining the optimal timing of interventions in information security management. Using utility theory, we derive the limiting condition under which, given a potential or realized risk, a decision to invest, delay, or abandon can be justified. Our primary focus is on the decision to defer costly deterministic investments, such as the removal of a service or implementation of a security patch, when the costs associated with future security vulnerabilities are uncertain. We outline an investment function with irreversible fixed costs that introduces a rigidity into the investment decision-making profile. This rigidity introduces delay in the implementation of security measures, resulting in cyclical investments in information security, as the decision-maker determines the optimal investment horizon. We therefore show that cycles emerge endogenously given the policy-maker's chosen trade-offs between investment and the deterioration of the system attributes.

*Part of this work was carried out whilst Pym was employed at HP Labs, Bristol, England, UK

C. Ioannidis (✉)
Department of Economics, University of Bath, Bath BA2 7AY, England, UK
e-mail: c.ioannidis@bath.ac.uk

D. Pym
School of Natural and Computing Sciences, King's College, University of Aberdeen, Aberdeen AB24 3UE, Scotland, UK
e-mail: d.j.pym@abdn.ac.uk

J. Williams
Business School, University of Aberdeen, Aberdeen AB24 3QY, Scotland, UK
e-mail: julian.williams@abdn.ac.uk

B. Schneier (ed.), *Economics of Information Security and Privacy III*,
DOI 10.1007/978-1-4614-1981-5_8,
© Springer Science+Business Media New York 2013

1 Introduction

Decision-making in information security problems has traditionally been understood in the context of the equalization of marginal cost of, and marginal benefit from, investments. An alternative approach is to formulate the same problems in terms of strategic behaviour, such as Bayesian games. For a classic example among many, consider Fultz and Grossklags' paper on distributed security attacks [15]. This approach is useful for garnering certain stylized facts about behaviour that can guide the formulation of security policies and the design of incentive structures for policy-makers in information systems. Because these models rely upon high levels of abstraction from the detail of the system's design and its security management, such approaches are not easily mapped to deployable decision-support tools. In this paper, we argue that the appropriate formulation of the decision-support problem is as a decision-under-uncertainty problem for a representative policy-maker.

We formulate this optimization as a utility maximization problem under uncertainty; that is, framing the decision problem as a one-dimensional single-equation reaction function, with multivariate stochastic innovations in the system architecture, representing the risks that undermine the system attributes. This is, in effect, an Arrow–Pratt [6, 25] approach to optimal decision making under uncertainty for a risk-averse policy-maker. Using this approach, we are able to derive a closed-form limiting condition for decision-making using all the information and intervention technologies that are available to the decision-maker[1].

The assumption of risk aversion is justified as a reasonable choice because: in the context of government, a precautionary approach to risk management is the usual guiding principle; in owner-manager businesses, the capital of the firm is intimately connected to the capital of the policy-maker; in businesses in which management and ownership are separated, transaction costs associated with change of employment inhibit the policy-maker's risk appetite.

An economics-based perspective on the management of information security operations has been discussed in a series of papers [2–4]. In [16, 17], a microeconomic analysis of the costs and benefits of defences against given vulnerabilities is presented. Recent work by the present authors has applied ideas from utility theory and dynamic optimization to information security. More specifically, we have presented a dynamic model of trade-offs between confidentiality, availability, and investment in information security operations [19, 20][2]. The aggregate timing of decision-making—in product cycles, consumption cycles, and investment cycles—is explored in, for example, the recent work of Bloom [10].

In the case of risk management and mitigation of vulnerability, this is a utility-of-action problem, which has been explored extensively in applied, commercial, contexts in [8, 9, 24], work which has directly informed the present paper. To demonstrate this issue appropriately in a timing framework, we treat system

---

[1]The solution includes the stochastic process that represents the threat environment.

[2]Modelling multiple trade-offs can be accommodated within the same methodology.

vulnerabilities as being stochastic discount factors that erode the attributes of a system. The discount factors are assumed to be arrive through a poisson process and have jump intensities driven by a multivariate log-normal distribution. Whilst this is a simple specification, the purpose of this paper is to demonstrate a methodology and the steps involved in implementing it.

In this paper, we introduce the notion of a security investment cycle. The key components of this idea are the following:

- Investments in IT systems are a major cost for firms;
- These systems are subject to security vulnerabilities, which typically compound over time;
- Accordingly, IT system managers plan investments in information security operations;
- These investments typically include irreversible (e.g., up-front) fixed costs;
- This rigidity (e.g., derived from up-front costs) inhibits rapid implementation of new security measures in response to emerging threats, since the fixed costs may outweigh the immediate benefits;
- To exhibit this situation, consider how the two system attributes of performance and security trade off against each other, and jointly against investment costs.

An example of this situation is provided by the question of when to deploy patches. Indeed, the importance of timing vulnerability management in networks in the presence of externalities has been addressed by [7]. They show that software vendors can offer rewards to encourage timely patching when vulnerabilities occur in both proprietary software and freeware and, given the differential costs of patching to users, conclude ([7], p. 1718) that "a 'one-size-fits-all' approach is unlikely to be an immediate remedy". In addition, for situations in which the actions of users impact upon the welfare of others, they develop a set of incentive structures for the implementation of effective patch management. The timing of vulnerability disclosures by vendors is modelled by [5], where it is shown that, with no regulation, the vendor releases a patch less frequently than is socially optimal. In [11], the relationship between the release of patches by vendors and their implementation by users is studied. They classify patching cycles into time-driven and event-driven. They show that social loss is minimized when vendor releases are synchronized with the time-driven cycles of the system operator. When such synchronization cannot be achieved because it is costly, the imposition of liability on the vendor cannot achieve the socially timing optimal of disclosures. Finally, in [11], the authors calculate the socially optimal window of exposure and decompose the patching process into time- and event-driven incidents in a game-theoretic setting. In [18], a financial model using real options—in particular, deferment options— is employed to offer an integrated framework encompassing the decision to delay patching in the presence of known vulnerabilities. When system operators employ a variety of applications, patch arrivals will appear as random events, without apparent periodicity. From previous studies described, it is apparent that the time of patch deployment is important because such an action involves costs and mistiming exacerbates their impact.

Table 1 Glossary of terms

Phrase	Definitions
Vulnerability	A flaw in the architecture of an information system that may lead to a compromise of, for example, CIA or CS (criticality, sensitivity)
Exploit	A malicious tool that facilitates the exploitation of a vulnerability
Mitigation	A system update that mitigates the vulnerability, partially or completely impairing the function of an exploit

The methodology suggested in this paper can be described succinctly in the following steps: first, we map the preferences of decision-makers to a well specified utility function defined in terms of the system's attributes and control variables[3], such as confidentiality, integrity, and availability, or sensitivity and criticality; second, we derive the moment expansion of the utility function, using a Taylor expansion; third, we postulate the stochastic risk environment and substitute the moments of this process into the higher-order terms of the system's attributes, in addition to the moments of the control variable; finally, we compute the maximum of the expected utility by adjusting the properties of the control variable.

In this paper, we consider the security investment cycle more generally. In Sect. 2, we explain how some fundamental utility theory can be used to formulate the preferences of a representative policy-maker choosing forward-looking investment profiles. In Sect. 3, we derive an approximation to the solution space for expected utility maximization for a given functional form of investment in the presence of stochastic threats to system security. In Sect. 4, we set out a specific stochastic threat space and solve for the equilibrium timing of investment. We illustrate three cases of investment implementation: address vulnerabilities on arrival; never invest; and delay investment for a finite time.

The remainder of the paper employs a range of technical terms defined, for our purposes, in Table 1.

2 A Utility Theory of Vulnerability Management

Our first goal is to orientate the vulnerability management problem in an expected utility-maximization framework. We seek to construct a objective function, whose solution at the maximum is equivalent to the expected utility maximization condition. We state the policy-maker's objective function as

---

[3]Well specified, in this case, implies that preferences represented by this utility function are consistent with rational choice. For a full exposition of axiomatic utility theory and decision making see [14].

$$\mathbb{E}\left(\mathfrak{U}(t,T)\right) \triangleq \max_{K(t)} \int_t^T e^{-\beta t} u\left(x(t); K(t)\right) d\mathbb{P}\left(\omega(t)\right) \tag{1}$$

where

- T is the terminal time,
- $K(t)$ is a choice of investment function,
- $x(t) = \{x_1, \ldots, x_n\}$ is a n-vector of real-valued system attributes that is stochastic, because of threats, defined over the probability space $(\Omega, \mathscr{F}, \mathbb{P})$ [26],
- $u(x(t); K(t))$ is an instantaneous real-valued twice-differentiable utility function over the system attributes x, with exogenous parameters the investment function, $K(t)$,
- β is a global discount rate, and
- $\omega(t) \in \Omega$ is an experiment in the probability space $(\Omega, \mathscr{F}, \mathbb{P})$ [26].

Here the idea is that we vary the investment function $K(t)$ in order to maximize expected utility at time t by choosing a future investment time $t^* \geq t$.

Equation (1) provides a general characterization of a variety investment problems. As such, it is difficult to derive general analytic solutions and so we reduce the problem space to a polynomial approximation of (1) for which solutions can be found.

In this paper, we assume a risk-averse policy-maker. In the case of a risk-neutral policy-maker, our analysis collapses to a polynomial approximation to the real options solution for the investment timing problem [28].

2.1 The Power Utility Family

We explore the general problem described above in the case in which $n = 2$. This is the simplest case that fully illustrates our approach. Examples of this case would include the security attributes confidentiality and availability, and we have explored, in less generality, the way in which these attributes trade off against each other elsewhere [19, 20]. In [19], for example, we exogenously imposed an investment cycle on the representative firm within the model. In contrast, in this paper, we demonstrate how an investment cycle arises from investment rigidities.

In economics and finance, the power utility family of functions is the predominant mechanism for defining preferences for inter-temporal decision problems. Whilst for most of our derivation we are agnostic to choice of utility function (our interest is restricted to the ratio of the derivatives), some discussion of the higher level of functional form is relevant and useful for future applied work. The basic power utility construct for a consumption variable $x_i \in \{x_1, x_2\}$, suppressing the control variable K, has a partial utility function defined as

$$u_i(x_i) = \frac{x_i^{1-\gamma_i}}{1-\gamma_i} \tag{2}$$

where γ_i is the coefficient of relative risk aversion $\mathfrak{R}$, for the ith attribute. Combining the partial utility functions with cross power utility would yield and over utility function of

$$u(x_1, x_2) = \frac{1}{1-\gamma_1} x_1^{1-\gamma_1} + \frac{1}{1-\gamma_2} x_2^{1-\gamma_2} + 2 \frac{|x_1 x_2|^{1-\gamma_{12}}}{1-\gamma_{12}} \qquad (3)$$

Several extensions of the power utility have been proposed in the literature and several of these innovations have useful interpretations for information security problems. From this point onward, for ease of exposition, we shall concentrate on the partial utility functions. Kahneman and Tversky [21] suggest the inclusion of a fixed point, or kink point, k, to discriminate between aversion to risk of loss and aversion to risk of gain. The power utility representation of this approach is

$$u_i(x_i) = \begin{cases} \frac{1}{1-\gamma_i} x_i^{1-\gamma_i} & \forall x_i > k \\ \frac{1}{1-\tilde{\gamma}_i} x_i^{1-\tilde{\gamma}_i} & \forall x_i \leq k \end{cases} \qquad (4)$$

where $\tilde{\gamma}_i \neq \gamma_i$. The inclusion of the fixed point adds a significant complication to the type of optimization suggested herein as the derivatives of $u(x)$ are now discontinuous.

An alternative augmentation is to include a utility profile of the consumption of system attributes at some future point in time. This nesting of future utility allows for a substitution between current expected utility and future expected utility and has been used extensively since first being suggested in [13]. The power utility form is compactly presented as

$$u_i(x_i(t)) = (1-\zeta_i) x_i^{\frac{1-\gamma_i}{\theta_i}} + \zeta_i \mathbb{E}_t \left(u(x_i(t+\Delta t))^{\frac{1}{\theta_i}} \right)^{\frac{\theta_i}{1-\gamma_i}} \qquad (5)$$

where θ_i is the anticipated future coefficient of relative risk aversion at $t + \Delta t$, ζ_i is the inter-temporal elasticity of substitution—that is, the substitution between current and future expected utility.

The last type utility function we have considered in our applied work is the "inside and outside of habit" utility function, suggested by [1]. This sets expected utility as being relative to a peer group represented by an index (of consumption), ξ_i, of the variable x_i. In our notational scheme, the power utility version of this type of utility function is (as usual, suppressing $K(t)$) defined as

$$u_i(x_i) = \frac{\left(x_i \xi_i^{-1} \right)^{1-\gamma}}{1-\gamma} \qquad (6)$$

There are obvious circumstances where each of these definitions of preferences will be appropriate. Augmentations to cater for non-zero cross products

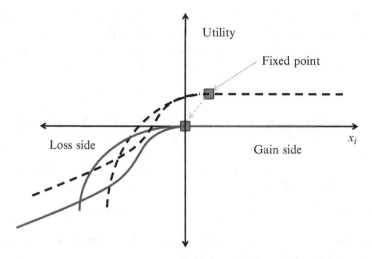

Fig. 1 Illustration of the projection of a family of utility functions, $u(x_i)$, for a single attribute. The markers represent the fixed points in the utility problem. The fixed points can be located anywhere within this plane. For example, the *dashed* represents a curve with a fixed point at positive value of x_i. For our purposes, we assume the fixed point is at the origin (the *dark grey line*) and that deviations from steady state are always to the left of the origin

(i.e., supermodularity or submodularity) are also relatively trivial. For instance, fixed points are common in many aspects of information security: in particular, on the loss side—essentially, improvements over targets are relatively under rewarded.

Figure 1 outlines an example of this structure.

2.2   The Policy-Maker's Problem

We begin with a quick review of several key results for properties of utility functions and in particular the structure of risk aversion. Absolute risk aversion ($\mathfrak{A}$) in two-variable (i.e., $n = 2$) multi-attribute decision problems is defined as follows:

$$\mathfrak{A}(x_1,\cdot) = \frac{u''_{x_1}(x_1,\cdot)}{u'_{x_1}(x_1,\cdot)} \qquad \mathfrak{A}(\cdot,x_2) = \frac{u''_{x_2}(\cdot,x_2)}{u'_{x_2}(\cdot,x_2)} \tag{7}$$

where we suppress in the notation the exogenous parameter, $K(t)$. This is then simply mapped to a relative risk aversion ($\mathfrak{R}$) context

$$\mathfrak{R}(x_1,\cdot) = \frac{-\gamma_{x_1} u''_{x_1}(x_1,\cdot)}{u'_{x_1}(x_1,\cdot)} \qquad \mathfrak{R}(\cdot,x_2) = \frac{-\gamma_{x_2} u''_{x_2}(\cdot,x_2)}{u'_{x_2}(\cdot,x_2)} \tag{8}$$

where γ_{x_1} and γ_{x_2} are the coefficients of relative risk-aversion (i.e., the marginal rate of change in risk-aversion with respect to $u(\cdot)$) for each of the system attributes.

Both $\mathfrak{A}$ and $\mathfrak{R}$ are useful tools in summarizing the properties of specific utility functions: in addition to the risk aversion properties, the cross products for the attributes are useful in elucidating the preference structure. In the bivariate context, there are three main combinations. Consider the following decomposition

$$u(x_1, x_2) = u_1(x_1) + u_2(x_2) + u_{12}(x_1, x_2) \tag{9}$$

where $u(x_1)$ and $u(x_2)$ are the partial utility functions with respect to system attributes x_1 and x_2 and $u_{12}(x_1, x_2)$ is the joint utility adjustment. In the general form of our modelling framework we maintain the general assumption that $u_{12}(x_1, x_2) \neq 0, \forall \{x_1, x_2\} \in \mathbb{R}^2$. For our final analytic solutions, however, we have assumed *separable additivity*; that is,

$$u''_{x_1, x_2}(x_1, \cdot) = 0 \quad \forall x_2 \qquad u''_{x_1, x_2}(\cdot, x_2) = 0 \quad \forall x_1 \tag{10}$$

The contrasting assumptions that maybe made on the shape of the multi-attribute utility function are *supermodularity* whereby

$$u''_{x_1, x_2}(x_1, \cdot) > 0 \quad \forall x_2 \qquad u''_{x_1, x_2}(\cdot, x_2) > 0 \quad \forall x_1 \tag{11}$$

and *submodularity* whereby

$$u''_{x_1, x_2}(x_1, \cdot) < 0 \quad \forall x_2 \qquad u''_{x_1, x_2}(\cdot, x_2) < 0 \quad \forall x_1 \tag{12}$$

Discussion of the appropriate application of these properties is usually driven by game-theoretic models of incentives. For instance, most problems can be treated as separably additive, and as such the attributes rolled in a single linear function. However, in the authors' experience of working with industry and government, compound attacks on multiple system attributes are often more damaging than attacks (of similar component-wise magnitude) that occur at different times. In this case, utility functions incorporating a degree of supermodularity would be most appropriate for describing policy-maker preferences. Cases of submodular preferences are much rarer, although not unheard of. For instance, in a confidentiality, integrity, and availability (CIA) framework, a distributed denial of service (DDOS) attack mixed with a breach of confidentiality could, for certain institutions such as retailers, be understood as being submodular: to some extent, the DDOS mitigates the effectiveness of the confidentiality attack as the system's availability (to the confidentiality attacker) is compromised. A fuller exploration of supermodular and submodular preferences is deferred to future work.

3 Constructing the Expected Utility Function

For simplicity of exposition, we now simplify the decision under uncertainty problem to a policy maker choosing a forward looking investment profile from an initial time t_0; that is, at a point where no existing vulnerabilities are present.

The resulting expected timing of investment $t^* > t_0$ is the ex-ante expected amplitude of the investment cycle. Future work will address the "steady-state" equilibrium investment horizon at time $t > t_0$.

For a given choice of utility function $u : \mathbb{R}^n \to \mathbb{R}$ operating over $n=2$ system attributes—consumption variables in an economic context—the dynamic representation of the utility function is defined from the terms of the Taylor expansion as

$$u(x_1(t_0) + \Delta x_1, x_2(t_0) + \Delta x_2) = u(x_1(t_0), x_2(t_0))$$
$$+ (u_{x_1}(x_1(t_0), x_2(t_0)) \Delta x_1 + u_{x_2}(x_1(t_0), x_2(t_0)) \Delta x_2)$$
$$+ \frac{1}{2} u_{x_1, x_1}(x_1(t_0), x_2(t_0)) (\Delta x_1)^2$$
$$+ \Delta x_1 \Delta x_2 (u_{x_1, x_2}(x_1(t_0), x_2(t_0)))$$
$$+ u_{x_2, x_2}(x_1(t_0), x_2(t_0)) (\Delta x_2)^2 \tag{13}$$

where $x_1(t_0)$ and $x_2(t_0)$ denote initial values, which is a valid approximation as Loistl [23] demonstrates that under fairly mild conditions the remainder converges to zero.

Assuming that the moment generating process is fully described by its first two moments, the following notation applies:

$$\mu_{x_1}(t) = \mathbb{E}_t(x_1(t) - \bar{x}_1) \tag{14}$$

$$\mu_{x_2}(t) = \mathbb{E}_t(x_2(t) - \bar{x}_2) \tag{15}$$

$$\sigma_{x_1}(t) = \mathbb{E}_t(x_1(t) - \bar{x}_1)^2 \tag{16}$$

$$\sigma_{x_2}(t) = \mathbb{E}_t(x_2(t) - \bar{x}_2)^2 \tag{17}$$

$$\sigma_{x_1, x_2}(t) = \mathbb{E}_t(x_2(t) - \bar{x}_2)(x_1(t) - \bar{x}_1) \tag{18}$$

where $\bar{x}_1$ and $\bar{x}_2$ are long-run targets and $\mathbb{E}_t$ is the instantaneous expectation at time t. Substituting these into the utility function above results in the following expected utility function:

$$\mathbb{E}(u(x_1(t), x_2(t))) = u(x_1(t_0), x_2(t_0)) + (u_{x_1}(x_1(t_0), x_2(t_0)) \mu_{x_1} + u_{x_2}(x_1(t_0), x_2(t_0)) \mu_{x_2})$$
$$+ \frac{1}{2} u_{x_1, x_1}(x_1(t_0), x_2(t_0)) \sigma_{x_1}(t) + \sigma_{x_1, x_2}(t)(u_{x_1, x_2}(x_1(t_0), x_2(t_0)))$$
$$+ u_{x_2, x_2}(x_1(t_0), x_2(t_0)) \sigma_{x_2}(t) \tag{19}$$

Assuming the existence of threats that degrade the system, induce utility losses, and continuously compound, and which are such that, for all t, $x_1(t) \geq 0$ and $x_2(t) \geq 0$, then the utility function will obey

$$u(\bar{x}_1, \cdot) \geq u(\bar{x}_1 + x_1(t), \cdot) \qquad \forall t \tag{20}$$

$$u(\cdot, \bar{x}_2) \geq u(\cdot, \bar{x}_2 + x_2(t)) \qquad \forall t \tag{21}$$

Table 2 Policy parameters

Parameter	Description
w_{x_1}	Policy weighting applied to first system attribute
w_{x_2}	Policy weighting applied to second system attribute
v_{x_1}	Sensitivity (risk aversion) to variance in first system attribute
v_{x_2}	Sensitivity (risk aversion) to variance in second system attribute
v_{x_1,x_2}	Sensitivity to covariance first and second system attributes

where $\cdot$ is a placeholder in the function. This results in decreasing marginal utility with respect to loss:

$$\frac{\partial u(\bar{x}_1,\cdot)}{\partial x_1} \geq \frac{\partial u(\bar{x}_1+x_1(t),\cdot)}{\partial x_1(t)} \qquad \forall t \tag{22}$$

$$\frac{\partial u(\cdot,\bar{x}_2)}{\partial x_2} \geq \frac{\partial u(\cdot,\bar{x}_2+x_2(t))}{\partial x_2} \qquad \forall t \tag{23}$$

We define the following policy parameters, as described in Table 2:

$$w_{x_1} = -u_{x_1}(x_1(t_0),x_2(t_0)) \tag{24}$$

$$w_{x_2} = -u_{x_2}(x_1(t_0),x_2(t_0)) \tag{25}$$

$$v_{x_1} = -2u_{x_1,x_1}(x_1(t_0),x_2(t_0)) \tag{26}$$

$$v_{x_1} = -2u_{x_2,x_2}(x_1(t_0),x_2(t_0)) \tag{27}$$

$$v_{x_1,x_2} = -u_{x_1,x_2}(x_1(t_0),x_2(t_0)) \tag{28}$$

Each of these has a simple interpretation, as described in Table 2.

From the asymmetric preference structure, the policy-maker's problem can be expressed as maximizing an expected utility function. The expected utility from the state of the system attributes is defined by the following integral that represents the cost of inaction:

$$\mathfrak{U}(t_0,T|w_{x_1},w_{x_2},v_{x_1},v_{x_2},v_{x_1,x_2}) = \int_{t_0}^{T} e^{-\beta t}\ell(t|w_{x_1},w_{x_2},v_{x_1},v_{x_2},v_{x_1,x_2})\,dt$$

$$= \int_{t_0}^{T} e^{-\beta t}(w_{x_1}\mu_{x_1}(t) + w_{x_2}\mu_{x_2}(t) + v_{x_1}\sigma_{x_1}(t)$$

$$+2v_{x_1,x_2}\sigma_{x_1,x_2}(t) + v_{x_2}\sigma_{x_2}(t))\,dt \tag{29}$$

where

$$\ell(t|w_{x_1},w_{x_2},v_{x_1},v_{x_2},v_{x_1,x_2}) = w_{x_1}\mu_{x_1}(t) + w_{x_2}\mu_{x_2}(t) + v_{x_1}\sigma_{x_1}(t)$$

$$+2v_{x_1,x_2}\sigma_{x_1,x_2}(t) + v_{x_2}\sigma_{x_2}(t) \tag{30}$$

The additional separable component in the policy-maker's loss function is defined with respect to the additional investment required in the presence of disclosed vulnerabilities. The objective is to find the policy-maker's cycle time to investment; that is, the upper limit of integration, T, which satisfies the equality of utility of action and utility of inaction. We denote this value as t^*.

3.1   The Investment Function

We assume the following investment function:

$$K(t) = \begin{cases} 0 & \text{if } t < t^* \\ \hat{K} + K_0 e^{\delta t} & \text{if } t = t^* \end{cases} \tag{31}$$

where $\hat{K}$ is the fixed cost, K_0 is the initial investment, and δ is the growth rate in variable cost, and, as defined above, t^* is the timing of the future investment. We assume that the investment function has a deterministic schedule: that is, there is no stochastic variation in the investment profile.

The policy-maker's credibility is defined in terms of deviation from a preset investment profile. That is, the policy-maker's utility is eroded by deviations from target investment. Specifically, we assume the following utility function for K:

$$u(\bar{K}) \geq u(\bar{K} + K(t)) \quad \forall t \tag{32}$$

$$\frac{\partial u(\bar{K})}{\partial K} \geq \frac{\partial u(\bar{K} + K(t))}{\partial K} \quad \forall t \tag{33}$$

Note that the utility of investment is always lower for deviations from the target investment profile, and that the change in utility is increasing with $K(t)$.

Taking the series expansion and integrating yields the cost of action:

$$\mathfrak{U}_K(t_0, T | w_K, v_K) = \int_{t_0}^{T} e^{-\beta t} \left(w_K \mu_K(t) + v_K \sigma_K(t) \right) dt \tag{34}$$

where, for initial investment K_0, $w_K = -u_K(K_0)$, $v_K = -2u_{KK}(K_0)$, $\mu_k(t) = \mathbb{E}(K(t) - \bar{K})$ and $\sigma_k(t) = \mathbb{E}(K(t) - \bar{K})^2$. The complete policy-maker's problem brings together the two additively separable components of the loss function:

$$\mathfrak{D}(t_0, T | w_{x_1}, w_{x_2}, v_{x_1}, v_{x_2}, v_{x_1, x_2}) = \mathfrak{U}(t_0, T | w_{x_1}, w_{x_2}, v_{x_1}, v_{x_2}, v_{x_1, x_2})$$

$$-\mathfrak{U}_K(t_0, T | w_K, v_K) \tag{35}$$

In the case of our system attributes, preferences, and investment function, we have

$$\mathfrak{D}(t_0, T \mid \cdot) = \int_{t_0}^{T} e^{-\beta t} \left(w_{x_1} \mu_{x_1}(t) + w_{x_2} \mu_{x_2}(t) + v_{x_1} \sigma_{x_1}(t) + 2v_{x_1, x_2} \sigma_{x_1, x_2}(t) + v_{x_2} \sigma_{x_2}(t) \right) dt$$

$$- \int_{t_0}^{T} e^{-\beta t} \left(w_K \mu_K(t) + v_K \sigma_K(t) \right) dt \tag{36}$$

The components of the decision structure in (35) have the following interpretation: the first denotes the cumulative loss from undertaking no additional investment, and the second is the cumulative loss incurred because of the extra expenditure, in the presence of disclosed vulnerabilities.

Equating utility of action and utility of inaction in (35) yields:

$$\mathfrak{D}(t_0, T \mid w_{x_1}, w_{x_2}, v_{x_1}, v_{x_2}, v_{x_1, x_2}) = 0 \tag{37}$$

Notice that the utility function given in (1) uses a Lebesgue integral to handle the stochastic structure of the problem, whilst in (29) the same problem is expressed, via the second-order approximation of the utility function, as a finite integral in terms the first two moments of the underlying distribution.

The decision system represented in (35) is a general device for a wide range of optimal control problems depending on the choice of moment functions, $\mu_K(t)$, $\mu_B(t)$, $\mu_{x_2}(t)$, $\sigma_K(t)$, $\sigma_{x_1}(t)$, $\sigma_{x_2}(t)$ and preferences w_K, w_{x_1}, w_{x_2}, v_K, v_{x_1}, v_{x_2}, v_{x_1, x_2}.

4 The Threat Environment and Decision-Making

We have developed the decision-making rule without taking into account explicitly the stochastic nature of vulnerability disclosure. We now proceed to give a detailed description of these stochastic processes, and integrate them into the policy-maker's decision-making algorithm.

The model is explicitly derived in terms of pre-defined target levels, $\bar{x}_1$ and $\bar{x}_2$. The impact of disclosure of vulnerabilities degrades these attributes by a factor Y, which is driven by an underlying vector stochastic process $y(t)$. The key feature of this setting is that the longer a system is left vulnerable, the greater the degradation to the system attributes. The stochastic process, $y(t)$, that characterizes the vulnerabilities/threats, is described by the following stochastic differential equation:

$$dy(t) = (\mu(y(t)) dt + \sigma(y(t)) dW_t) dJ_t \tag{38}$$

where $\mu(\cdot)$ is a vector/matrix function of the driving factors, $\sigma(\cdot)$ is a càdlàg variance generating function and, as such, discontinuities are entirely driven by the one-dimensional jump process J_t, with time-invariant intensity parameter, or rate, λ.

This form provides for a whole family of jump processes with random step sizes. We can think of this as being a compound of a smooth variational system (in the Brownian motion) and a discontinuous jump model driven by a poisson process. We now define μ_1 and μ_2 as being the time-homogenous drift-terms, and σ_1, σ_2 and σ_{12} are the time-homogenous elements of the covariance matrix of the underlying multivariate normal random variable driving the jump sizes of $y(t)$; see Appendix.

The process is driving a continuous stochastic discount factor, a very useful way of approaching the timing problem, as in essence we are comparing the evolution of a stochastic discount rate (for the potential and realized vulnerabilities) and a deterministic discount rate for the cost function.

The evolution of the individual system attribute x_i is written in integral form as

$$x_i(t_0, T) = x_i(t_0) \exp\left(\int_{t_0}^{T} y_i(t)\, dt \right) \tag{39}$$

The terminal distribution (at time $t + \Delta t$) is assumed to be log-normal with compounded jumps (see [27]). The useful properties of this terminal distribution are that the moments can be defined explicitly as products of the moments of the log-normal distribution and the intensity parameter, λ, from the jump process, as given in (38).

We now explain the timing solution space for the expected loss equation. First we find the derive the form of the solution (Proposition 1), and then we establish the existence of solutions (Theorem 1).

Proposition 1 (Form of Equilibrium Solution). *Let t^* be the expected time of investment. The equilibrium decision function (at t_0) in expectations is the following:*

$$
\mathfrak{D}\left(t_0, T \middle| w_{x_1}, w_{x_2}, w_k, v_{x_1}, v_{x_2}\right)
$$

$$
= e^{-t\beta} x_2(t) \left(\frac{e^{e^{2\mu_2 + \sigma_2^2}\left(-1 + e^{\sigma_2^2}\right)t\lambda}}{-\beta + e^{2\mu_2 + \sigma_2^2}\left(-1 + e^{\sigma_2^2}\right)\lambda} v_{x_2} + \frac{e^{e^{\mu_2 + \frac{\sigma_2^2}{2}}t\lambda}}{-\beta + e^{\mu_2 + \frac{\sigma_2^2}{2}}\lambda} w_{x_2} \right)
$$

$$
+ e^{-t\beta} x_1(t) \left(\frac{e^{e^{2\mu_1 + \sigma_1^2}\left(-1 + e^{\sigma_1^2}\right)t\lambda}}{-\beta + e^{2\mu_1 + \sigma_1^2}\left(-1 + e^{\sigma_1^2}\right)\lambda} v_{x_1} + \frac{e^{e^{\mu_1 + \frac{\sigma_1^2}{2}}t\lambda}}{-\beta + e^{\mu_1 + \frac{\sigma_1^2}{2}}\lambda} w_{x_1} \right)
$$

$$
- e^{-t\beta} \left(\frac{\hat{K}}{\beta} + \frac{e^{t\delta} K_0}{\beta - \delta} \right) w_K \Bigg|_{t=t_0}^{t=T} \tag{40}
$$

In this decision function, the first two terms represent the discount factors of the system attributes given the threat environment. The third term represents the dynamic evolution of investment in information security as the decision-maker

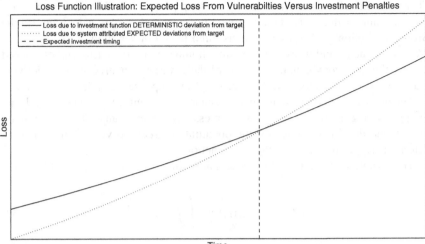

Fig. 2 Graphical Illustration of the expected and deterministic losses from deviations from system attributes and investment targets. The rigidity is given by $\hat{K}$, which is the height at which the *solid line* cuts the loss (vertical) axis

determines the appropriate time horizon, T. In effect, we are mapping the expected loss from the first two terms into the deterministic investment function $K(t)$; see Fig. 2. Setting $\mathfrak{D}(t_0, t^*) = 0$ defines the expected investment cycle (the vertical broken line in Fig. 2).

Thus Proposition 1 describes the equilibrium condition assuming the existence of a solution t^*. The proof of Proposition 1 is outlined in Appendix A.1.

We now give a characterization of the conditions for the existence of such a solution.

Theorem 1 (Existence of Equilibrium). *The existence of a solution t^* is subject to the following inequalities obtaining:*

$$e^{-t\beta} x_1(t) \left(\frac{e^{e^{2\mu_1 + \sigma_1^2}\left(-1+e^{\sigma_1^2}\right)t\lambda} v_{x_1}}{-\beta + e^{2\mu_1 + \sigma_1^2}\left(-1 + e^{\sigma_1^2}\right)\lambda} + \frac{e^{e^{\mu_1 + \frac{\sigma_1^2}{2}}t\lambda} w_{x_1}}{-\beta + e^{\mu_1 + \frac{\sigma_1^2}{2}}\lambda} \right)$$

$$> e^{-t\beta}\left(\frac{\hat{K}}{\beta} + \frac{e^{t\delta}K_0}{\beta - \delta} \right) w_K \quad \forall t > 0 \tag{41}$$

$$
e^{-t\beta} x_2(t) \left(\frac{e^{e^{2\mu_2+\sigma_2^2}\left(-1+e^{\sigma_2^2}\right)t\lambda} v_{x_2}}{-\beta + e^{2\mu_2+\sigma_2^2}\left(-1+e^{\sigma_2^2}\right)\lambda} + \frac{e^{e^{\mu_2+\frac{\sigma_2^2}{2}}t\lambda} w_{x_2}}{-\beta + e^{\mu_2+\frac{\sigma_2^2}{2}}\lambda} \right)
$$

$$
> e^{-t\beta} \left(\frac{\hat{K}}{\beta} + \frac{e^{t\delta} K_0}{\beta - \delta} \right) w_K \quad \forall t > 0 \tag{42}
$$

To derive the existence of equilibrium we impose certain reasonable assumptions on the model parameters. First, the global discount factors, $\delta > 0$, $\beta > 0$, are assumed positive and unbounded. Second, the derivatives are assumed to be in the risk aversion domain, and therefore w_{x_1}, w_{x_2}, w_K, v_{x_1}, $v_{x_2} > 0$. Finally, the initial expected investment point is assumed to be positive and unbounded; that is, $\hat{K} > 0$, indicating investment is always costly. The proof of Theorem 1 is presented in Appendix A.2.

4.1 Alternative Cases Under Equilibrium

For the decision function $\mathfrak{D}(\cdot)$, the inequalities presented in Theorem 1 provide three discrete cases:

- If, for all t, the decision function is strictly positive, then the policy-maker addresses vulnerabilties on arrival;
- If, for all t, the decision function is strictly negative, then the policy-maker, in expectations, never anticipates deviation from long-run investment;
- If there is a crossing solution for a positive t, then, in expectations relative to rest, there is an expected investment timing; that is, an investment cycle.

4.2 Discussion

For practical purposes, orientating the security management problem as suggested in Proposition 1 and Theorem 1 has been a useful exercise. Proposition 1 allows us to build a model of timing, by ascribing the system parameters exogenously from data and mapping preferences via a case-study approach to hypothesized events, in the manner of [22]. In related work, to be reported elsewhere, we have used a simulation approach along the lines of [12] and [9], whereby the system architecture of the candidate organization is modelled explicitly, using a location–resource–process systems model. The stochastic properties of the system's attributes are then mapped to our simpler stochastic process and the investment cycle timing.

Subsequently, we can orient the problem using actual data from the organisation on security threats (e.g., using a library such as the NISC CVSS[4] dataset) to populate the inequalities suggested in Theorem 1. We can then orient the free parameters of the system, to see which domains are feasible (i.e., calibrate the stated preferences in the systems model).

In organizations for which confidentiality and availability are of the utmost importance, that is for which the parameters w_a, w_{x_1}, etc. have high values compared to w_K, investment cycles in security will occur relatively more frequently compared to organizations for which investment in information security has high opportunity cost.

For example, in the context of the example of patching policy, a state organization which places very high value on confidentiality, whilst facing soft resource constraints as represented by a low value of w_K, will patch on arrival. A small firm, however, that is severely resource constrained, will avoid undertaking additional investment in information security, that is above $\hat{K}$, to shorten the window of vulnerability. In the strictly negative case of Sect. 4.1, the model indicates indefinite waiting for investment in the presence of vulnerability threats.

5 Conclusion

In this paper, we have derived (a quadratic approximation to) an analytic solution to the problem of optimal timing of security investments in the presence of existing and future threats. A key aspect of our approach is to introduce the concept of a security investment cycle that is analogous to the classical Keynesian treatment of rigidities.

An interesting potential application of this approach could be in cloud computing, whereby one of the potential macroeconomic benefits is in reducing the amount of capital (fixed) investment. In general, this should reduce vulnerability to negative shocks and, in effect, mitigate business cycles. However, rigidities in security costs could reduce the impact of this effect.

Appendix

A.1 Proof of Proposition 1: Decision Function Equilibrium

The vector random variable z has n univariate log-normal marginal distributions and correlation structure driven by $\Sigma = \mathbb{E}(\log z - \mu)(\log z - \mu)'$. Where $\prime$ denotes the conjugate transpose, $\mu = \{\mu_1, \ldots, \mu_n\}$ is a vector of time-homogenous central

---

[4]National Institute of Science and Technology (NIST), www.nist.gov; Common Vulnerability Scoring System (CVSS).

expectations, and $\Sigma = [\sigma_{ij}]$ is a time-homogenous covariance variance matrix. Setting $n = 2$, the observed moments and co-moments of z are defined as

$$\mathbb{E}(z_1) = e^{\mu_1 + \frac{\sigma_1^2}{2}} \tag{43}$$

$$\mathbb{E}(z_2) = e^{\mu_2 + \frac{\sigma_2^2}{2}} \tag{44}$$

$$\mathbb{E}(z_1 - \mathbb{E}(z_1))^2 = \mathrm{var}(z_1) = e^{2\mu_1 + \sigma_1^2}\left(-1 + e^{\sigma_1^2}\right) \tag{45}$$

$$\mathbb{E}(z_2 - \mathbb{E}(z_2))^2 = \mathrm{var}(z_1) = e^{2\mu_2 + \sigma_2^2}\left(-1 + e^{\sigma_2^2}\right) \tag{46}$$

$$\mathbb{E}(z_1 - \mathbb{E}(z_1))(z_2 - \mathbb{E}(z_2)) = \mathrm{cov}(z_1, z_2) = e^{\mu_1 + \mu_2 + \frac{1}{2}(\sigma_1^2 + \sigma_2^2)}\left(-1 + e^{\sigma_{12}}\right) \tag{47}$$

where μ_1 is the expected value of the generating normal distribution for the system attribute x_1, μ_2 is the expected value of the generating normal distribution for the system attribute x_2, σ_1 is the standard deviation of the underlying normal distribution for x_1, σ_2 is the standard deviation of the underlying normal distribution for x_2, and σ_{12} is the covariance of the underlying normal. distribution.

Consider an arrival rate λ. The expected number of events over the interval $[t_0, T]$ is then $\lambda(T - t_0)$. Let $t_0 \leq t \leq T$ and set $t_0 = 0$. The combined jump process $y(t) \in \mathbb{R}^2$, with poisson arrivals with count $\lambda(t)$, yields the expected moments of the threat environment discount factors for the interval $[0, t]$ as follows:

$$\mathbb{E}(y_1) = e^{\mu_1 + \frac{\sigma_1^2}{2}}\lambda(t) \tag{48}$$

$$\mathbb{E}(y_2) = e^{\mu_2 + \frac{\sigma_2^2}{2}}\lambda(t) \tag{49}$$

$$\mathbb{E}(y_1 - \mathbb{E}(y_1))^2 = \mathrm{var}(y_1) = e^{2\mu_1 + \sigma_1^2}\left(-1 + e^{\sigma_1^2}\right)\lambda(t) \tag{50}$$

$$\mathbb{E}(y_2 - \mathbb{E}(y_2))^2 = \mathrm{var}(y_1) = e^{2\mu_2 + \sigma_2^2}\left(-1 + e^{\sigma_2^2}\right)\lambda(t) \tag{51}$$

$$\mathbb{E}(y_1 - \mathbb{E}(y_1))(y_2 - \mathbb{E}(y_2)) = \mathrm{cov}(y_1, y_2)$$
$$= e^{\mu_1 + \mu_2 + \frac{1}{2}(\sigma_1^2 + \sigma_2^2)}\left(-1 + e^{\sigma_{12}}\right)\lambda(t) \tag{52}$$

Combining the moments of the system process from (39) with the instantaneous expectations from (14–18), yields

$$\mu_{x_1}(t) = e^{e^{\mu_1 + \frac{\sigma_1^2}{2}}(t)\lambda}x_1(t) \tag{53}$$

$$\mu_{x_2}(t) = e^{e^{\mu_2 + \frac{\sigma_2^2}{2}}(t)\lambda}x_2(t) \tag{54}$$

$$\sigma_{x_1}(t) = e^{e^{2\mu_1 + \sigma_1^2}\left(-1 + e^{\sigma_1^2}\right)(t)\lambda}x_1(t) \tag{55}$$

$$\sigma_{x_2}(t) = e^{e^{2\mu_2+\sigma_2^2}\left(-1+e^{\sigma_2^2}\right)(t)\lambda}x_2(t) \tag{56}$$

$$\sigma_{x_1,x_2}(t) = e^{e^{\mu_1+\mu_2+\frac{1}{2}\left(\sigma_1^2+\sigma_2^2\right)}(-1+e^{\sigma_{12}})(t)\lambda}x_2(t)x_1(t) \tag{57}$$

Substituting these into (30) gives the explicit instantaneous loss function, for compactness we assume separable additivity, therefore all the covariance terms drop out as follows:

$$
\begin{aligned}
\ell\left(t|w_{x_1},w_{x_2},v_{x_1},v_{x_2},v_{x_1,x_2}\right) &= e^{e^{2\mu_2+\sigma_2^2}\left(-1+e^{\sigma_2^2}\right)(t)\lambda}x_2(t)v_{x_2}\\
&+e^{e^{2\mu_1+\sigma_1^2}\left(-1+e^{\sigma_1^2}\right)(t)\lambda}x_1(t)v_{x_1}\\
&+e^{e^{\mu_1+\mu_2+\frac{1}{2}\left(\sigma_1^2+\sigma_2^2\right)}(-1+e^{\sigma_{12}})(t)\lambda}x_2(t)x_1(t)v_{x_1,x_2}\\
&+e^{e^{\mu_2+\frac{\sigma_2^2}{2}}(t)\lambda}x_2(t)w_{x_2}\\
&+e^{e^{\mu_1+\frac{\sigma_1^2}{2}}(t)\lambda}x_1(t)w_{x_1}
\end{aligned}
\tag{58}
$$

Integrating and discounting over the policy-maker's time horizon yields the expected loss function at time t_0,

$$
\begin{aligned}
\mathfrak{U}\left(t_0,T|w_{x_1},w_{x_2},v_{x_1},v_{x_2},v_{x_1,x_2}\right) &= -e^{-t\beta}x_2(t)\frac{e^{-e^{2\mu_2+\sigma_2^2}\left(-1+e^{\sigma_2^2}\right)(t)\lambda}}{\beta+e^{2\mu_2+\sigma_2^2}\left(-1+e^{\sigma_2^2}\right)\lambda}v_{x_2}\\
&-e^{-t\beta}x_2(t)\frac{e^{-e^{\mu_1+\mu_2+\frac{\sigma_1^2}{2}+\frac{\sigma_2^2}{2}}(-1+e^{\sigma_{12}})(t)\lambda}}{\beta+e^{\mu_1+\mu_2+\frac{\sigma_1^2}{2}+\frac{\sigma_2^2}{2}}(-1+e^{\sigma_{12}})\lambda}x_1(t)v_{x_1,x_2}\\
&-e^{-t\beta}x_2(t)\frac{e^{-e^{\mu_2+\frac{\sigma_2^2}{2}}(t)\lambda}}{\beta+e^{\mu_2+\frac{\sigma_2^2}{2}}\lambda}w_{x_2}\\
&-e^{-t\beta}x_1(t)\frac{e^{-e^{2\mu_1+\sigma_1^2}\left(-1+e^{\sigma_1^2}\right)(t)\lambda}}{\beta+e^{2\mu_1+\sigma_1^2}\left(-1+e^{\sigma_1^2}\right)\lambda}v_{x_1}\\
&-e^{-t\beta}x_1(t)\frac{e^{-e^{\mu_1+\frac{\sigma_1^2}{2}}(t)\lambda}}{\beta+e^{\mu_1+\frac{\sigma_1^2}{2}}\lambda}w_{x_1}\Bigg|_{t=t_0}^{t=T}
\end{aligned}
\tag{59}
$$

A.2 Proof of Theorem 1

Let $T < \infty$. For $t^* \in (t_0, T)$, the cost function at t_0 is defined as

$$
\mathfrak{U}(t_0, T | w_k) = \int_{t_0}^{T} e^{-\beta t} \left(\hat{K} + e^{t\delta} K_0 \right) w_k dt
$$

$$
= e^{-t\beta} \left(-\frac{\hat{K}}{\beta} + \frac{e^{t\delta} K_0}{-\beta + \delta} \right) w_k \Bigg|_{t=t_0}^{t=T} \tag{60}
$$

The subsequent trade-off decision-making function relative to the cost function from 35 is now

$$
\mathfrak{D}\left(t_0, T | w_{x_1}, w_{x_2}, w_K, v_{x_1}, v_{x_2}, v_{x_1, x_2}\right) = -e^{-t\beta} x_2(t) \frac{e^{-e^{2\mu_2 + \sigma_2^2}\left(-1 + e^{\sigma_2^2}\right)\lambda(t)} v_{x_2}}{\beta + e^{2\mu_2 + \sigma_2^2}\left(-1 + e^{\sigma_2^2}\right)\lambda}
$$

$$
-e^{-t\beta} x_2(t) \frac{e^{-e^{\mu_1 + \mu_2 + \frac{\sigma_1^2}{2} + \frac{\sigma_2^2}{2}}(-1 + e^{\sigma_{12}})\lambda(t)} x_1(t) v_{x_1, x_2}}{\beta + e^{\mu_1 + \mu_2 + \frac{\sigma_1^2}{2} + \frac{\sigma_2^2}{2}}(-1 + e^{\sigma_{12}})\lambda}
$$

$$
-e^{-t\beta} x_2(t) \frac{e^{-e^{\mu_2 + \frac{\sigma_2^2}{2}}\lambda(t)} w_{x_2}}{\beta + e^{\mu_2 + \frac{\sigma_2^2}{2}}\lambda}
$$

$$
+x_1(t) \left(-\frac{e^{-e^{2\mu_1 + \sigma_1^2}\left(-1 + e^{\sigma_1^2}\right)\lambda(t)} v_{x_1}}{\beta + e^{2\mu_1 + \sigma_1^2}\left(-1 + e^{\sigma_1^2}\right)\lambda} - \frac{e^{-e^{\mu_1 + \frac{\sigma_1^2}{2}}\lambda(t)} w_{x_1}}{\beta + e^{\mu_1 + \frac{\sigma_1^2}{2}}\lambda} \right)
$$

$$
+ \left(\frac{\hat{K}}{\beta} + \frac{e^{t\delta} K_0}{\beta - \delta} \right) w_k \Bigg|_{t=t_0}^{t=T} \tag{61}
$$

It is now trivial to see that the inequalities in Theorem 1 are obtained by subtracting last term of (61) from each side and setting either $x_1(t_0)$ or $x_2(t_0)$ to zero.

References

1. Abel R (1990) Asset prices under habit formation and catching up with the Joneses. Am Econ Rev 80(2):38–42
2. Anderson R (2001) Why information security is hard: an economic perspective. In: Proceedings of 17th Annual Computer Security Applications Conference, pp 358–265. IEEE

3. Anderson R, Böhme R, Clayton R, Moore T (2007) Security economics and the internal market. Report to the European Network and Information Security Agency (ENISA)
4. Anderson R, Moore T (2006) The economics of information security. Science 314:610–613. Extended version available at http://www.cl.cam.ac.uk/~rja14/Papers/toulouse-summary.pdf
5. Arora A, Telang R, Xu H (2008) Optimal policy for software vulnerability disclosure. Manag Sci 54(4):642–656
6. Arrow K (1971) The theory of risk aversion. In: Essays in the theory of risk bearing. Markham Publ. Co. pp 90–109 (Reprinted from: Aspects of the Theory of Risk Bearing, by Yrjo Jahnssonin Saatio, Helsinki, 1965)
7. August T, Tunca T (2006) Network software security and user incentives. Manag Sci 52(11):1703–1720
8. Beres Y, Griffin J, Shiu S, Heitman M, Markle D, Ventura P (2008) Analysing the performance of security solutions to reduce vulnerability exposure window. In: Proceedings of the 2008 Annual Computer Security Applications Conference. IEEE Computer Society Conference Publishing Services (CPS), pp 33–42
9. Beres Y, Pym D, Shiu S (2010) Decision support for systems security investment. In: Network Operations and Management Symposium Workshops (NOMS Wksps), 2010. IEEE/IFIP, pp 118–125, Doi: 10.1109/NOMSW.2010.5486590, ISBN: 978-1-4244-6037-3, INSPEC Accession Number: 11502735
10. Bloom N (2009) The impact of uncertainty shocks. Econometrica 77(3):623–685
11. Cavusoglu H, Cavusoglu H, Zhang J (2008) Security patch management: share the burden or share the damage. Manag Sci 54(4):657–670
12. Collinson M, Monahan B, Pym D (2010) Semantics for structured systems modelling and simulation. In: Proceedings of Simutools 2010. ICST: ACM Digital Library and EU Digital Library. ISBN: 78-963-9799-87-5
13. Epstein LG, Zin SE (1989) Substitution, risk aversion, and the temporal behavior of consumption growth and asset returns I: a theoretical framework. Econometrica 57(4):937–969
14. Fishburn PC (1970) Utility theory for decision making. Wiley
15. Fultz N, Grossklags J (2009) Blue versus red: towards a model of distributed security attacks. In: Dingledine R, Golle P (eds) Proceedings of the Thirteenth International Conference Financial Cryptography and Data Security (FC'09), Springer Verlag, pp 167–183, LNCS 5628, ISBN: 978-3-642-03548-7
16. Gordon L, Loeb M (2002) The economics of information security investment. ACM Trans Inform Syst Secur 5(4):438–457
17. Gordon L, Loeb M (2006) Managing cybersecurity resources: a cost-benefit analysis. McGraw Hill
18. Gordon L, Loeb M, Lucyshyn W (2003) Information security expenditures and real options: a wait-and-see approach. Comput Secur J 19(2):1–7
19. Ioannidis C, Pym D, Williams J (2009) Investments and trade-offs in the economics of information security. In: Dingledine R, Golle P (eds) Proceedings of Financial Cryptography and Data Security '09, LNCS, Springer, vol 5628, pp 148–166. Preprint available at http://www.abdn.ac.uk/~csc335/IoannidisPymWilliams-FC09.pdf
20. Ioannidis C, Pym D, Williams J (2011) Information security trade-offs and optimal patching policies. Eur J Oper Res. 216(2):434–444
21. Kahneman D, Tversky A (1979) Prospect theory: an analysis of decisions under risk. Econometrica 47: 313–327
22. Keeney R, Raiffa H (1976) Decisions with multiple objectives: preferences and value trade-offs. Wiley
23. Loistl O (1976) The erroneous approximation of expected utility by means of Taylor's series expansion: analytic and computational Results. Am Econ Rev 66(5):904–910
24. Mont MC, Beres Y, Pym D, Shiu S (2010) Economics of identity and access management: providing decision support for investments. In: Network Operations and Management Symposium Workshops (NOMS Wksps), 2010, IEEE/IFIP, pp 134–141, Doi: 10.1109/NOMSW.2010.5486588, ISBN: 978-1-4244-6037-3, INSPEC Accession Number: 11502733

25. Pratt J (1964) Risk aversion in the small and in the large. Econometrica 32:122–136
26. Rogers D, Williams L (2000) Diffusions, Markov processes, and Martingales. Cambridge Mathematics Library
27. Ross S (1995) Stochastic processes. Wiley
28. Taksumi K, Goto M (2010) Optimal timing of information security investment: a real options approach. In: Moore T, Pym D, Ioannidis C (eds) Economics of Information Security and Privacy. Proceedings of WEIS 2009, Springer, London

Are Home Internet Users Willing to Pay ISPs for Improvements in Cyber Security?

Brent Rowe and Dallas Wood

Abstract One strategy for improving cyber security would be for Internet service providers (ISPs) to take a more active role in curtailing criminal behavior over the Internet. However, few ISPs today are offering robust security to their customers, arguing that home Internet users are unwilling to pay for improvements in cyber security. This lack of ISP involvement in improving cyber security has led some industry experts to support government solutions that encourage ISPs to take a more active role in security. Yet no prior studies have attempted to evaluate empirically whether home Internet users are willing to pay the monetary and nonmonetary costs of ISP-based security solutions. This makes it difficult to determine whether government intervention is necessary, what form the intervention should take, and what the welfare impacts of intervention would be. Our research takes the first step in filling this gap in the literature. Specifically, we used choice-based conjoint analysis to examine the preferences of US Internet users. We found that home users are indeed willing to accept price increases, ISP-required security training, and security related interruptions of their Internet service in exchange for reductions in the risk of their computer slowing down or crashing, the risk of their identity being stolen, or the risk that others will be affected by their insecurity. This finding suggests that Internet users would be willing to pay for ISPs to take a more active role in security if the benefits of ISP-based security solutions were clearly communicated to them.

Keywords Internet service providers • Botnets • Home Internet users • Demand • Willingness to pay • Willingness to accept • Perceptions • Behaviors • Economics • Modeling • Knowledge • Attitudes • Beliefs • Incomplete information • Incentives • Disincentives

B. Rowe (✉) • D. Wood
RTIInternational, San Francisco, CA, USA

B. Schneier (ed.), *Economics of Information Security and Privacy III*,
DOI 10.1007/978-1-4614-1981-5_9,
© Springer Science+Business Media New York 2013

1 Introduction

Cyber attacks resulting from the current insufficient state of Internet security have led to large financial losses for businesses, governments, and individuals. Home Internet users are a large contributor to this problem because they typically do not maintain adequate security measures on their computers, which leaves them vulnerable to becoming part of a botnet, spreading viruses, or propagating other threats to cyber security.

Industry opinion and past research suggest that Internet service providers (ISPs) are in an ideal position to improve the security of home users [5, 8, 17, 25]. Specifically, ISPs can identify and quarantine subscribers that have malware on their machines, provide their subscribers with security software, and educate them on the importance of cyber security. However, few ISPs are taking such steps to improve home Internet user security. It is commonly argued that this is because home Internet users are unwilling to pay ISPs for improvements in cyber security, especially improvements in the security of others [1, 25, 27]. This belief has led several researchers to propose a variety of government solutions to encourage ISPs to take more steps to improve cyber security [4, 14, 15]. Yet, no previous study has attempted to assess empirically how much home users are actually willing to pay for ISP-based security solutions. This information could be useful for determining whether government intervention is required, what form that intervention should take, and what the welfare consequences might be.

Our paper takes the first step in filling this gap in the literature. Specifically, we address three research questions. First, we quantify US Internet users' preferences regarding ISP security solutions using choice-based conjoint analysis. We hypothesize that Internet users have clear preferences over several features of ISP security packages, favoring packages that impose fewer costs and provide greater reductions in cyber security risks. Second, we use the conjoint analysis results to explore how much Internet users are willing to pay for changes in individual ISP security package features (holding all other features constant). We hypothesize that the mean Internet user is willing to pay positive sums to improve their own security and the security of others. Lastly, we explore how much Internet users would be willing to pay for hypothetical security packages that combine multiple benefits and non-monetary costs. We hypothesize that the mean Internet user is willing to pay positive sums for these ISP security packages, even when those packages only benefit others.

2 ISP-Based Security Solutions and Home User Demand for Security

Recent studies and security experts have suggested that ISPs are in a good position to cost-effectively prevent certain types of malicious cyber behavior, such as the operation of botnets on home users' computers [5, 8, 17, 25]. ISPs are critical control points because they provide home users with access to the Internet. This allows them to observe traffic flowing into and out of their networks, placing them in a position to identify traffic spikes that could be associated with excessive malicious traffic (e.g., caused by worms or spam bots).

Once an ISP identifies signs of infection or misbehavior, they can pursue a number of security solutions. In general, these ISP-based security solutions can be grouped into two main categories:

1. *Internal solutions*: These solutions are implemented inside the ISP and involve monitoring traffic so that suspicious activity is addressed (e.g., responding to traffic spikes or other signs of infection by cutting off the infected user's Internet access until their machine has been repaired).
2. *External solutions*: These solutions help Internet subscribers improve their own security, either by providing them with security advice (e.g., how to set up a firewall) or with free security products (e.g., antivirus software). Fundamentally, these solutions rely on user action to improve security (and are therefore "external" to the ISP).

When these solutions are pursued, they can impose a variety of costs on ISP customers. First, they can lead to increases in the price home users pay for Internet access, because quarantining infected or malicious subscribers or offering antivirus software will increase the cost of doing business for ISPs. Second, home users may have to spend time each month taking advantage of security advice or installing and updating their antivirus software for those solutions to influence their security. Lastly, home users might have to suffer the inconvenience of having limits placed on their Internet access if they have malicious software on their machines.

However, home Internet users would not have to incur these costs for no reason. If internal and external solutions were pursued, they could serve to protect Internet users from malware and other threats. Specific benefits of ISP-based security solutions would include the following:

- Improved performance of a home user's computer: By removing malware that uses the scarce computing resources of a user's computer, users may see an increase in the performance of their machine.
- Reduced risk of a home user's identity being stolen: By removing malware from a user's computer and blocking spam from their e-mail accounts, ISP-based security solutions can reduce the risk of a person's identity being stolen.
- Reduced risk to other individuals and businesses from a home user's insecurity: By helping to mitigate the presence of botnets on home users' computers, ISP-based security solutions can help reduce the risk that businesses or other individuals would be harmed by them.

Although home Internet users may benefit from ISP-based security solutions, existing information suggests that few ISPs are pursuing these options. Currently, most ISPs do not pursue internal solutions like those described above. According to the 2009 Worldwide Infrastructure Security report, only 28% of the ISPs surveyed said that they use automated techniques for quarantining infected or malicious subscribers [3]. In terms of external solutions, many ISPs (such as Comcast and AOL) provide antivirus software to their home Internet customers for free [19]. However, no data exist that enable us to determine how effective these solutions, which require voluntary action on the part of home users, have been in improving overall cyber security. One ISP interviewed for this study[1] indicated that only 50% of their customers have downloaded a security software package that is free with their subscription.

It is typically argued that ISPs do not engage in more security activity because they do not have the proper incentives . Specifically, ISP customers are believed to be unwilling to incur the costs associated with ISP security solutions, and the ISP itself is immune from liability for its role in creating and propagating malware [1, 14, 25]. Therefore, a number of government solutions have been proposed to provide ISPs with a financial incentive to take a greater role in promoting cyber security [4, 14, 15]. Yet, no previous study has attempted to empirically determine how much home users are willing to pay for ISP-based security solutions. This information could be used to evaluate the welfare impacts of these proposed government solutions and thereafter to determine the appropriate government involvement (if any involvement is warranted).

For example, many proposals for government involvement involve forcing ISPs to pay for damages caused by botnets and other threats emanating from their networks. Specifically [14], argue that ISPs should be made strictly liable for the damages caused by their subscribers when they are infected with malware. Similarly, in a commissioned report for the European Network and Information Security Agency [2], recommend that ISPs be charged a fixed penalty if they do not quarantine infected individuals in a timely manner once they have been notified of their activities. They argue that this approach avoids several stumbling blocks with trying to impose strict liability on ISPs, such as the potentially high transaction cost of lawsuits and the difficulty of valuing the monetary losses associated with individual events. In either case, encouraging ISPs to take a more active role in security will still impose costs on home Internet users like those described above. They may also lead ISPs to pursue other options not discussed, such as requiring their subscribers to meet basic security requirements. For example [14], note that "ISPs have a direct contractual relationship with their subscribers and so surely a liable ISP will require each of its subscribers to adopt rudimentary precautions... [b]etter still, these contract terms can be enforced by technology, which is to say that an ISP can block any subscriber whose virus definitions are horribly out of date or whose firewall is malfunctioning" (p. 27).

Government involvement could also help encourage ISP-based security solutions by reducing the costs ISPs incur in pursuing them. For example, it is commonly known that the largest cost to ISPs in helping to providing additional security and remove bots from their networks is the cost of operating a call center that contacts users who show signs of infection, responding to questions, and helping them clean

---

[1]Participation by this ISP required that their name be kept confidential.

up their computers (e.g., [4]). These costs could be reduced substantially if the government were to operate a centralized call center to which ISPs would send all infected home Internet users, as is being done in the Netherlands [26].

However, the welfare impacts of pursuing these types of government policies cannot be evaluated until the demand of home Internet users for ISP-based security solutions has been assessed. This study aims to take the first step in filling this gap in the literature. Although no study has attempted to estimate the amount home users are willing to pay for ISP-based security solutions, several studies have tried to assess the demand for cyber security services in general. For example, a 2004 study of consumers in the United Kingdom found that 58% would be willing to pay $3 or more per month for greater protection. In the same study, 66% of consumers said that they would switch ISPs to one that offered "clean" Internet service [23]. In a more recent study [6], interviewed a small sample of home Internet users and found that more than 50% spend more than $20 per year on security products or subscription services. More than half also indicated they would be willing to pay their ISP 10% more for additional security. It is important to note that all of these past studies used simple opinion surveys that did not allow users to express their demand in terms of various cost trade-offs and specific security service components. This study uses choice-based conjoint analysis to better quantify home user demand for security, which are described in more detail in the following section.

3   Methods for Quantifying Home Internet Users' Demand for Improvements in Cyber Security

The primary purpose of this study is to assess the demand of home Internet users for improvements in cyber security. In order to answer this question, we must first conceptualize how the various costs and benefits of these ISP-based security solutions contribute to an individual Internet user's utility. Based on the discussion in the previous section, we can identify three costs to home users:

- Increases in the cost of Internet access,
- Time spent complying with ISP security requirements, and
- Limits placed on Internet access.

- We can also identify three types of benefits that may be received in exchange for accepting these costs:

- Reduced risk of a user's computer slowing down or crashing,
- Reduced risk of a user's identity being stolen, and
- Reduced risk to other individuals and business from a user's insecurity.

Although other costs and benefits could be considered in relation to ISP-based security solutions, we believe that these are the ones that would most concern Internet users. Therefore, we can conceptualize Internet user utility as a function that takes the form of

$$U = f(F, T, A, P, I, O)$$

where F is the additional fee ISPs charge Internet users for pursuing the security strategy, T is time users must spend complying with ISP-based security solutions, A is a measure of the user's ability to access the Internet, P is a measure of the risk a user's computer will slow down or crash, I is a measure of the risk of identity theft, and O is a measure of the risk that others will incur losses as a result of an individual Internet user's lack of security.

We hypothesize that increases in the cost of Internet access decrease personal utility ($\partial U/\partial F < 0$), increases in the time it takes to comply with ISP security requirements decrease personal utility ($\partial U/\partial T < 0$), improvements in a user's access to the Internet increase utility ($\partial U/\partial A > 0$), increases in the risk of a user's computer slowing down or crashing decrease utility ($\partial U/\partial P < 0$), increases in the risk of identity theft decrease utility ($\partial U/\partial I < 0$), and increases in the risk that others will incur losses as a result of a user's insecurity decrease utility ($\partial U/\partial O < 0$).

We operationalize this conceptual model using choice-based conjoint analysis. Choice-based conjoint analysis is a stated-preference survey method in which survey respondents are asked to choose between hypothetical products or policies. Conjoint analysis has been extensively used by market researchers for the past 30 years to evaluate the market potential of new products and to create pricing strategies [16]. In recent years, conjoint analysis has also been increasingly used to value the net benefits of government health and environmental policies [7], as well as types of security policies [18, 22]. Evidence supporting the reliability of conjoint analysis for making credible estimates of purchasing decisions has also been obtained through field experiments [13].

For the purposes of this study, we created conjoint choice tasks that required survey respondents to choose between ISP security "packages" that were differentiated by the costs they would impose on the respondent and the security benefits they would provide. In the following sections, we describe how the survey was developed, how it was administered, and the statistical methods used to evaluate the survey data collected.

3.1 Survey Development and Design

Data for this study were collected through a survey instrument, the primary component of which was a set of seven forced-choice questions that included a no-choice alternative (an opt-on) follow-up question (see Fig. 1 for an example). Each question described two hypothetical security packages that an ISP might offer Internet customers. After the respondent selected which of the two hypothetical packages they most preferred, they were asked if they would actually support their own ISP pursuing the package they selected. For the purposes of this study, we consider this choice task as being composed of three alternatives: Option A (if a person selected Option A and indicated that he would support his ISP pursuing that option), Option B (if a person selected Option B and indicated that he would support

	Option A	Option B
ISP Strategies to Improve Security		
Adding a fee to your bill to provide security services to Internet subscribers	$4 per month	$7 per month
Requiring you and other Internet subscribers to comply with security requirements and training	0.5 hours per month	0.5 hours per month
Limiting Internet access for you or other subscribers who show signs of malicious or illegal activity	ISP can never limit your access to the Internet	ISP can never limit your access to the Internet
Cyber Security Outcomes		
Reduced risk of your computer slowing down or crashing	Greatly Reduced	Greatly Reduced
Reduced risk of your identity being stolen	Not Reduced	Not Reduced
Reduced risk to other individuals and business from your insecurity	Not Reduced	Greatly Reduced
If these were the only options available, which would you choose?	☐	☐

Suppose your ISP was going to pursue the strategies for improving security that are included in your preferred option and that these strategies resulted in the outcomes described in the table above. Would you support your ISP pursuing these strategies?

☐ Yes, I would support my ISP pursuing these strategies
☐ No, I would not support my ISP pursuing these strategies

Fig. 1 Example choice question

his ISP pursuing that option), and a no-choice alternative (if a person selected either Option A or B but then indicated that he would not support his ISP pursuing that option).

Each hypothetical ISP security package was presented as being composed of the six costs and benefits (known as package "features" or "attributes") we used to conceptualize Internet user utility. However, in order to make the description of these attributes tractable in an experimental setting, we had to establish a set of finite descriptors known as "levels" to describe each attribute in a way the average Internet user would understand. We attempted to create levels for each of the six attributes so that they would include the set of plausible extremes. For example, the levels chosen for the attribute for limiting access to the Internet range from the ISP never having the ability to limit one of its customers' access to the ISP being able to totally disconnect a customer from the Internet if her computer appears to be infected by malware.

However, choosing the levels for the cyber security outcomes (benefits) attributes proved to be more difficult. We considered using quantitative measures of the how much various threats could be reduced (for example, saying the risk of identity theft would be reduced by 50%) but were concerned that (1) respondents would find these questions difficult to comprehend and (2) respondents would be answering

Table 1 Attributes and levels for choice experiment design

Attributes	Levels
Fee	$4 per month
	$7 per month
	$12 per month
Require Internet users to follow certain security policies and be trained regularly	0.5 h per month
	1 h per month
	3 h per month
Limit Internet access of customers whose computers show signs of being hacked	ISP can never limit a user's access to the Internet
	ISP can restrict a user's usage to certain functions or Web sites if the ISP suspects the user has been hacked
	ISP can cut off a user's connection to the Internet entirely if the ISP suspects the user has been hacked
Reduced risk of a user's computer slowing down or crashing	Not reduced
	Somewhat reduced
	Greatly reduced
Reduced risk of a user's identity being stolen	Not reduced
	Somewhat reduced
	Greatly reduced
Reduced risk to other individuals and businesses from a user's insecurity	Not reduced
	Somewhat reduced
	Greatly reduced

questions from different baselines as to what the current risks were. Therefore, three qualitative levels were chosen for each attribute to indicate whether the package in question greatly reduced a given threat, somewhat reduced it, or did not reduce it at all. A summary of the attributes and levels used in the final survey instrument are presented in Table 1.

Given the six attributes and three levels described above, 729 ($3 \times 3 \times 3 \times 3 \times 3 \times 3$) possible hypothetical packages could be created. However, one of the primary benefits of conjoint analysis is that only a small fraction of these potential packages have to be evaluated by actual respondents if each attribute being considered is assumed to add linearly to a person's utility. When this assumption is made and a proper subsample of the 729 hypothetical package profiles is chosen (this subsample is referred to as the "experimental design"), then statistical analysis can be used to predict how respondents would answer the remaining hypothetical choice tasks [16]. A "proper subsample," or statistically efficient experimental design, is one that possesses several properties [9, 28], such as the following:

- *Level balance*: The levels of an attribute occur with equal frequency.
- *Orthogonality*: The occurrences of any two levels of different attributes are uncorrelated.
- *Minimal overlap*: Cases where attribute levels do not vary within a choice set should be minimized.

- *Utility imbalance*: The probabilities of choosing alternatives within a choice set should be as efficient as possible. For example, for two alternatives the probabilities should be approximately 0.75 and 0.25 [9].

Unfortunately, it is often impossible to achieve both level balance and orthogonality in small designs. However [12], show that it is possible to produce relatively efficient designs that are neither balanced nor orthogonal. Such efficient designs can be produced using an iterative computer algorithm. The experimental design for our stated preference questions was created using Sawtooth Choice-Based Conjoint Software [20]

3.2 Survey Fielding and Sample Characteristics

After the survey instrument was completed, it was programmed for Web administration by comScore, Inc., and administered from November 2010 to December 2010 to 3,635 members of the comScore panel that had broadband Internet access, exceeded 18 years of age, and resided inside the United States. The comScore panel is a large opt-in consumer-panel that comScore, Inc maintains to be representative of the online population and projectable to the total US population. The panelists are recruited across thousands of sites not used by other panel suppliers and they do not have to be willing to answer surveys to be accepted to the panel. We decided to include only broadband Internet users from the comScore panel in our sample because they are the users that would be most affected by ISP security packages.

To determine the proper sample size for this survey, we used the technique recommended in [16] as a starting point. This approach relies on the number of total questions per respondent (t), the maximum number of attribute levels (c), the number of alternatives in the trade-offs (a), and the number of respondents (n). In this study, $c = 3$ (all attributes possess only three levels), $a = 2$ (alternatives of A or B), and $t = 7$ main questions. Specifically, Orme recommends that ($nta/c \geq 500$), for a minimum sample size of at least $n = 107$ for each version of our survey. To improve the statistical power and reliability of our analyses, we sampled a significantly greater number $n = 3,635$.

Descriptive statistics of the sample we collected are provided in Table 2. The sample was approximately evenly split between males and females. Approximately half of the sample was under 40 years of age. The vast majority of survey respondents ($\sim$70%) were college educated. The majority of respondents (57%) had household incomes exceeding \$50,000. The vast majority of the sample was white (81%). The majority of respondents pay more than \$40 per month for broadband Internet access (54%). Specifically, the mean monthly Internet bill was estimated to be \$46.

To determine how well this sample compares with the US broadband Internet population, we compared it with a sample collected by the Pew Research Center in May 2010 and used in its 2010 Home Broadband Adoption study [21]. Their sample

Table 2 Sample characteristics (N = 3,635)

	2010 Survey (N = 3,635)	Pew 2010 Survey (N = 1,413)
Gender		
Male (%)	49	45
Female (%)	51	55
Age		
18–24 years (%)	11	12
25–34 years (%)	31	15
35–44 years (%)	15	16
45–54 years (%)	26	22
55–64 years (%)	12	21
65 years or older (%)	5	12
Don't know/refused (%)	0	2
Education		
High school diploma or less (%)	21	27
Some college (%)	30	30
College graduate (%)	49	43
Don't know/refused (%)	0	0
Annual Household Income		
< $50,000 (%)	44	33
$50,000–$99,000 (%)	36	32
$100,000+ (%)	21	20
Don't know/refused (%)	0	15
Race		
White (%)	81	80
Nonwhite (%)	19	20
Monthly Broadband Internet Bill		
< $20 (%)	8	2
$20–$39 (%)	38	33
$40+ (%)	54	36
Don't know/refused (%)	0	29

was intended to be representative of the US adult population as a whole, not just broadband users. A combination of landline and cellular random digit dial (RDD) samples was used to represent all adults in the continental United States who have access to either a landline or cellular telephone. Of this sample, 86% was composed of broadband Internet users. The demographic characteristics of these broadband Internet users are compared with the characteristics of those in our sample. As we can see, the demographic characteristics are relatively similar across both samples. However, it is important to note that our sample does appear to be slightly younger and slightly more educated than the broadband Internet users included in the Pew sample.

3.3   Statistical Analysis of Survey Data Collected

The first research question of this paper is to quantify US Internet user preferences. However, the data collected through the survey described above do not allow us to quantify Internet user preferences directly, as we only observe the choices they make between hypothetical ISP security options. Instead, we can only quantify these preferences if we make a series of assumptions regarding the average Internet user's utility function. Specifically, we estimate Internet user preference parameters using a random utility maximization (RUM) model.

The RUM model assumes that utility is defined as a function of the six attributes used to define a hypothetical ISP security package option and some random component. More formally, we define the utility a person receives from ISP security option j on choice task t by

$$u_{jt} = v_{jt}(\mathbf{X}_{jt}) + \varepsilon_{jt}, \quad j = 0, 1, 2, \quad t = 1, \ldots, 7, \tag{1}$$

where v_j is the deterministic (observable) component of utility that depends on the attribute levels that compose security option j in choice task t (represented as the vector $\mathbf{X}_{jt}$) and ε_j is a random error that represents the component of utility that is unobservable to the researcher.

We follow convention and assume that the deterministic portion of the utility function (v_j) follows a linear specification for utility such that preferences for the three alternatives on a given choice occasion are given by

$$U_{isppackage} = \beta_{fee} * \textit{fee}^i + \beta_{time} * \textit{time}^i$$

$$+ (\beta_{neverlimit} + \beta_{restrictifuserhacked} + \beta_{cutoffifuserhacked}) * x^i_{\text{isp access}}$$

$$+ \left(\beta_{notreduced} + \beta_{somewhatreduced} + \beta_{greatlyreduced} \right) x^i_{\text{comp crash}}$$

$$+ \left(\beta_{notreduced} + \beta_{somewhatreduced} + \beta_{greatlyreduced} \right) x^i_{\text{ident theft}}$$

$$+ \left(\beta_{not\_reduced} + \beta_{somewhat\_reduced} + \beta_{greatly\_reduced} \right) x^i_{\text{risk\_to\_others}} + \varepsilon^i_{isp\_package} \tag{2}$$

$$U_{neither\_package} = \beta_0 * D^i_{\text{neither\_package}} + \varepsilon^i_{neither\_package}$$

where $\textit{fee}^i$ is the price of alternative i, $\textit{time}^i$ is the time associated with complying with ISP security requirements in alternative i, $x^i_{\text{isp access}}$ is a vector of three indicator variables for different levels of the "limits placed on Internet access" attribute, $x^i_{\text{comp crash}}$ is a vector of three indicator variables for different levels of "improved computer performance" attribute, $x^i_{\text{ident theft}}$ is a vector of three indicator variables for the "reduced risk of identity theft" attribute, $x^i_{\text{risktoothers}}$ is a vector of three indicator variables for the "reduced risk to other individuals and businesses from your insecurity" attribute, and $D^i_{\text{neitherpackage}}$ is an indicator variable equal to 1 if alternative i is "neither package."

The RUM model presented above was estimated using a mixed-logit model in Stata 11[2]. In this estimation, variables fee and time were entered as continuous variables in the regression, while indicator variables for the other four attributes were entered as effects coded variables. A primary advantage of this approach is that it allows us to interpret the β parameters as relative importance weights. Specifically, $(-\beta_{fee})$ represents the marginal utility of income and $(-\beta_{time})$ represents the marginal utility of time. The remaining β parameters can be interpreted as relative importance weights (also known as part-worth utilities), where larger values of β indicate greater utility.

After the RUM model has been estimated, the β parameters can be used to make the calculations required to address the remaining two research questions of this paper, which deal with estimating willingness to pay (WTP) metrics. First, the estimated RUM parameters are used to calculate how much the average Internet user is willing to pay for changes in the levels of a particular ISP security package attribute (also known as a marginal WTP). A marginal WTP can be estimated by dividing the difference between the part-worth utilities of the two attribute levels in question by the marginal utility of income.

For example, the mean marginal WTP to move from a package where the US government had unlimited access to one's personal information to a package where the government had no access equals the difference between the part-worth utilities for these two levels divided by the marginal utility of money: $[(\beta_{neverlimitaccess} - \beta_{cancutoffaccesifuserhacked})/(-\beta_{fee})]^3$. Standard errors and confidence intervals for these estimated marginal WTP measures were estimated using a Krinsky-Robb bootstrapping procedure with 10,000 iterations [10, 11].

Second, the estimated RUM model results are used to estimate the maximum amount the mean Internet user would be willing to pay for a hypothetical security package offered by ISPs relative to having no package. For the purposes of this study, we consider two hypothetical security packages. First, we consider the package that would be most preferred by home Internet users. This package would include 0 h each month complying with ISP security requirements, the ISP can never limit the user's Internet access, the risk of the computer slowing down is greatly reduced, the risk of identity theft is greatly reduced, and the risk to other individuals from user insecurity is greatly reduced. Although this package would likely be unfeasible from the perspective of the ISP, the WTP estimated for this package would represent the most Internet users would ever pay for ISP-based security solutions.

---

[2]Mixed logit was chosen over simpler methods of estimation, like conditional logit, because it treats variation in respondent preferences as a statistical property, which greatly improves the fit of the model.

[3]The intuition behind this calculation is that the difference between the part-worth utilities of the two levels under consideration provides one with the number of "utils" gained from making the package change. These "utils" are converted to monetary units by dividing by the marginal utility of income $(-\beta_{fee})$.

The second hypothetical package we consider in this study is one that is similar to the type of ISP-based security solutions discussed above. Specifically, this package would "quarantine" users that were identified as having malware on their machines and require them to spend time removing this malware from their machine. This package would certainly benefit individuals besides the user herself because such a package would go toward preventing the spread of botnets and other cyber security threats. However, it is readily apparent how much benefit the Internet user herself would receive from this package. Therefore, to achieve a conservative WTP, we assume she receives no direct benefit. In terms of the attribute levels used in the choice experiments, this package would be described as including 1 h of time each month complying with ISP security requirements, the ISP can entirely cut off the user's Internet access if the ISP suspects the user has been hacked, the risk of the computer slowing down is not reduced, the risk of identity theft is not reduced, and the risk to other individuals from user insecurity is greatly reduced.

After the hypothetical packages have been selected, the maximum amount Internet users would be WTP for this package can be calculated by estimating the difference between the total utility a given security package yields and the total utility a no-package alternative yields, which is done using what is known as the "log-sum" formula (derived in [24]). For example, say we wanted to estimate the maximum WTP (relative to the no-package alternative) for the most preferred ISP security package. This would be estimated as follows:[4]

$$
\begin{aligned}
\text{Max Mean WTP} = (-1/\beta_{\text{fee}}) * \Big[&\ln \Big(\exp \Big(\beta_{\text{time}} * 0 + \beta_{\text{never limit access}} \\
&+ \beta_{\text{crash risk greatly reduced}} + \beta_{\text{id theft risk greatly reduced}} \\
&+ \beta_{\text{others risk greatly reduced}} \Big) \\
&+ \exp(\beta_0 - \beta_{\text{fee}} * \$7.15 - \beta_{\text{time}} * 1.40) \Big) \\
&- \ln(\exp(\beta_0 - \beta_{\text{fee}} * \$7.15 - \beta_{\text{time}} * 1.40)) \Big]
\end{aligned}
\tag{3}
$$

Here again, standard errors and confidence intervals for these estimated marginal WTP measures were estimated using a bootstrapping procedure with 10,000 iterations.

---

[4]Please note that the $7.15 and 1.40 h are the mean dollars and time shown to respondents in the hypothetical choice tasks. The subtraction of $\beta_{\text{fee}}^* $7.15 and $\beta_{\text{time}} * 1.40$ from the alternative-specific constant, β_0, is necessary because we used continuous fee and time terms and effects-coding for the other parameters.

4 Estimation Results

4.1 Quantified US Internet User Preferences

For the first research question, Table 3 presents results from our mixed logit model, which quantifies preferences for US Internet users. Based on the size and sign of model coefficients, we can see that user preferences coincide well with the hypotheses stated in constructing our conceptual model. Specifically, increases in the cost of Internet access decrease personal utility, increases in the time it takes to comply with ISP security requirements decrease personal utility, improvements in a user's access to the Internet increase utility, decreases in the risk of a user's computer slowing down or crashing increase utility, decreases in the risk of identity theft increase utility, and decreases in the risk to other individuals and businesses from the user's insecurity increase utility.

We can also see from these results that the cyber security outcome (or benefit) that matters most to Internet users is reduction in the risk of identity theft. This is demonstrated by the fact that the part-worth utility associated with great reductions in the risk of identity theft (0.43) is larger than the part-worth utility associated with great reductions in the risk of the computer slowing down or crashing (0.32) or risk to others (0.21).

4.2 Marginal Willingness to Pay for Changes in ISP Security Package Features

For the second research question, we calculate the mean marginal WTP estimates for changes in each ISP security package feature from their least to their most favored level. Table 4 reports these mean marginal WTP estimates as well as 95% confidence intervals. As hypothesized, the mean US Internet user is willing to pay positive sums for improvements in their security as well as the security of others (as the confidence intervals indicate, all values are statistically different from zero at the 5% significant level). Specifically, respondents were willing to pay $6.51 per month to greatly reduce the risk of identity theft (other things being equal). If ISPs could achieve and charge for such an improvement, this would represent a 14% increase in ISP revenue over the current mean monthly Internet bill. In terms of improvements in other cyber security outcomes, respondents were willing to pay $4.40 per month to greatly reduce the risk of their computer crashing and $2.94 per month to greatly reduce the risks of cyber security threats to others that may result from their personal insecurity. This third result conflicts with past views (e.g., [1, 27]) that doubted whether Internet users would be willing to pay to improve the security of others.

In terms of nonmonetary costs associated with ISP security packages, we see that because these have negative impact on utility that Internet users are willing to pay to

Table 3 Preference parameter estimates (coefficients from mixed logit model)

	Estimated mean coefficient	Standard error of the mean	Estimated standard deviation	Standard error of the standard deviation
Add a fee to provide security services to Internet subscribers	−0.14***	0.00	NA	NA
Require Internet users to follow certain security packages and be trained regularly	−0.10***	0.01	NA	NA
Limit Internet access for customers whose computers show signs of being "hacked"				
Never limit access	0.31***	0.02	0.51	0.03
Only restrict access	−0.01***	0.02	0.00	0.05
Entirely cut off access	−0.30***	0.02	NA	NA
Reduced risk of the user's computer slowing down or crashing				
Not reduced	−0.30***	0.02	0.26	0.05
Somewhat reduced	−0.02***	0.02	−0.09	0.08
Greatly reduced	0.32***	0.02	NA	NA
Reduced risk of the user's identity being stolen				
Not reduced	−0.49***	0.02	−25.23	0.00
Somewhat reduced	0.06***	0.02	0.92	0.36
Greatly reduced	0.43***	0.02	NA	NA
Reduced risk to other individuals and businesses from the user's insecurity				
Not reduced	−0.21***	0.02	−0.10	0.08
Somewhat reduced	0.00***	0.02	−0.01	0.04
Greatly reduced	0.21***	0.02	NA	NA
No choice alternative (adjusted)	−0.46***	0.07	1.17	0.42

Note: (1) Effects-coded variables were used for all attributes except fee and time spent complying with security requirements. (2) Standard errors on omitted coefficients were estimated by Krinsky-Robb parametric bootstraps. (3) *** denotes $p < 0.01$,** denotes $p < 0.05$,* denotes $p < 0.10$.

avoid these costs or could be made indifferent to them through cash compensation (such as reductions in their monthly internet bill). For example, the mean WTP to avoid 1 h spent complying with ISP security requirements was only $0.73 per month. Alternatively, this means respondents would only have to be paid $0.73 per month to be indifferent to these requirements (all else being held constant). Such a payment would represent a 1.6% decrease in the mean monthly Internet bill of respondents participating in the survey ($46 per month).

Table 4 Mean willingness to pay for improvements in ISP security package features

	Estimated WTP ($/month)	95% Confidence interval
Time spent complying with ISP security requirements: WTP to avoid 1 h of time complying with security requirements	0.73	[0.57–0.92]
Limiting Internet access: WTP to move from ISP being able to entirely restrict access to not restrict access at all	4.32	[3.72–4.92]
Risk of computer slowing down or crashing: WTP to move from not reduced to greatly reduced	4.40	[3.83–4.97]
Risk of identity theft: WTP to go from not reduced to greatly reduced	6.51	[5.86–7.16]
Risk to other individuals and businesses: WTP to go from not reduced to greatly reduced	2.94	[2.44–3.45]

Note: 95% confidence interval was estimated using Krinsky-Robb parametric bootstrapping technique.

By contrast, US Internet users were willing to pay more to avoid limitations on their Internet access. Specifically, we estimate the mean WTP to shift from allowing ISPs to entirely cut off one's Internet access to never being allowed to restrict one's access would be $4.32 per month. Or, alternatively, respondents have to be paid $4.32 per month to be indifferent to a shift in the other direction (all else being held constant). This would represent a 9% reduction in the mean monthly Internet bill.

4.3 Maximum Willingness to Pay for Hypothetical ISP Security Packages

For the third research question, we estimate the maximum amount the mean Internet user is willing to pay for two hypothetical ISP security packages—the first is the package most preferred by Internet users and the second is the package where respondents would be subject to "quarantine." Table 5 summarizes the results of our analysis.

The mean WTP for the most preferred ISP security package was $7.24. This estimate represents the most an average Internet user would ever pay for an ISP security package that offers all the benefits considered in our experiment. We estimated a 95% confidence interval for this WTP by using Krinsky-Robb parametric bootstraps and found the lower confidence limit to be $6.51 per month and the upper confidence limit to be $7.97 per month.

The mean WTP for the quarantine package is $1.22 with a 95% confidence interval from $1.03 to $1.41. Although this WTP estimate is 83% lower than the mean WTP for the most preferred ISP security package, it is based on very conservative assumptions and is still significantly different from zero. This suggests that the average Internet user would indeed be willing to pay for a package that

Table 5 Willingness to pay for hypothetical ISP security package

	Estimated WTP ($/month)	95% Confidence interval
Most preferred package: 0 h each month complying with ISP security requirements, ISP can never limit the user's Internet access, risk of computer slowing down is greatly reduced, risk of identity theft is greatly reduced, and risk to other individuals from user insecurity is greatly reduced.	7.24	[6.51–7.97]
Quarantine package: 1 h of time each month complying with ISP security requirements, ISP can entirely cut off the user's Internet access if the ISP suspects the user has been hacked, risk of computer slowing down is not reduced, risk of identity theft is not reduced, and risk to other individuals from user insecurity is greatly reduced.	1.22	[1.03–1.41]

Note: The 95% confidence interval was estimated using Krinsky-Robb parametric bootstrapping technique.

quarantined users infected with malware from the Internet until they had removed the harmful software from their machine. Again, this result conflicts with past views on this topic (e.g., [1, 27]).

5 Conclusions

The purpose of this paper was to explore three research questions. First we sought to quantify US Internet users' preferences. We found that Internet users have clear preferences over several features of ISP security packages and, not surprisingly, favor packages that impose fewer costs and provide greater reductions in cyber security risks. In particular, the security risk that Internet users care most about is the risk of identity theft.

Second, we explored how much US Internet users are willing to pay for changes in individual features of ISP security packages (holding all other features constant). The results of our analysis suggest that U.S. Internet users are indeed willing to pay positive and statistically significant sums to ISPs to achieve improvements in their own security as well as the security of others. Specifically, we found that home Internet users were willing to pay up to $6.51 per month to greatly reduce the risk of identity theft, $4.40 per month to greatly reduce the risk of their computer crashing, and $2.94 per month to reduce the risks other individuals and businesses might face as a result of their personal insecurity. Additionally, we found that (when ignoring the benefits of ISP security packages) US Internet would require cash compensation (such as in the form of reductions in the monthly cost of

Internet access) to be indifferent to the nonmonetary costs of ISP security packages. For example, respondents would have to be paid $0.73 per month to be indifferent to spending 1 h complying with ISP-determined security standards. Given that the mean monthly Internet bill for the sample was $46 per month, this compensation would correspond to a 1.6% the monthly cost Internet access on average. Similarly, we found that home users would have to receive a $4.32 decrease in their monthly Internet bill (a 9% reduction in the monthly cost of Internet access) to be indifferent between ISPs never being able to interrupt an individual's Internet access and allowing ISPs to entirely cut off a person's Internet access if the security of their computer is compromised.

However, in the real world, Internet users would be asked to weigh the costs and benefits of a particular ISP security package simultaneously. Therefore, in investigating the final research question we estimated the maximum WTP for several hypothetical ISP security packages. We found that the most an average Internet user will pay for an ISP security package is approximately $7.24 per month, which would represent a 16% increase in the current average monthly Internet bill in the U.S. Furthermore, we found that, on average, Internet users were willing to pay for ISP security packages that primarily improved the security of other individuals. Specifically, the mean WTP for a package that required all individuals to spend 1 h complying with ISP security requirements each month, enabled ISPs to entirely cut-off the internet access of users with machines infected with malware, and only reduced the risk to others from the user's own insecurity was $1.22.

Overall, these results indicate that US Internet users are willing to accept both monetary and nonmonetary costs to improve their security and the security of others. This could suggest government intervention is not required to encourage ISPs to take a more active role in security, because they could offer improvements in security to customers in exchange for higher prices. However, if this were the case, we must ask why ISPs are not already pursuing this opportunity.

One possible reason is that individuals participating in our study were told how effective the hypothetical ISP security packages would be at improving their security. Yet, this kind of information is not available to ISP customers in the real world, and no [25] adequate market signals exist that enable users to distinguish ISPs based on the level of security they provide their users [25]. Therefore, developing a means of communicating the benefits of ISP-based security solutions may be a more cost-effective method for improving overall cyber security than other policy options being considered.

A second possible reason we do not observe more ISPs engaged in improving user security is that home users are not willing to pay enough to make pursuing improvements in security profitable. For example, if it costs ISPs more to implement a particular security plan than their customers are willing to pay, then implementing the plan would not ultimately be profitable. Yet, relatively little information is available on the costs of ISP-based security solutions, so we cannot say at this time whether they pose a barrier to ISPs taking a more active role in security. However, if it is the case that most ISP-based security solutions are cost prohibitive, it is important to note that the majority of Internet users are typically ill-informed about the true threat that malware or botnets pose. Therefore, it may be that Internet users would be willing to pay ISPs more for security packages if they were better informed of the dangers associated with cyber security threats. This possibility should also be taken into account when considering how best governments can work to improve cyber security.

References

1. Anderson R (2001) Why Information security is hard: an economic perspective. In: Proceedings of the 17th Annual Computer Security Applications Conference
2. Anderson R, Bohme R, Clayton R, Moore T (2008) Analyzing barriers and incentives for network and information security in the internal market for e-communication. http://www.enisa.europa.eu/act/sr/reports/econ-sec. Accessed 1 June 2011
3. Arbor Networks (2010) 2009 Worldwide infrastructure security report. http://www.arbornetworks.com/report. Accessed 21 Feb 2010
4. Clayton R (2010) Might governments clean-up malware? http://weis2010.econinfosec.org/papers/session4/weis2010_clayton.pdf
5. Evers J (2005) ISPs versus the zombies. Cnet News.com. http://news.cnet.com/ISPs-versus-the-zombies/2100--7349_3--5793719.html. Accessed 24 Apr 2009
6. Gallaher M, Rowe B, Rogozhin A, Link A (2006) Economic analysis of cyber security and private sector investment decisions. Report prepared for the U.S. Department of Homeland Security. Research Triangle Park, NC: RTI International
7. Hensher DA, Rose JM, Green WH (2005) Applied choice analysis: a primer. Cambridge University Press, Cambridge, UK
8. Huang Y, Xianjun G, Whinston A (2007) Defeating DDoS attacks by fixing the incentive chain. ACM Trans Internet Technol 7(1):1–5. http://portal.acm.org/citation.cfm?doid=1189740.1189745. Accessed 30 Apr 2009
9. Kanninen B (2002) Optimal design for multinomial choice experiments. J Mark Res 39:214–227
10. Krinsky I, Robb A (1986) On approximating the statistical properties of elasticities. Rev Econ Stat 68:715–719
11. Krinsky I, Robb A (1990) On approximating the statistical properties of elasticities: a correction. Rev Econ Stat 72:189–90
12. Kuhfeld WF, Tobias RD, Garratt M (1994) Efficient experimental design with marketing research applications. J Mark Res 31:545–557
13. List J, Sinha P, Taylor M (2006) Using choice experiments to value non-market goods and services: evidence from field experiments. Adv Econ Anal Policy 6(2):1–37
14. Lichtman D, Posner E (2004) Holding Internet service providers accountable. In: John M Olin Law and Economist Working Paper, Vol 217. University of Chicago. http://www.law.uchicago.edu/files/files/217-dgl-eap-isp.pdf. Accessed 1 June 2011
15. Moore T (2010) The economics of cybersecurity: principles and policy options. Int J Crit Infrastruct Prot 3(3–4):103–117
16. Orme B (2010) Getting started with conjoint analysis. Research Publishers, LLC, Madison, WI
17. Richards J (2007) Make firms bear the cost to improve information security, says Schneier. Computer Weekly. http://www.computerweekly.com/Articles/2007/05/22/223959/make-firms-bear-the-cost-to-improve-information-security$\neg$says-schneier.htm. Accessed 24 Apr 2009
18. Robinson N, Potoglou D, Kim C, Burge P, Warnes R (2010) Security at what cost? In: Critical infrastructure protection IV: IFIP advances in information and communication technology. 342:3–15

19. Rowe B, Wood D, Reeves D, Braun F (2011) Economic analysis of ISP provided cyber security solutions. https://www.ihssnc.org/portals/0/Rowe_IHSS_Cyber_Final_ReportFINAL. pdf. Accessed 3 June 2011
20. Sawtooth Software, Inc. (2010) SSI Web v.6.6.12: choice based conjoint [Computer Software]. Sequim, WA
21. Smith A (2010) Home broadband adoption 2010. http://www.pewinternet.org/$\sim$/media// Files/Reports/2010/Home%20broadband%202010.pdf. Accessed 3 June 2011
22. Smith V, Mansfield CA (2006) Valuing airline security: an analysis of the MANPADS program. Paper presented at the Workshop on Benefit Methodologies for Homeland Security Analysis, Washington, DC, June 8–9
23. StreamShield Networks (2004) Consumers prepared to pay extra for clean and safe Internet service. Press release. http://www.streamshield.com/index.php?option=com_content& task=view&id=59&Itemid=130. Accessed 24 Apr 2009
24. Train K (2003) Discrete choice methods with simulation. Cambridge University Press, Cambridge
25. van Eeten M, Bauer J, Asghari H, Tabatabaie S (2010) The role of Internet service providers in botnet mitigation: an empirical analysis based on spam data. http://www.oecd. org/LongAbstract/0,3425,en_2649_33703_46396507_119684_1_1_1,00.html. Accessed 1 June 2010
26. van Eet3n M, Asghari H, Bauer J, Tabatabaie S (2011) Internet service providers and botnet mitigation: a fact-finding study on the Dutch market. http://www.rijksoverheid.nl/ bestanden/documenten-en-publicaties/rapporten/2011/01/13/internet-service-providers-and-botnet-mitigation/tud-isps-and-botnet-mitigation-in-nl-final-public-version-07jan2011.pdf. Accessed 1 July 2011
27. Varian H (2000) Managing online security risks. The New York Times. http://www.nytimes. com/library/financial/columns/060100econ-scene.html. Accessed 3 June 2011
28. Zwerina K, Huber J, Kuhfeld WF (1996) A general method for constructing efficient choice designs. SAS Working Paper. http://support.sas.com/techsup/technote/mr2010e.pdf. Accessed 3 June 2011

Economic Methods and Decision Making by Security Professionals

Adrian Baldwin, Yolanta Beres, Geoffrey B. Duggan, Marco Casassa Mont, Hilary Johnson, Chris Middup, and Simon Shiu

Abstract Increasing reliance on IT and the worsening threat environment mean that organisations are under pressure to invest more in information security. A challenge is that the choices are hard: money is tight, objectives are not clear, and there are many relevant experts and stakeholders. A significant proportion of the research in security economics is about helping people and organisations make better security investment and policy decisions.

This paper looks at the impact of methods based on security economics on a set of decision makers. Importantly, the study focused upon experienced security professionals using a realistic security problem relating to client infrastructure. Results indicated that the methods changed the decision processes for these experienced security professionals. Specifically, a broader range of factors were accounted for and included as justifications for the decisions selected. The security professional is an (important and influential) stakeholder in the organization decision making process, and arguably a more complete understanding of the problem is more suitable for persuading a broader business audience.

More generally the study complements all research in security economics that is aimed at improving decision making, and suggests ways to proceed and test for the impact of new methods on the actual decision makers.

A. Baldwin (✉) • Y. Beres • M.C. Mont • S. Shiu
HP Labs Bristol, England, UK
e-mail: first.last@hp.com

G.B. Duggan • H. Johnson
University of Bath, England, UK

C. Middup
Open University, England, UK

B. Schneier (ed.), *Economics of Information Security and Privacy III*,
DOI 10.1007/978-1-4614-1981-5_10,
© Springer Science+Business Media New York 2013

1 Introduction

The growing threat environment and increasing reliance on IT mean that security investment and policy decisions are becoming more difficult and more business critical. In large organisations, security decisions involve many stakeholders, including IT, finance, compliance, business and risk managers. This makes the decision process more complex as different stakeholders all have different knowledge, expertise, and incentives relating to security. For example, the security team normally has the subject matter expertise, but lack the business context to properly make the business case for an investment.

A key element with security decisions is the complexity of the problems. Typically, a decision to implement one or another security procedure requires the consideration of a huge range of inter-dependent factors, some of which vary in complex ways. Moreover, it is difficult to know or predict the actual impact of different choices on these factors. Extensive background knowledge about security and the company, prior experience of making similar decisions, and established standards such as ISO27000, see [19], help security professionals to cope with some of this complexity. Nonetheless, there is plenty of evidence indicating that even experts find it difficult to accurately trade-off multiple variables simultaneously [27]. This is essentially a problem of limited cognitive processing capacity—the decision maker is unable to hold all of the required information in mind whilst carrying out the necessary computations.

The most common tool for supporting decision making in this way is simply a pen and paper. Writing information down lessens the amount of information being held in working memory and frees up cognitive resources. In a sense, users "download" cognition to the environment. Payne, Howes and Reader [28] show that users adaptively allocate resources between internal and external cognition to maximize performance.

In this paper we describe a study with 12 experienced security professionals to examine how security decisions are made and justified. Including preparation of scripts and tools, practice runs, iterations, finding appropriately experienced security professionals, and conducting the actual interviews the study took over 6 months to complete. The study focused on the economic utility based approach developed and described in our earlier work [6] together with a system modeling and simulation based on the Gnosis toolset [5, 8].

Our economic utility based method aims to help decision makers identify and prioritise the trade-offs between the business outcomes of a security decision, and as a result extracts a form of utility relevant for a decision maker and/or their organisation. We start from the assumption that at least three outcomes, such as cost, productivity and security risk, trade-off against one another. The decision maker is guided through multiple steps where he/she has to prioritise the outcomes, select appropriate measures that can be used as proxies for the outcomes, and finally express the targets for these measures and the preferences in meeting them. Results from Gnosis based system modeling and simulation are then used to help the stakeholders gain a better understanding of their assumptions and to show the predicted effect that a security decision has on the selected measures and business outcomes.

The study was designed so as to examine the difference (if any) these techniques make to the security decision making process. Specifically, if and how they effect:

- The conclusions or decisions made,
- The thought process followed,
- The justifications given, and
- The confidence the stakeholder has in the final conclusions or decisions made.

The focus was upon the way our methodology and related software tools influence the security professionals as a precursor to understanding how in turn this may influence organisational decision processes. To this end, the security decision problem for the study and the possible alternative solutions were chosen to require participants to make different trade-offs between security, productivity and cost. There was not an expectation that the use of the methodology and tools should lead to any particular decision outcome to be favored. This reflects the multi-factorial and often ill-specified decision making typically undertaken by the security professionals.

This paper describes the process followed through the study, the economic based methods used, and the analysis of the results. It is organised as follows. Section 2 discusses related work; Sect. 3 describes the economic framing and system modeling approaches used; Sect. 4 outlines the study goals; Sect. 5 describes the structure of the controlled study and the phases carried out by all participants; Sect. 6 describes the economic and modeling interventions that half the participants followed; Sect. 7 describes the data analysis and results; Sect. 8 provides a discussion and interpretation of the results; and Sect. 9 summarizes and draws conclusions.

2   Related Work

There have been many examples of economic methods being applied to improve or explain security outcomes [1, 2]. Of most relevance to this study is the work that proposes techniques or suggestions for how organisations should make or justify their security investments. Gordon and Loeb [16] describe methods for how to provide a return on investment justification for security decisions. Schneier [30] further discusses the challenges of security decisions and suggests cost benefit analysis as providing a more appropriate framework for justifying business decisions. The UK Government funded collaborative project on "Trust Economics" [33] provides a series of examples where economic, modeling and empirical methods are combined to improve security decision making. These include studies of USB stick policy [7], tool support [25], human factors [7], patching policy [18], de-perimeterisation [6] and identity management [8]. Related to the trust economics project and specific to the case studies and tools used in the study methodology are the examples on vulnerability and threat management [5] and identity and access management [8]. By providing an analysis of how the security professionals and decision makers actually make a decision, and how they may be influenced, this work is complementary to all of the above.

There is a large body of research on decision making and support [14]. Keeney and Raiffa [21] provide a comprehensive description of approaches to multi-stakeholder, multi-objective, multi-attribute decisions many of which are similar to the economic framing process used in our study. Security is an especially difficult and rich area for decision support. Most major security decisions involve multiple stakeholders with multiple objectives. In addition the stakeholders do not have shared understanding of the context, lack common language; have to make decisions with very little empirical data, continually changing threats, technology and best practices; and any predictions can only be made with high degrees of uncertainty.

With the study described in this paper we aim to better understand how the multi-objective decision support approaches that have been applied in other areas of decision support can be used in the security domain.

The factors in the security decision process detailed above mean that it is impossible for a security expert to precisely weight all the relevant variables and derive the optimal solution accordingly. The literature on decision making under uncertainty indicates that the way individuals cope with such problems is by employing heuristics or rules of thumb [20]. These shortcuts are relatively easy to implement and have been shown to be remarkably effective [15]. Nonetheless, they can also lead to systematic biases in performance.

A bias that has been well documented within the psychological literature is the tendency for people to seek information that confirms their viewpoint rather than information that contradicts their viewpoint. This bias does not refer to a conscious, deliberate attempt to selectively gather information to support a particular perspective as, for example, is undertaken by lawyers in a court case. Rather it refers to a less explicit, unwitting selection of evidence without intent to bias the conclusion (see [24]).

This confirmation bias can affect decision making carried out by security professionals. Security professionals are by definition experts in security and, even where this is not the case, they are motivated to be perceived as knowledgeable about security. This expertise can lead to a high level of confidence in any initial decision made making it less necessary to pursue alternative solutions. Another consequence is that any disconfirming evidence could be challenging to their self-concept as an expert.

This confirmation bias was demonstrated using simple reasoning tasks which found that individuals tested a hypothesis by seeking information that was consistent with the hypothesis rather than seeking inconsistent information that would disprove the hypothesis [35]. Studies have since demonstrated that the confirmation bias applies both when a decision has been made and prior to the decision [32]. Further, there is evidence that a preexisting preference can lead to the distortion of new information in favour of the preferred alternative [29].

Outside of the laboratory the confirmation bias has been observed within contexts as diverse as policy making during the Vietnam war [34], medical diagnosis by physicians [12] and the development of scientific theory [23]. These real world case studies illustrate that expertise within a particular area does not preclude the operation of the bias. Moreover, they show the generalizability of the bias to complex environments where decision makers must balance multiple variables against one another.

In this work we examine the impact of the confirmation bias upon security decision making and discuss how our methods aim to address this bias.

3 Economic Framing and System Modeling

Figure 1 shows the overall approach from security problem to iteration between eliciting preferences and utility through economic framing, and exploring and predicting consequences through system modeling.

Organisations need to determine an appropriate policy, process, and technological response to the threat faced by the organisation in the context of operational requirements and security budget. Among the many attributes that must be considered are information confidentiality and integrity, system availability, assurance, and business performance. Moreover, this multi-objective, multi-attribute decision problem must be solved in a highly variable, highly dynamic environment.

There are many approaches based on security economics that address this problem. In this study we have focused on the combination of economic framing

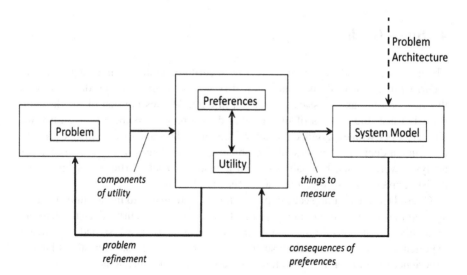

Fig. 1 Iterating between economic framing and system modeling

and system modeling that has been developed from a series of previous case studies including vulnerability and threat management [5], USB stick policy [3], de-perimeterisation [6], and identity and access management [4].

In this approach economic framing is used to identify and prioritise between the multiple objectives. The framing is provided by a form of multi-criteria utility function. In practice, it is very difficult to extract a formal utility function direct from the organisation. We approach this with a multi step process that guides participants to select outcomes and preferences relevant to their organisation. This includes choosing how these outcomes can be measured, which are the most important, at which points performance in a particular outcome becomes "intolerable" and predicting what effect the security decision could have on the multiple outcomes. A fuller exposition of the method is given in [6], and further discussion and examples of applying and using this style of utility function are given in [3, 18].

System modeling and simulation are used to help the decision maker explore the effect the different security controls have on the selected set of outcomes. For example, following empirical work to construct a model we simulate the effect that restricting admin rights might have on reducing risk exposure to malware-type threats and model its impact on user satisfaction.

In this study system models are built and explored using the Gnosis language and tools [10]. Gnosis is a discrete process simulation language, and can be used to explore complex concurrent interactions of processes and resources (at locations) under numerous assumptions and stochastic conditions. This approach is particularly useful for exploring the combined effect of various operational processes and technological solutions. Much work has been done on the mathematical foundations behind the Gnosis language and its suitability to modeling security problems [9].

4 Study Goals

The goal of this study was to explore how security economics can change the way security professionals think about and justify security decisions. In order to address this question it was necessary to conduct in-depth studies not just of the decision itself but also the process of making that decision. To maximize the validity we chose to work with experienced security decision makers and to examine the process by which a decision to a presented problem is made. This strategy meant that our analyses were primarily qualitative and considered each participant's individual decision process for similar approaches see [11, 22, 26].

Overall twelve current security professionals were involved in the study. Careful selection ensured each had many years of experience of security decision making in a mixture of consulting, operational and policy roles. Most had significant experience of security in public sector and financial services, with others having experience of commercial, retail telecoms and energy organisations.

It is unusual and therefore novel to have this amount of time with a significant number of professionals. The intention was to explore if they could use the information provided, whether it was deemed relevant and whether it figured in their justifications. For example, do the techniques lead to professionals asking more questions, making more causal links, and being aware of different trade-offs. If so then this small-scale study will have explored and illustrated some of the value of our economic approaches.

Each participant was presented with the same security problem and four possible security decision options. The decision problem involved making improvements in the vulnerability and threat management for client infrastructure in an organisation. The organisation was fictitious with a number of key attributes established. These included company size, regulations that applied, structure and size of the IT workforce, history of security incidents, IT architecture, critical business processes, mobility of workforce and so on.

Four decision options were presented: (1) investing to improve software patching, (2) buying and deploying client based host intrusion prevention technology (HIPS), (3) introduce changes in when users have admin privileges, and (4) do nothing. Our previous work in the area of vulnerability and threat management with several large organisations [5] provided confidence that the problem selected was realistic and representative, and meant we can call on our experience for how the security stakeholder's opinion and role affects the organisation decision process.

Even though the decision problem is restricted to four investment options, it is still a complex multi-objective problem with a high degree of uncertainty with how well the options might meet the organisations business objectives. From one point, each security investment address different types of security risk. For example, investing in patching might ensure the operations team does a better job of getting infrastructure sufficiently patched within policy deadlines; investing in HIPS might provide quicker protection for a significant class of threats; and investing in lockdown may prevent privilege escalations that in turn reduce the spread of malware. Each option is also likely to have a different impact on productivity, costs, compliance. For example, doing nothing presumably does not reduce security risk, but does have the advantage of not affecting capital or operational costs, and of not impacting productivity of users, IT operations or business processes.

Though all participants were introduced to the problem in the same way, only half of the participants (participants in each group were matched in terms of experience) were guided to use the economic utility based methodology (with the help of specifically designed software tools) and the results from simulations of the system model. This group (the intervention group) was challenged to think through preferences for how the different strategic outcomes trade-off, and to use a system model and associated results to help explore the effects of the four decision options on these outcomes. The other half acted as a comparative control group, and was asked to make the decisions without the help of the extra tools. This second group functioned as a control or baseline against which to compare the intervention group's performance.

For reasons of brevity in this paper, types of questions and justifications for each participant were simply aggregated to highlight differences between the groups. Further analysis is being done to look at the trajectory of each individual participant question/justifications, to see the different processes within individuals and to discern any patterns within and between groups, and for the intervention group whether and where information from the interventions were mentioned or used in later questions and justifications.

An interview lasted 30–45 min for a participant from the control group, and 60–75 min for participants from the intervention group. Each interview had two subject matter experts; one running the interview and ensuring consistency of protocols for introducing information, tools and moving through the various stages, and a second acting as a member of a security team of the fictitious organisation as well as an expert of the tools used (when required), answering all questions that the participants asked. All the sessions were recorded and transcribed, and the tools captured choices made and screens viewed.

5   Study Structure and Common Phases

Figure 2 shows the scripted phases followed by the intervened and control groups. The problem description, decision options, choice and justification and introspection phases were the same for each group. The only difference for the intervened group was that we included phases 5a and 5b where the participants worked through economic framing and system modeling. Below we describe details relevant to each of the main phases shown in the diagram.

Study Phase 1. Session Introduction

All participants were given a standard introduction to the session. This included an introduction to the experimenters, an outline of the role they were expected to play, and the incentive for doing this to the best of their ability. In addition they used a web based tool to record their security experience.

Study Phase 2. Problem Description

All participants were given a standard written description of the problem. Essentially they were presented with the scenario that they had just joined the security

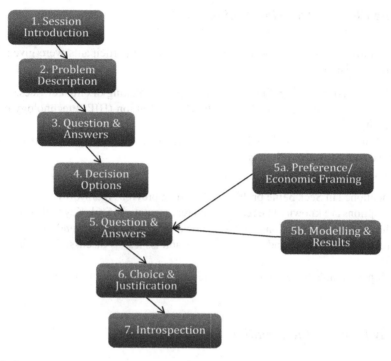

Fig. 2 Schematic of study phases for each group

team of a company, that the CISO was concerned about protections on client infrastructure, and was looking for a recommendation for whether and how to proceed.

Study Phase 3. Question and Answers

At this point they were encouraged to ask any questions they thought relevant to the problem and the expert used a script sheet to provide consistent answers. For example, there were scripted answers for the type of business, compliance culture, history of incidents, the different needs, behaviours and expectation of staff in different functions, and so on. If a subject asked a question that was not part of the script, the expert made up an answer and this was recorded to ensure consistency in future interviews.

All participants were given 10 min to ask questions at which point if they had not asked or been told about the patching policy and processes they were given a sheet describing this. This allowed us to explore what order participants sought information, but ensured all participants had certain key information that we deemed relevant to the problem, before being asked to provide a decision.

Study Phase 4. Decision Options

To simplify the problem and the results analysis the participants were given four discrete decision options:

1. Process and technology investment to improve patching of client devices,
2. Investment to deploy host based intrusion prevention (HIPS) technology on all clients,
3. Rolling out a policy to lockdown all clients so that only the IT department would have administrative privileges, or
4. To do nothing.

As mentioned in Sect. 3, the problem is based on previous real world case studies so these options are known to be realistic and representative [5,6]. Key to this study the implications of these options are well known to security experts and they represent interesting and distinct trade-offs, concerns and issues, as discussed in more detail in [5].

All participants were invited to provide an initial view at this point.

Study Phase 5. Intervention

This phase was only followed by the intervention group. The two parts (5a and 5b) and described in section.

Study Phase 6. Choice and Justification

Whilst we welcomed discussion on how combinations of other solutions, and how combination or sequenced strategies would make sense, we were clear we wanted a preferred option. Once they had given their preferred option all the participants were asked to fill out a form for each option describing pro's and con's, and a confidence level (1–7 Likert scale).

Study Phase 7. Introspection

After the participants had completed their justifications they were encouraged to introspect on how they had solved the problem, why they sought certain information, and how it had been used. For the intervened group we asked what, if any difference they felt the tools had made to their thinking.

6 The Intervention Phases

This section describes the way the intervention group was exposed to the economic framing and system modeling approach described in Sect. 3. These interventions are specifically designed to deal with the challenges decision makers have dealing with multiple factors and predicting the actual impact of choices. In both phases a number of tools and materials were used and so these are explained ahead of the actual phase description.

6.1 Tool Support for Economic Framing

This phase involved a complex workflow where participant's choices about business priorities would affect which proxy measures and trade-off graphs would make sense to display and process. A preference elicitation tool was used to capture, process and display information in support of this process. The high level overview of this tool is provided in Appendix 9. Figure 3 provides various screenshots of this tool, for the different steps, including: the initial questionnaire to gather information about the interviewed person; elicitation of outcomes of relevance, elicitation of relevant proxy measures; and trade-off graphs between chosen proxy measures.

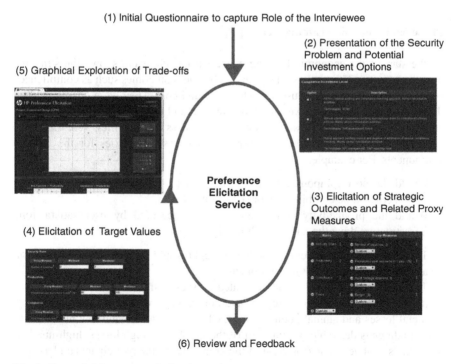

(1) Initial Questionnaire to capture Role of the Interviewee

(2) Presentation of the Security Problem and Potential Investment Options

(5) Graphical Exploration of Trade-offs

Preference Elicitation Service

(4) Elicitation of Target Values

(3) Elicitation of Strategic Outcomes and Related Proxy Measures

(6) Review and Feedback

Fig. 3 Screenshot from economic framing tool

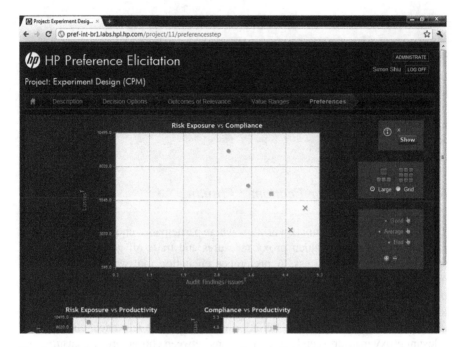

Fig. 4 Screenshot of trade-off graphs from the preference elicitation tool

Phase 5a. Economic Framing (see Fig. 2)

At the start of the economic framing phase participants were shown the strategic outcomes screen. This suggested significant business outcomes such as compliance, (security) risk, (business or user) productivity and cost. They were encouraged to think of other components we may have missed, and then to reduce to three main components that seemed most relevant to the business decision they were making.

Participants were then shown a series of metrics, or proxies for the chosen components. For example:

– Would the cost component best be measured by impact on operational cost, capital cost, some combination, or something else?
– Would the productivity component best be measured by user satisfaction, infrastructure downtime, or something else?

They were asked to select the one they thought would serve as the best proxy for measuring performance of the component.

The tool took these inputs and generated a series of trade-off graphs, see Fig. 4. In the figure the components are risk and compliance, with proxy measure being financial losses and annual audit findings. Clearly low losses and low numbers of audit findings is desirable (bottom left of the graph) and high losses, high number of findings is undesirable (top right of the graph). Once the participants understood this they were asked discuss (and mark) how they felt relatively about the areas that trade off, i.e., is it better to be in the lower right (low losses, but higher number of audit findings), or upper left (higher losses, but low audit findings).

This ensured that we could record the prioritized preferences expressed, and have some confidence they properly considered both strategic outcomes and the way they trade off.

6.2 Tools and Material Support for System Modeling and Results Analysis

In previous case studies the stakeholders were involved in the empirical work to construct a model. This was not possible for this study, instead we used a model developed to support a similar problem. Figure 5 shows the system diagram of the model used in the study. The boxes represent processes, event generators and decision points, and show the paths that can be taken once a vulnerability is discovered. A simulation allows these paths to run concurrently, and to collect metrics such as the time taken from vulnerability discovery, to "some" mitigation being in place.

The red section within the model represents the external environment of vulnerabilities, exploits, malware and patches. This includes statistics observed from the external world. *The blue section* represents the security controls and processes within the organisation, such as patching and AV Mitigations. Patching is split into testing and deployment sub-processes and further separated to capture accelerated patching when the vulnerability is deemed critical (decisions for when to accelerate are represented by the complex set of logic gates) and an emergency patching when it is critical and no other protections are in place. The *additional red boxes* represent the additional security investments in HIPS and lockdown that are added to the model for some simulations. Investment in patching is represented by making different assumptions about how long patch test, deploy and acceleration would occur. A more detailed description of this model can be found in [5].

The model was configured to produce statistics relating to the proxies discussed in the economic framing. Based on previous experience we added details about the effect on user satisfaction, impact on the productivity of operations staff, and associated costs. Overall we had data for nine measurements that could be contrasted for each of the four decision options:

- *Machine days exposed to know malware*—# of machine and # days each of them is exposed from the time that malware is known in the wild.
- *Exposure window*—day's workstation environment is exposed (not mitigated) from vulnerability discovery time.
- *Malware infection*—# of machine infections.
- *Helpdesk calls*—number of helpdesk calls per each vulnerability.

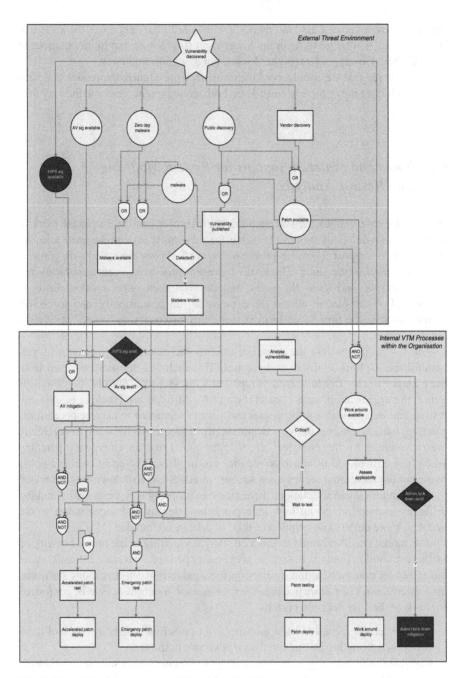

Fig. 5 Schematic of the system model used for the study

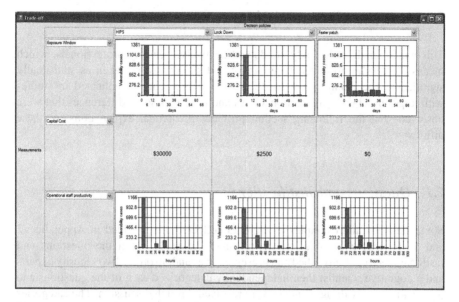

Fig. 6 Screenshot of the system model results tool

- *Productivity of operational staff*—number of hours spent by operational staff doing security tasks.
- *User satisfaction*—level of user satisfaction between 0–4.
- *Policy violations*—% of vulnerability cases where mitigations took longer to be deployed than policy dictated timeline.
- *Capital cost*—one off dollar value.
- *Operational cost*—dollars spent yearly.

We created a results tool to mine this data and produce comparative views. For example, Fig. 6 shows a screenshot from this tool which compares results for cost, exposure and staff productivity for three of the decision options.

Study Phase 5b. Modeling and Results (see Fig. 5.2)

After economic framing the participants were shown a schematic of the system model, seeFig. 5. The interviewer explained that domain experts had verified that the model was a reasonable representation of the system, that simulations could be run to see the effect of the different decision options under a range of conditions and that the results of simulations provided reasonable evidence of expected behavior and outcomes in each of the simulated situations.

The participants were introduced to the results tool and shown results for options and proxies they had prioritized earlier in the interview, see Fig. 6. They were then able to select different proxy and decision option combinations so they could compare multiple outcomes from different choices.

7 Results and Data Analysis

This was a small-scale study conducted on twelve security professionals, which means the results presented here cannot and should not be taken as statistically significant. The results point to differences that might be replicated in studies with larger numbers. This section shows and describes some differences that were observed, and the following section provides theoretical explanations for these differences.

7.1 Questions and Justifications

Some statistics and examples of the data collected are provided in Appendices 2 and 3. To ensure an objective approach to the analysis, all the questions and justifications were transcribed and presented in a random order. Two security experts and a cognitive scientist then independently categorized each of the questions and justifications. Any disagreements were resolved through discussion. The categories were:

Cost	Meaning the question/justification was about finance or budget considerations
Compliance	Meaning the question/justification was about regulation constraints
Productivity	Meaning the question/justification was about effect on business or user productivity
Evidence	Meaning the question/justification was about historical data, events, or incidents
Security	Meaning the question/justification was about improving security

The remaining questions and justifications did not fit into the above, and did not form any other grouping, and so were all labeled "other".

The proportion of questions and justifications in each of the categories are given in Figs. 7 and 8. For the questions in Fig. 7, the distribution across the categories was similar in both groups. This is unsurprising given the questions were asked prior to the intervention. The majority (just over 63% in both groups) of questions referred to security issues and there were very few questions about costs or productivity implications.

By contrast there was a clear difference between the groups in the proportion of justifications allocated to each of the categories. Figure 8 shows that security remained dominant in the control group (with 51% of justifications), this dropped considerably (to 36% of justifications) in the intervention group. Moreover the emphasis on cost and productivity was considerably higher in the intervention group than the control group. These results suggest that the economic framing and system modeling led to a broader range of reasons being produced to justify the decision in the intervention group.

To ensure that this greater breadth in justifications was not at the expense of depth in reasoning the justifications were scored according to depth of explanation.

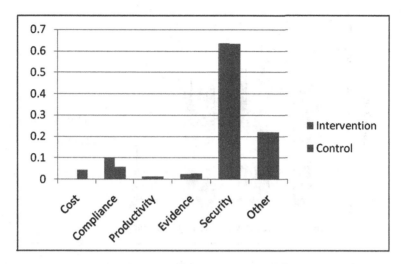

Fig. 7 Proportion of questions in each category for intervention and control groups

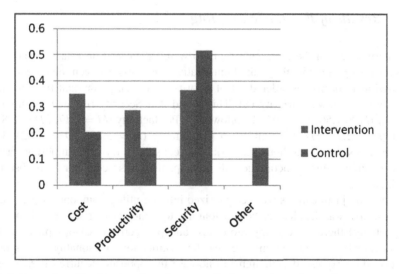

Fig. 8 Proportion of justifications in each category for intervention and control groups

For example, simply mentioning cost would score 1, explaining the impact in terms of operational costs would score 2, whereas explaining the cost impact in comparison with the gain/loss of productivity would score 3. As with the other categorization this was carried out by security experts. Based on this analysis more justifications were provided by the intervention group (81) than for the control group (68), and there was a small increase in depth of explanation per justification, intervention group: $M = 1.91, SD = 0.24$; control Group: $M = 1.8, SD = 0.34$.

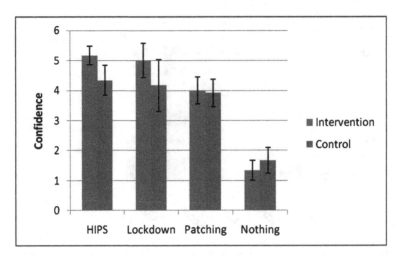

Fig. 9 Mean confidence and standard error for each decision options

7.2 Results of Economic Framing

The participants in the intervention group were asked to drop a factor, and then express on a graph how they felt about relative trade-offs between the others. This allowed us to derive an ordered set of priorities for each participant from highest priority (1) to lowest priority (4). This found that Security risk had the highest priority ($M = 1.50$, $SD = 0.77$), followed by Productivity ($M = 2.17$, $SD = 0.82$), Cost ($M = 2.75$, SD 0.76) and then Compliance ($M = 3.58$, $SD = 1.02$). The preferences show that although Security was considered the most important factor the economic framing encouraged all participants to also consider both cost and productivity.

When the justifications were categorized into the utility components (i.e., each pro and con was labeled as best belonging to either cost, risk, compliance or productivity) there were many more cost and productivity reasons provided by the intervention group. In most cases the justifications reasonably represented the priorities expressed, although in one case the opposite occurred (i.e., where compliance and risk were expressed as the priorities the justifications were actually expressed only in terms of cost).

7.3 Results of Choices and Likert Scale Confidences

Decision outcomes were similar in both groups with three participants selecting HIPS and three selecting lockdown in the intervention group. In the control group three selected lockdown, two selected HIPS and one selected patching. Mean confidence for each of the four options in both groups is given in Fig. 9. There was slightly higher confidence for both the HIPS and Lockdown options in the intervention group. Mean confidence for the selected option was 5.83 ($SD = 0.75$) in the intervention group and 5.50 ($SD = 1.05$) in the control group.

7.4   Introspection Results

The main themes from the introspection were that intervened participants valued the results tool but not the economic framing. Specifically, for the results tool they liked the quantitative results of simulations and the ability to easily compare results of different options. Conversely for the economic framing, they typically reasoned that they were already well aware of the main outcomes and trade-offs. This makes the result that the intervention did seem to affect the richness and range of their justifications more interesting.

8   Interpretation of the Data Analysis and Results

The results from the study provide a clear indication that the decision processes of security professionals were affected by the economic framing and system modeling tools. Initially, participants gathered information about the problem by asking questions and in both groups, the majority of questions focused upon security related factors. Having made a decision, participants were required to explain their reasoning for each of the decision options. In the control group the majority of these justifications related to security issues. However, in the intervention group, the type of justifications produced for the decision focused upon factors such as cost and company productivity as well as security related factors.

Confirmation Bias

The high proportion of security related questions asked in both groups suggests that security professionals typically focus on factors that are related to their expertise. This confirms our initial view that the confirmation bias described in Sect. 2 affects the decision making carried out by security professionals.

We can also observe that the economic utility based approach encouraged the alternative factors to be considered which worked against this confirmation bias. Firstly, it shifted the focus away from purely security factors and secondly, by representing different trade-offs explicitly to security professionals and by encouraging them to consider interactions between variables, there was greater opportunity for disconfirming evidence to be evaluated.

Cognitive Dissonance

Interestingly, despite the differences between the two groups in the reasons cited to support their decisions, the intervention group participants claimed that their decision making was unaffected by the economic framing and system modeling. At one level this is unsurprising, it is well documented that self-reports can be unreliable measures of behaviour—people have limited access to their internal cognitive processes [24]. Indeed the reason that process measures were included in conjunction with self-report measures was to compensate for potential inaccuracies in reporting. Nonetheless, to understand the effectiveness or otherwise of our tools it is helpful to understand why this discrepancy exists.

A theoretical account for the confirmation bias can also provide an explanation for the failure to acknowledge an effect of the tool despite the shift in reasons provided for the decision. Cognitive dissonance [13] refers to the discomfort experienced when two conflicting cognitive elements (e.g., beliefs) are held by the same person. One way to reduce this discomfort is to alter one of the beliefs to make it consistent with the other belief. Importantly, it may sometimes be easier to modify an accurate belief than an inaccurate one. This can be seen with post-hoc rationalizations when an expected outcome is not attained, for example, "I didn't try my hardest which was why I didn't win the race". Some beliefs are more integral to an individual's self concept or worldview than others and they will be more resistant to change. Thus, to reduce dissonance an alternative cognitive element is altered.

In our study, the participants were experts and were employed as such. Further, they were required to make a decision prior to using any tools. Thus, any additional insights provided by using the tools could be interpreted by the participants as a challenge to their internal perceptions of expertise. One way to reduce this cognitive dissonance is to minimize the perceived worth of the tools. We do not mean to imply security professionals will not adjust their decisions or are not open-minded. Indeed, we would argue that the shift in justifications for their decision implies that our participants did account for the tools within their reasoning. Rather, we wish to emphasize that they might not be fully aware of any benefits gained from using the tools.

Notwithstanding this, it is possible to conjecture that cognitive dissonance could negatively affect the quality of decision making by security professionals. Because the correct solution to a security problem is often open to debate it is difficult for a security professional to receive accurate feedback on decisions. Where there is not clear evidence against a decision the desire to reduce cognitive dissonance can mean counterevidence is understated. (See [17] for evidence of similar behaviour by mutual fund investors.)

The additional tools used by the intervention group can be seen as a solution to this as they provide information about alternative decision options. The tools lessen any confirmation bias the security professionals might have by providing both confirming and disconfirming information.

Effect of Results from System Modeling

The other noteworthy finding from the introspection was that the system modeling tool was valued as a decision aid. This supports our contention that providing external information could support the internal processing carried out by security professionals. Perhaps more importantly, it also indicates that the external support provided was in an appropriate form and was relevant for the processing required to address the problem.

Generalizability of Findings and Future Research

The actual decisions made in the two groups did not differ as a result of the interventions, however, we do not view this as problematic. The problem and the alternative solutions were chosen to be representative of actual security decisions and the focus was on providing sufficient complexity to enable an understanding of the process both with and without economic interventions. We were primarily interested in the gathering of information and any subsequent reasoning which was why the questions asked and the justifications provided were of interest. Future work could focus on the actual decision by devising problems that specifically discriminated between different decision criteria yet were equivalent on other criteria. However, here our focus was upon capturing the complexity of a typical security decision where multiple attributes were traded off against each other.

As explained in Sect. 4, our goal was to look at the way actual security decision makers solved realistic security problems and to investigate how the economic framing and system modelling tools affected this process. To this end, we have provided a theoretical explanation for the differences in behaviour associated with using the tools. In-depth study of relatively small participant sample sizes is often a richer and more fertile method for theoretical development than larger more evaluative approaches [31]. We feel the findings and ideas suggested by our study reinforce this conclusion and our methodological approach. Nonetheless, we recognise the value of complementary studies that build upon the results here and generalize the conclusions to alternative problems and larger populations.

Timing of the Introduction of the Tools

The timing of the intervention also seems an important factor. Our participants were allowed to ask questions about the problem and then asked to make a decision prior to the intervention. This facilitated a controlled comparison across groups, however, it would also be interesting to study the decision process when participants were provided with the tool at the same time as the problem. This would enable our tools to be integrated with the information gathering phase of the decision. The introspection results suggested that many of the selections were based on knowledge of best practice. Providing our tools from the start would mean their benefits could be realized before or during the test for best practice. Of course, an alternative view is that best practices represent a reasonable way forward in most cases, and that our tools should be reserved for broader questions.

Multiple Stakeholders

This experiment focused on the security (expert) stakeholder. Our tools are designed to allow multiple stakeholders with different levels of expertise and accountability to work through and share their priorities, preferences and assumptions. Different organisations will have different structures and processes in place to ensure due diligence on these kinds of decisions. In some cases, a risk committee may handle policy changes, whereas the CIO will make IT investment choices. Intuitively, we expect any improvement by the security professional in their understanding or ability to explain a decision should help in all these cases. However, these observations suggest further work is needed to investigate the impact of our tools upon non security stakeholders. A simpler and smaller study would be to explore whether the broader justifications are more convincing to the non-security stakeholders. A more ambitious challenge is to design a study to look at the effect our tools (or any security decision making method) have on the range of organisation decision processes.

9   Conclusions

Organisations' increasing reliance on IT, and the hostile threat environment mean that it is crucial to make good security investment and policy decisions. The area is complex, changing and has multiple stakeholders so making good decisions is likely to remain difficult. Security economics provides many useful approaches and techniques to improve this decision process. Trust economics [33] is an example project in this realm.

This study has looked at the impact of economic framing and system modeling on a set of decision makers. Crucially, the study focused upon experienced security professionals using a realistic security problem. Integrating findings from the decision-making literature into this security context has highlighted the potential for security professionals to favour information that confirms their initial viewpoint over information that does not. By externally representing alternative aspects of the problem and trade-offs between different factors our method can thus support decision making.

Results indicated that the interventions changed the decision processes for these experienced security professionals. Specifically, a broader range of factors were accounted for and included as justifications for the decisions selected. The security professional is one (important and influential) stakeholder in the organisation decision making process, and arguably the richer arguments are more suitable for persuading a broader business audience.

More generally the study complements all research in security economics that is aimed at improving decision making, and suggests ways to proceed and test for the impact of new methods on the actual decision makers.

Appendix 1: System Architecture of the Preference Elicitation Tool

The figure below provides a high-level view of the system architecture behind this tool. It is based on an engine that executes preference elicication workflows. Each step in the workflow can be configured in terms of the information that will be requested to the user and its graphical representation. The tool stores the gathered information into a centralised database, allowing for further post-processing and data mining.

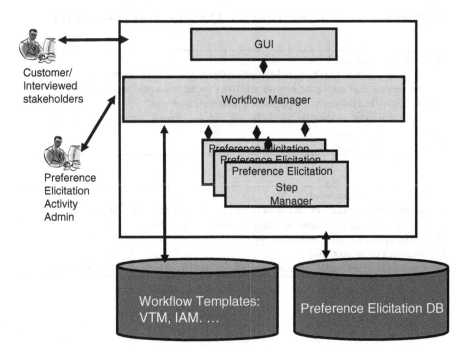

Appendix 2: Summary of Data Analysis

Phase	Result/Data collected	Analysis
3. Questions and answers	173 questions	Various, but main result was based on ratio of security related questions between the control and intervened groups
6. Choice & justification	152 justifications	Various, but main results were based on ratio of security related justifications, and complexity of justifications between the control and intervened groups
5a. Preference/Economic framing	Six ordered preferences over four components (Appendix 4)	Participants preferences were compared with justifications
6. Choice & justification	12 choices and 48 Likert scores (Fig. 9)	Comparison between control and intervened groups
7. Introspection	Judgments on the interventions	See discussion

Appendix 3: Example/Illustration Question and Justifications

Example questions included:

Q1. What processes [do we have] to keep anti-malware up to date on clients?

Q2. Do we have anything on the network that looks for unusual traffic, maybe an IPS?

Q3. Is training and [following of] procedures measured in any way?

Q4. To what regulations these customers [of our company] have to comply with, e.g., data protection legislation, etc.?

Q5. Precisely which countries do we operate in

Example justifications included:

J1. Reduces ability for malware infections to gain admin rights on client systems

J2. Reduces threat vector for zero day / early exploited vulnerabilities

J3. Zero cost [and] no acceptance issues

J4. Can impact on productivity

J5. High impact on user satisfaction and productivity [and] more expensive than HIPS option

Appendix 4: Preferences Expressed by the Intervention Group in Phase 5a

Component	Intervened subject 1	Intervened subject 2	Intervened subject 3	Intervened subject 4	Intervened subject 5	Intervened subject 6
(Security) Risk	1	1 =	1 =	1	1	3
Compliance	4	4	1 =	4	4	4
Cost	2	3	4	3	2 =	2
Productivity	3	1 =	3	2	2 =	1

References

1. Anderson R, Moore T (2006) The economics of information security. Science 314:610–613
2. Anderson R (2001) Why information security is hard: an economic perspective. In: Proceedings of 17th annual computer security applications conference (ACSAC)
3. Beautement A, Coles R, Griffin J, Ioannidis C, Monahan B, Pym D, Sasse A, Wonham M (2009) Modelling the human and technological costs and benefits of USB memory stick security. In: Managing information risk and the economics of security. Springer
4. Baldwin A, Mont M (2009) Simon Shiu - using modelling and simulation for policy decision support in identity management. In: IEEE 10th symposium on policies for distributed systems and networks, ieee policy 2009 symposium, 20–22 July. London
5. Beres Y, Griffin J, Shiu S, Heitman M, Markle D, Ventura P (2008) Analysing the performance of security solutions to reduce vulnerability exposure windows, in annual computer security applications conference (ACSAC) CA IEEE. pp 33–42
6. Beres Y, Pym D, Shiu S (2010) Decision support for systems security investment. In: Network Operations and Management Symposium Workshops (IEEE/IFIP, NOMS Wksps
7. Beautement A, Sasse A, Wonham M (2008) The compliance budget: managing security behaviour in organisations. In: New Security Paradigms Workshop (NSPW) 2008, Plumpjack Squaw Valley Inn, Olympic, California, USA, pp 22–25
8. Casassa Mont M, Beres Y, Pym D and Shiu S (2010) Economics of identity and access management: providing decision support for investments. In: Network Operations and Management Symposium Workshops (IEEE/IFIP, NOMS Wksps
9. Collinson M, Monahan B, D Pym (2009) A logical and computational theory of located resources. J Logic Comput (in press) DOI: 10.1093/logcom/exp021
10. Collinson M, Monahan B, Pym D Semantics for structured systems modelling and simulation. In: Proceedings of simutools 2010, ACM digital library and EU digital library
11. Ericsson KA, Lehmann AC (1996) Expert and exceptional performance: Evidence of maximal adaptation to task constraints. Ann Rev Psychol 47:273–305
12. Elstein AS, Shulman LS, Sprafka SA (1978) Medical problem solving: an analysis of clinical reasoning. MA: Harvard University Press, Cambridge
13. Festinger L (1957) A theory of cognitive dissonance. Stanford University Press, Stanford, CA
14. French S, Maule J, N Papamichail (2009) Decision behavior, analysis and support. Cambridge University Press
15. Gigerenzer G, Goldstein D (1996) Reasoning the fast and frugal way: Models of bounded rationality. Psychol Rev 103:650–669
16. Gordon LA, Loeb MP (2006) Managing cybersecurity resources: a cost-benefit analysis. McGraw Hill

17. Goetzmann WM, Peles N (1997) Cognitive dissonance and mutual fund investors. J Financ Res 2:145–158
18. Ioannidis C, Pym D, Williams J (2009) Investments and Trade-offs in the Economics of Information Security. In: Proceedings of financial cryptography and data security 2009, LNCS 5628. Springer, pp 148–162
19. ISO 27000 series of standards for information security and security management. see http://www.27000.org/
20. Kahneman D (2003) A perspective on judgment and choice: Mapping bounded rationality. Amer Psychol 58:697–720
21. Keeney RL, Raiffa H (1976) Decisions with multiple objectives: preferences and value tradeoffs. Wiley, New York. Reprinted, Cambridge Univ. Press, New York (1993)
22. Lipshitz R, Klein G, Orasanu J, Salas E (2001) Taking stock of naturalistic decision making. J Beh Dec Mak 14:331–352
23. Nickerson RS (1998) Confirmation bias: a ubiquitous phenomenon in many guises. Rev General Psychol 2:175–220
24. Nisbett RE, Wilson TD (1977) Telling more than we can know: verbal reports on mental processes. Psychol Rev 84:231–259
25. Parkin S, van Moorsel A, Inglesant P, Sasse A (2010) A stealth approach to usable security: helping it security managers to identify workable security solutions. In: The proceedings of the new security paradigms workshop (NSPW) 2010. Concord, MA, USA
26. Payne JW (1976) Task complexity and contingent processing in decision making: an information search and protocol analysis. Org Behav Human Perform 16:366–387
27. Payne JW, Bettman JR, Johnson EJ (1993) The adaptive decision maker. Cambridge University Press, New York
28. Payne SJ, Howes A, Reader WR (2001) Adaptively distributing cognition: a decision-making perspective on human-computer interaction. Behav Inform Technol 20(5): 339–346
29. Russo JE, Medvec VH, Meloy MG (1996) The distortion of information during decisions. Org Behav Human Dec Processes 66:102–110
30. Schneier B (2008) Security ROI, in Schneier on security blog. 2 Sept see http://www.schneier.com/blog/archives/2008/09/security_roi_1.html
31. Salkovskis PM (2003) Empirically grounded clinical interventions: cognitive-behavioural therapy progresses through a multi-dimensional approach to clinical science. Behav Cognitive Psychother 30:3–9
32. Schulz-Hardt S, Frey D, Luthgrens C, Moscovici S (2000) Biased information search in group decision making. JPers Soc Psychol 78:655–669
33. UK Government technology strategy board (TSB) funded collaborative research project. see http://www.trust-economics.org/
34. Tuchman BW (1984) The march of folly: from Troy to Vietnam. Ballantine Books, New York
35. Wason PC (1966) Reasoning. In: Foss B (ed) New horizons in psychology. Penguin, Harmonsworth, Middlesex, England, pp. 135–151

Real Name Verification Law on the Internet: A Poison or Cure for Privacy?

Daegon Cho

Abstract As the internet media has become more widely used over time, public opinions formed by internet discussions affect political and social issues more critically. While the internet space guarantees equal status for every participant and equal opportunity in terms of freedom of speech based on anonymity, baseless rumors, personal defamation, and privacy invasion against particular individuals and groups are more likely to happen rather than in the face-to-face offline communications. In order to prevent this undesirable effect, the South Korean government implemented Real Name Verification Law in July 2007 by which discussion participants should pass verification process in order to express their opinions in most websites. This study examines the effects of Real Name Verification Law in several aspects. By applying content analysis to abundant data of postings in a leading discussion forum that is subject to the law, the results suggest that Real Name Verification Law has a dampening effect on overall participation in the short-term, but the law did not affect the participation in the long term. Also, identification of postings had significant effects on reducing uninhibited behaviors, suggesting that Real Name Verification Law encouraged users' behavioral changes in the positive direction to some extent. The impact is greater for Heavy User group than for Light and Middle User groups. Also, discussion participants with their real names showed more discreet behaviors regardless of the enforcement of the law. By analyzing the effect of this policy at the forefront of internet trends of South Korea, this paper can shed light on some useful implications and information to policy makers of other countries that may consider certain type of internet regulations in terms of privacy and anonymity.

D. Cho (✉)
School of Information Systems and Management, The H. John Heinz III College,
Carnegie Mellon University, Pittsburgh, PA 15213, USA
e-mail: daegonc@andrew.cmu.edu

B. Schneier (ed.), *Economics of Information Security and Privacy III*,
DOI 10.1007/978-1-4614-1981-5_11,
© Springer Science+Business Media New York 2013

Keywords Anonymity • Pseudonymity • Deindividuation • Computer-mediated communication • Real name verification law • Freedom of speech • Content analysis

1 Introduction

"The incident, 'Dog Shit Girl[1]' (in South Korea), involves a norm that most people would seemingly agree to clean up after your dog. But having a permanent record of one's norm violations is upping the sanction to a whole new level... allowing (internet) bloggers to act as a cyber-posse, tracking down norm violators and branding them with digital scarlet letters." (Daniel Solove, Washington Post, 7/7/2005)

"Internet space in our country has become the wall of a public toilet." (A member of South Korean National Assembly) (...) Widespread verbal abuse on the web has become a growing social problem, and efforts to stamp it out have become a government priority. (The New York Times, 10/13/2008)

Long ago, Plato raised a concern in his Phaedrus: he expressed the fear that the *emerging technology of writing* would destroy the rich oral literacy that was central to his culture [34]. Plato preferred *speech* to *writing* due to his suspicion of writing as a threatening new technology. He worried that people's thoughts would become unwavering by written documents, and this would ruin the root of democracy by preventing a variety of free discussions. Plato's concern is analogous to the present worries with regard to a newly emerged technology, *the internet or computer-mediated communication (CMC)*[10].

With the growth in sociality and interaction around online discussion forums, these mediums are increasingly becoming places for communities to discuss and address common issues [5]. Through this intermediary based on cutting-edge technology, our opinions are delivered and shared rapidly, and the history of communications via the internet is cumulated exponentially. That is, internet-based information technologies have enabled the emergence of new types of communicative practices [12]. The other unique characteristic of the internet communication is *anonymity or pseudonymity*. People want to surf the web, purchase online, and post messages or comments without exposing their identities, interests, and activities to others [1]. On the one hand, participants in online discussion forums are all equal under the anonymous condition, no matter what their backgrounds and circumstances are. Minorities and neglected classes of people in the real world can have equal opportunities to express their thoughts: freedom of speech is guaranteed

---

[1] 'Dog Shit Girl' case has changed public sentiment in favor of Real Name Verification Law, as discussed more specifically in Sect. 2.

more highly thanks to online anonymity. The immensely popular and large-scale interactions are associated with distilling expertise and opinions from thousands of participants who may or may not know each other.

However, on the other hand, anonymity mitigates the social norm and establishes conditions to neglect principles of mutual respect. Malicious profanities and groundless online rumors can proliferate quickly under this circumstance, and those online slanders can lead to serious privacy invasion and personal defamation. Not surprisingly, there have been a variety of conflicts surrounding freedom of speech and anonymity on the cyberspace, particularly in South Korea, a country that is the most highly networked in the world. According to a recent research[2], South Korea's household broadband penetration reached 95%, which was the highest rate among those of all 57 surveyed countries.[3] This fact indicates that cyberspace has become an important part of daily life for South Koreans than people in any other countries. In spite of several positive impacts of this advanced network, radical changes have created several spillover effects in South Korea's society. For instance, online harassment in anonymous cyberspace has constantly occurred, such as the 'Dog Shit Girl' case[4].

This study examines the impact of policy that was firstly taken into effect in 2007 by which internet users should verify their real identification when they write on widely-used internet websites. The paper proceeds as follows: Sect. 2 discusses the description of legislation and related literature. Section 3 lays out the research model and hypotheses and Sect. 4 describe the data and methods of analysis. Main results in terms of policy impacts are specified in Sect. 5. Finally, Sect. 6 provides a discussion and conclusion of the results.

2   Backgrounds and Relevant Literature

2.1   History and Description of Real Name Verification Law

The initial debate was ignited by political domain. Presidential election in 2002 was a turning point from a traditional campaign to an internet-oriented one. In the

---

[2]http://www.strategyanalytics.com/default.aspx?mod=PressReleaseViewer&a0=4748

[3]Second: Singapore (88%), 3rd: Netherlands (85%), USA (60%) (at the end of 2008).

[4]When a girl riding a South Korean subway refused to clean up her dog's excrement, a witness took pictures of her and posted them on a popular website, along with an account of her misbehavior. Within hours, she and her dog were recognized everywhere they went. Within hours, she was labeled "dog-shit-girl" and her pictures and parodies were everywhere on the cyberspace. Within days, her identity and her past were revealed. Request for information about her parents and relatives started popping up and people started to recognize her by the dog and the bag she was carrying as well as her watch, clearly visible in the original picture. All mentions of privacy invasion were shouted down with accusations of being related to the girl.(Source:http://boingboing.net/2005/06/29/woman_doesnt_clean_u.html)

election, it was believed to some extent that young voters' assertive online activities and campaigns in favor of a particular candidate upset the election result. Some conservative members of National Assembly enacted Real Name Verification Law for the first time in 2005. Under this rule, only verified users with their real identity can leave postings and comments on the website. The suggested bill contained that the rule would be applied to election-related online discussion boards before 90 days of the Election Day. They believed that this policy would protect the privacy of candidates and promote more reliable online discussions. Due to the constant social issues caused by online slanders, the extended version of Real Name Verification Law was built in July 2007. By this law, all websites that have average daily viewership of over 300,000 went into effect. Once again, this law was strengthened to websites that have average daily viewership of over 100,000 in 2009. Accordingly, 37 websites had been subject to the law in 2007, but 153 websites[5] were concerned with the law in 2009. In order to verify a user's identity, resident registration number (RRN)[6] is used at the associated websites.

The original policy goal is to prevent widespread online abuse in postings and comments that can seriously cause privacy invasion and personal defamation by legal enforcement and penalties. However, this strict law can discourage users' willingness to express, which is not desirable. In this context, research questions are as follows: was Real Name Verification Law effective? Did people's online behaviors change due to the law? Which factor is more influential to behaviors of users between an anonymous condition with the law and condition with revealed real identity? Relevant literature is reviewed in the following section.

2.2 Anonymity and Pseudonymity

As noted above, Real Name Verification Law can be regarded as a changed rule-setting in terms of anonymity. First of all, the relevant terminology should be clearly defined. According to [20], *anonymity* is the state of being not identifiable within a set of subject. *Unlinkability* and *unobservability* are accompanied with anonymity. The distinction between anonymity and *pseudonymity* is another important matter. Pseudonymity indicates that the user maintains one or more persistent pseudonyms that are not connected to the user's physical identity [8]. Pseudonymity comprises all degrees of linkability to a subject. For example, third parties (website operators) may have the possibility to reveal the identity of the holder (users) in order to provide

---

[5]It is not an exaggerated statement that almost all frequently-visited websites by South Korean people came to be laid under this restriction

[6] Resident registration number is equivalent to social security number in the US. This is a 13-digit number issued to all residents of South Korean citizens. It is used to identify people in various private transactions such as in banking and employment. It is also used extensively for online identification purposes.

means for investigation or prosecution. In online communications, pseudonyms contain a variety degree of anonymity [6]. High linkable *public pseudonyms* indicate that the link between pseudonym (or nickname) and a real identity is publicly known or easy to discover. *Unlinkable pseudonyms* mean that system operators or third parties cannot detect a certain pseudonym's real identity [20]. Real Name Verification Law led to the cyberspace to switch from an unlinkable pseudonymous condition to a publicly pseudonymous condition.

2.3 Deindividuation

The paper is directly associated with a large body of literature of the social value of anonymous communication and deindividuation research. Social psychology has a long history of studying the effect of anonymity and its disinhibiting effect on individual's behaviors. Two main streams are existent with regard to anonymous communication: positive and negative aspects. On the positive side, anonymity communications enable minorities to express their own opinions and to maintain privacy protection [7]. An anonymous environment is helpful in promoting more active involvements without revealing personal identity [26]. Also, anonymous speech helps to settle the imbalance of information through revelation of autonomous personal identity [35]. According to the social identity model of deindividuation effects (SIDE) model that was built by [24], anonymity should accentuate the effects of the salient social identity and the dominant normative response associated with it. From Information Systems literature, anonymity led to a reduction in behavioral constraints and enabled individuals to engage in behavior they would not engage in when identified [9].

On the other hand, opponent groups argue that it is more likely that defamation, threat, insulting words, and slander can occur under an anonymous communication environment [2]. According to classical deindividuation theory, anonymity in the group can lead to reduced self-awareness and influence of social norms that ultimately correspond to antinormative behaviors [23].

2.4 CMC and Deindividuation

Finally, according to recent literature on impacts and influence of CMC, reduction of identifiable information reduces self-awareness and stimulates antinormative behavior [15]. However, aforementioned SIDE model proposes that certain feature of CMC can intensify social influence and enhance normative behavior [22, 27].

The main limitation of the previous studies is that they are based on designed experiments. None of these studies have investigated actual behavioral changes of online communications by using real-world data. Real Name Verification Law provides a proper condition to examine the actual behavioral change of users.

Moreover, previous studies regarding anonymity have been conducted from legal and economic aspects. There is little research of empirical aspects of anonymity which are associated with behaviors of people and impacts of a particular policy.

3 Research Model and Hypotheses

The goal of Real Name Verification Law is to reduce undesirable and antinormative postings by changing the level of anonymity in which linkability and traceability are enhanced. Previous studies found that the anonymous condition is negatively associated with privacy invasion, such as more slanders and defamation [4, 28]. However, at the same time, if this strict legal enforcement leads to discouragement of willingness-to-express related to freedom of speech to the internet users, the law is dysfunctional and the results may yield undesirable spillover effects [17, 33]. For this reason, some privacy experts and groups in South Korea also criticize this policy which enables a person's real identity to be fully traceable. Some researchers tried to examine the impact of Real Name Verification Law in South Korea. Most argued the legal aspects and appropriateness of the policy [[10, 13], Myung, 2005]. More recently, [32] pioneered the empirical study to explore the effects of the law with real world dataset, and their findings are the following: the number of postings decreased, slanderous and swear words in postings did not decrease, but those in replies (or comments) decreased in replies after the implementation of the law. However, the study only observed each 10 days before and after the law implementation and did not examine the long term impact. Not surprisingly, users would be more cautious led by excessive sense of alarm right after the law. This paper explores both short term and long term effects of the law with abundant data from several sources. The research model has been designed for this purpose, as shown in Fig. 1.

Figure 1 shows the main factors to be examined and the structure of the research. Site 1 and Site 3 use nickname policies at their online discussion forums; by contrast, Site 2 uses real name policy regardless of the existence of the law. In other words, Site 2 is with more enhanced level in terms of exposing users' real identity, compared to other two sites. Site 1 and Site 2 are subjected to Real Name Verification Law, but Site 3 is not applied to the law due to its smaller number of daily visitors. Site 1 is of main interest in the study in order to see policy effects and users' behavioral change, and it is compared to those in Site 2 and Site 3 for the robustness check. By comparing Site 1 to Site 2, I can observe how users behave differently when they write messages with their real identity. In addition, Site 3 is a reference of Site 1 for verifications.

Real Name Verification Law gives participants the feeling that others can observe and track their posting history. For example, government's inspection authority may be involved and punished in case that a particular user's postings lead to negative social cues. This in turn can affect the quantity of interaction and the richness of discussion in the online forums. Not surprisingly, anonymity has been found to

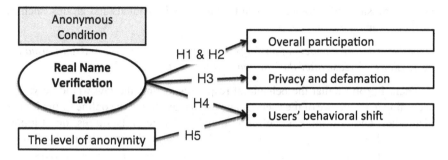

Before Real Name Verification Law

Policy Level of anonymity	Pseudonym (nickname)	Real name
No regulation	**Site 1** and Site 3	Site 2

Creation of traceability

Policy Level of anonymity	Pseudonym (nickname)	Real name
Subject to Real Name Verification Law	**Site 1**	Site 2
Not applied	Site 3	--

Fig. 1 Research model

increase actual participation over identified groups [Kahai et al. 1998]. In addition, when members are originally reticent to participate, anonymity frees them from evaluation and apprehension and leads to more participation [21]. Thus, the freeing of participants from surveillance and traceability seems to be a pronounced effect on participation. Since the enforcement of Real Name Verification Law was widely reported by the mass media and websites that were applied to the law at the point of its implementation, it is assumed that most internet users were aware of it. The first two hypotheses are to measure whether the law directly discouraged the willingness-to-express at the online forum:

Hypothesis 1: Participants decrease after the law comes into effect.

Hypothesis 2: The number of postings decreases after the law comes into effect.

Next, I measure how effective the law was in terms of reducing swear words and antinormative expressions. Excessive slanders and abuse are closely associated with privacy invasion and defamation against particular individuals and groups, such as politicians and political parties.

Hypothesis 3: The numbers of postings that include swear words and antinormative expressions decrease after the law comes into effect.

Then, I propose that the behavioral responses against the law would be varied according to the nature of the users. Some users may stay in the online forum longer than others and post more. Other users may participate in the discussion of topics in which they are particularly interested. I conjecture that people involved more heavily in the discussion were affected by the law rather than temporary users.

Hypothesis 4: The heavy users are more influenced by the law than the light users.

Also of interest is how the operating policy of the online discussion board influences users. I assume that users behave more responsibly and discreetly with their real name, because writings with real name cannot be separated with their real-world identity.

Hypothesis 5: There are less abusive and antinormative postings in the real-name discussion forum than those in the pseudonym-based discussion forum.

4 Data and Methods

4.1 Data

Data is collected from Site 1, which is the most popular online discussion forum in the South Korea's top portal website[7], using a web-crawling method. I chose a discussion board with the topic of political issues. Political and diplomatic issues, including topics relevant to North Korea, public policy, elections are more arguable in the online discussion; therefore, it provides a higher likelihood to represent users' thoughts and emotions directly. Since it was unlikely for users to change their nicknames in the given period, it is assumed that each nickname represents each separate individual.

During the period from January 2005 to December 2010, 2,024,274 postings written by 207,124 participants (nicknames) are collected, and the mean of postings and participants per month are 28,114 and 2,798 respectively. Figure 2 illustrates the trends in the number of postings and participants. A vertical solid line in the middle of the graph is the point of Real Name Verification Law, and the oval

---

[7]http://agora.media.daum.net/ According to the official announcement of the portal operator, the total number of postings in all categories of forums was 784,107 by 74,949 participants in the period April 1, 2008–June 18, 2008, and the number unique visitors were 7.9 million in April, 2008

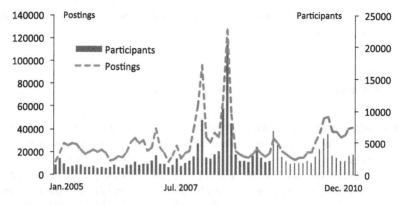

Fig. 2 The trend of number of postings and participants at Site 1 (2005–2010)

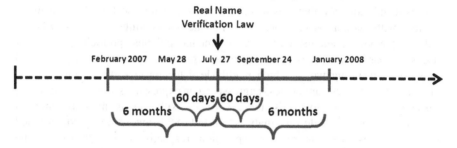

Fig. 3 Two periods (short term and long term) of the study

around the line is the period of interest in this study. In the long term point-of-view, it is seemingly conjectured that the number of postings and participants were more influenced by particular politically disputable issues rather than by the law. Two kinked points in the rectangular were caused by two nationwide striking issues, the recent presidential election in December 2007 and the dispute against the government's decision to import American beef respectively.

In order to see behavioral changes and policy impacts more directly caused by Real Name Verification Law, I selected two separate periods of short term and long term, which are 60 days and 6 months, as shown in Fig. 3.

For the supplemental study, two websites, Site 2[8] and Site 3[9], are considered: Site 2 is a discussion forum of a leading newspaper site and Site 3 is a debate forum specialized in political issues. As noted above, Site 1 and Site 2 have been subject to Real Name Verification Law since July 2007. In these Sites, only users who passed real identity verification process could leave postings in the latter period. By contrast, Site 3 is not associated with the law, because its daily visitor was less than

---

[8]http://www.chosun.com/

[9]http://www.freezone.co.kr/

300,000. Anybody can express their opinions with their own nicknames without any authorization process in Site 3.

4.2   Methods

First of all, several terms have to be clearly defined. *Posting* is a message that is written by an individual (nickname), and each posting is represented with time, date, writing number by time order, and nickname set by each user. Content analysis is based on two criteria: *swear words* and *antinormative expressions*. Even though it is certain that these two standards are closely correlated, each factor indicates salient meaning. Postings with swear words[10] can be regarded as the most aggressive behaviors. This is closely associated with privacy invasion and defamation as well as deindividuation that was discussed in the previous section. Contrastingly, postings with antinormative expressions indicate that writings include slanderous and abusive words against certain governmental policies, politicians, or other discussion participants. It is common to use irrational contractions of words and transformed insulting words which readily lead to conceive the original words. Although these expressions are less aggressive than expressing swear words directly, it is assumed that participants use these words by exploiting anonymous condition in the online forum. To do this analysis, 34 and 585 keywords are predetermined for swear words and antinormative expressions respectively. In order to examine the behavioral shift across the nature of users, six categories and three groups of users are defined as following criteria on the basis of the number of postings per month: (1) one posting and (2) two postings: light user, (3) three posting and (4) 4–10 postings: middle user, (5) 11–15 postings and (6) more than 15 postings: heavy user.

The following technical approach is implemented. To run and display content on the browsers, web data such as HTML and JavaScript are downloaded to the client side (Site 1). This data stream can be read and its target content can be parsed, a concept known as "crawling and parsing". A web crawler is designed to reconstruct all URLs, also known as the seeds of the target sites, and retrieve content from those pages using Java and MS-SQL. Based on extracted data from the target sites, data mining and filtering methods can be implemented to retrieve postings with specific keywords—swear words or antinormative expressions.

---

[10]Most discussion board systems automatically block writings with well-known swear words by their own filtering algorithm, so it is common for participants to use these words in a slightly different way. These words were regarded as homogeneous words to the original swear words in this paper.

5　Results

5.1　The Change in the Number of Postings and Participants

Before I examine the change of postings based on 60 days and 6 months windows, the change in each 3 weeks before and after Real Name Verification Law is illustrated in Table 1 and Fig. 4. Salient decrease at the point of the implementation of the law on July 27, 2007 is observed in Fig. 4, and the average number of daily postings in the discussion has decreased from 477 to 379, and the difference is statistically significant. The average number of daily participant has also decreased from 124 to 115, but the difference is not significant. This can be interpreted that some users might be more cautious in posting their opinions right after the law enforcement.

Regardless of this result, it is difficult to conclude that users' willingness-to-express was discouraged due to the law. It was straightforwardly expected that the number of postings would decrease in this short time period, because the implementation of the law was highly disputable through online and offline and offline media at that time. Thus, I examine the impact of the law on the basis of short term (60 days) and long term (6 months) by each user group, and the

Table 1 The comparison between before and after the law (3-week windows)

	Before the law	After the law	Change (%)	t-statistic (p-value)
Average daily posting	477	379	−98 (−20.5)	2.28** (0.014)
Average daily participants	124	115	−9 (−7.6)	1.08 (0.14)
Average posting per user	3.78	3.25	−0.53 (−14.0)	2.61*** (0.006)

* significant at 10%; ** significant at 5%; *** significant at 1%

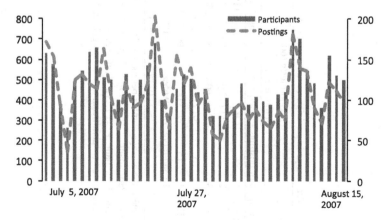

Fig. 4 The trend of postings and participants at Site 1 (July–August 2007)

Table 2 The change in participants and postings by each user group

| User Group | # of postings | (1) Short term (60 days) | | | | (2) Long term (6 months) | | | |
| | | Before the law | | After the law | | Before the law | | After the law | |
		Participants	Postings	Participants	Postings	Participants	Postings	Participants	Postings
Light User	1	1,026 (52.80%)	1,026 (5.11%)	962 (51.38%)	962 (5.30%)	839 (51.60%)	839 (4.59%)	1,775 (45.86%)	1,775 (3.99%)
	2	251 (12.93%)	503 (2.50%)	265 (14.15%)	529 (2.92%)	219 (13.44%)	438 (2.39%)	572 (14.77%)	1,143 (2.57%)
Middle User	3	128 (6.60%)	385 (1.92%)	128 (6.85%)	384 (2.12%)	109 (6.72%)	327 (1.80%)	300 (7.75%)	900 (2.20%)
	4 ~ 10	291 (14.98%)	1,758 (8.76%)	281 (15.02%)	1,682 (9.28%)	239 (14.67%)	1,430 (7.83%)	649 (16.76%)	3,894 (8.76%)
Heavy User	11 ~ 15	59 (3.04%)	809 (4.03%)	60 (3.19%)	700 (3.86%)	51 (3.13%)	645 (3.53%)	146 (3.76%)	1,859 (4.18%)
	16 and more	187 (9.65%)	15,603 (77.69%)	176 (9.42%)	13,875 (76.52%)	170 (10.44%)	14,591 (79.86%)	429 (11.10%)	34,903 (78.48%)
Total		1943 (100%)	20,083 (100%)	1,871 (100%)	18,132 (100%)	1,626 (100%)	18,269 (100%)	3,870 (100%)	44,473 (100%)

Each value is the average number per month. The % value in parenthesis is a proportion out of total value in the last row

Short-term: Participant: $\chi^4 = 1.67\ df = 5$, $p = 0.89$, Postings: $\chi^4 = 13.90^{***}$, $df = 5$, $p = 0.016$

Long-term: Participant: $\chi^2 = 15.72^{***}$, $df = 5$, $p = 0.89$, Postings: $\chi^4 = 46.38^{***}$, $df = 5$, $p = 0.000$

* significant at 10%, ** significant at 5%, *** significant at 1%

result is provided in Table 2. First, while the number of postings is decreased by about 10% from 20,083 to 18,132 in the short term, the number of participants is slightly reduced by 3.7%. The difference of postings is statistically significant, but the difference of participants is not. When it comes to the long-term, the numbers of both postings and participants are strikingly increased. As noted previously, the main reason that more participants expressed their opinions was the disputable political issues in South Korea in the late 2007–2008, but, at the same time, this is clear evidence that Real Name Verification Law is not associated with users' willingness-to-express on the Internet unlike prevalent concerns by experts and activists in South Korea [10, 32]. In other words, active discussions are maintained according to the political issues, so Hypothesis 1 and 2 are rejected based on the long term perspective. This result is somewhat conflicting with the findings by [32] in which they concluded that Real Name Verification Law affected users' intention to post negatively. It should be noted that the period of their study was only 20 days around the point of the law, and their result is along with the narrow time period result that is specified earlier. As they specified that the short time period as the limitation of their study, examination based on the longer periods is required to see the effect of the law in terms of freedom of speech at the online space. However, I should be cautious to interpret the result. My conclusion is that Real Name Verification Law does not seem to be related to overall participation in the long term, according to Figs. 2 and 4. This means that there is no causal relationship between the law and the participation.

Comparison with Site 2 and Site 3

I checked relatively fewer postings after the law in the short term, but no relevance to the law in the long term from Site 1. In order to make this argument more concrete, I compared the trend of the number of postings in Site 2 (a site with real-name posting policy and applied to Real Name Verification Law) and Site 3 (a site with pseudonym policy and not applied to the law) in the same period. It is possible that some users in Site 1 who were sensitive to the law implementation might move to the other discussion forums to which Real Name Verification Law was not applied. Nevertheless, it would be difficult to create a new actively debating place, since all popular websites including newspaper websites, portals, and social networking sites are subject to the law. Yet, some debate-specialized websites, such as Site 3, can be alternative choices for some users as their shelter. Thus, I checked if there was a significant change in other relevant and equivalent websites. If there is a sign that the significant increase in the number of postings and participants, Real Name Verification Law would cause an undesirable spillover effect. As shown in Fig. 5, no striking shifts in Site 2 and Site 3 unlike somewhat radical variations in Site 1 are observed around the point of the implementation of the law even in the short term.

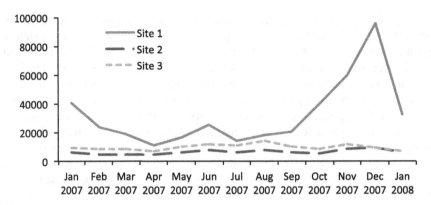

Fig. 5 The trend of postings and participants at Site 1 (July–August 2007)

5.2 The Change in the Number of Postings with Swear Words and Antinormative Expressions

The main interest of this study is to see how much participants' behaviors in terms of using swear words and antinormative expressions were shifted after the implementation of the law. These negative postings are associated with privacy invasion and defamation, and the reduction of these postings is the primary policy goal. The results are reported in Table 3. The proportion of each category which is specified in the parenthesis is calculated by the number of postings with swear words divided by the number of total postings in each category of the given period. While the proportions of swear words and antinormative expressions in Light User group are mostly greater than those in Middle and Heavy User groups, the actual numbers of bad postings in Heavy User group is greater than those in Light and Middle User groups across all columns. The proportions of swear words and antinormative expressions in the first row of Light User group are around 20% and 30%, compared to around 2% and 5% in the last row of Heavy User group in Table 3. There are two reasons for this finding. First, a few heavy users post far greater number of postings, several hundred in each month; therefore, the distribution is highly skewed to this group. Second, participants in Light User group usually post one or two postings according to their interests, and these postings are more likely to contain either swear words or antinormative expressions.

When it comes to the shift between two periods, the proportions of swear words and antinormative expressions are reduced in all cases, and all differences are statistically significant. In particular, behavioral shifts are observed more saliently in Heavy User group and this mainly lead to the difference of total proportions between two periods. Assuming that these heavy users' frequent postings influence the mood of discussion forum more critically, this result is meaningful in terms of the effects of Real Name Verification Law. That is, if their behavioral shift is truly maintained, this may affect behaviors of both Light and Middle User groups

Table 3 Trends of using swear words and antinormative expressions

User Group	# of postings	(1) Short term (60 days)				(2) Long term (6 months)			
		Before the law		After the law		Before the law		After the law	
		Participants	Postings	Participants	Postings	Participants	Postings	Participants	Postings
Light User	1	195 (20.00%)	282 (28.78%)	166 (16.06%)	261 (25.26%)	171 (20.91%)	244 (29.92%)	334 (17.92%)	509 (27.54%)
	2	82 (17.75%)	130 (26.37%)	77 (12.96%)	146 (24.87%)	84 (19.80%)	132 (30.71%)	153 (13.43%)	285 (25.29%)
Middle User	3	71 (17.49%)	90 (27.08%)	53 (12.88%)	98 (23.20%)	61 (18.20%)	92 (29.19%)	104 (12.66%)	169 (20.09%)
	4~10	241 (13.73%)	447 (26.22%)	176 (9.46%)	402 (21.29%)	247 (17.18%)	413 (28.93%)	312 (9.28%)	664 (19.53%)
Heavy User	11~15	111 (13.45%)	137 (16.24%)	96 (14.30%)	160 (20.23%)	108 (17.84%)	184 (30.63%)	119 (8.93%)	252 (16.54%)
	16 and more	323 (1.77%)	1,184 (6.93%)	150 (1.03%)	589 (4.03%)	355 (2.33%)	987 (6.49%)	330 (1.01%)	1,116 (3.62%)
Total		1,022 (4.83%)	2,269 (10.85%)	717 (3.71%)	1,655 (8.54%)	1,025 (5.58%)	2,051 (11.13%)	1,351 (3.26%)	2,996 (7.38%)

Each value is the average number per month

Short-term: Swear words: $\chi^4 = 26.99^{***}$, $df = 5$, $p = 0.000$, Antinormative expressions: $\chi^4 = 112.65^{***}$, $df = 5$, $p = 0.000$

Long-term: Swear words: $\chi^2 = 49.14^{***}$, $df = 5$, $p = 0.000$, Antinormative expressions: $\chi^2 = 75.57^{***}$, $df = 5$, $p = 0.000$

* significant at 10%; ** significant at 5%; *** significant at 1%

in positive directions. In addition, it is noted that the discrepancies in the long term are greater than those in the short term. This fact can be interpreted that the effect of policy is accelerated over time. Unlike the noticeable change in Heavy User group, there were less significant shifts in Light and Middle User groups. In these groups, it is highly likely that users who posted swear words before the law implementation are different from those who posted after the law. That is, it seems that new participants after the law did not change their behaviors and Real Name Verification Law did not affect the fundamental shift of behaviors. There are some limitations of this study and caveats in interpreting results. Undoubtedly, postings which are involved in negative emotional expressions notably depend on the level of disputes surrounding the political issues. In addition, since the number of postings by a few heavy users is quite great, their behavioral change led to this result. In order to solve these problems, future research should explore the consistency of the results from other websites and by tracking political issues more precisely. Nevertheless, the findings of this study indicate that the governmental intervention was effective to reduce swear words and antinormative expressions that might cause privacy invasion to some extent, and Hypothesis 3 and 4 are supported. This result is also consistent to the findings from experimental designs in the previous research that argued people would behave more politely and conformingly under the identifiable condition rather than anonymous condition.

5.3   The Behavioral Changes of Particular Individuals

In the previous sections, I checked the trends in the number of postings and participants as well as the reduction of bad postings after Real Name Verification Law. Even if swear words and nonnormative expressions can be detected through text mining and filtering techniques, the result could be downward biased, because some slanderous postings may not contain selected keywords in the predetermined algorithm. Thus, as supplemental analysis, I conducted additional content analysis in greater details by investigating directly[11]. The same approaches for detecting slanderous and abusive postings which may or may not include swear words and antinormative expressions are conducted. By doing this, I can also check the robustness of the previous analysis and more precise behavioral changes across user groups. Since I am interested in postings around the implementation of the law, I selected participants who wrote their postings in July and August 2007. Thousand two hundred and eighty nine users posted at least one message in July 2007, and

---

[11]Two independent coders rated each set of postings on the basis of the provided standards, and cross-checked for coding reliability. Both coders are Ph.D students in social science fields in the US, whose native language is Korean.

120 participants[12] are randomly selected for this study. In order to examine the behavioral shift, I only need to see users who write postings before and after the law; therefore, 41 users are taken into account.

Table 4 reports the results. In Column (1), the total number of postings increased, and this difference is not statistically significant. This finding is associated with the previous conclusions in terms of the trends in the number of postings in which the participation in the discussion is not relevant to the law enforcement. The results in terms of the number of swear words and antinormative expressions are reported in Column (2) and Column (3). Some interesting findings are as follows. First, the proportions of swear words and antinormative postings are greater than the previous results, which were the pre-coded detection algorithm. The main reason could be that more number of postings is classified to these bad postings by detailed content analysis by coders. In particular, some postings can be regarded as antinormative postings without containing significant informal expressions, such as serious slanders against the other discussion participants. Other possible reasons are due to smaller sample size and shorter period of analysis. For example, there are only three users in some categories. Second, the proportions of swear words and antinormative postings have decreased, and the differences are statistically significant. However, salient finding is that the differences between two periods are smaller than those in the previous section (5.2). It can be interpreted that some users still behaved in aggressive ways even after the law, but the usage of explicitly abusive words might be decreased. Thus, it should be more cautious to conclude whether Real Name Verification Law has achieved its policy goal. The decrease in swear words and antinormative expressions can be positively associated with less slanders and defamation, but the finding suggests that this is not guaranteed by counting the words they used. That is, it is required to explore in more details in order to assess the policy impacts properly. Nevertheless, main results in terms of the reduction of swear words and antinormative expressions are supported and consistent with individual-level data.

5.4 Postings with Real Name Versus Postings with Pseudonym

The last part of study is to examine how the level of anonymity affects users' behaviors. Regardless of whether a form of legal enforcement by a regulatory authority existed or not, encouraging normative behaviors can be achieved by the other mechanism, such as self-regulation by website operators[13]. I argue that users behave more responsibly and discreetly with their real name regardless of the

---

[12] After sorting by the number of postings in the given period, every tenth of participants are selected.

[13] Some websites including Facebook.com hold their own policy in terms of using users' real names rather than their nicknames.

Table 4 Detailed content analysis across groups

User Group	# of postings	(1) Postings		(2) Swear words		(3) Antinormative	
		Before the law	After the law	Before the law	After the law	Before the law	After the law
Light user	1 (11)	11	45	3 (27.27%)	9 (20.00%)	5 (45.45%)	20 (44.44%)
	2 (3)	6	8	2 (33.33%)	2 (25.00%)	2 (33.33%)	3 (37.50%)
	3 (3)	9	17	2 (22.22%)	3 (17.65%)	3 (33.33%)	5 (29.41%)
Middle user	4 ~ 10 (10)	78	102	12 (15.38%)	14 (13.73%)	18 (23.08%)	21 (20.59%)
Heavy user	11~15 (3)	47	44	6 (12.77%)	4 (9.09%)	12 (25.53%)	7 (15.91%)
	16 and more(11)	548	762	24 (4.38%)	26 (3.39%)	70 (12.77%)	72 (9.38%)
Total (41)		699	978	49 (7.01%)	58 (5.89%)	110 (15.74%)	128 (13.01%)

The percentage value in parenthesis of "# of postings" column is the number of samples in each category

The percentage value in parenthesis of column (2) and (3) is the proportion out of total postings in each row

Postings: tvalue= 1.36, $df = 5$ $p = 0.11$, Swear words: tvalue= 3.67***, $df = 5$ $p = 0.007$

Antinormative expressions: tvalue= 1.48*, $df = 40$ $p = 0.09$

* significant at 10%; ** significant at 5%; *** significant at 1%

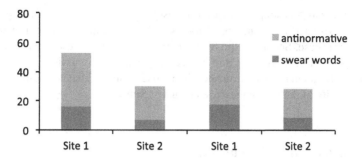

Fig. 6 Comparison between Site 1 and Site 2 (swear words and antinormative expressions)

Table 5 Participation frequency and rate in Site 1 and Site 2

	Topic 1 (Before the law)		Topic 2 (After the law)	
	Site 1	Site 2	Site 1	Site 2
1	79 (90.1%)	62 (81.6%)	73 (86.9%)	53 (74.6%)
2	3 (3.4%)	7 (9.2%)	8 (9.5%)	10 (14.1%)
3	2 (2.2%)	5 (6.6%)	2 (2.4%)	7 (9.9%)
More than 3	3 (3.4%)	2 (2.6%)	1 (1.2%)	1 (1.4%)
Total	87 (100%)	76(100%)	84 (100%)	71 (100%)

The percentage value in parenthesis is the proportion out of total value in the last row

existence of the law. Writings with real name cannot be separated with their real-world actual identity. Site 1 and Site 2 are used for this study: as aforementioned, both websites are subject to Real Name Verification Law, but the only difference is that the messages are posted with *pseudonym* at Site 1, but users have to post with *real name* at Site 2. Two controversial political issues are chosen; the each discussion topic was in May 2007 and in May 2009 respectively, which are before and after the law implementation. Then, 100 postings are randomly selected at each discussion topic from both Site 1 and Site 2. I followed the method and the procedure conducted by [19]. They found that postings in the discussion board with real name showed less emotional behaviors and less grammatical errors than those in pseudonym-based online boards. I selected different topics and additional periods as well as different criteria, compared their study.

Topics:

- Construction of Grand Canal Project (May 2007)
- Administrative capital relocation plan and new policies (May 2009)

The results are reported in Fig. 6 and Table 5. Firstly, as shown in Fig. 6, the results are clearly distinguishable between two Sites. Site 2 shows less postings that contain swear words and antinormative expressions than Site 1 for both topics in two periods. It is noted that Topic 2 seems to be more disputable than Topic 1; therefore, there are more postings that contain swear words and antinormative expressions even after the law. The salient finding in this study is that participants with their real identity show more prudent behaviors than those with pseudonyms.

Thus, Hypothesis 5 is supported with this result. Since the number of bad postings is closely correlated to the nature of topics, it is not meaningful to compare both periods in this case. Secondly, the result in Table 5 shows that users participated in the discussion more actively at Site 2. Real-name online discussion board (Site 2) shows more frequent participation rates than those in Site 1. That is, one-off postings are the majority in the nickname-based board of Site 1.

6 Discussion and Conclusion

6.1 Discussion

There is an interesting analogy in terms of real identity between analyzed South Korean websites and famous social networking services, *Facebook and MySpace*. Users can usually be identified by their real names on Facebook under its self-regulation policy[14]. By contrast, a constant criticism of MySpace is that real names were hidden when users see someone's profile. According to an article[15], anonymity is great when you do not want your actual identity to get in the way of whatever fantasy life you are living online. But, it is also one of the reasons Facebook, which identifies users by their real names, is gaining so quickly on MySpace. That is, people make online social connections on the basis of real-world networks. Users are willing to reveal more private stories and to share their opinions on Facebook that are consistent with their true thoughts in the real world. Abundant use of language containing abuse, slander, and aggressive slang terms on MySpace might have caused the declining use of the website. Moreover, a further study that may be highly relevant could include that of the controversial but widespread commenting systems of Facebook[16], whose advanced features were officially launched in March 2011. Even if this is helpful if users are interested in tying their non-Facebook activity to the social-networking site, this might discourage users to leave comments in sensitive topics.

---

[14]"Impersonating anyone or anything is not permitted. To encourage people to use their real names on Facebook, we limit the number of times names can be changed.", "Your account was disabled because the name under which it was registered was fake. We do not allow users to register with fake names, to impersonate any person or entity, or to falsely state or otherwise misrepresent themselves or their affiliations. In addition, Facebook accounts are intended for use by single individuals, so groups, clubs, businesses, or other types of organizations are not permitted to maintain accounts." *(excerpt from Help Center at Facebook.com)*

[15]http://techcrunch.com/2008/12/17/myspace-quietly-begins-encouraging-users-to-use-their-real-names/

[16]The update to Facebook's comments box plugin was intended to make comments more relevant. Users to a particular site see comments from Facebook friends first and Facebook added public information about users next to their names. (http://www.pcmag.com/article2/0,2817,2381630,00.asp)

6.2   Conclusion

This paper analyzed privacy and anonymous issues surrounding Real Name Verification Law in South Korea. The law was established in order to prevent indiscreet postings on the web; as a result, the country's cyberspace has become more traceable to users' identity as well as more vulnerable to guarantee freedom of speech.

The results suggest that Real Name Verification Law has a dampening effect on overall participation in the short-term, which is consistent with Haines et al. (2006), Kahai et al. (1998), and [32]; however, it is more closely associated with the nature of issues. Thus, the law did not affect the participation of the discussion in the long term. Furthermore, identification of postings had significant effects on reducing uninhibited behaviors (swear words and antinormative expressions), suggesting that Real Name Verification Law encouraged users' behavioral changes in the positive direction to some extent. The impact is greater for Heavy User group than for Light and Middle User groups. Also, discussion participants with their real names showed more discreet behaviors regardless of the enforcement of the law. It seems that users have recognized that the level of anonymity was shifted by the law, from complete dissociation of real and online identities to only visual anonymity by pseudonyms in which their real identity can be detectable. By analyzing this unprecedented policy at the forefront of internet trends of South Korea, this paper can shed light on some useful implications and information to policy makers of other countries that consider a certain type of internet regulation in terms of privacy.

This study contains some limitations. Only a few websites have been considered for analysis and comparison. If more websites are examined in each category and this significant difference is still maintained, the suggested results will be more convincing. Another limitation is *self-selection* problem. Presumably, some users who are reluctant to show their real identity might use pseudonym-based online discussion forums, and they are more likely to be assertive and abusive. In other words, it is reasonable to say that more discreet users prefer to participate in real name boards, and more violent users prefer to discuss in a pseudonymous board. Notwithstanding these limitations, users' behaviors on online boards may be affected by anonymous conditions and topics rather than loosely proclaimed legal enforcement.

There are several promising future research agenda. First, future research can be conducted by collecting data from more discussion boards in the given period. People usually have their own frequently-visiting websites and participate in the discussion in those spaces. Thus, when more discussion forums are included in the study and current results are still maintained, the argument in this paper becomes highly strengthened and reasonable. Second, as noted previously, this study is linked to the next step of research in terms of the impact of recently-implemented commenting systems with real identity by popular social networking service providers in the US. Morio and Buchholz [16] pointed out that cross-cultural differences affected interpersonal motivation (autonomy vs. affiliation) when individuals decided whether or not to remain anonymous in the online communication. Their conclusion is that Western societies will gravitate toward online communities that allow lower levels of anonymity, while individuals in Eastern societies will be more likely to seek out online communities that promote higher levels of anonymity. However, currently-implementing social comments systems in the US is more relevant to higher levels of anonymity. It would be interesting to observe whether users' behaviors are shifted when they post comments with their real personalities and how this result differs from the findings in this study.

References

1. Acquisti A, Dingledine R, Syverson R (2003) On the economics of anonymity. In: Camp J Wright R (eds) Financial cryptography (FC'03). Springer-Verlag, LNCS
2. Cohen JE (1996) The right to read anonymously: a closer look at "copyright management" in cyberspace. Conn L Rev 28:981
3. Cohen JE (2000) Examined lives: information privacy and the subject as object Stan L Rev 52:1373–1398
4. Danielson P (1996) Pseudonyms, Mailbots, and virtual letterheads: the evolution of computer-mediated ethics In: Ess C (ed) Philosophical perspectives on computer-mediated communication. State University of New York Press, Albany
5. Diakopoulos N, Naaman M (2011) Towards quality discourse in online news comments. In: Proceedings of the ACM 2011 conference on computer supported cooperative work
6. Froomkin MA (1995) Anonymity and its enemies. J Online L Art 4
7. Froomkin MA (1996) Flood control on the information ocean: living with anonymity, digital cash, and distributed database. J Law Commerce 15(2):395–507
8. Goldberg I (2000) A pseudonymous communications infrastructure for the internet. PhD thesis
9. Jessup LM, Connolly T, Galegher J (1990) The effects of anonymity on GDSS group process with an idea-generating task. MIS Quarterly 14:3: 313–321
10. Hwang Y (2007) Critical approach to the implementation of real-name system on bulletin board of the internet: exploring right of anonymous communication, (in Korean). Media Soc 15(2):97–130
11. Kahai SS, Sosik JJ, Avolio BJ (2003) Effects of leadership style, anonymity, and rewards on creativity relevant processes and outcomes in an electronic meeting system context. Leader Q 14:499–524
12. Karyda M, Kokolakis S (2008) Privacy perceptions among members of online communities. In: Acquisti A, Gritzalis S, Lambrinoudakis C and De Capitani di Vimercati, S (eds) Digital Privacy: theory, technologies and practices. Auerbach Publications, Boca Raton pp 253–266
13. Kim K (2009) The technical, legal and business issues of the real-name-verification requirement (in Korean). Hum Right Justice 7:78–97
14. Marx G (1999) What's in a name? some reflections on the sociology of anonymity. Inform Soc 15(2)
15. McLeod PL, Baron RS, Marti MW, Yoon K (1997) The eyes have it: Minority influence in face-to-face and computer-mediated groups. J Appl Psychol 82:706–718
16. Morio H, Buchholz C (2009) How anonymous are you online? examining online social behaviors from a cross-cultural perspective. AI Soc 23:297–307
17. Myers DG, Lamm H (1976) The group polarization phenomenon. Psychol Bulletin 83: 602–627
18. Myung J (2003) Trace of the implementation of real-name system on the internet bulletin board in a public institution (in Korean). Center Law Inform Soc 5:2–13

19. Park CS, Go MK, Ki S (2008) The impact of anonymity on behavior of comments in online discussion board, manuscript
20. Pfitzmann A, Koehntopp M (2001) Anonymity, unobservability, and pseudonymity—a proposal for terminology. In: Hannes Federrath (ed) Designing privacy enhancing technologies - Proceedings of the International Workshop on Design Issues in Anonymity and Unobservability vol 2009 of LNCS Springer, New York, NY
21. Pinsonneault A, Barki H, Gallupe RB, Hoppen N (1999) Electronic brainstorming: the illusion of productivity. Inform Syst Res 10(2):110–133
22. Postmes T, Spears R, Lea M (1998) Breaching or building social boundaries: side-effects of computer- mediated communication. Comm Res 25(6):689–715
23. Postmes T, Spears R (1998) Deindividuation and antinormative behavior: a meta-analysis. Psychol Bulletin 123:238–259
24. Reicher SD, Spears R, Postmes T (1995) A social identity model of deindividuation phenomena. European Rev Soc Psychol 6:161–198
25. Reidenbach RE, Robin DP, Dawson L (1991) An Application and extension of a multidimensional ethics scale to selected marketing practices and marketing groups. J Acad Market Sci 19(2):83–92
26. Siegel J, Dubrovsky V, Kiesler S, McGuire TW (1986) Group processes in computer-mediated communication. Organ Behav Hum Decis Process 37:157–187
27. Spears R, Lea M, Lee S (1990) De-individuation and group polarisation in computer-mediated communication. British J Soc Psychol 29:121–134
28. Sproull L, Kiesler S (1986) Reducing social context cues: electronic mail in organizational communication. Manag Sci 32(11):1492–1512
29. Solove DJ (2004) The digital person: technology and privacy in the information age. New York University Press, New York
30. Solove DJ (2006) A taxonomy of privacy Univ Penn Law Rev 154(3):477–560
31. Solove DJ (2007) The future of reputation: gossip, rumor, and privacy on the internet Yale University Press New Haven, CT
32. Woo JW, Nah HS, Choi JM. (2010) An empirical analysis of the effect of real name system on internet bulletin boards South Korea J Pub Admin 48(1):78–96
33. Walther JB (1992) Interpersonal effects in computer-mediated communication. Comm Res 19(1):52–90
34. Wood A, Smith M (2001) Online communication: linking technology, identity, and culture. Mahwah NJ, Erlbaum
35. Zarsky TZ (2004) Thinking outside the box: considering transparency, anonymity, and pseudonymity as overall solutions to the problems of information privacy in the internet society, 58. Univ Miami Law Rev 991:1028–1032

The Privacy Landscape: Product Differentiation on Data Collection

Sören Preibusch and Joseph Bonneau

Abstract Whilst the majority of online consumers do not seem to take the privacy characteristics of goods and services into account with their consumption choices, a sizeable proportion consider differences in data collection and processing amongst alternative suppliers when deciding where to buy. Meeting their heterogeneous privacy preferences would require varied privacy regimes between different suppliers. Based on an empirical evaluation of 140 web sites across five industries, we consider two questions: (1) can privacy-conscious consumers find a privacy-friendly seller/provider? (2) is this alternative associated with higher prices? We interpret the empirical evidence using the economic model of horizontal differentiation. As an overarching conclusion, differentiation on privacy is more prevalent in markets where consumption is priced—an observation that confirms the prediction from theory. Surprisingly, sellers that collect less data charge lower prices, with high significance. Implications for regulation and for further study are discussed.

1 Competition on Privacy

The policy of self-regulation on consumer privacy, implemented prominently in the United States more than a decade ago as well as in other jurisdictions, assumes "market resolution of privacy concerns" [14]: a firm whose data collection and use are incompatible with consumers' privacy preferences will see its demand diminish. To some extent, ideally to the socially optimal extent, privacy-friendliness should be maximally profitable. Indeed, three out of four consumers state they would

S. Preibusch (✉) • J. Bonneau
Computer Laboratory, University of Cambridge, Cambridge, MA CB3 0FD, USA
e-mail: sdp36@cl.cam.ac.uk; jcb82@cl.cam.ac.uk

B. Schneier (ed.), *Economics of Information Security and Privacy III*,
DOI 10.1007/978-1-4614-1981-5_12,
© Springer Science+Business Media New York 2013

cancel their online shopping transaction if asked for personal information they are unwilling to provide. The majority of them indicate they would switch to an alternative web site [1].

Consumers exhibit heterogeneity in their privacy preferences, expressing different levels of discomfort in revealing different data items to commercial web sites [11]. Simply reducing the amount of personal information collected online cannot satisfy all users' preferences, though. Only 15% of web users would want to give up the personalisation benefits they receive in exchange for not revealing details about themselves [4]. Therefore, consumers' ability to choose a company whose privacy practices are aligned with their individual demand for data protection requires differentiation on the supply side. If failure to provide desirable levels of data protection becomes universal across firms, consumers will be unable to divert their demand due to lack of alternatives.

Dissatisfying security and privacy practices have been identified across many web industries: deployment of tracking technologies, data sharing with affiliates, and vague textual privacy notices are ubiquitous [7]. Three out of four web sites across popularity strata and audience use persistent cookies that allow re-identifying users over multiple visits [13]. Few studies, however, have looked at privacy differences within a given industry. For instance, whilst P3P adoption has been reported to vary strongly across industries, the within-industry variance has not been studied [5].

A distinction between accessibility of privacy policies and actual privacy practices was found in online social networks by Bonneau and Preibusch [2]. Amongst online social networking sites competing for members worldwide, privacy practices varied considerably, but were rarely used as a promotional argument. There was nonetheless a trend that social networking sites offering premium, that is, priced accounts, collected less personal information from their members. At the national level, a similar comparison was performed by Fraunhofer SIT, concluding that platform operators over-collected personal information compared to the technical minimum for service provision. None of the market players was found to be leading on privacy in general; instead, different platforms excelled at different aspects of data protection [6]. Privacy practices of competing firms have also been assessed against one another by consumer watch organisations in areas including online social networks, online dating platforms, music downloads, online travel agents or webmail providers—all of these studies being aimed at guiding consumption choices [18].

Empirical evidence regarding consumers' reactions towards differentiated supply in privacy is scarce. In laboratory experiments, users of a product search engine were found to choose companies with good privacy reviews despite higher prices when shopping for sensitive items [16]. However, when shopping for DVDs, consumers' consumption choices were dominated by price, rather than privacy concerns [1].

We investigate privacy practices at competing web sites within specific industries. To the best of our knowledge, this is the first endeavour to search for such evidence of privacy competition on the web. We studied five industries that supply goods and services over the web, some of which are offered for a fee or price, others

Table 1 Overview of studied web sites and industries

Industry	Product	Pricing	No. sites
Consumer electronics retail (cameras)	Good	Priced	29
Entertainment retail (DVDs)	Good	Priced	22
Social networking	Service	Zero-price	23
Web search	Service	Zero-price	18
Blogging	Service	Zero-price	42

at a zero price. In total, 130 competing web sites were analysed (Table 1), plus ten non-competing web sites. While merchants differentiated on data collection, little variation was found for zero-price services. For e-commerce sites, higher prices were associated with more abundant data collection. Web sites facing little competition tend to collect significantly more personal details than other services offered for free.

2 Methodology

This study is driven by one over-arching research question: do competing online firms differentiate themselves on privacy? As a corollary, we also investigate whether privacy differentiation, if any, is related to different pricing behaviour. We further study what impact the absence of competition has on data collection.

2.1 Hypotheses

Web operators have been observed to exhibit differing privacy regimes. Social networking sites, for instance, exhibit pronounced variation in the amount of personal information collected from their users. Some sites promote themselves as privacy-friendly, and although this promotional claim is often not met in practice, some sites do seem to occupy a privacy niche [2]. Several German social networking sites tried to turn data protection into a positively distinguishing feature in early 2010, a time when Facebook was overtaking the former national incumbents [12]. Differences have also been observed regarding the care for user passwords amongst web sites offering free sign-up. However, better security was not used as an argument to entice users, and practices differ more strongly between industries rather than within industries [3].

Economic theory predicts that firms differentiate their products to evade price competition that would drive their profits towards zero as prices approach marginal costs.

Horizontal differentiation, introduced by Hotelling, describes the concept of products differentiated along a characteristic for which there is no universal better or worse, but for which consumers develop a taste. The taste characteristic of privacy has been established in the context of online social networking [9]; our own research indicates that a vertical ordering cannot be established even for data items of seemingly obvious sensitivity levels: in comparing the data items "home address" and "hobbies", both of which might be used alternatively for personalising entertainment recommendations, 58% of consumers are more willing to provide the latter, but 20% are more comfortable with revealing the former [1].

Heterogeneous preferences are conceptualised as a distribution of consumers along a taste interval of length 1. The position of a consumer on the interval is determined by her preference for something on the left over something on the right. For instance, someone at position 0 would strongly prefer revealing one's home address over revealing one's hobbies, and vice versa for a consumer located at position 1. The strategic behaviour of competing firms facing such a demand is well studied in economics [[15], chap. 7]. Two antagonistic effects determine their choices of prices and positions on the interval, meaning their practices within the privacy space.

Given a structure of positive prices, firms want to increase their market share by moving closer to each other, towards the centre of the interval: a firm on the "left" side of the interval serves all customers located between itself and the left edge, and by symmetry, the firm on the "right" side is the preferential supplier for those located between it and the right edge. In expanding these monopolistically served regions, firms have a tendency to move towards the middle. However, as firms are close to one another, price competition becomes stronger. In the extreme case, firms located at the same position are no longer differentiated and compete solely on price. In order to relax competition, maximum differentiation is sought by the firms when they charge prices [15]. A differentiated product can establish a profitable niche. Our first research hypothesis is therefore:

Hypothesis 1: Web sites offering the same product at a positive price will differentiate on privacy

A principle of minimum differentiation applies instead if price competition disappears, typically due to exogenous effects. Many services on the web are offered at zero price, which is effectively fixed by consumer expectations. With no price competition to avoid, firms must compete for the same consumers at this given price. Web operators would group around the consumer with average privacy concerns. The entire market is then split proportionally amongst the alternative vendors, yielding a higher demand than a fully occupied small privacy niche. Application of this principle would also explain why competing web sites offering free registration exhibit similarly good or bad security practices without making it an aspect of differentiation. Our second research hypothesis is therefore:

Hypothesis 2: Web sites offering the same product at zero price will differentiate less on privacy.

If firms have successfully escaped price competition through discrimination, they may charge an above-market price without losing all customers. A priori, as data protection is a horizontally rather than a vertically differing characteristic, it is unclear whether a company collecting more data will be cheaper or more expensive. Experience suggests that additional personal information can be used for price discrimination, enabling firms to better extract rent from consumers. In comparing industries with and without the ability to price discriminate, one often observes that in the presence of personalised pricing, firms sell to more customers some of which are charged lower prices. Additionally, personal information can be monetised directly by increasing sales with targeted advertising or indirectly through selling or renting this data to third parties. Consumers buying from a company collecting more information would thus subsidise the retail price through the monetary value of the data they provide. Moreover, empirical evidence suggests that privacy awareness and social status increase concordantly amongst consumers. Privacy concerns and disposable income would have a common antecedent and thus be positively associated. A more privacy-friendly firm would attract buyers with a higher willingness to pay [17]. In summary, our third research hypothesis is therefore:

Hypothesis 3: If the same product or service, differentiated on privacy, is offered by two competing web sites, it will be offered more cheaply at the less privacy-friendly firm.

Further, the absence of competition would imply that consumers have to consume from a given web site regardless their tastes. If this applies to a service offered for free, the markup would be in the amount of collected and monetisable data, rather than in the price. In analogy to the under-supply of quality by monopolists, our fourth research hypothesis is therefore:

Hypothesis 4: Web sites facing little competition are less privacy-friendly.

2.2   Operationalisation

The *relevant market* of a firm is delimited geographically, temporally, by product, and by the position in the value chain. For a homogeneous consumer product, we limit the market to substitute products available online at the same time, and in the same currency if the product is priced.[1]

Competition between two firms is assumed if they operate in the same relevant market and are perceived by consumers as substitutes. We do not adopt a metric of competition based on technological similarity or cross-price elasticity. For physical

---

[1]While modern payment cards usually can transparently make payments in foreign currencies, shipping costs often limit consumers to web merchants aimed at their own country. In addition, for both DVDs and digital cameras, which we studied, manufacturers often price products differently in different regions, in the case of DVDs using a specifically designed DRM system (region codes) to facilitate price discrimination.

products, we take a conservative approach in only considering identical offerings (the same DVD title or digital camera model) to be substitutes. We intentionally avoid comparing potentially similar products (such as DVD box sets and any of the component DVDs, or cameras of the same model but differing in colour or minor accessories). Two metrics are used as a proxy to determine the competitors of a given web site. First, co-occurrence in the web site category describing the relevant market on the open directory project (ODP); second, co-occurrence within search results for a given product.

The *privacy regime* of a company is measured by the amount of personal information the consumer is asked to provide explicitly during a registration prior to consuming a web site's product. We do not include technical data collected implicitly such as a users' IP address or stored third-party cookies. If no registration is required prior to consumption, the amount of explicitly collected personal information is nil. For a given data item, such as "first name", "email address" and so on, a company may collect this information on a mandatory basis, on an optional basis, or not at all. Added to the privacy regime are login options, the provision of a privacy notice, a visual distinction between mandatory and optional fields, and the means of seeking consent to data collection.

Differentiation in privacy regimes is assessed by the (existence or lack of) similarity between the privacy regimes across the entire industry. Testing for differentiation is distinct from establishing an ordering over the privacy regimes. In the absence of a definite statistic, we assess the disparity in privacy practices within a given market using two metrics. First, measuring sample *diversity* for nominal or ordinal data is not typically considered in basic statistics, although a number of indices of qualitative variation (IQV) exist. Amongst these, the "Variance Analog" (VA) metric is the only one that continuously extends to multivariate applications whilst offering computational ease [19]. The VA positions a population along a continuum ranging from homogeneity ($VA = 0$) to heterogeneity ($VA = 1$). It can be calculated from vector-based variables (such as those describing data collection regimes), any entries of which can be polytomous or dichotomous [10]. Despite its advantages, the VA suffers from not attaining its theoretical maximum of 1 even for orthogonal variables. Further, it is rather unstable when adding categories with low frequencies [19]. We therefore consider a second metric, Cronbach's alpha, which is also suitable for ordinal data, to measure agreement between all competing firms. For well-behaved data, alpha indicates how consistently the scores for each characteristic contribute to a global score for a latent concept: if one is unable to assess a concept of interest directly, a battery of scores is used instead. Alpha gives an indication how well those proxies, taken together, capture the original concept. A value of one would mean that assessing a web site by its collection/non-collection behaviour for a selection of data items is a perfect proxy for this website's overall data collection regime. A value of zero would mean that the individual scores cannot be combined into an aggregate score as they would not vary concordantly. However, Cronbach's alpha can reach negative values which cannot be given a sensible interpretation. This happens as the dimensions of assessment vary systematically discordantly. This may happen for bad choices of the individual scores, but also if

Table 2 Illustration of our procedure to compare price levels between two companies, using fictitious data

	Merchant A ($)	Merchant B ($)	Ordering	Merchant C ($)	Merchant D ($)	Ordering
Product 1	7	8	<	3	5	<
Product 2	6	8	<	3	5	<
Product 3	12	10	>	6	7	<
Product 4	4	4	=	6	7	<
Product 5	10	–	n/a	8	4	>
median	6.50	8.00	2 <, 1 >	6.00	5.00	4 <, 1 >
Significance in pairwise ordering counts			$p_G = 0.68$			$p_G = 0.31$

Two pairs of companies are compared, A and B on the one hand and C and D on the other hand. Merchant B does not sell product 4. Comparison is done using the median price and the consistency in pairwise ordering counts.
Both metrics typically agree, although one may encounter data where this does not apply.

the data is not drawn from a single population. In light of the critiques this statistic has received, we interpret alpha as a measure of *internal consistency* rather than measurement reliability.

Ordering privacy regimes is achieved pairwise by comparing the amount of personal information collected by two companies. A *strict subset relation* is used: a company is said to collect less data if and only if the other company collects all plus at least one additional data item. Given a pair of companies, privacy regimes can only be ordered if all of the data items one of the companies collects are also collected by the other company. The order of privacy regimes may therefore be undefined using the subset relation. We deliberately make no attempts to compare the data collection regimes of companies when both of them have unique data items. Although average sensitivity scores are available for commonly asked personal information, this approach would be incompatible with our assumption of horizontally differentiated consumers. When using the subset test, optional and mandatory data items are treated alike.

Ordering companies by price is done by first ordering all products they both sell by price, which is a metric variable. We use quoted prices for a given product in new condition and excluding bundles. Prices are only compared if they are in the same currency. A company is then said to be cheaper than another if it sells common products consistently cheaper. Consistency is desirable since the proliferation of personal information when buying from a newly chosen retailer each time is typically more privacy-invasive than committing to one seller. We use two complementary approaches to assess this consistency. Table 2 illustrates the procedure.

First, across all studied products, for a given pair of companies, we compare the number of cases in which the product is sold at a strictly lower price to the number of occurrences of a strictly higher price. Equal prices (ties) are discarded. Products not sold by either or both companies are removed from the price comparison. A 2×2 G-test is used to assess whether there is a consistent difference in prices, at

$p = 0.10$, benchmarked against a half-split (note that the G-test allows non-integer counts). Second, for each company, the median price across the products it offers is computed. Again using strict inequalities, a company is said to be cheaper if its median price is lower than the one of a competing firm. This implements the rationale that customers may themselves compare multiple prices during explorative browsing to get a feel for the prices offered at a site.

2.3 Selection of Industries and Web Sites

Industries were selected which provide goods and services typically consumed online. We operationalised this typicality as popularity according to Alexa "top sites", where the US country ranking was used to guide our choice of industries: Google was ranked first, Facebook second, then Yahoo!, YouTube, Amazon.com fifth and Blogger sixth, eventually leading to the inclusion of search engines, social networking sites, retailing, and web blogging into our sample. Top web sites were used as seeds to discover other web sites in the same industry. The mapping from web sites to industries is not functional, however. The most visited web sites in particular often supply multiple services and which sites they compete with depends on the service under consideration. For instance, we consider Bing as a competitor for Google in the market of search engines, but Microsoft Advertising is not included since they compete in different markets.

Sites we considered not to face substantial competition were excluded, as described in Sect. 2.3.3, since their practices are explicitly outside the scope of our research agenda of examining the existence of privacy-friendly alternatives.

2.3.1 Sampling Positive-Price Web Sites

Online retailing was found to be the only industry where products were not offered for free. The ability to buy from an alternative vendor is determined by the availability of the same product. An online clothing store and an online book store are not direct competitors. The sampling of online merchants was thus realised by the sampling of products, yielding a list of electronic retailers selling an acceptably high proportion of them.

For our study, we desired products which are distinctly branded independently of individual merchants so that they can be easily compared across sites. We chose to consider sellers of DVDs and digital cameras, both of which have a large number of online sellers and come in a relatively small number of distinctly labelled varieties. This choice of products is also appropriate for reasons of external validity and pragmatic consideration: DVDs and cameras are typically bought online, they are homogeneous so that the choice of the retailer does not impact on perceived quality, they are not price-regulated (unlike, for instance, books or train tickets), they are, as far as we know, not price-discriminated (unlike air travel or hotels), and the title or product identifier are unique enough to identify the same product across different stores.

For digital cameras, we obtained a list of 31 best-selling cameras for the year 2010. The complete list is provided in Appendix A.2 (Table 8). Using Google Product Search (products.google.com), we then compiled the list of all shops listed as selling any of our top cameras, and kept the 29 sites which offered the largest proportion of our cameras. We consider the sampling bias introduced by Google to be small if not desirable. Price information was then recorded automatically using the Google Product Search interface. We recorded only the "base price" for a new product with no accessories, excluding shipping and handling costs. We also recorded a seller rating for each of these merchants, as well as the availability of Google Checkout as an alternative to registration with the site.

For DVDs, we selected a random sample of 20 film titles from the list of 500 highest-grossing films of all time provided by imdb.com. The complete list is provided in Appendix A.1 (Table 7). The set of competing online sellers was compiled via dmoz.org and Alexa, using the same methods as for non-priced products (Sect. 2.3.2). For each film, we recorded the price for each merchant, in a semi-automated manner. For films with multiple versions (extended versions, collector's editions, etc.), the cheapest version offered was chosen, excluding Blu-ray discs. Four sites were excluded because their selection turned out to be too limited (shop.abc.net.au, shopto.net, game.co.uk, mymemory.co.uk, homeshopping.24ace.co.uk), leading to a sample of 22 sites.

2.3.2 Sampling Zero-Price Web Sites

Sampling through Google Product Search is unavailable for products which are not sold, but offered at a zero price. As an alternative, a manual inspection of categories under which a top web site was listed in the ODP, accessed via dmoz.org, was used to determine the most relevant market for a web site. By region/language, categories are organised in trees, which are similar in structure. For top web sites, hundreds of categories are returned. The most sensible category can be identified quite easily though.[2]

As a guiding principle, the English-language tree was used, and "Computers" was expected to show up as the first sub-category. Once the representative category of a top site was determined, all other web sites in this category were manually inspected to decide whether they should be considered as competitors. Sites listed in the same category needed to be excluded if they were inaccessible, discontinued

---

[2]For Flickr, for instance, the first two categories are "Recreation: Outdoors: Urban Exploration: Image Galleries" and "Society: Death: Death Care: Cemeteries: Image Galleries". Links therein include http://www.flickr.com/groups/abandonded_gas_stations/ or http://www.flickr.com/groups/cemeterygates/. A link to the homepage http://www.flickr.com/ is found in category "Computers: Internet: On the Web: Web Applications: Photo Sharing", listed 73th and one of only three categories listed under "Computers".

Table 3 Examples of "Related Links", as provided by Alexa. Whilst the listings typically exhibit convincing face validity, they require a manual inspection

cam.ac.uk	facebook.com	amazon.com
University of Cambridge	Facebook	Amazon.com
Stanford University	Xanga	Buy.com, Inc.
University of Oxford	Myspace	Amazon UK
Massachusetts Institute of Technology	LinkedIn	eBay
Cambridge University Press	Google	Barnes & noble.com
The Gates Cambridge Scholarships	Friendster	ABC shop online
Ucas: Universities & Colleges	University life	Alibris
Admissions Service	Student life and culture	CD universe
QS Top Universities: study abroad	archival program	CBC Boutique
guides, The QS World University	Zynga Inc.	Buy sell rent media
Rankings, Bach	YouTube	AOL
National Rail Enquiries	Yahoo!	google.com/
London School of Economics and	Facebook.com	
Political Science (LSE)		
www.cambridge.ac.uk/		

Shown is the complete list per site, in its original formatting of the Alexa output, including inconsistent capitalisation and trailing slashes. (The site cam.ac.uk is shown for illustrative purposes only and not part of the sample.).

or temporarily "under construction", not functioning properly, not directed towards consumers or documentation about a service rather than offering the service itself.

The web site sampling via dmoz.org was complemented by sampling using a seed web site's "Related Links", as provided by Alexa. According to the rather vague definition given by Alexa, construction of related links takes into account characteristics of the sites, but also click paths by users, resulting in not necessarily symmetric relations. Listings typically include alternative web sites, which can be interpreted as competitors. Highly popular sites, however, are often found clustered together, as by definition the web population is likely to visit several of the top sites (for instance, Google-Facebook-Yahoo!-YouTube, ranked 1–4). Non-competing sites, which match the interests of the audience are also included and must not be counted as competitors. Taking the example of the University of Cambridge, Stanford, Oxford etc. are competitors on the global market for higher education, but the railway is rather a means of getting to the University and cambridge.ac.uk is just a redirect to the institution's site (see Table 3).

2.3.3 Excluded Web Sites

From the outset, we excluded industries for which we had currently no ability to determine accurate pricing behaviour or for which we concluded that the sites were not offering a homogeneous product. This notably excluded airlines or car rental companies. Also excluded were markets for which there was an exogenously given consumption constraint, such as banking sites, ISPs or mobile phone operators.

Amongst those web sites identified as being part of a chosen relevant market, we excluded all that had discontinued their service, locked registration, technically failed during registration after retries, required an upfront payment or were identified as duplicates of other web sites in the sample.

For the top 25 according to Alexa, we set aside web sites and thus industries for which we were unable to identify a set of competitors that sufficed our expectations of face validity. As an indicator, we used the absence of same-industry web sites in Alexa's "related links", leading to the exclusion of YouTube, Twitter, or eBay amongst other. These web sites were recorded to form a "monopolies" sub-sample.[3] This would include Flickr, for instance, ranked 22nd amongst US top sites: web sites such as Blogger, Fotolog, Photobucket, Webshots or Twitter could all be considered competing sites, in markets for photo viewing, uploading or sharing, or photo-centric or other self-presentation, but based on the related-links indicator and our judgement, we concluded otherwise (similarly for aol.com, despite it facing competition as a search engine).

2.4 Data Collection Procedure

Assessment of all web sites in our sample was manual, although supported by tools. Data was collected using a fresh profile in the Firefox browser, version 3.6.10, using the extensions "Autofill Forms", "CipherFox", "Ghostery", and "View Cookies", all in the latest version as of March 10th, 2011. A UK Internet connection was used; forced redirects to regional sites (e.g. aol.co.uk instead of aol.com) were followed. Data collection was assessed by completing the sign-up forms of each web site, sometimes spanning multiple web pages. All fields marked as mandatory were filled in before submitting; fields not marked as mandatory were left blank. A constant set of personal information was used representing a male in his late thirties with an imaginary residence in California. Changes to this standard sign-up profile were made only to adhere to site-specific requirements, such as (un-) availability of the test username, addresses from UK or lookup-based postcode checks for California. Valid email addresses were provided at all times, tailored to the specific site. Emails received as part of creating an account were opened and links for account "verification" were clicked.

2.5 Data Standardisation and Analysis Procedures

Conservatively, data items collected by a given web site were coded "1", regardless of whether disclosure was mandatory or optional. Data items not collected during initial sign-up were coded "0". Potentially, optional data items could be assigned

---

[3]We do not claim that web sites listed in this sub-sample are monopolists, but rather that we were unable to find competing web sites.

any score between 0 and 1, denoting the extremes of absent respectively present collection. We treated them no different from mandatory items because visual indicators that would discriminate between optional and mandatory items were often missing (as discussed below). We certainly noticed a tendency amongst web sites not to indicate a certain data item was optional despite it not being required for successful registration. We further observed the practice of placing a heading "all field are required" above the form and adding "optional" in fine print to some fields. If present, such visual indicators are often overlooked, in particular for standard forms. Also, automatic form fillers are typically oblivious to compulsiveness so that consumers making use of them will reveal even optional items. We further note that the classification of an input field as "mandatory" or "optional" may not be clear-cut: for gender enquiry, we encountered drop-down lists with a third option of "unspecified" and "decline to state".

Cronbach's alpha, a statistic used to assess the internal consistency of characteristics exhibited by several entities, was calculated for all five markets. The coefficient alpha is sensitive to the number of characteristics; we therefore took a constant set of data items across all industries. Name details (first name, surname, full name) were lumped into one synthetic data item "name" if at least one of them was collected. Across all web sites in our sample, the collection of first name and last name is highly positively correlated ($\rho = 0.93$). The cases when both are collected in separate fields largely outnumber the cases of collection as "full name" (68 vs. 15).

We similarly lumped into one characteristic all address data, that is street address, city, state, and postal code. This also follows the rationale that in countries such as the UK, there is almost a functional relationship between the postal code and the street address. Country was not included in this list, as we felt that country information alone was not of comparable sensitivity to the other fine-grained address requirements. For date of birth, we collapsed the day, month, and year components (which were again often collected in conjunction, $\rho = 0.85$); for telephone number, the collection of any or specifically mobile or landline was equally collapsed. We thereby avoided inflating the measured consistency of data collection practices, by removing items that vary concordantly per se.

As a measure of outlier correction, we did not include in our analysis data items only collected by very few sites, such as "I identify myself as" (Blackplanet only), years of attending and rating of college and university (Perfspot only), tax identification number (Howard only), species (NuTang only), boat name (SailBlogs only), and "interested in" (once amongst social networking sites, thrice amongst camera retailers, thrice amongst weblog hosts; note the differing semantics).

We systematically recorded but excluded from the analysis the occurrence of input fields to type twice one's password, username, email or to enter a CAPTCHA.

Both our measures for statistical dispersion, Cronbach's alpha and the Variance Analog are sensitive towards changes in the number of characteristics. For the latter, standardisation is expressively discouraged and considered inappropriate [10], making comparisons between datasets with varying numbers of characteristics misleading. To ease cross-market analyses, we therefore excluded items just appearing in a single industry. In particular, this meant excluding blog title (only appearing amongst weblogs) and company name (mainly for camera retailers, otherwise once amongst weblogs and DVD retailers each).

For retailers, an adjusted coefficient alpha was calculated, $\alpha^\dagger$, which will be used subsequently: name and address details were removed, as those are exogenously given minimum data requirements for an online shop that ships physical goods. Moreover, we noticed that sites fell into two regimes, varying on whether a shipping address was collected during sign-up or during the first checkout. Differentiating on this behaviour would not provide a valid assessment of a company's data practices.

Eight characteristics were used to calculate VA and α, six for $\alpha^\dagger$. For coefficient alpha, the commonly used cut-off value of 0.80 was used to ascertain that an industry does not have differentiated data collection practices.

Price comparisons were evaluated using median prices and by pairs of companies within each market, subdivided between currencies were applicable, as described in Sect. 2.2. Given the symmetry of the evaluation, $N \times (N - 1)/2$ pairs of companies were thus compared given a market of N suppliers.

For comparisons of prices and privacy regimes, only strict inequalities are taken into account. Cases of equal prices or equal data collection schemes are ignored. When privacy and price orderings are considered together across the sample, only cases for which both comparisons are decidable and significant are counted. Again, this is a conservative approach.

3 Results

We collected statistics for 140 sites spread across the five categories. The overall frequency of collection for different data items is shown in Table 4. In addition to these items, we notice variance in other privacy-related presentation choices. For example, only 11% of sites included a checkbox indicated agreement to the site's privacy policy, and 23% a textual reference to the agreement. Less than one third of the web sites highlight mandatory form fields. A fair share of 19% of sites displayed privacy seals during the signup process (most of them commercially issued), counting also more general seals such as "VeriSign Secured" or "McAfee secure". We also noticed several compelling differences between industries in the type of data collected. For example, only 19% of weblog hosts required an address, while 50% of online merchants did prior to any purchase. However, 87% of social networking sites required a date of birth, while only 26% of the other sites across all industries in our sample did.

Amongst DVD retailers, one retailer, dvdstreet.co.uk was selling through the Amazon.com platform; the data collection scheme from the perspective of the consumer, is thus the same as for Amazon itself, and the web site was excluded when assessing the industry-wide variance in data collection. Five web sites were found to operate as front-ends to the same shopping system "elysium": sendit.com,

Table 4 Privacy communication and data collection practices: for each sub-sample, i.e. market, the proportion of sites are given that indicate mandatory input fields in their registration forms, that link to their privacy policy from there, and respectively, that collect certain items of personal information. The average for a market (pen-ultimate column) gives the proportion of data items collected across the web sites in that sub-sample. The last column gives the significance at which non-competing web sites collect more data items than other web sites that offer services for free.

Market	Mandatory items are marked (%)	Privacy policy is linked (%)	Some name (%)	Email address (%)	Username (%)	Password (%)	Some telephone (%)	Some address (%)	Some DOB (%)	Gender (%)	Average (%)	Significance p_t
Camera retailers	66	72	79	86	7	86	59	59	10	3	49	
DVD retailers	28	78	83	100	17	100	39	44	33	17	54	
Social networking sites	22	100	74	100	35	96	0	43	87	91	66	0.9
Search engines	17	17	17	44	33	50	6	28	28	28	26	0.004
Weblog hosts	33	67	50	98	88	88	2	19	29	24	50	0.03
Non-competing sites	30	90	60	100	80	100	20	60	50	50	65	

whsmithentertainment.co.uk, zavvi.com, thehut.com, and asda-entertainment.co.uk. WHSmith Entertainment was chosen as the representative in assessing market-wide differentiation on privacy and the other four sites were discarded. These duplicate sites were again taken into consideration when assessing the correlation of pricing and data collection practices.

Search engines are the only market for which data collection is consistent, with a large proportion of web sites collecting no data. The market for online social networking exhibits a negative coefficient alpha, with a low variance analog, suggesting that sites in this market may fall into multiple, internally consistent camps by collecting broadly non-overlapping data items—and may thus be offering services which cannot be regarded as competing. Further analysis of this phenomenon would require an expanded sample size and is thus left for future work. Weblogs have a moderate variance analog and coefficient alpha, which may stem from the strongly diversified market in terms of general purpose and niche blogging sites. Both electronic commerce markets, for DVDs and for cameras, exhibit differentiated data collection practices, when compared to the other markets we studied.

4 Analysis and Interpretation

All studied markets on which homogeneous products are sold at a positive price, that is, sales of DVDs and cameras, exhibit differentiated data collection practices. In the light of aforementioned shortcomings with both dispersion metrics, we consider a market to be differentiated on privacy if it is amongst the three out five most dispersed web site populations according to both metrics. A G-test reveals that these results are significant despite the small sample size ($p < 0.01$). We also note that web sites selling goods rather than providing a service for free are very significantly more likely to highlight which input fields are mandatory (two-tailed t-test for difference in arithmetic means, $p < 0.01$). Unlike the existence of a privacy policy, typically mandated by regulations, the open communication of data collection practices is a voluntary best practice. Thus, Hypothesis 1 is supported; web sites selling goods at a positive price do differentiate on privacy.

Web search engines, which offer an online service at zero-price, exhibit higher consistency in their data collection practices than any of the industries selling products at a positive price (Table 5). Results are inconclusive for social networking sites, as discussed in Sect. 3 and borderline for weblog, for which VA is moderately high. We conclude that Hypothesis 2 is supported; web sites offering free services differentiate less on privacy than those selling goods for a positive price.

Hypothesis 3 states a negative association of the amount of personal information collected by a firm and the prices it charges. We test this hypothesis for the markets of retailing cameras and DVDs only, as web search and online social networking are not priced. For UK DVD retailers, 24 pairs of strict inequalities could be established, 17 for US DVD retailers, and 300 for camera retailers,

Table 5 Summary of assessed web sites, per industry

Industry and sites	Sites / α	VA
Camera retailers: www.abesofmaine.com, www.adorama.com, www.amazon.com, www.antarespro.com, www.aztekcomputers.com, www.beachaudio.com, www.bestbuy.com, www.buydig.com, www.capitolsupply.com, www.cdw.com, clickfrom.buy.com, www.compnation.com, www.compsource.com, www.compuplus.com, www.daxmart.com, www.ecost.com, www.futurepowerpc.com, www.govgroup.com, www.homemylife.com, www.howardcomputers.com, www.neobits.com, www.nextdaypc.com, www.nextwarehouse.com, www.pcrush.com, www.ritzcamera.com, www.tekmentum.com, underbid.com, www.valleyseek.com, www.walmart.com	29 sites $\alpha = 0.80$ $\alpha^{\dagger} = 0.63$	VA = 0.27
DVD retailers: www.101cd.com, www.alibris.com, amazon.com, www.borders.com, www.buy.com, www.cdplus.com, cdquest.com, www.cduniverse.com, www.chapters.indigo.ca, www.dvd.co.uk, www.fye.com, www.gohastings.com, hmv.com, www.moviesandgamesonline.co.uk, www.play.com, www.tesco.com, www.wherehouse.com, www.whsmithentertainment.co.uk	18 sites $\alpha = 0.64$ $\alpha^{\dagger} = 0.44$	VA = 0.28
Social networking sites: www.2befriends.net, badoo.com, www.bebo.com, www.blackplanet.com, facebook.com, fropper.com, hi5.com, www.linkedin.com, www.livejournal.com, www.meinvz.net, www.mocospace.com, multiply.com, www.myspace.com, www.myyearbook.com, www.netlog.com, www.orkut.com, www.perfspot.com, www.plaxo.com, signup.live.com, www.skyrock.com, www.sonico.com, www.tagged.com, www.xanga.com	23 sites neg. α	VA = 0.23
Search engines: www.amfibi.com, www.aol.co.uk, uk.ask.com, www.bing.com, www.chacha.com, cluuz.com, www.entireweb.com, www.google.com, www.hakia.com, kalooga.com, www.mahalo.com, middlespot.com, www.mozdex.com, www.searchhippo.com, www.spiderline.net, www.ulysseek.com, www.wotbox.com, www.yahoo.com	18 sites $\alpha = 0.89$	VA = 0.38
Weblog hosts: www.aeonity.com, www.blog.com, www.blog-city.info, www.blogdrive.com, www.blogger.com, bloghi.com, www.blogigo.com, blogmyway.com, www.blogomonster.com, blogs.scriptologist.com, blogs.trhonline.com, en.blogspirit.com, www.blogster.com, www.blogstudio.com, blogtext.org, www.efx2blogs.com, www.fotopages.com, www2.globbo.org, hubpages.com, www.inube.com, www.kitehost.org, lifewithchrist.org, www.ohblog.com, ohlog.com, moblog.net, www.mycookingblog.com, www.nutang.com, www.problogs.com, www.sailblogs.com	42 sites $\alpha = 0.55$	VA = 0.26
Non-competing sites: aol.com, cnn.com, craigslist.org, ebay.com, flickr.com, msn.com, paypal.com, twitter.com, youtube.com, wikipedia.org	10 sites n/a	n/a

Cronbach's alpha is indicated as a statistic of internal consistency in data collection; in the case of online retailers, $\alpha^{\dagger}$ indicates the value adjusted for base data collection (name and address), and with companies operating on the same web platform collapsed into one subject (DVD retailers only). The non-standardised Variance Analog (VA) is given.

Table 6 Trend and significance of associations between prices and the amount of data collection

prices:	UK DVD retailers data collected:		US DVD retailers data collected:		Camera retailers data collected:		prices:
	more	less	more	less	more	less	
higher	8	2	9	0	76	48	higher
lower	5	9	0	8	74	102	lower
	$p_G < 0.028$		$p_G < 0.0000012$		$p_G < 0.0010$		

For each sub-market, the number of co-occurrences of higher/lower prices and more/less data collected is given. Strict inequalities are used for comparison, using median prices across assortments and subset relations, as described in Sects. 2.2 and 2.5. Significance levels as determined by a G-test.

using the median price for comparisons of price levels (Table 6). There is a highly significant, positive association between the amount of data collection and price level. Companies charging higher prices collect more personal information. These results are confirmed using the median method for comparing prices across assortments, as described in Sect. 2.5. Hypothesis 3 is rejected; priced goods are not offered more cheaply by more privacy-friendly firms.

We note that the empirical evidence regarding prices and privacy regimes is in fact the opposite of the hypothesised relationship. Further investigation reveals that this result cannot be attributed to differences between top sites and lower tier sites or between online-only and multichannel retailers. Any attempt to explain this phenomenon would be post-hoc and thus speculative. Plausible, although not tested intra-sample effects include brand effects or a positive relationship between data collection and perceived service quality through personalisation. Price discrimination does not seem to be a plausible explanation, since there is no evidence that online retailers in our study charged individualised prices.

All web sites operating without major competition in our sample are offering free services. We therefore relate their data collection practices to other markets that provide free services. With the exception of online social networking, for which no difference was found, non-competing web sites are collecting more personal information than search engines and weblog hosts with high significance (both $p < 0.05$ in a two-tailed t-test). Hypothesis 4 is, therefore, supported.

We note that the non-competing web sites in our sample also enjoy high popularity, which, however, we do not consider a convincing explanation for over-collection of personal information: previous research has indicated a positive relationship between good privacy practices and high popularity [2]. Plus, one can assume that more popular sites are also under stronger privacy scrutiny from the media and other interest groups.

5   Conclusions and Critical Review

5.1   Summary

When shopping online, consumers are faced with a supply that is differentiated in privacy. They may choose to buy from a company whose data protection practices are compatible with their own preferences. Our empirical evidence suggests that electronic retailers compete on privacy. However, at high levels of significance, consumers do not face a trade-off between privacy and price. In choosing a privacy-friendly retailer for DVDs or digital cameras, consumers are also likely to get a better deal more than half of the time and to pay less across the assortment of the seller.

Consumers may choose from a broad variety of hosts for their weblog, and they have fair chance of finding a provider whose privacy regime matches their preferences. They have less choice when using web search engines. Although they all offer a basic service without registration requirements, there is little variance in the data one needs to provide when signing up for a personalised service.

Web sites which do not face strong competition are significantly more likely to ask for more personal information than other services provided for free, such as web search or blogging. Social networking sites, however, collect data to an extent otherwise seen only for sites for which the risk of losing customers to competitors is low. Our findings on the variety in and the amount of data collection depending on price and market structures are in line with the predictions economic theory makes. The co-occurrence of more privacy and lower prices, however, comes as a surprise and mandates further study.

5.2   Limitations

We address several limitations. First, our operationalisation of privacy as the extent of data collection ignores the importance of use and sharing of personal information—which may be even more important than data collection. However, these facets of data protection are typically unobservable to the user. Second, our economic model may have been too simplistic, although it did explain the observed phenomena reasonably well. Neither lock-in effects, particularly prevalent in service consumption, nor differences in quality between service alternatives are considered. We only consider one-time consumption without accounting for the effect of repeated purchases. Third, data collection was largely resistant against automation, in particular as determining the relevant market and competitors therein requires judgement. Inevitably, this also introduces sources of human error. Fourth, we have only studied five industries so far. Our sample does not include paid-for services, physical goods offered for free, or services delivered beyond the web. Finally, regarding our conclusions, online merchants may differentiate on privacy for other reasons than competing on privacy.

5.3 Managerial and Regulatory Implications

In the case of search engines or online social networking, one may conjecture that service providers are too close to one another from a social welfare perspective. Welfare could be increased if there were more variance in privacy regimes. A social planner would mandate that search engines and online social networks were more spread out over the continuum of privacy preferences. Higher dispersion would also mean that more web users start using social network sites, who, at the time being, would incur prohibitively high "transportation costs" in signing up for the service. Given the difficulty—or "impossibility" [8]—to regulate sites like Facebook, Google and its global competitors, transforming them into paid-for services could be a viable approach, to incentivise differentiation on privacy in the operators' own interests.

From a managerial perspective, there is an incentive to introduce new products and occupy several positions in the product space as a single company. Several markets with dominating firms exist on the web, including online social networking, web search, online auctions, or video sharing. Current quasi-monopolists might therefore increase their market shares and attract new customers by differentiating into a multi-brand monopoly.

Appendix

A.1 DVDs Used for Price Comparison

Table 7 The list of films used to compare prices of entertainment retailers. It represents a random sample from the top 500 highest-grossing films worldwide, provided by imdb.com as of March 2011

50 first Dates	Jumanji	The Nutty Professor
An Officer and a Gentleman	Jurassic Park III	The Sixth Sense
Beverly Hills Cop II	My Big fat Greek Wedding	The Sting
Charlie's Angels: Full Throttle	Saving Private Ryan	Top Gun
Enemy of the State	Shrek	True Lies
Fun with Dick and Jane	Sleeping with the Enemy	Tropic Thunder
Ghostbusters II	The DaVinci Code	

A.2   Digital Cameras Used for Price Comparison

Table 8 The list of cameras used to compare prices of electronics retailers. It was taken from a 2010 holiday camera shopping guide published at cnet.com

Canon PowerShot G12	Fujifilm FinePix S1800	Olympus Stylus Tough 6020
Canon PowerShot S95	Fujifilm FinePix XP10	Panasonic Lumix DMC-FZ35K
Canon PowerShot SD1300	Kodak EASYSHARE C143	Panasonic Lumix DMC-ZS7
Canon PowerShot SD1400	Kodak EASYSHARE M590	Pentax Optio W90
Canon PowerShot SX20	Nikon Coolpix L22	Pentax X90
Canon PowerShot SX30	Nikon Coolpix P100	Sony Cyber-shot DSC-H55
Casio EXILIM G EX-G1	Nikon Coolpix S8100	Sony Cyber-shot DSC-HX1
Casio EXILIM EX-Z35PE	Olympus E-PL1	Sony Cyber-shot DSC-HX5V
Fujifilm FinePix JV100	Olympus FE-47	Sony Cyber-shot DSC-TX9
Fujifilm FinePix W3	Olympus SP-800UZ	

References

1. Beresford A, Preibusch S, Kübler D (2010) Unwillingness to pay for privacy: a field experiment. IZA discussion papers 5017, Institute for the Study of Labor (IZA)
2. Bonneau J, Preibusch S (2009) The privacy jungle: on the market for data protection in social networks. The eighth workshop on the economics of information security (WEIS)
3. Bonneau J, Preibusch S (2010) The password thicket: technical and market failures in human authentication on the web. The ninth workshop on the economics of information security (WEIS)
4. Personalization Consortium (2000, 2005) Personalization & privacy survey, via Internet Archive
5. Cranor LF, Egelman S, Sheng S, McDonald AM, Chowdhury A (2008) P3P deployment on websites. Electron Commerce Res Appl 7(3):274–293
6. Fraunhofer Institut für Sichere Informationstechnologie SIT (2008) Privatsphärenschutz in Soziale-Netzwerke-Plattformen.
7. Gomez J, Pinnick T, Soltani A (2009) KnowPrivacy. School of Information, UC Berkeley
8. Leutheusser-Schnarrenberger S (2011) Regulierung im Netz: Ihr Reflex greift zu kurz. Interviewers: Hildebrandt T, Wefing H
9. Lewis K, Kaufman J, Christakis N (2008) The taste for privacy: An analysis of college student privacy settings in an online social network. J Computer-Mediated Comm 14(1):79–100
10. Lieberson S (1969) Measuring population diversity. Am Socio Rev 34(6):850–862
11. Preibusch S (2010) Privacy types revisited. http://talks.cam.ac.uk/talk/index/22536. Accessed 1 Jan 2011
12. Preibusch S (2011) Datenschutz-Wettbewerb unter social network sites [Privacy competition amongst social networking sites]. In. Neumann-Braun K, Autenrieth UP (eds) Freundschaft und Gemeinschaft im Social Web: Bildbezogenes Handeln und Peergroup-Kommunikation auf Facebook & Co. Nomos Verlag
13. Tappenden AF, Miller J (2009) Cookies: a deployment study and the testing implications. ACM Trans Web 3:9:1–9:49
14. The White House (1997) The framework for global electronic commerce. Washington, DC
15. Tirole J (1988) The theory of industrial organization. The MIT Press

16. Tsai J, Egelman S, Cranor L, Acquisti A (2007) The effect of online privacy information on purchasing behavior: An experimental study. The sixth workshop on the economics of information security (WEIS)
17. Varian H, Wallenberg F, Woroch G (2004) Who signed up for the do-not-call list? workshop on economics and information security
18. Warentest Stiftung (2011) Suche "Datenschutz" [Search "Privacy"] http://www.test.de/suche/?q=Datenschutz. Accessed 1 Mar 2011
19. Wilcox AR (1973) Indices of qualitative variation and political measurement. West Polit Q 26(2):325–343